Law and Justice around the World

LAW AND JUSTICE AROUND THE WORLD

A Comparative Approach

Mikaila Mariel Lemonik Arthur

UNIVERSITY OF CALIFORNIA PRESS

University of California Press
Oakland, California

© 2020 by Mikaila Mariel Lemonik Arthur

Cataloging-in-Publication Data is on file at the Library of Congress.

Names: Arthur, Mikaila Lemonik, author.
Title: Law and justice around the world : a comparative approach /
    Mikaila Mariel Lemonik Arthur.
Description: Oakland, California : University of California Press,
    [2020] | Includes bibliographical references and index.
Identifiers: LCCN 2019021375 (print) | LCCN 2019981582 (ebook) |
    ISBN 9780520300019 (paperback) | ISBN 9780520971585 (epub)
Subjects: LCSH: Comparative law.
Classification: LCC K583 .A78 2020 (print) | LCC K583 (ebook) |
    DDC 340/.2--dc23
LC record available at https://lccn.loc.gov/2019021375
LC ebook record available at https://lccn.loc.gov/2019981582

Manufactured in the United States of America

29 28 27 26 25 24 23 22 21 20
10 9 8 7 6 5 4 3 2 1

To Benjamin

Contents

Illustrations and Tables

TABLES

CASE STUDY ILLUSTRATIONS

Acknowledgments

This book has been nearly a decade in the making. In the summer of 2009, I sat down to start preparing a new course, Comparative Law and Justice. Rhode Island College had hired me a year earlier in part to teach this course, which was cross-listed between anthropology and sociology and also served majors in justice studies and international business, but I had managed to delay its initial offering while I prepped several other courses I was teaching for the first time. The learning curve for Comparative Law and Justice was, let's just say, staggering. And the available textbooks were of little help, as none conformed to my vision for how the course should be taught. Over the years since I began prepping this course, it has undergone many revisions with the help of many people, ultimately taking the form I have recorded in this book. All of their support and advice has made this a better product.

Conversations I had with Michael Friedson when I first conceived of this course helped established a solid foundation for the book. While I was writing the final text, discussions with Carse Ramos, who has taken on the responsibility of teaching the course while I serve as department chair, have immeasurably strengthened it. Michael and Carse also introduced me to some of the film selections shared in the ancillary materials. Carse additionally contributed two important case studies that enhanced the book, and our colleague Geoff Harkness provided another. I also want to thank Silvia Oliviera for giving a campus presentation on Portuguese drug strategy that sharpened my thinking and enhanced my knowledge of that case. Dragan Gill and Tish Brennan provided excellent reference support, and Deryl Freeman made sure all the e-resources I endlessly consulted were working. Many colleagues in sociology, political science, anthropology, and other fields at Rhode Island College took part in innumerable discussions about content and pedagogy that strengthened the book. It would take up every remaining word of my word limit to do justice to thanking them all.

Audiences at the American Sociological Association, the Law and Society Association, and the Mid-Atlantic Law and Society Association provided useful questions and feedback when I discussed some of the pedagogy behind this book, sharpening my perspective on what I was trying to do with this course. It was a presentation at the American Sociological Association that brought my work to the attention of Maura Roessner, and I cannot overstate my appreciation to her for seeing the potential in the project even before I could. Maura shepherded this book from a kernel of an idea to the finished product. Madison Wetzel and Sabrina Robleh provided additional editorial assistance, and I am also grateful to the marketing professionals at the University of California Press for their vision and support. A series of reviewers, some anonymous and others named, provided important feedback on this project. Thanks to Tammy Castle, Gary Feinberg, Darrell Hamlin, Anna King, Jennifer Renee Trombley, Michelle

VanNatta, and especially to Yvonne Zylan, who not only provided comments on the manuscript but also has been a valued colleague for many years. The reviewers' enthusiastic support for the vision of this text kept me going, and their careful reading and suggestions made the final product immeasurably better.

A variety of individuals provided resources, data, and support that were essential to making this text a reality. Seth Dixon refreshed my memory on how to use GIS and provided me with the tools necessary to craft the maps on these pages, and Dan Ryan provided useful technological advice. Joyce Fife provided excellent administrative support that made my life easier for all the months that I worked on this project. Anne Holland helped me better understand the publishing process. Sami Arthur is responsible for the original artist's rendering of the elephant ball in chapter 7, which enabled me to include one of my favorite images without fear of copyright infringement. Stefán Ólafsson and Rósa Guðrún Erlingsdóttir helped me learn about the Icelandic equal pay law, and Ethan Michelson provided access to his cross-national data on lawyers.

Since that day in 2009 when I first sat down to develop the Comparative Law and Justice course, I have taught it twelve times to a total of over 320 students. I thank them for letting me work out my ideas and pedagogy with them, and for the many insights they contributed that have found their way into these pages. My students at Rhode Island College come from all over the world, and they brought to class their own knowledge about and perspectives on topics like Islamic family law, marital naming conventions, and compulsory voting. During the course, they completed projects on the legal systems of other countries, enhancing my own understanding of the global diversity of approaches to law and justice. Some of these students deserve far more credit than I can give for their contributions to this work.

I began writing this book in 2017, as the United States and the world around it changed in ways that had previously been inconceivable. It was easy to think that a text like this could make little impact on a world so broken when there was so much other work to be done. There were places I did not go and meetings I did not make because I was writing. And thus I must thank the amazing women of Rhode Island who reminded me with their optimism in seeking office and working to get other women elected why this work of writing was important and why understanding law and justice matters and who cheered me on even when it meant I was not there for them. I'll try not to have a project this big in 2020 so I can do better by all of you next time.

This genre of acknowledgments always closes with family. Many Finkelstein relatives enthusiastically listened to my plans for the book and asked good questions that helped me refine my elevator pitch. I must most of all thank my parents, Baila Lemonik and Dwight Arthur, for their support of this project and of me. Baila happily provided a respite when I needed to step away from writing and also translated some French, and Dwight was always available to help troubleshoot my technical problems. And it is their indulgence of my youthful curiosity about the world that provided the foundation for the career that has led me here. Finally, Benjamin Ledsham provided a lawyer's perspective on many of the thorny issues included here, debugged my spreadsheets, and enabled me to consult Russian and Japanese sources, but he did so much more. He listened as I worked through the arguments of this text, and he made sure dinner was on the table when I was buried in a flood of typing. *Ani ohevet otto mipoh layarayach vehazara.*

Preface

Law and Justice around the World is designed to introduce readers to comparative law and justice, including cross-national variations in legal and justice systems and global and international justice. The text is distinctive for two reasons. First, it covers law and justice broadly rather than limiting its focus to criminal justice systems. This broader perspective provides the opportunity to examine topics of pressing global concern in our contemporary moment—such as election systems, forms of government, environmental regulations, and migration and refugee status—without compromising coverage of core criminal justice topics such as crime, law enforcement, criminal courts, and punishment. While students in law and justice classes may first come to these areas of study due to their interest in criminal law, *noncriminal* issues are just as important to the operations of national and global legal systems. For example, in U.S. district courts, under 20 percent of new cases filed in 2017 were criminal—and criminal cases account for an even smaller percentage of federal courts' business when bankruptcy and other administrative matters are included (Administrative Office of the U.S. Courts 2017). Students thus cannot develop a robust understanding of (or effectively seek careers in) law and justice with attention only to criminal justice.

Second, *Law and Justice around the World* provides a comprehensive global perspective, with an emphasis on examples from the global south. This comprehensiveness is especially important given the growing frequency of cross-national interactions around issues like trade, migration, and crime between the nations of the global north and those of the global south. Effectively reaching readers and educating them for the increasingly globalized futures in which they will live and work requires attention to all areas of the world, not just Europe, North America, and East Asia. Unlike texts that take a country-by-country perspective, selecting several key nations that exemplify different patterns of legal structures and illuminating their legal systems in detail, this text is organized topically, allowing for a more nuanced exploration of each topic. Examples from specific countries—including countries from the global south—are used to illustrate topics, but the specific countries vary from chapter to chapter so that the most pertinent details can be included. Furthermore, all chapters incorporate basic information about the U.S. legal system so that readers are equipped with the knowledge and background necessary to understand similarities and differences across nations.

In addition, this text foregrounds a sociological perspective that emphasizes the implications of both culture and structure for legal systems. But it does so while incorporating concerns and ideas from various other disciplines that study comparative law and justice, including political science, criminology, anthropology, legal studies, international relations, philosophy, and geography.

PLAN OF THE BOOK

As noted above, this book will take readers on a tour of legal systems around the world. Unlike many other books focused on comparative law, it is not limited to just a handful of countries but rather explores all aspects of legal systems (not just criminal justice). As you read, you will learn how systems vary and what they have in common. Chapter 1 begins this tour by introducing the study of comparative law and justice. Chapter 2 provides an overview of families of law, or basic types of legal systems into which most countries can be categorized.

The next seven chapters each concentrate on a particular aspect of legal and justice systems. Chapter 3 focuses on the organization of government and the electoral process. Chapter 4 explores crime itself, including variations in crime rates, the measurement of crime, and cross-border crime. Chapter 5 discusses law enforcement, and chapter 6 explores dispute resolution processes, especially courts. Chapter 7 examines social control and punishment practices. Chapters 8 and 9 move away from the criminal justice context. Chapter 8 covers family law—marriage, divorce, and children—and chapter 9 explores human, civil, and universal rights.

The final three chapters broaden in perspective, attending to more global issues. Chapter 10 provides an introduction to global and international law, including the International Criminal Court. Chapter 11 examines the concept of legal culture and how it might help us understand global differences and work together across them. Finally, chapter 12 explores the future of comparative law and considers how it can continue to enhance understanding in our increasingly globalized world.

HOW TO USE THIS BOOK

This text is designed to enable its readers to understand cross-national and historical variation in elements of law and justice systems; evaluate the many factors shaping cross-national differences in law and justice practices; analyze the consequences of these differences in law and justice practices for societies and nations; understand the role of international law and international justice institutions in relation to contemporary global problems; and apply knowledge of diverse law and justice practices when evaluating options for responding to national and local problems.

Each chapter begins with clear learning objectives, and the text includes a complete glossary of key terms. Chapters are enhanced with detailed case studies that enable readers to delve more deeply into a specific issue or context relevant to that chapter's focus. Additional online resources to support teaching and learning include suggested supplemental books, articles, films, videos, websites, and data sources; open-ended questions for writing assignments or in-class discussions; a test bank; and slide decks ready for instructor use containing full-color versions of maps featured in the text. In addition, a transition guide for those interested in converting a U.S.-focused law and society course into a globally focused comparative law and justice course is available. The goal of these resources is to provide readers, students, and instructors with the support necessary to ensure an engaging and thought-provoking learning experience.

The pedagogical approach featured in this book and its associated ancillaries has been used to teach comparative law and justice to hundreds of students, and it works to expand their knowledge of the world, open their minds to the possibilities of comparative analysis, and enhance their social scientific understanding of legal and justice systems. It was written to bring that approach to a broader audience, as learning more about the world and its variations is one of the most essential tasks of education.

—Mikaila Mariel Lemonik Arthur

The Study of Comparative Law and Justice

CHAPTER GOALS

1. Understand why the study of comparative law and justice is an important area of study and how it can be useful for justice and legal system professionals.
2. Become familiar with basic terminology used in the study of comparative law and justice.

Consider map 1. You will see that the countries of the world are each colored black or one of three shades of grey. What do you think these shades represent? What do Brazil, Kazakhstan, and Israel have in common? Russia, Algeria, and Papua New Guinea? Mexico, South Africa, and Iceland? Or perhaps hardest to explain, the United States, Saudi Arabia, Belarus, and Somalia? Take a moment, and make a guess.

Those who contemplate this map often struggle with the question of what it depicts, and they come up with a variety of explanations, ranging from aspects of world history to issues of global economics. The actual answer is that the map depicts countries' policies about the death penalty (Amnesty International 2017). The lightest grey countries, like Mexico, South Africa, and Iceland, have completely abolished the death penalty—no one can be sentenced to death in those countries. The medium grey countries, like

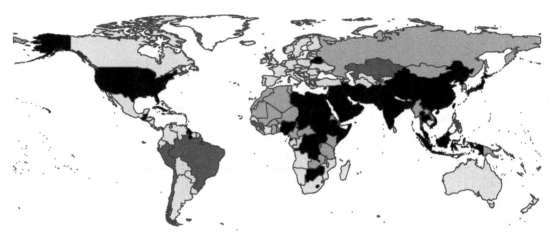

Map 1 A map of the world.

Russia, Algeria, and Papua New Guinea, still have the death penalty on the books but have abolished it in practice, meaning they do not currently sentence people to death or carry out judicially imposed executions. The darkest grey countries, like Brazil, Kazakhstan, and Israel, retain the death penalty, but only for cases of extraordinary or exceptional crimes, such as treason or military offenses. Finally, the black countries, like the United States, Saudi Arabia, Belarus, and Somalia, retain the death penalty for ordinary crimes—whether only for murder, as in the United States, or for a wider variety of offenses.

The study of comparative law and justice can help us understand patterns like those we observe in map 1. People who study comparative law and justice have done the work of gathering and compiling the data that lets us group and categorize countries. More sophisticated analytical work can then be carried out to try to understand why countries do what they do and what the consequences of these differences might be. Some of these explanations regarding the death penalty can be found in chapter 7. But for now, let's consider why we study comparative law and justice in the first place.

WHY STUDY COMPARATIVE LAW AND JUSTICE?

People often think of law, crime, and justice as local issues. In countries like the United States, Canada, India, and Australia especially, law is fairly localized, with different states, provinces, and regions taking somewhat different approaches to law enforcement, punishment, and criminalization. So why, then, is it important to take a global perspective on these issues?

Well, there are a number of reasons. First of all, we live in an increasingly globalized world. The sociologist George Ritzer defines **globalization** as "the worldwide diffusion of practices, expansion of relations across continents, organization of social life on a global scale, and growth of a shared global consciousness" (Ritzer 2011:166). Let's consider what each of these four elements means.

By the *worldwide diffusion of practices*, Ritzer means that things that are done in one place become done everyplace. There are a wide variety of examples of such diffusion. Pizza and sushi are found all over the world today, not just in Italy and Japan, respectively. Similarly, many religions are practiced worldwide rather than solely in a specific nation or region. Soccer, cricket, and other sports are played around the globe. And movies—whether they come from Hollywood, Bollywood, or Nollywood—are viewed in countries far from those in which they were produced.

By the *expansion of relationships*, Ritzer is referring to the growth in connections between people and governments across the globe. Before globalization took hold, people would generally have known only others living nearby, and governments would have had ties only with neighboring nations. Now, countries on opposite sides of the world can forge alliances, and people can build and maintain personal and business relationships across oceans. Such relationships, and the practices embedded in them, lead to *new ways of organizing social life*. Consider the example of stockbrokers' work schedules. When financial markets were local, traders worked the hours their local stock exchanges were open. But today, with global economic relationships and trades across multiple exchanges, brokers' work lives have been reshaped to reflect the global marketplace. Thus, a stockbroker in New York may need to start work at 4 A.M. so they can talk to clients in London as their workday begins or check in with the Tokyo office as the day there comes to a close. Finally, Ritzer argues that globalization has brought with it a new level of *global consciousness*. By this, he means that we see ourselves as part of a global world and are conscious of the interconnections between people and between nations.

Another definition of globalization, which takes a slightly different perspective, refers to globalization as "the intensification of worldwide social relations which link distant localities in such a way that local happenings are shaped by events occurring many miles away and vice versa" (Giddens 1990:64). While it is clearly the case that some local events always affected distant areas—for example, when volcanoes erupt, they result in not only local destruction but also global weather changes—globalization as a social phenomenon emerged with the development of global travel and global communications technologies. Therefore, we can say that globalization began during the ages of exploration and colonization in the 1500s and 1600s and that its pace intensified in the 1800s with the development of steamships (see figure 1) and telegraphs.

Figure 1 The SS *Great Western*, the first purpose-built transatlantic steamship, in 1838 (lithography created by Napoleon Sarony, A. Robertson, and H. R. Robinson).

Globalization has led to increased interaction among countries in relation to issues of law, crime, and justice. Our world must grabble with global problems like environmental catastrophe, world war, cross-border crime and terrorism, and human migration. Without a global approach, we cannot understand how and why these problems arise, what their consequences are, and what approaches might most effectively reduce the harm they can cause. Limiting this harm, whether by intervening when problems arise or by working to prevent them from arising in the first place, requires countries to work together. And working together requires that people understand one another's perspectives, approaches, norms, and values.

As countries have worked together on various global and regional problems, they have built a complex array of global justice institutions. Historically, these institutions were limited to bilateral or multilateral treaties and alliances between nations. Today, though, we have many more global organizations and institutions. Some of these are global, like the World Trade Organization, and others are regional, like the African Union. Some, like the United Nations and the European Union, deal with a broad spectrum of issues, and others, like Interpol and the International Criminal Court, deal with a narrow set of topics and tasks. Without people who are willing to work with those from quite different national contexts to find solutions that are acceptable everyone, such global institutions could never be built. Again, this type of work requires understanding across legal, political, and value systems.

Taking a global perspective on issues of law, crime, and justice therefore enhances our international understanding in our increasingly globalized world, and it establishes the basis for cooperation between countries. But that is not all it does. It also allows people who work within or make policy for legal and justice systems in a particular national context to learn from the ways that other groups or nations do things (Breyer 2018). For example, Norway has an unusual prison system, discussed in chapter 7, which provides prison inmates with much more freedom of activity and movement and treats them much more like they would be treated outside the prison walls (Slater 2017). Yet Norwegian prisoners are much less likely than prisoners in many other countries to be returned to prison in the first few years after their release. Could prison authorities in other countries learn something from Norway's approach? Would adopting some of Norway's practices reduce recidivism elsewhere? Questions like these can extend to any area of the legal system, whether it is an analysis of the effects of making Election Day a national holiday in the United States, a study of the consequences of requiring all employers to provide paid vacation time to their employees, or an investigation into what happens if most police officers are not permitted to carry firearms.

Thus, it is clear that it is important for people who care about legal and justice systems, whether as policymakers, employees, or observers, to learn about what other countries do. There are even career paths devoted to working specifically on questions of global justice, often through **nongovernmental organizations** (NGOs). These include global NGOs focused on specific issues or causes, as well as those focused more generally on global access to justice. For example, The Hague Institute for Innovation of Law (HiiL), based in the Netherlands, works to develop policies to ensure that people all over the world have access to justice and legal services when they need them to help resolve disputes (HiiL 2017). Other options include employment in a global governance organization like the United Nations, in a country's foreign service, or as a consultant who works with countries struggling with particular issues. For example, Independent Diplomat is a consulting firm that helps countries develop political strategies and navigate international law (Independent Diplomat n.d.). It has worked on issues as disparate as how the low-lying Marshall Islands will be able to cope with climate change and sea-level rise and how the non-self-governing territory of Western Sahara can work toward autonomy.

But even if your career will not ever relate to global law and justice or directly benefit from an understanding of how legal and justice systems in other countries have addressed particular problems and issues, it is still useful to learn about and pay attention to the rest of the world. In our increasingly globalized context, what happens on the other side of the planet can have real consequences for our lives, whether by shaping our economic opportunities, contributing to climate change, or creating or avoiding a global military conflict. And so many of us are caught unaware by these processes—from the military service member who has not learned enough world geography to know where the countries to which he or she may be deployed are located to the small business person planning to import a trendy new food product without developing an understanding of the complex dynamics of cross-border trade regulations, from the parents planning an international adoption to the senior citizen sitting in a recliner and trying to follow the incredibly complicated stories of global interaction that are part of our daily news in today's world.

THE ROOTS OF THE FIELD

So we see that studying comparative law and justice is important. But where did this field of study come from, and how are such investigations carried out today? It is likely that for as long as governments and legal systems have existed, there have been individuals within those systems who have committed themselves to understanding how things worked across the border (borders are a relatively modern invention, actually, but the turn of phrase is still useful). Throughout recorded history, there is documentation of emissaries traveling from one kingdom to another and settling down to learn about and observe governmental behavior. But as an area of academic study, comparative law is much younger. According to legal scholars Konrad Zweigert and Hein Kötz (1988), the academic and applied study of comparative law in the Western world did not become a serious practice until the 1800s. Many early scholars of comparative law focused their research on the historical development of legal systems and on the question of why and how it is that we have law in the first place.

They developed their analysis against the backdrop of legal philosophy that had begun to emerge in seventeenth-century Europe. The central debate here concerns the origin of government and legal systems, and it is exemplified by the different perspectives of Thomas Hobbes and John Locke. In his book *Leviathan* (see figure 2), Hobbes argued that before the development of government, humans existed in the "state of nature," living lives that were "solitary, poor, nasty, brutish, and short" and characterized by a war of all against all (Hobbes 1909–14). To Hobbes, then, law is what makes the building of society possible by regulating the rampant conflict between people that would otherwise destroy any chance to create and maintain social bonds. Thus, he believed that a lawless society is not a society at all. Locke's perspective is quite different. He argued that people are by nature social and cooperative beings who live in a state of fundamental equality and have a sense of moral right and wrong. This means, according to Locke, that people will strive to live in peace, even without a government or a ruler. Locke did believe, though, that leadership and law would tend to emerge as a structured and orderly way to ensure justice and the protection of property (Locke [1690] 2008).

Regardless of which of these perspectives you find more persuasive, it is important to note that the fact that governmental and legal systems exist across societies does not mean that they always look like contemporary Western people expect them to look. There are many different ways to organize

Figure 2 The frontispiece of the 1651 edition of Hobbes's *Leviathan* (engraving by Abraham Bosse).

systems designed to ensure justice or maintain social order. Thus, early scholars of comparative law began to construct research agendas involving detailed studies of various societies. While some such scholars came from legal backgrounds and confined their study to the formal legal texts of European nations (Zweigert and Kötz 1988), others were anthropologists who extended their study far beyond formal legal institutions. Such scholars lived among the populations they studied for extended periods, often years, engaging in ethnographic observations of all aspects of social life, including dispute resolution and social control. What they found was that while all societies have ways to resolve disputes and maintain order or compliance with norms, the mechanisms and methods they use vary widely, ranging from tribunals that might closely resemble modern court systems to a variety of processes modern observers might not see or understand as law, like contests or witchcraft. In fact, as you will see in chapter 6 when you learn about the history of trials, European societies used to use methods of dispute resolution that were much like those the early legal anthropologists encountered on far-flung Pacific islands (though by the time these anthropologists came around, few European scholars were eager to recall their own history).

Today, scholars of comparative law and justice have even more traditions to draw on. They come from a vast array of disciplines, including (but not limited to) law and legal studies, sociology, anthropology, geography, political science, and history, and many do interdisciplinary work. And they use a wide variety of methodological strategies (Bracey 2006). For example, many anthropologists, especially in the earlier days of legal anthropology, used descriptive ethnographic methods. They observed dispute resolution and rule-making processes, whether complex modern systems or simple small-group traditions, and recorded how those processes worked. As more and more descriptive studies of legal systems became available, scholars became more able to develop comparative cross-cultural studies of these systems. Such studies enabled scholars to understand many of the ways systems differ as well as to begin to generalize about characteristics that groups of systems have in common (a topic taken up in chapter 2).

Contemporary scholars of comparative law and justice go beyond simply describing or comparing. They look to understand what sorts of dynamics might have led to particular legal arrangements—for example, are there complex relationships of conflict and compromise between different groups in a given society? And they study the consequences of particular legal and justice processes—for example, what sorts of punishments are correlated with higher or lower levels of crime? Finally, they engage in applied analysis, using the comparative study of law in more practical contexts. This includes the ways described above, looking at how countries seek to work together as well as investigating approaches that might improve their own internal systems. It also includes using legal study to explain cultural conflicts within systems, such as when different groups of immigrants with different legal and cultural traditions find themselves in conflict.

Because the study of comparative law and justice draws on so many disciplinary traditions, it is common for two people to talk about the same kind of phenomenon using very different language. This can be a real obstacle for the field, though it also presents opportunities to discover new things by blending various approaches. It does mean, however, that those who are writing about comparative law and justice should be clear about where they are coming from. This book, for example, comes from a sociological perspective. That has certain consequences—in particular, it means that the analysis presented here will pay close attention to structural characteristics of legal and justice systems and will take notice of the ways in which inequality and stratification might be related to those systems. But it will also explore other kinds of issues, even those that are not typically a central focus of sociologists. It will consider the role of culture, look at geographical data, and provide some historical background.

LEGAL CULTURE VERSUS LEGAL STRUCTURE

The debate over the roles and importance of culture and structure is central to many social science topics, including the study of law. So what do these very important terms mean? Well, **social structure** refers to patterns of social arrangements, relations, and institutions within a given society (S. Hunt 2011). **Culture**, in contrast, refers to ways of life and ways of making meaning among groups (Jenks 2011; Spillman 2011). While different social sciences use slightly different definitions of culture, they all typically include elements such as the use of symbols to represent human experience, including modes of artistic and linguistic expression; the norms and values (not laws!) governing social life; and the distinct ways of life of people in different parts of the world, comprising their beliefs, traditions, and habits, including a variety of spheres of activity such as the economy, religion, and family patterns.

While culture and structure are general terms, they can be used in the specifically legal context as well. The term **legal culture** refers to "the network of values and attitudes relating to law, which determines when and why and where [and how] people turn to law or government or turn away" (Friedman 1969:34). In contrast, **legal structure** refers to the institutions, processes, and personnel that make up the legal system. In other words, legal culture is the set of perceptions, values, and opinions about the law, while legal structure refers to the institutions, rules, and processes that support and shape the legal system. Table 1 provides a set of examples of elements of legal structure and related elements of legal culture from the United States legal system.

Social scientists who study a wide variety of social institutions and organizations have found that culture tends to change much more quickly than do social structures. Thus, even when legal culture changes, legal structures tend to remain in place—even when these structures lend themselves to processes and outcomes that make little sense. As Oliver Wendell Holmes, Jr., a United States Supreme Court Justice (see figure 3), wrote in an 1897 article: "It is revolting to have no better reason for a rule of law than that so it was laid down in the time of Henry IV. It is still more revolting if the grounds upon which it was laid down have vanished long since, and the rule simply persists from blind imitation of the past" (Holmes 1897:469).

This book will focus on both legal culture and legal structure—on both what law says it is and what it does, and on both the official institutions and the unofficial practices. It will consider the functions of law that social theorists have long understood—social control, conflict resolution and dispute settlement, and the maintenance of justice—as well as functions that law can hide under

Table 1   Legal structure and legal culture in the United States

Legal structure	Legal culture
The Constitution	Originalism, textualism, activism, pragmatism, and realism are among the various schools of thought about how to interpret or use the Constitution. • For example, consider the arguments around Eighth Amendment standards related to the use of the death penalty and whether there are "evolving standards of decency" or those standards are stuck in the eighteenth century.
Adversarial legalism	People pursue lawsuits as a weapon in disputes, sometimes using them just to make the other party suffer. They are likely to draw on the courts as a way to resolve interpersonal and interorganizational disputes (rather than pursuing means of dispute resolution that do not require legal interventions). • For example, consider the New Jersey family court case in which a divorced couple went to court to argue about whether it was acceptable to take an eleven-year-old to a Pink concert (Shrayber 2015).
Separation of powers	Beliefs about the extent to which it is legitimate for senators to use the filibuster, the president to use executive orders or the veto, or members of Congress to intervene in foreign affairs.
Criminal codes laying out potential punishments for different crimes	Beliefs about the degree to which punishment "should be" harsh or "should provide" access to rehabilitation. • Consider debates about drug-crime sentences and the solitary confinement and lifelong incarceration of juvenile offenders.
Criminal defendants are "innocent until proven guilty beyond a reasonable doubt"	The assumption that anyone on trial must have done something to deserve it and that no one would confess to a crime they did not commit.
The courts favor live witness testimony in trials	Juries expect to see DNA and other forensic evidence, murder weapons, etc.

the surface, with effects that can be just as profound. These might include enabling or preventing social change, maintaining or restraining civil liberties and individual freedoms, expressing societal morals and values, perpetuating or reducing social inequality of various types, and making legal matters more complex and inaccessible to nonlegal personnel. Of course, sometimes these more subtle functions, and the legal culture and unofficial practices that enable them, are easier to see and explore, but we cannot always understand the detailed dynamics of systems we have not observed first-hand and come to inhabit fully. It is important to remember that law is not just a set of texts and the institutions that follow these rules—it is a living, dynamic system that works in all kinds of ways in accordance with the cultural norms and societal priorities of the people who are part of it.

Figure 3 Justice Oliver Wendall Holmes, Jr., circa 1924 (Library of Congress).

A QUICK INTRODUCTION TO LEGAL SYSTEMS

As will be discussed in chapter 3, the particular fashion in which countries arrange the various parts of their legal systems varies widely. But there are some common features of legal systems worth reviewing as you begin your study of comparative law and justice: the branches of government, key types of law, and central varieties of legal texts.

Scholars of governance talk about three branches of government: the **legislative branch**, the **executive branch**, and the **judicial branch**. The legislative branch is responsible for making laws. The executive branch is responsible for enforcing those laws and carrying out the functions of government. Finally, the judicial branch is responsible for resolving disputes and, in some countries, adjudicating challenges to actions or decisions of the other branches. In some countries, like the United States, these three branches are quite separate, and there is a system of **checks and balances** to ensure that no branch is able to dominate the others. In countries run as dictatorships, the three branches may be combined under the power of one ruling individual. Other countries have systems that lie somewhere between these two extremes.

Countries make, enforce, and adjudicate various types of law. The first to come to mind is typically **criminal law**, which is a body of law having to do with defining particular actions or behaviors as criminal, assessing penalties to such actions and behaviors, and explaining how particular instances of these actions or behaviors are to be adjudicated in courts. But criminal law is only a small part of what legal systems do. **Civil law** concerns relationships, rights, and duties between people and organizations. For example, if you have a contract with a roofer to repair your roof, but the roof still leaks after his work is done, no crime has been committed—but you still have a legal dispute. Does the roofer have to come back and fix the job? Can you refuse to pay the full fee and use the remaining money to hire a different roofer? These are the kinds of questions civil law is designed to deal with. **Administrative law** deals with the functioning of the government and its subsidiary agencies. In many legal systems, there are other areas of law that are treated as their own specialized fields, such as family law, commercial law, labor law, or agricultural law.

These areas of law are often—but not always—spelled out in legal texts, most notably in **statutes**, which are written laws that have been enacted by the legislature. In some countries, these statutes are collected into a written **legal code**—an organized and systematic set of laws covering all elements of law. Not all systems have legal codes, however, and in those that do, the codes may cover only certain areas of law (for example, there may be a criminal code but not a civil code). In some countries, as will be discussed in chapter 2, a large portion of law comes not from statutes at all but rather from **precedent**—previous decisions made by courts that are now considered binding law. In addition, many—though not all—countries have **constitutions**, which are written documents laying out the fundamental legal principles of a country's legal system.

For now, before we get into the specific ways in which the organization of countries' legal systems may vary, consider one example of how differently things can work in two countries we might think to be quite similar, the United States and the United Kingdom ("two countries divided by a common language," as the old joke goes). This example concerns the process by which an individual elected to the national legislative body resigns their seat. In the United States, doing so is a fairly straightforward process. An individual who wishes to resign simply announces that he or she will do so as of a specified date, and then, on that date, they leave office. The legislator is then replaced, either by a special election (for members of the House of Representatives and for senators in a few states) or by appointment by the state's governor for Senators in the remaining states.

In the United Kingdom, special elections can also be held to fill vacant seats in Parliament. However, members of Parliament are not permitted to resign, as this would be considered dereliction of their duty to the people they represent. But of course it is not unusual for circumstances to arise that give elected officials reason to resign. In 1680, Parliament passed a law stating that any members who accepted a paying office from the Crown (in other words, a position in the executive branch, run by the King or Queen) were obligated to leave their Parliamentary posts due to the possibility of conflict of interest (U.K.

CASE STUDY 1.1

An International Child Custody Dispute

In June 2004, a young mother boarded a plane with her four-year-old son at Newark Liberty International Airport in New Jersey. The pair were headed to her native Brazil for a trip to see her family, with her husband—the father of her child—due to join them a week later. But before he was scheduled to depart, his wife called him up to say that neither she nor their son would be returning to their life in New Jersey (Semple 2009). This phone call was the opening shot in what became a protracted international struggle involving the Goldman family—mom Bruna, dad David, and child Sean.

David and Bruna met in Italy, where he was a model and she a student of fashion design. They married in 1999 and moved to New Jersey, with Sean coming along shortly thereafter (Semple 2009). David worked as a boat captain, and Bruna found a job as a teacher. After Bruna left the country with Sean, David embarked on a complex, multinational legal battle to try to regain custody of his son. He filed suit in the New Jersey courts, where he quickly won a ruling that Sean should be returned. But Bruna did not comply with the ruling.

In cases such as this, the United States, Brazil, and more than sixty other countries who have signed on (as shown in CS 1.1 map a) are governed by the Hague Abduction Convention, a multilateral international treaty designed to "secure the prompt return of children wrongfully removed to or retained in any Contracting State and to ensure that rights of custody and of access under the law of one Contracting State are effectively respected in the other Contracting States" (Convention on the Civil Aspects of International Child Abduction 1980). While the convention is complicated, it generally holds that children under age sixteen cannot be removed from their place of residence and taken to another country without permission of all custodial parents, and that if such an abduction takes place, the child should be returned—"unless it is demonstrated that the child is now settled in its new environment."

Thus, when Bruna failed to return Sean to his father, David's lawyer turned to the United States Department of State for assistance in enforcing the convention. The United States then contacted the Brazilian government, and at the same time,

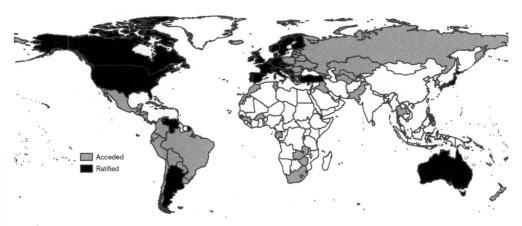

CS 1.1 Map a State parties to The Hague Abduction Convention as of March 2017 (Hague Conference on Private International Law 2019).

David sued in Brazil. Even the Brazilian courts agreed that Sean has been taken from New Jersey illegally, but they referenced the convention's clause about children being settled in their new environment to rule that Sean should stay in Brazil (Semple 2009). David continued to appeal this ruling in the Brazilian courts, and the United States continued to put pressure on Brazil to return Sean to his father. Indeed, the United States repeatedly cited Brazil as noncompliant with the convention, noting dozens of other cases in which children were taken to Brazil (Semple 2009).

In the meantime, Bruna divorced David. She then remarried, wedding a lawyer who had been working on her case, and became pregnant with a daughter. In August 2008, four years after she left New Jersey with Sean, she died in childbirth (Goldman 2012). As soon as he heard the news, David flew to Brazil, seeking to be reunited with the son he had not seen in four years. But the Brazilian courts refused to grant him custody or even visitation, appointing João Paulo Lins e Silva, Bruna's widower, as Sean's legal guardian.

While the Hague Abduction Convention does not differentiate between Bruna and her second husband as abductors, there is of course a difference in how we understand a mother's decision to bring her child to her native country versus a man with no prior legal or biological connection to a child deciding to keep him away from his father. One of the things that remains so fascinating about the Goldman case is how different people respond to it; there are so many varying assumptions we can make about the motivations guiding Bruna's decision and the actions taken by her Brazilian relatives, as well as about what David's role in all of this may have been.

Eventually, in February 2009, David was allowed a few hours of supervised visitation with his son. After almost a year of additional litigation and further diplomatic pressure from the United States, the Brazilian courts issued a unanimous ruling that Sean be returned to his father (Bring Sean Home Foundation 2012). But the Goldmans' legal ordeal was not over. Sean's Brazilian grandparents sued in both Brazilian and U.S. courts, ultimately culminating in a ruling that the surviving Brazilian grandmother should be able to visit him in New Jersey (*D.G.G. v. B.B.G., v. R.R.F. and S.B.R.* 2012). Sean had a long, hard adjustment back to life in New Jersey with his father, and he remained in the public eye, appearing on television specials into his early teens (Flam 2014).

In 2014, President Obama signed into law a bill sponsored by New Jersey representative Christopher Smith, who had worked with David, that was designed to enhance the United States' strategies for dealing with cases violating of the Hague Abduction Convention (Sean and David Goldman International Child Abduction Prevention and Return Act of 2014). This law includes provisions for annual reporting on abduction cases, supplies a set of potential actions for the State Department to take in such cases, and provides for the establishment of interagency training and cooperation to prevent international child abductions. However, any additional strategies or provisions provided for in this law apply only to the U.S. government—and even then, only if the executive branch decides to use them. As will be discussed in more detail in chapter 10, most international treaties are not built with any kind of enforcement mechanism, and thus any country from which a child is abducted can only attempt to pressure the country to which the child has been taken into returning him or her. As important as a child like Sean is, when that country is a valued ally and trading partner, as Brazil is to the United States, extreme actions like military force or even economic sanctions are probably not going to be used in seeking the child's return.

Parliament n.d.). Therefore, when members wish to resign, they can request that the Crown appoint them to one of two pointless Crown offices that exist only for this purpose (the Crown Steward and Bailiff of the Chiltern Hundreds or of the Manor of Northstead), and then Parliament disqualifies them from continuing to serve. They hold this office only until the next member wishes to resign, which can be as little as a matter of minutes, but they are permitted to run in the subsequent special election should they so choose.

CONCLUSION

Studying comparative law and justice—reading this book—will give you a new perspective on the complexity and diversity of legal and justice systems around the world. You will learn what kinds of things countries tend to have in common, and in what ways countries have found themselves on (or chosen) more distinct paths. You may find that your own country has much to learn from the ways that other countries do things, or you may find that your country is what Kristijane Nordmeyer, Nicole Bedera, and Trisha Teig (2016) call a "model country"—one that provides an example other countries can learn from. Should you embark on a career in law, justice services, government, or another area of law or justice systems, learning about these differences will help you to evaluate the policies and programs that are part of your career and make suggestions for improvements that are based on global best practices.

But even if you do not plan to work in field related to law or justice, learning about comparative law and justice is important. It will help you understand the complex dynamics that shape all kinds of issues in our increasingly globalized world, from cross-border crime to international conflict, from environmental protection to migration. And it will help you better understand the law and justice system in which you live by situating it in a broader, more comparative context. Thus, by studying comparative law and justice, you will become more familiar with all the moving parts of your own legal structure and be able to better comprehend the nature of your own legal culture.

So, on with the journey.

World Legal Systems

CHAPTER GOALS

1. Understand the utility of categorizing legal systems and the central questions useful in the process of categorizing.
2. Describe five main world legal systems and identify the central similarities and differences between them.
3. Explain the processes of change that shape legal systems.
4. Become familiar with the idea of the rule of law.

In the year 1500, the country we now know as the Philippines—a nation consisting of over seven thousand islands and over one hundred million people—was made up of a number of distinct kingdoms. These kingdoms were shaped by a vast array of ethnic and religious traditions. Some had adopted Hindu or Buddhist philosophies from India, some were influenced by Islam, and some were part of the Chinese orbit, while others continued their own indigenous traditions. In 1521, Ferdinand Magellan landed on an island in the Filipino archipelago during his circumnavigation of the globe. He is generally considered to have been the first European to visit the territory. By 1565, the Spanish were actively involved in colonizing the Philippines, and they imported both the Catholic faith and, later, the Spanish legal code. In 1898, the United States defeated Spain in the Spanish-American War and claimed the Philippines as a prize. The country was occupied by Japan during World War II and finally became an independent nation in 1946 (Santos-Ong 2015).

Scholars believe that traditional legal codes existed in some Filipino kingdoms before the arrival of the Spanish. The Spanish added to or replaced these legal codes, first with individual laws and then, by the 1880s, with a complete legal code. While some of these Spanish laws remained in effect during the United States occupation, others were replaced with new laws, a process that was repeated after the country gained independence. This complex history left the Philippines with a complex legal system that combines elements of Spanish civil law, United States common law, Islamic religious law, and indigenous traditional law (Santos-Ong 2015). The country also spent several years—both under Japanese military occupation and under dictator Ferdinand Marcos (who was in power from 1972 to 1986)—with authoritarian governments and legal systems. There are even multiple types of courts: *katarungang pambarangay,* or neighborhood justice courts, are state-administered organs of traditional law (Merry 1988); Shari'a courts dispense Islamic justice for the Muslim population; and regular state courts draw on the particular combination of civil and common law that is the Filipino legal regime. Understanding the complexities the Philippines presents requires that we first learn about these different types of legal systems, each of which has its own history and approach to legal thinking and decision-making, among other characteristics.

THE RULE OF LAW

In thinking about the classification of world legal systems, it helps to start with the concept of the **rule of law**. Most fundamentally, the rule of law means that law is written down, publicly available, and fairly applied (O'Donnell 2004). A legal system that exhibits the rule of law follows clear rules and guidelines rather than acting in an arbitrary way, and it ensures that no one is above the law and that people have access to knowledge about law and to legal institutions (Waldron 2016). This concept has a long history in political thought, stretching back as far as Aristotle.

The specific details of what the rule of law entails, beyond this general framework, are disputed. According to the World Justice Project (n.d.), the essential features of the rule of law are that both government and private individuals are legally accountable; that laws are clear, accessible, fairly applied, and protect fundamental rights; that the processes of lawmaking and enforcement are accessible and fair; and that dispute resolution is administered fairly, impartially, and accessibly. According to Lord Thomas Henry Bingham, Lord Chief Justice of the United Kingdom from 1996 to 2008, the rule of law requires

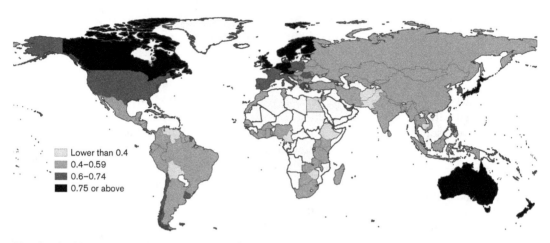

Map 2 Rule of law score (World Justice Project 2017).

that laws are accessible and intelligible, that they are equally applicable to all, that human rights are given adequate protection, that there are provisions for fair dispute resolution, that the laws comply with international law, that government officials exercise their duties appropriately, and finally that decisions are made fairly and based on rules rather than discretion (Bingham 2007). Some scholars even argue that the rule of law requires that individuals comply with legal authority, including in cases where they disagree with rules or decisions (Waldron 2016). Other scholars argue that the rule of law is a Western notion that has been rhetorically imposed on countries in other parts of the world (Ohnesorge 2007). Empirical analysis has found a correlation between particular national cultures and the rule of law (Licht, Goldschmidt, and Schwartz 2007), which supports the argument that the rule of law is a culturally specific formulation. Scholars also point out that the rule of law often falls short in reality of what it promises in theory (O'Donnell 2004; Waldron 2016).

Nevertheless, the rule of law remains a useful concept for considering differences among legal systems. As map 2 shows, there is wide variation between countries in the degree to which they uphold the rule of law. A score of 1 would represent a country with complete adherence to the rule of law; a country with no adherence would have a score of 0. This analysis was calculated based on data for forty-seven factors; the data was gathered from local experts and via household surveys. Note that a number of countries (those that appear shaded in white on the map) have not been given a score; this is due to missing data. Among these missing countries, there are those that would have scored low and those that would have scored high were they to have been included. Bermuda and Iceland, for instance, are among those with insufficient data, yet they are not countries we generally assume to be without the rule of law. Among countries with sufficient data to calculate a rule of law score, Venezuela (0.29) and Cambodia (0.32) scored lowest, while Sweden (0.86), Finland (0.87), Norway (0.89), and Denmark (0.89) scored highest (World Justice Project 2017). But the rule of law is only one dimension of variation among legal systems—there are many others.

DEFINING LEGAL SYSTEMS

While each country's legal system has its own unique characteristics, scholars of comparative law group them into different categories of legal systems within which countries share some characteristics in common, often called **families of law**. Families of law are an example of what social theorists call **ideal types** (Weber 1949)—abstract concepts generalizing from phenomena common to most instances or examples of the thing being described. Although no real instance might include all elements of an ideal type, the ideal type enables us to create sensible categories. For example, if we were to think about a set of ideal types of furniture, we might include "tables" as one category. Tables typically have flat tops at least a foot or so above the ground and have one or more legs holding them up. But if you encountered a dining room where the table was suspended from the ceiling, or a coffee table with an uneven surface, you would still be able to identify the item as a table.

This chapter lays out five **legal systems**, or families of law, each of which should be understood as an ideal type. No actual country may exactly match up to the descriptions provided, but this system allows us to determine where any particular country fits (although we must remember that some countries have mixed legal systems that incorporate elements from two or more of these categories). Note that scholars have developed a variety of different taxonomies of world legal systems—some propose slightly different categories than this text does, while others propose a greater number of categories. This text categorizes legal systems as **civil law**, **common law**, **theocratic law**, **authoritarian law**, or **traditional law**. Civil law is a system of law based on legal codes that first developed in continental Europe. Common law is a system of law based on **precedent**—"something done in the past that is appealed to as a reason for doing the same thing again" (Landes and Posner 1976:3). Theocratic law is based on systems of religious belief. Authoritarian law stems from the control of a dictator or other authoritarian leader. And traditional law is, as it sounds, a system based on tradition. While no particular legal system has a monopoly on the rule of law, traditional systems are less likely to function in the fashion it requires, and authoritarian systems do not exhibit it. Each of these systems will be discussed in more detail below.

In describing each of these five categories of legal systems, there are a series of clarifying questions we can ask (Zweigert and Kötz 1988). We can start by

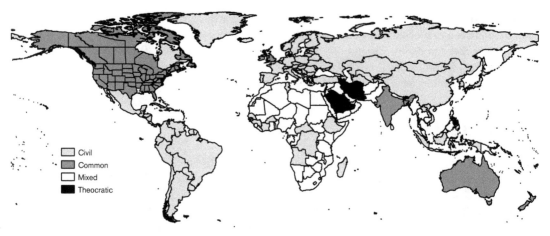

Map 3 Map of world legal systems.

understanding a category's historical development, leading up to where it is found today. Then we can ask about its mode of legal thinking and sources of law and authority. Next, we can ask about its central legal institutions, such as the procedures for decision-making and dispute resolution. Finally, we can ask about its ideology or central beliefs and any other special characteristics it may exhibit.

So where are our five families of law found? Map 3 shows the distribution of families of law across the globe. As you can see, common law is concentrated in English-speaking countries, including England, Canada, the United States, India, Australia, New Zealand, and other former British colonies. Civil law is concentrated in Europe, Asia, and Latin America. Mixed systems are found in Africa, the Middle East, and South and Southeast Asia, as well as in some island nations. There is less of a geographic pattern in the location of countries that have theocratic law, since they can be based on any given body of religious belief. As will be discussed later in the chapter, few countries rely entirely on traditional law, so countries with traditional elements to their legal system show up on the map as among the group of mixed legal systems. Finally, there are no countries shown as having authoritarian legal systems. This is because countries tend not to admit that they are authoritarian in nature; thus, authoritarian regimes construct legal systems resembling those of some other family of law, even if authoritarian power is truly at the root of the system.

Common Law

England has a long legal history, with periods during which it was ruled by different conquering forces, including the Romans, who each brought their own legal traditions with them. The concept of common law first emerged when England was under Norman rule as the body of law applying to the people of England. The Norman rulers built a population of judges to extend their rule over local populations and consolidate their authority, and as the judges needed to be able to read and write, they were often recruited from among the literate clergy. Thus, early English law was deeply influenced by religious law. This complex mixture of Roman, Norman, and religious legal traditions became the backdrop for the later development of modern common law, beginning in the period after the Norman conquest in 1066.

Since there was no body of codified law of the sort that will be discussed in the section on civil law systems, England developed a special process for facilitating court action. The king would issue a **writ**, a set of written instructions for addressing particular kinds of disputes. Court cases could be initiated only in compliance with some particular writ, and there were not that many to choose from—only about seventy-five existed even by the early 1800s (Glenn 2007). If there was no writ that addressed the circumstances of a given dispute, disputants had to either make do without the court or craft complex legal fictions to make the case relevant to an existing writ. When cases were heard, judges made legal decisions—but they drew on local people to form juries that made decisions of fact. This probably increased the public's acceptance of the king's role (Glenn 2007) and enabled courts to move away from trials by ordeal or combat (Zweigert and Kötz 1988). Throughout this period, special religious courts worked alongside the more secular courts, and they were charged with hearing cases relating to family law, religious offenses, and the clergy.

In the 1830s, legal reforms began to reshape the English common law system into something more like what we would recognize today. New court procedures were established that moved courts away from the use of specific writs and made it possible for people to bring cases as they wished (Glenn 2007). The courts themselves were systematized to make it clearer who had jurisdiction over what (Zweigert and Kötz 1988). Religious courts were largely abolished, though some of their influences remained. Similar reforms took place in the United States, though it had never had religious courts.

Today, common law remains the legal system of England, Wales, and Northern Ireland and part of the legal system of Scotland. It was also imported by the British into countries they colonized, including the United States, Canada, Australia, India, and others all around the world. Unlike civil law, common law has not been adopted by countries unless those countries were colonized by or heavily influenced by another common law country. This is because common law is extremely complex. Civil law, as will be discussed in the following section, can be easily imported, as it largely consists of written legal codes. But common law relies on a long history of accumulated court decisions and thus cannot reasonably be adopted by countries that have not been part of this history.

The most important source of authority for common law is precedent, the prior decisions of courts as part of an accumulated body of knowledge. Early in the history of common law, precedent was not binding—judges could use it to guide their reasoning, but they could also depart from prior rulings. As the common law developed, precedent became more entrenched, and today a central principle of common law is **stare decisis**, literally "let the decision stand" (Glenn 2007). What this means is that when judges are confronted with a case dealing with the same issues as a prior case, they are expected to conform their decision to the prior decision. Precedent thus exists as law to be followed. Of course, not all court decisions truly adhere to this principle. There are always ways for courts to argue that a given case is not so much like any prior ones (Zweigert and Kötz 1988). It is also worth noting that precedent can be shared across jurisdictions that use common law, since they have common history (Glenn 2007), though not all countries with common law systems choose to do this.

Precedent may sound a lot like tradition, but they are not the same thing (K. Bartlett 1995). Precedent exists strictly within the legal system; tradition exists outside it, or encompasses both legal and nonlegal contexts. Precedent carries more weight the more recent it is, while tradition carries more weight the longer it has existed. Finally, there are ways to overrule precedent, but tradition cannot be overruled; changing tradition is possible only gradually.

Trial procedures in common law legal systems are adversarial in nature. While the adversarial process will be discussed in more detail in chapter 6, the most important feature of **adversarial trials** is that they involve two competing sides that present oral arguments before a judge. Central to the history of adversarial trials is the presence of a **jury**. In jury trials, the **judge** decides questions of law, while the jury decides questions of fact. However, not all common law jurisdictions retain a strong role for juries. Jurisdictions also differ on other elements of trial procedure, such as whether judges can question witnesses (Glendon, Carozza, and Picker 2008).

Appeals are an important part of common law. While all courts, even the most local, are empowered to make decisions, those of higher courts have additional precedential authority. Judicial review of legislative decisions often has a strong role to ensure that new laws are in line with precedent. Judges in common law countries are typically part of an independent judiciary and are not subject to direct control by other branches of government (Glenn 2007).

While England remains without a legal code today, many common law jurisdictions have constructed legal codes for at least some portion of the issues they deal with (Glenn 2007). Even where formal legal codes do not exist, legislatures in common law legal systems are empowered to create law by passing legislation enacted as statutes. Thus, the common law legal systems of today have extensive bodies of written law, though some or all of it may remain uncodified. Criminal and procedural law are more likely to have been codified than civil law. It is important to note that in some common law jurisdictions,

CASE STUDY 2.1

Cannibalism and Common Law

To understand the distinction between tradition and precedent, it might help to consider one of the classic cases of common law that law students learn about: *Regina v. Dudley and Stephens* (1884). The origins of this case involve the journey from England to Australia of a fifty-two-foot vessel with a crew of four men: three adults with sailing experience—Edwin Stephens, Ned Brooks, and Thomas Dudley—and one seventeen-year-old orphan boy, Richard Parker. While sailing the South Atlantic, the ship sank suddenly. The four crew members managed to escape the wreck in a thirteen-foot boat, but they did not have time to grab any provisions other than two cans of turnips. And they were very far from land. After about twenty days of drifting, with very little water and nothing to eat but the turnips and a turtle they caught, Dudley killed Parker, with the agreement of Stephens, and all three men set about eating Parker's corpse. They were rescued a few days later by a German vessel. Upon their return to England, they were arrested and charged with murder (Simpson 1981).

It was clear to all that a murder had occurred; the legal question the case raised was whether necessity, in this case the need for sustenance, was a legitimate defense to murder charges. Eventually, a panel of judges ruled that it was not and sentenced Dudley and Stephens to death; charges against Brooks had been dismissed earlier, as he had not participated in the killing and was willing to serve as a witness. But eventually, the death sentence was revoked, and after serving six months in prison, Dudley and Stephens were pardoned (Simpson 1981).

What is important to note here is that the propriety of cannibalism was never a legal question—Dudley and Stephens were convicted for the killing, not for eating the body. Cannibalism may be viewed with moral outrage by many, but cannibalism at sea was not uncommon in the 1800s. Many oceanic accidents resulted in a lack of food, and deaths on board were frequent. Thus, crews would resort to eating their dead comrades. The Dudley and Stephens case is not even the only one in which sailors killed a crew member in order to eat him. However, sailors were expected to draw lots to determine who would be killed, and Dudley and Stephens did not draw lots—though Dudley had tried to convince the other men that they should do this—because Parker was already close to death, having consumed seawater. Of course, it is likely that proper lots were not drawn in other cases either, but Dudley and Stephens were perhaps overly honest about what had transpired on their lifeboat. It is clear from the recorded history that cannibalism at sea, and even murder as a means to obtain the meat, was a tradition of sorts, at least in extreme circumstances (Simpson 1981).

There is a side note to the *Dudley and Stephens* case: in fact, the trial was a bit of a setup. Dudley, Stephens, and Brooks were all men from well-respected seafaring families, and public sentiment was on their side. While the British government wanted to make an example of them to put a stop to the tradition of cannibalism at sea, it did not want to risk too much public outrage. Thus, a deal was reached to find the men guilty but ensure a minimal punishment (Hojecká 2003). *Regina v. Dudley and Stephens* established the common law principle that necessity is not a defense to murder (Hojecká 2003), which has been incorporated into the body of precedent in many countries with common law legal systems. The legal precedent it established paid no heed to the longstanding tradition of cannibalism at sea, and indeed that sort of cannibalism remained traditional, even as the new *precedent* aimed to stop the practice.

legislatively enacted statutes are not considered to have the force of law until they are judicially interpreted (Glendon, Carozza, and Picker 2008).

When judges interpret laws, they may do so literally or they may draw on other information to develop an understanding of context and legislative intent (Glendon, Carozza, and Picker 2008). Similar strategies of interpretation are used in applying precedent, as it is rare for two cases to be exactly alike. When judges engage in interpretation, they begin with the facts and reexamine the law in light of those specific facts.

Common law is a system of mutual obligations, with early cases focusing much attention on issues like land ownership and the obligations of landlords and tenants. Thus, it provided little room for the development of individual rights throughout most of its history (Glenn 2007). Today, many common law jurisdictions do have robust protections for at least some individual rights, and they can provide access to justice and fair procedures. Thus they are able to uphold the rule of law. However, in contrast with civil law, common law is not very transparent to regular people. Mastering a body of precedent is not easy, and so those without legal education in common law jurisdictions may not find the law clear or intelligible.

Civil Law

Civil law is sometimes called code law. This other name focuses on the most central characteristic of civil law: the presence and fundamental importance of a written legal code. Note that the term "civil law" has two meanings. The one that refers to civil law as a legal system will be discussed here; the other, which refers to civil law as a category of law that exists in all legal systems and deals with private, noncriminal relations, will be discussed in chapter 6.

The Romans established a system in which certain types of disputes could be brought before designated officials to be heard and decided. Many of these decisions were written down, and thus it became possible to be learned in the law (Glenn 2007). As Rome expanded its territories through conquest, the complexity of legal matters and disputes grew, and thus in the sixth century, the emperor Justinian ordered that a body of Roman written law and legal decisions be codified. But as the Roman Empire fell, Roman law largely disappeared from Europe. In the Middle Ages, Roman law was rediscovered as a source for academic study, and because scholars were familiar with that body of knowledge, it was to Roman law they turned when they began the task of codifying national legal systems in the 1800s (Glenn 2007).

France created the first national legal code in 1804, and Germany and Austria followed soon after (Glenn 2007). While the French legal code was crafted in just a few years as a revolutionary project, the German and Austrian codes emerged from a painstaking intellectual endeavor that took decades (Glendon, Carozza, and Picker 2008; Zweigert and Kötz 1988). The French legal code spread, with modifications, to Italy, Spain, and Portugal; today, Franco-Roman civil law is still found in those countries, as well as in the many countries in Latin America, Africa, Southeast Asia, and the Pacific that France, Italy, Spain, and Portugal colonized. It is also found in a number of Middle Eastern countries, some of which were under French authority after the collapse of the Ottoman Empire. Many Muslim countries looking to codify their secular law imported the Egyptian legal code, which was developed under French rule (Zweigert and Kötz 1988). French civil law is also found in Quebec, in Canada, and Louisiana, in the United States, while Portuguese civil law had an important influence on the Indian state of Goa. The Germanic civil law system spread to Switzerland and the Netherlands and the colonies of these countries (Zweigert and Kötz 1988), and it influenced the development of Russian law as well as the legal systems of Eastern Europe, Central Asia, and many communist countries.

The written legal code, along with other legislation, is the primary source of law in civil law systems (Glendon, Carozza, and Picker 2008). In deciding cases, courts may also look to local customs, their own prior decisions in similar circumstances (though these are not binding), and the writings of legal scholars. Judges use interpretation of written laws to guide their decision-making, particularly when written laws are ambiguous or do not fully address a given situation (Glendon, Carozza, and Picker 2008). However, they have only modest ability to shape law itself. The authority of these codes comes from the legitimate authority of the state that enacts them.

Civil law countries can, at any time, decide to adopt a new legal code (Glendon, Carozza, and Picker 2008). They may do this because of regime change, or they may simply decide the code needs a refresher due to societal changes. Short of this, it is easy to create some change in civil law legal systems simply by passing new laws (Glendon, Carozza, and Picker 2008). Though civil legal codes initially drew on older Roman models, they were themselves contemporary creations, and they can be modified at any time through lawmaking processes (Glenn 2007). In formally democratic civil law countries, new law is created through the legislative process; in other types of regimes, the executive branch or ruler may create law.

The trial process in civil law courts is inquisitorial. While this model will be discussed in more detail in chapter 6, the most important elements of **inquisitorial trials** are that judges directly question witnesses, including those accused of crimes, and that juries are rare (Glendon, Carozza, and Picker 2008). In recent years, some civil law countries have adopted a more adversarial model for their trials while retaining other aspects of the civil law system. Appeals are possible, but the decisions of appellate courts do not become binding precedent as they would in the common law system.

The outcomes of cases in civil law courts do not become law—there is no role for precedent, and courts rarely refer to prior judicial decisions in their rulings. Also, there is little or no role for judicial review—judges and courts cannot overturn the actions of the legislature as an ordinary matter of course. However, as will be discussed in chapter 6, many civil law countries have developed special constitutional courts that are charged with reviewing the constitutionality of new laws (Zweigert and Kötz 1988). Judges in civil law courts are typically civil servants; the judiciary is not independent of other branches of government (Zweigert and Kötz 1988).

Civil law scholars believe that writing down laws *creates* them—laws do not exist prior to their creation, though they may be based on broader moral, ethical, or religious principles (Glendon, Carozza, and Picker 2008). When engaging in legal reasoning, scholars and judges begin with a solid foundation in the law and then apply that law to facts.

As the civil law system evolved, central European thought developed a notion of individual legal rights (Glenn 2007), another factor that marks this system as different from other families of law. This helped give rise to the modern conception of the rule of law. Not all civil law legal systems uphold the rule of law, of course—some engage in arbitrary behavior, do not have transparent processes, or do not guarantee fundamental rights. But modern civil law, especially in democratic countries, is quite hospitable to the rule of law.

Theocratic Law

Theocratic law is a system of law based on religious belief. It can also be called religious law or ecclesiastical law. While the term "ecclesiastical" technically refers only to Christian religious practices and beliefs, it is widely used to refer to religion more generally. The roots of theocratic law are in the practice of religion, which extends far into history. Hindu and Jewish law are the oldest recorded continuous legal traditions, with histories stretching back several millennia. Jewish law, called *halakha* in Hebrew, is rooted in the text of the Old Testament and the later Talmudic commentaries. Hindu law is similarly based on a body of religious texts, including the Vedas and Sastras. Other theocratic legal systems found today include Islamic law and Roman Catholic canon law, though any religion can be the source of a theocratic legal system. Islamic law, called **Shari'a** in Arabic, comes most fundamentally from the Qur'an, Islam's sacred text. Additional sources of Islamic law are the *hadith*, the collected sayings of the Prophet Muhammed and accounts of his daily life believed to contain revelations of law and moral guidance; and *ijma*, the consensus of Islamic scholars (sometimes only those from early in the history of Islam, but sometimes extended to more modern scholars). Catholic canon law, or *jus canonicum*, has been codified in the Code of Canon Law, which was first issued in 1917 (there are separate versions for Roman and Eastern Catholics); before then, Catholic law depended on a variety of texts (Peters 2013).

Today, theocratic law is found primarily in Islamic countries, some of which have purely theocratic legal systems, some of which have mixed legal systems combining theocratic law with other systems, and some of which have formally secular systems with limited Islamic influence. In some of the countries with mixed systems, secular law predominates, while in others, secular law is used only for issues not sufficiently addressed in Islamic texts. The countries with legal systems that are most purely Islamic in nature are Iran and Saudi Arabia. Another purely theocratic entity is the Vatican, the seat of Catholicism. Jewish law is used for family law issues in Israel, as is Hindu (and other) religious law in India. Thailand's complex mixed legal system also has some historical Hindu influences.

While theocratic law is written and codified, its authority stems not from the text itself but rather from the fact that it was revealed by whatever higher power the religion believes in. Thus, the divine is the source of authority rather than the secular state. Religious and legal authority are often conflated in theocratic legal systems, even if personnel are formally separate. For example, Iran has a Supreme Leader, a religious figure who holds office for life, and a president, who is elected and carries out executive functions. Furthermore, while theocratic law is based on texts, like civil law, it is harder to change than is civil law. In civil law, new laws can be passed; in contrast, foundational religious texts cannot be edited. Yet despite their unchanging texts, theocratic systems can have multiple schools of thought and diverse interpretations of the implications of the texts for legal rules (Shahidulah 2014).

The central mode of legal thinking in theocratic legal systems is reasoning from the texts. In circumstances where the legal issues presented to judges are closely consistent with rules outlined in the text, judicial reasoning from the text is easy. Where more novel circumstances or questions are presented, theocratic authorities must interpret texts and reason from analogy (Glenn 2007). It is also important to note that theocratic legal texts, especially those of Judaism, played an important role in the development of modern secular legal codes. This is in large part due to the fact that Jewish legal codes already existed in textual form prior to the development of modern civil law codes and thus could be used as example texts.

Theocratic legal systems can easily—but do not necessarily—fulfill some of the criteria of the rule of law. They have clear, and usually accessible, legal systems to which all people are equally subject. And there are rules about dispute resolution, which are not arbitrary. Processes of decision-making are specific to each religion. They are less significant today in Jewish and Hindu religious law, as these exist only within the context of secular legal systems. Canon law is subject to the authority of the Pope, who is elected by the College of Cardinals. Systems of legal decision-making in countries with Islamic legal systems vary. In Iran, for instance, such decision-making is in the hands of the Supreme Leader, while in Saudi Arabia, the king has primary power and consults with religious authorities.

Similarly, dispute resolution procedures depend on the specific religion in question. It is worth noting that both Islamic and Jewish law retain some procedural rights and protections for the accused, including the right to a trial with witnesses, that are supposed to protect people from arbitrary punishment. However, these may not always be followed, especially where systems mix theocratic law with traditional or authoritarian law. Jewish and Islamic law do not use lawyers; judges are typically clergy and may not require any special training beyond that which all clergy receive. In canon law, lawyers and judges must be specifically trained in canon law at special canon law schools; while clergy do have some understanding of canon law, they are not generally qualified for official roles in dispute resolution (Peters 2013).

The fundamental ideology of theocratic legal systems is the ideology of whichever set of religious beliefs underlies that system. Theocratic legal systems may not protect individual rights, and individual rights are always subjugated to religious values. Indeed, religious traditions tend to focus heavily on individual obligations, such as the Ten Commandments or the Hindu notion of dharma, leaving limited room for individual rights.

Authoritarian Law

Authoritarian law, sometimes also called autocratic law, is the system of law found in countries with **authoritarian governments**, such as dictatorships and totalitarian monarchies (to be discussed further in chapter 3). As authoritarian countries can emerge anywhere, there is no particular geographical location or type of country in which authoritarian legal systems are concentrated. Current examples of authoritarian legal systems include North Korea, Syria, Belarus, and Eritrea. There is also no generalized historical process leading to the emergence of authoritarian law, as it simply comes into being with the rise of an authoritarian government. In such countries, the trappings of some other legal system—often civil or theocratic—may exist, but the country is not actually bound to that system. Rather, what the ruling body says (whether it is a dictator, a king or queen, some kind of military council, or something else) goes.

The ruler is the source of law and authority in authoritarian countries. Some authoritarian rulers believe, or convince the population to believe, that they rule because they have been blessed by the heavens. Yet the authority remains vested in the rulers themselves. While there may be a codified body of law that retains some authority, the ruler can undermine it without restraint. Thus, there is no rule of law in authoritarian legal systems. At best, the legal system represents the current embodiment of administrative policies; at worst, codified law is a convenient hypocrisy for the country's leadership.

Despite the fact that the ruler exercises authoritarian control, authoritarian legal systems do still have legal institutions. Many retain legislative bodies, though their actions may be strictly controlled by the ruler. They also tend to retain courts. However, the judiciary is not independent of the authoritarian structure, and so its decision-making power is constrained. One way to constrain judicial power is to ensure that prosecutors—acting on orders from the leadership—are more powerful than judges. In the case of ordinary disputes and petty crimes, the courts may even function similarly to courts in less authoritarian contexts. But for more significant crimes or in cases of state interest, trials will not be fair. They may not be conducted at all, with suspects tortured and/or executed, or the country may mount **show trials** with predetermined outcomes (discussed further in chapter 6).

Authoritarian legal systems can be formed around all kinds of different legal and political philosophies and ideologies, from communism to fascism, from secularism to religious fundamentalism. What they tend to have in common is a belief in the supremacy of the leader and the state over the people. This has particular consequences for criminal law, as it means that the ruler is likely to establish a category of crimes against the state, defined as actions taken in opposition to official state ideologies. Spreading anti-government propaganda and expressing anti-government sentiment or sentiment in opposition to government ideology are classic examples of such crimes, as is treason (though that is typically a crime even in democracies with freedom of thought and political association). Insulting the ruler can also be a crime, which is called **lèse-majesté** (literally "injured majesty"). In Thailand, for example, anyone who "defames, insults or threatens the king, the queen, the heir-apparent or the regent" is subject to imprisonment, and offenses can be as minor as liking a social media post (*BBC News* 2017). Communist countries may also define a set of economic crimes, or actions that undermine the state's control of the economy. For example, in China, market speculation has at times been illegal (Shultz 1989).

Traditional Law

Traditional law is law primarily shaped by tradition. It can also be called customary law, as in law based on customs. Some scholars refer to it as chthonic law, or law dwelling in the earth (Glenn 2007). Of course, all legal systems are based in some part on tradition (Glenn 2008). What differentiates traditional law from other legal systems is that this tradition has not been written down or institutionalized into formal structures. Traditional law has no historical "point of origin" (Glenn 2007:60). Rather, it has been handed down through tradition, usually orally, and is resistant to formalization and encoding, though it is possible to create written codes of traditional law. Historically, nearly all societies would have had traditional legal systems, as it was only with the development of more complex bodies of law and legal institutions that other types of systems were possible. And it is only after colonial conquest or other imperial forms of domination that indigenous legal systems became defined as examples of something called traditional law (Merry 1988)—earlier, they would have been known simply as the law. Few countries today have legal systems dominated by traditional law. It tends to be found in more remote areas, where modern central government has limited reach, such as tribal areas of Afghanistan or widely scattered Pacific islands. However, traditional law can also be found as part of some mixed legal systems.

The source of authority in traditional legal systems is tradition itself. Tradition can be expressed in many ways, such as through stories and legends or the memory of elders. Often, there are religious or supernatural elements. The distinction between theocratic and traditionally religious law can sometimes be unclear, but the central difference is that theocratic law is governed by the word of the divine as expressed in encoded rules while traditional law is governed specifically by tradition, although that tradition may have rich religious content. While it is theoretically possible for a traditional legal system to uphold the rule of law, this is not very likely, largely because law in traditional systems is generally not written down and not accessible to ordinary people. Rather, the law is typically part of an oral tradition that is passed down to those tasked with leadership and dispute resolution.

Legal authorities in traditional legal systems do not consult books for the answers to legal questions. Rather, they consult human authorities. These may be elders with a link to the past, sometimes ruling as a **gerontocracy**. Or they may be tribal leaders, such as chiefs. Typically, decision-making occurs in consultation with those considered wise in the law. Alternatively, power may be granted based on strength or skill, which is demonstrated by winning a duel, for example, or bringing large prey back to the village. Regardless of how authority is determined, traditional legal systems tend to grant supremacy to family, tribe, and clan connections rather than to some external legal order.

Traditional legal systems do not typically have legal institutions that are fully separate from other areas of life, though some countries today have established standing courts that implement traditional law principles. All societies have ways of engaging in social control and dispute resolution, but these methods vary considerably between different countries with traditional legal systems. Key examples of traditional dispute resolution practices, some of which will be discussed further in chapter 6, include duels or battles, contests, vigilantism and blood feuds, divination or oracles, and hearings or tribunals presided over by chiefs, elders, other authorities, or the entire tribe or village. It is important to remember that such practices were part of Western history until relatively recently. Disputants still fought duels to the death in Europe and the Americas in the mid-1800s.

While the specific ideologies of traditional legal systems are shaped by the individual society and its values, a common thread is loyalty to the small group. Typically, traditional legal systems value the collective more than any one individual and emphasize collective rights rather than individual rights. Law in traditional legal systems is interwoven with other beliefs, norms, and values rather than existing as some separate institutional arrangement.

It is also important to note that traditional law can function only in relatively small societies without too much complexity. Large and complex societies would make it unmanageable to administer law without standing rules and legal institutions. Where traditional law is part of mixed legal systems, countries tend to establish a local traditional law apparatus that, when needed, feeds into a national system with structures and elements derived from common, civil, and/or theocratic law.

Other Legal Systems

There are a variety of other legal systems that have existed throughout human history, some of which are lost to us and some of which continue to influence and be part of modern legal systems. For example, prior to the Chinese Communist Revolution, China had a Confucian legal system, and some elements of Confucianism continue to influence the Chinese system today (Glenn 2007). China had written legal codes as far back as the third century BCE, though the written law focused on criminal and administrative matters (Zweigert and Kötz 1988). Extensive mediation procedures were used for personal disputes.

Some scholars argue that Scandinavian law represents its own separate world legal system (Zweigert and Kötz 1988). While Scandinavian law was influenced by Roman law, it has a somewhat different history than civil law in the rest of continental Europe. Local areas within Scandinavia began keeping written law as early as the twelfth century, and these were codified nationally in Denmark, Norway, and Sweden (Finland was ruled by Sweden for much of this period) by the seventeenth and eighteenth centuries (Zweigert and Kötz 1988). Some Roman influences are present in these codes, but they are primarily based on older legal traditions.

Scholars also argue over whether the Soviet Union developed a separate world legal system grounded in communist principles that then influenced the national legal systems of other communist countries. Those who hold the view that Soviet law established a separate world legal system point to the presence of single-party rule, the subordination of law to economic policy, the expansion of public law and corresponding contraction of private law, and the lack of individual rights (Quigley 1989). However, these features may not be so distinct from what is found in other families. Indeed, many of these features are found in authoritarian societies with other ideological bents, such as fascism. Furthermore, communist countries have tended to retain in large part or to develop legal codes that draw heavily on the French or German traditions. So it may be more accurate to speak of a Soviet tradition within civil law rather than to characterize communist societies as having a separate world legal system (Quigley 1989). In any case, few communist countries remain today—North

Korea, Vietnam, Laos, China, and Cuba are the only countries that claim a communist identity, and several of those countries are undergoing rapid transformations that may reduce the communist features of their economic systems. Postcommunist countries may retain some Soviet influences, but they are no longer a part of a Soviet legal system.

Mixed Systems

In many countries, more than one legal system coexists. For example, a country that has a history of colonization might use a combination of traditional law and the civil or common law system its colonizer imported. For countries that were colonized by multiple foreign powers, such as the Philippines (as discussed at the beginning of this chapter), things can get even more complicated. And many highly religious countries combine a theocratic system with a civil legal code that address areas of law not specifically spoken to in religious texts. For example, Bangladesh's legal system is a mixture of common law imported by British colonizers and Islamic religious law, while Rwanda has a mixture of German and Belgian civil law and traditional law (Central Intelligence Agency n.d.-a). South Africa has a mixture of British common law, Dutch civil law, and indigenous traditional law. Scholars call such systems **mixed legal systems** or **legal pluralism** (Merry 1988). Despite the mixing that occurs in such systems, it is typically the case that one particular type of legal system is more dominant (Bracey 2006).

In other cases, a particular region of a country will maintain a legal system that is somewhat different from the one used by the rest of that country. Louisiana, in the United States, and Quebec, in Canada, both regions originally colonized by the French, have legal systems based on the Napoleonic Code, France's first legal code, established in 1804, while the rest the United States and Canada—including the national governments—are based on common law. Scotland has a legal system that combines some elements of common law with longstanding Scottish legal traditions. Over time, these traditions were influenced by disparate sources, from church law to Scandinavian law. It also developed its own body of common law, different from England's. But as Scotland is part of Great Britain, British common law has had considerable influence on the modern Scottish legal system. In southern Europe, Catalonia, the region of Spain that includes Barcelona, has a separate legal code with more traditional influences than does the rest of Spain.

CHANGE AND CONTINUITY

Legal systems are not permanent—they have changed over time and will continue to change in the future. Change can occur at a variety of levels of the legal

The Aztec Legal System

Scholars of comparative law tend to focus their attention on world legal systems that exist today and the historical examples that gave rise to them. However, there are other legal systems that have existed in the past that are worthy of study, including those that were ended by the forces of European colonization. One such example is the Aztec legal system. The term "Aztec" does not refer to a specific ethnic or tribal group but rather to a political entity located in an area called the Valley or Basin of Mexico. At its largest, it stretched from the Gulf of Mexico to the Pacific Ocean, including the area that is now Mexico City. It emerged around 1428 as an alliance between three ethnically Nahua city-states—Mexico-Tenochtitlan, Texcoco, and Tlacopan—and conquered surrounding areas, ruling until it was defeated in 1521 by Spanish conquistadores.

Records detailing the specifics of Aztec law are largely lost to history, despite the fact that the Aztec people did author texts. However, these complex and pictorially rich texts did not stand alone. Rather, they were used as reference sources or tools in complex performances including songs, and it is these performances that communicated the full body of Aztec legal thought (Offner 2017). Much of what has been recorded was written down by Spanish friars, who may not have fully understood the phenomena they were describing, and who may have ignored or left out important aspects of the legal systems; the best surviving text is the Codex Mendoza, housed at Oxford's Bodleian Library, which contains pictographic explanations of Aztec life and government. There were likely also considerable variations in legal rules and procedures between towns and regions (Offner 2017), so the records we do have access to may only represent practices as they were carried out in one part of the territory.

The ruler of the empire was chosen by a council of electors consisting of Aztec nobles and the kings of allies; usually rulers were warriors, but they could be priests, as was Montezuma, the last ruler (Carter 1964). Rule was not hereditary, though rulers were generally selected from among the brothers or nephews of prior rulers (Seus 1969). There was no legislature, so rules were made either by the emperor or through tradition. Major laws were recorded in pictographic texts (Avalos 1994).

The Aztec empire had a robust legal system, including courts designed to deal with all matter of issues, from criminal offenses to the distribution of land and property (Offner 2017). Records suggest there were four types of courts: specialized courts dealing with commercial matters, ecclesiastical matters (those relating to clergy or religious issues), and family matters, and general courts (Carter 1964). Some areas may also have had specialized tax and military courts (Seus 1969). Despite the specialization of courts and the fact that courts had specific geographical jurisdictions, it seems that there were no full-time judicial personnel. Instead, nobles heard cases and also carried out other official functions (Rounds 1977), and they were trained through lengthy apprenticeships (Avalos 1994). Cases could be appealed to at least two higher courts (Avalos 1994).

It also seems that there were no lawyers and that those accused of crimes testified on their own behalf (Carter 1964), though they could bring friends or relatives to assist them (Avalos 1994). All witnesses took oaths (Avalos 1994; Seus 1969). A wide variety of evidence was used, and judges directly questioned witnesses as well as parties to the case (Avalos 1994). Detailed records were kept of cases (Carter 1964; Seus

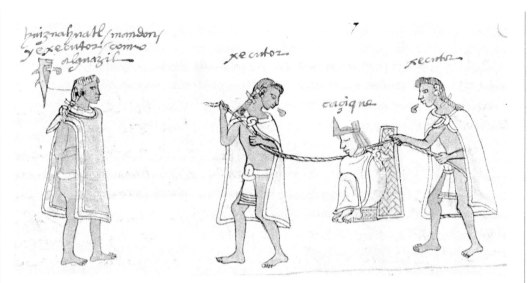

CS 2.2 Figure a An Aztec execution as depicted in the Codex Mendoza (folio 66r from the Codex Mendoza, held by the Bodleian Library, University of Oxford, CC BY 4.0).

1969), which were prohibited from extending for more than eighty days (Avalos 1994).

The empire collected taxes on manufactured goods, land, and other things (Carter 1964). There was robust regulation of the market, including price controls (Almazán 1999). Civil suits could be settled through payment of damages or the taking of the offender as a slave (Seus 1969). Although slavery was legal, it was governed by complex rules. Slave owners were not generally permitted to sell their slaves (Carter 1964), and there were a variety of ways for slaves to become free (Seus 1969).

Marriages could be contracted permanently or only until the birth of the first son. Legal separations were possible on certain grounds, including incompatibility, though those who were separated could not remarry. In the case of separation, fathers gained custody of sons and mothers gained custody of daughters, and property was divided according to premarital ownership, except in the case of fault, where the harmed spouse was

granted half of the offender's property. While women were not entitled to inherit, fathers could leave property to them.

The Aztecs had even developed their own body of international law, which included protections for ambassadors and rules of engagement for military action, such as a mandated day of rest from hostilities (Seus 1969). Except in times of military hostilities, roads and borders were kept open for the free movement of people (Almazán 1999).

Crimes could be punished in a variety of ways, ranging from execution by stoning to selling the criminal as a slave (Offner 2017). One such punishment is shown in CS 2.2 figure a. While some forms of physical punishment short of death were used, criminals were not whipped (Seus 1969). Offenders' heads might be shaved for drunkenness or when priests misbehaved (Pardo 2006). Adultery by women was punished by execution, and though men seem to have gotten away with adultery, they were not permitted to carry out vigilante justice by killing their adulteress wives' partners (Offner 2017; Seus 1969). During legal proceedings and before punishments could be carried out, the accused were detained in prisons of a sort (Offner 2017), such as secured wooden cages.

What we know about Aztec law may not be sufficient to enable a complete description of it as one of the world legal systems discussed above. But it is clear that it was indeed its own legal system, developing to an advanced state without the influence of other advanced legal systems. Scholars have compared Aztec law to common law, as judges seemed to rely on similar prior cases to guide their decision-making (Avalos 1994), but Aztec law is not common law, as it did not stem from British practice. Customs and traditions also played an important role, but Aztec law is not best understood as a traditional legal system given the importance of written records and rules.

When the Spanish conquered the Aztecs, they put into place their own legal system (Zion and Yazzie 1997). Initially, the missionaries working among the Aztecs opposed this path, seeing it as a disruption of the fundamental task of converting indigenous people to Catholicism. However, the Spanish government believed it necessary to create a distinction between religious and secular authority through the creation of courts according to the Spanish system (Pardo 2006). Thus, the religious and secular systems coexisted, and both were imposed on the indigenous population. Punishments such as public whipping and shaving the heads of offenders as a form of stigmatization were prescribed for engaging in actions contrary to Christian teachings, such as divination, idolatry, and drunkenness (Pardo 2006). Over time, Aztec traditions—and the documents in which they were recorded—were lost to history, a situation scholars call a dead tradition (Glenn 2008). But it was once very much alive.

system. **Micro**-level change is change at the smallest level, affecting one or just a few individuals. **Meso**-level change is change at the organizational or institutional level—such as the implementation of a new voting procedure or a reform of court procedures. **Macro**-level change is change at the societal or national level. When an existing legal system goes through a macro-level change, it may emerge as an entirely different kind of legal system. This is what happened to the Aztecs, as discussed in this chapter's case study: through the colonization process, their existing legal system was eradicated and ultimately replaced with a new civil law legal system imported by the Spanish.

This pattern is one of the main ways in which legal systems can experience wholesale change. Colonial powers all around the world imported civil or common law legal systems and imposed them on the lands they occupied. Preexisting legal systems, which were often based on traditional law but were sometimes based on theocratic law or some other unique system of law that no longer exists, were generally suppressed, though in some cases, certain features of preexisting legal systems were incorporated into the new imported systems. Similar dynamics shape the legal systems of other conquered or subjugated countries, such as the Eastern European nations that were incorporated into the USSR and subjected to Soviet communist rule and those that fell under Muslim rulers who spread Shari'a law. When colonized or conquered countries gained independence, many kept the basic legal system that had been imposed on them rather than attempt to start over, even as they drew up new constitutions and political institutions.

In other cases, former colonies did develop entirely new legal systems, sometimes as dictators seized power in the postrevolutionary moment. In these cases, the change in legal systems is more akin to what occurs in revolutionary regime change. For example, France established its first legal code in 1804 under Napoléon Bonaparte, a military commander during the French Revolution who became the ruler of the country. In Iran, the Iranian Revolution replaced a civil law system with a theocratic one based on Islamic law. But revolutions do not necessarily result in profound changes in legal systems. The United States broke from England through a process of revolution and crafted a new form of government quite different from what had come before, but it kept the common law legal system that England had imposed, including the body of British precedent.

CONCLUSION

The different world legal systems vary in a number of ways, from their history to their source of law and authority, from their dispute resolution procedures to their ideology and mode of legal thinking (Zweigert and Kötz 1988). But despite these profound differences, there are some commonalities across legal systems. All legal traditions express norms essential to their foundation, and these norms serve as guidelines for how to act in legal and nonlegal contexts (Glenn 2007). All are complex, exhibiting internal diversity (Glenn 2007) and incorporating elements of other systems (Merry 1988). Aztec law, a legal system that existed in only one part of the world, still had internal diversity since it incorporated multiple city-states and ethnic groups. Common law, which emerged in England, has grown to express itself in different ways in different national contexts.

Knowing which legal system or systems a country has tells us only a little bit about their government and justice system, but it is an important starting place. Legal systems shape approaches to lawmaking, dispute resolution, and other national activities. Furthermore, the study of legal systems helps us understand how and when we can effectively compare countries—and when we cannot. One obstacle to the goal of comparing legal systems is the translation problem, the difficulty in finding words that express phenomena foreign in both language and system. Translation is necessary for the study of comparative law (Rotman 1995). Legal translators find that it is much easier to translate across language within one body of legal systems—for instance, from one civil law system to another—than it is to translate across both language and legal system (Rotman 1995), but they persist in their task and make translation possible. Some legal scholars have argued that national legal systems are **incommensurable**, or unable to be evaluated relative to one another (Glenn 2001), given their unique properties. But because legal traditions and systems have long been in contact with one another, it has been possible for scholars to outline a set of specific characteristics defining legal systems, making comparison possible in terms of these characteristics (Glenn 2001) even if legal systems as a whole remain difficult to compare.

Of course, the world legal systems found in various countries are only one small part of the story. A fuller understanding of law and justice in any given country requires that we learn about so much more: the type of government a country has, the patterns of crime it experiences, the working of law enforcement and courts, its approaches to punishment, how it handles family and other private matters, what legal rights it protects, and many other factors. World legal systems shape some of these dynamics—for instance, as this chapter has shown, world legal systems are important elements shaping the types of dispute resolution processes that countries utilize. But there is often as much diversity within any one category of world legal system as there is between the categories. Take types of governments, for example. Civil law countries can be run by elected leaders or authoritarian rulers or have monarchs alongside elected lawmaking bodies. And that is only a small selection of the possibilities. Thus, chapter 3 will delve more deeply into the ways in which national governments can vary, an important next step in understanding the nature of law and justice in countries around the world.

The Organization of State Power

CHAPTER GOALS

1. Understand the different ways countries can be governed.
2. Evaluate electoral systems in terms of representativeness, governability, and other important factors.
3. Be able to explain why knowledge of state structures is important to understanding justice systems.

You might be surprised to learn that the City of London, on the northern bank of the River Thames, is only one square mile within the area we typically think of as London. It predates the rest of London, and indeed England itself, such that the City claims to be "the oldest continuous municipal democracy" in the world (City of London 2018). First entering history when King Alfred the Great appointed a municipal governor in 886 (Royal Commission 1893), it existed before the Magna Carta, and indeed, the Magna Carta specifically preserves the historical "liberties and free customs" of the City from interference by the English monarch (Thompson 2016).

As befits something so old, the City of London has a government structure so complex it strains comprehension (City of London 2018). It is run by a Lord Mayor who serves a nonrenewable one-year term, a Court of Common Council charged with decision-marking, and other personnel—including a town clerk, a Court of Alderman, two sheriffs, and a ceremonial sword-bearer—and elections for these positions are held from each of its twenty-five wards. To vote in these elections, one need not necessarily be a resident of the City (though residence does qualify one to be entered into the Register of Voters); owning a business or owning or leasing property in the City also qualifies one to vote, as does being appointed as a voter by one's employer, if that employer is located in the City. There are also over one hundred livery companies, which are basically corporate guilds, which nominate candidates for Lord Mayor (subject to election by the Court of Alderman).

This bizarre government has an outsized influence on England and on our entire world. It owns and maintains the central courts of England and Wales, for example (City of London 2018). And it has long served as a center of global trade, both in the import and export markets of the past (Ramsay 1975) and in the insurance, banking, and global finance industries of today (A. Davies 2017). While there have been periodic efforts to unify London and the City, they have not succeeded (Royal Commission 1893), leaving the City as perhaps the most unique government system in the world.

The City's government is what enables it to play the role it does in global markets, allowing it to maintain legal structures that facilitate its economic and legal practices. The fact that it permits those who do not reside in the City to vote if they have appropriate economic ties to the City community perpetuates practices that enhance corporate opportunities, sometimes at the expense of other potential priorities. Similarly, the governance structures of all countries affect the kinds of policies and practices put into place within them.

Later chapters in this book will focus on specific aspects of justice systems, including law enforcement, courts, punishment systems, and legal rights. But it is impossible to fully understand these specific aspects without first undertaking a study of the basic structures of government. Governments provide the foundation for legal rights; they also administer and manage the law enforcement organizations, courts, and mechanisms for punishment that are part of their own justice systems. Laws are considered, refined, enacted, and revised within legislative and executive power structures, and these laws create definitions of crime, determine appropriate punishments, and organize administrative structures. Thus, this chapter will begin by laying out what states are and the different ways they can be organized, including types of government and the separation of powers between governmental branches. Then it will consider how elections work (in countries that have them) and what qualifies people to vote or run for office.

WHAT IS A STATE?

Sociologist Michael Mann defines a **state** as a set of institutions and personnel who have centrally located control over a specific territory, including control over rule making and over the **legitimate** use of violence (Mann 1986). Note that this definition is much closer to what people in the United States commonly call a country than it is to what they think of a state. These two uses of the term "state" can be confusing, but the state-as-country usage is typical in discussions of legal systems. A state, however, is not the same thing as a legal system. There are legal systems that are larger than states, such as those that are international or regional; there are also legal system that are smaller than states, like those of indigenous populations or autonomous areas. There are even legal systems that are not grounded in any territory at all, like that of the Catholic Church. But a state must be grounded in a physical place, be it a small place or a very large one.

Any complex society needs to have some kind of authority in place that is empowered to make rules (Mann 1986) and manage important state functions, such as maintaining internal order, common defense, systems for communication and transportation, and the distribution of economic resources. This authority includes people and institutions set up for the purpose of carrying out rulemaking and management, though as this chapter will show, those people and institutions can be organized in very different ways. The key is that a state must have **sovereignty**—authority over self-government (Herz 1957)—which gives it the power to make rules, enforce rules, and resolve disputes.

The final element of Mann's definition is that a state must have a monopoly on the legitimate use of violence. This idea has long been part of social theory, and some argue that it is the most fundamental element of state power. This does not mean that a state must use violence or that it is the only entity that can ever use violence, but rather that a state determines when violence is permissible and can impose consequences on those who use violence without such permission (Weber 1946). Thus, a state has a monopoly on the legitimate use of violence, regardless of whether it prohibits violence of all kinds and sends those who engage in violence to meditation camps; uses violence itself to suppress dissent; forswears violence but permits those who have been victimized by crimes to carry out violent retribution; or anything in between.

The smallest type of state is a **city-state**. City-states are individual cities or metropolitan areas with their own sovereignty that are independent of any other state. Monaco and the Vatican are examples of city-states. The largest type of state is an **empire**. Empires are states made up of many different territories all governed by the same central government. There have been empires throughout recorded human history, such as the Roman, Mongol, and Ottoman Empires in Eurasia, the Ajuran Sultanate in Africa, and the Inca Empire in South America. They are often formed through military conquest or economic coercion. Today, the only state called an empire is Japan, which is ruled by an emperor but is better understood as a **nation-state** (though some commentators think that states like the United States and Russia that continue to interfere in the internal affairs of other states should be understood as empires).

Nation-states are states in which the state is pretty well aligned with a nationality or ethnic group (J. Bartlett 2017). For example, you might think of Sweden as the country of Swedes. Any time an ethnic group and a country seem like the same thing, you probably have a nation-state.

In between city-states and empires are **unitary states** and **federations**. Unitary states, which may also be nation-states, are states where there is one government for a specified territory, without any smaller political subunits. Federations, in contrast, are political entities where subunits, like provinces, or what in the United States are called states, each have their own internal self-government but where there is also an overall national government. The extent to which the national government has control over the subunits varies. In some cases, it may be limited to mediating disputes between subunits and managing the common defense; in others, subunits are responsible only for fairly local issues.

An expanded form of federation is the **superstate**. Superstates are coalitions of multiple countries that have collectively formed one political entity. The best example today of a superstate is the European Union (EU). The entity that became the EU originated in a series of treaties signed after World War II, when countries in central Europe that had been devastated by the war sought to address their common interests in economic policy, atomic energy, and defense (Dinan 2014). Over the decades, the project grew and changed, resulting in the development of a common economic community to create an integrated single market.

In the early 1990s, European countries came together to begin negotiating what eventually became the EU. It was formed through the Maastricht Treaty, which laid out the initial EU structure. Additional treaties drafted in the 2000s refined the EU system (Dinan 2014). The EU's government has a complex structure (European Union 2018) set up by these treaties. The European Commission, made up of the heads of state of member countries and an elected president, sets the agenda for the EU. The EU has three different legislative bodies: the European Parliament, a representative body directly elected by citizens of the EU; the Council of the European Union, representing the governments of member countries; and the European Commission, designed to ensure the proper functioning of the EU. Typically, the Commission proposes legislation and the Parliament and Council vote on whether to adopt it. It is then the Commission's responsibility, along with that of individual member countries, to implement these laws. Other EU institutions include the Court of Justice, the European Central Bank, and agencies responsible for financial audits, foreign affairs and security, investment, data protection, and other specialized issues.

The treaties, most recently the 2016 Treaty on the Functioning of the European Union, also specify which issues fall under the exclusive jurisdiction of the EU and which are shared with member states (European Citizens' Initiative 2018). Monetary policy, market regulation and commercial policy, marine conservation, customs and border control, and certain types of international agreements are subject to the exclusive jurisdiction of the EU. Jurisdiction is shared between the EU and member states on a wide range of other topics, such as internal economic markets, agriculture, the environment, consumer protection, transportation, energy, public health, research and technology, humanitarian aid, and asylum and refugee policy. The EU also works to facilitate coordination between member states for such issues as employment, social security, and the like. Finally, member states are primarily responsible for policies and practices around health care, industry, culture, tourism, and education, though they can seek support from the EU.

As of 2019, twenty-eight countries belong to the EU, as shown in map 4; nineteen of them (along with seven non-EU countries) use the EU's common currency, the euro; and twenty-six countries participate in the Schengen border-free area, which permits travel without border checks (European Union 2018). However, one EU member country, the United Kingdom, is currently seeking to leave the EU in a process that has come to be known as Brexit. Brexit was initiated by a popular referendum in which 51.9 percent of voters in the United Kingdom voted to leave (Hunt and Wheeler 2019). To leave the EU with trade and other relationships intact, a country must come to a set of agreements with the EU within two years of the commencement of the leaving process. Securing such a deal has been difficult for the United Kingdom because of vast differences among the country's elected officials—some wish to find a way to stay in the EU, while others want to ensure the greatest possible disentanglement from the EU. One of the biggest sticking points is the desire to avoid a hard border between Northern Ireland (part of the United Kingdom) and the Republic of Ireland (a member state of the EU) while simultaneously exiting the customs union that controls international trade deals (Hunt and Wheeler 2019). It is impossible to predict what will happen going forward. The United Kingdom could call a new referendum and seek to reverse Brexit; it could leave without a deal; it could vote to accept the deal currently on the table, which it previously rejected; or a new, last-minute deal could be struck before the deadline the EU has set, a deadline that has already been extended twice as of this writing.

Types of Government

There are many types of government, and they differ most notably in terms of who runs the country and how they get selected. The most central distinction is between regimes that are authoritarian in nature and those that employ a democratic system, though there are some types of government that do not fit into either of these categories. In authoritarian governments, the central government—whether run by one person or a ruling party—exercises significant control over political life and decision-making, leaving little room for discussion

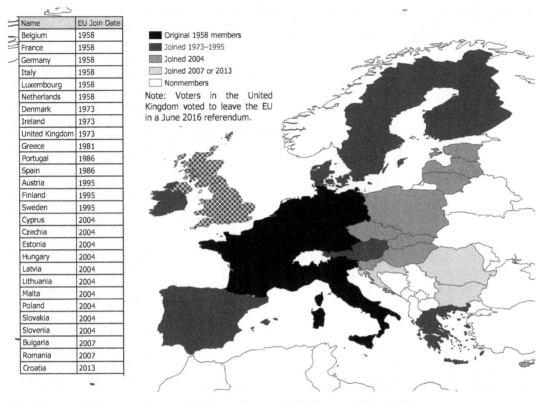

Name	EU Join Date
Belgium	1958
France	1958
Germany	1958
Italy	1958
Luxembourg	1958
Netherlands	1958
Denmark	1973
Ireland	1973
United Kingdom	1973
Greece	1981
Portugal	1986
Spain	1986
Austria	1995
Finland	1995
Sweden	1995
Cyprus	2004
Czechia	2004
Estonia	2004
Hungary	2004
Latvia	2004
Lithuania	2004
Malta	2004
Poland	2004
Slovakia	2004
Slovenia	2004
Bulgaria	2007
Romania	2007
Croatia	2013

Original 1958 members
Joined 1973–1995
Joined 2004
Joined 2007 or 2013
Nonmembers

Note: Voters in the United Kingdom voted to leave the EU in a June 2016 referendum.

Map 4 European Union countries, year of joining and map as of 2018 (European Union 2018).

or dissent. In contrast, democratic governments provide the opportunity for individuals to have input into the government, even if only through the electoral process. Both authoritarian and democratic regimes can be **republics**, governments in which the sovereign power of the state is vested in a legal system rather than a single individual. Republics have advanced legal systems that govern the government as well as the population, and they do not have hereditary rulers. Within each of these categories, there are a number of different types of government systems.

The most common types of authoritarian rule are **dictatorships**, **monarchies**, and **oligarchies**. Dictatorships and monarchies are both types of authoritarian governments run by a single leader who serves for life or until being ousted, but there are important differences between them. Dictators come to power without restraint by law and typically do not pass on their office to their children. They may seize power through military force or through an illegitimate manipulation of the political process. While **absolute monarchies** similarly are not bound by law, they do tend to be hereditary. However,

Indigenous Sovereignty

What does it mean to be **sovereign**? Dictionaries define sovereignty as entailing supreme governing power over a territory, not subject to any other authority. So, for example, the United States is sovereign, but the state of California is not, since the state is subject to the authority of the country. But it is not always this simple. The circumstances of indigenous populations who have been granted certain rights of self-government make the complexity of sovereignty and self-determination clear. In determining whether individual indigenous groups "merited" sovereignty, European theorists and colonizers applied Eurocentric models of nationhood, positing that politically organized societies engaged in settled agriculture qualified for nationhood and thus sovereignty while nomadic tribes did not have sufficient claim to the land (Perrin 2017).

At the formation of the United States, indigenous tribes were treated as foreign nations. Colonists fighting against the British had entered into treaties with tribes for mutual defense and protection. Early court cases held that U.S. states and the federal government had no jurisdiction or authority over indigenous lands (Fredericks 1999). However, as the young United States sought to expand its territory across North America, things changed. Later treaties were not negotiated in good faith; the U.S. government found ways to coerce or deceive tribes into signing away large tracts of land, and the courts held that Congress further had the power to withdraw unilaterally from treaties (Fredericks 1999). Today, where tribal lands have been maintained, tribes exercise self-government, administering their own courts, developing their own environmental standards, and the like. But there are many ways in which national governments intrude into the sovereignty of indigenous groups. For example, in the United States, federal prosecutors have the authority to prosecute crimes committed by indigenous people if those crimes are significant enough, even when they occur on reserved treaty lands (Washburn 2006). While tribes remain sovereign, their sovereignty is thus limited through their relationship with the United States (Fredericks 1999).

The relationship between indigenous groups and national governments continues to be negotiated. For example, a 1998 treaty between the Nisga'a Nation and the Canadian national and British Colombian provincial governments established, for the first time, a treaty right to self-government (Blackburn 2009). In Australia and New Zealand, indigenous groups have negotiated water rights treaties with the central national governments (Cornell 2015). And between 1979 and 2009, a series of legal changes enhanced the Inuit population of Greenland's control over its own affairs, including natural resources, without granting it status as a sovereign state—it remains part of Denmark (Shadian 2010). But such processes can be difficult, especially for indigenous groups whose populations have been decimated or that straddle international borders (Cornell 2015).

These examples highlight the limitations of a state-based perspective on sovereignty (Shadian 2010). Indigenous tribes had governance structures, territorial locations, and economic practices long before the arrival of conquering forces, and they have labored mightily to preserve all of these in the face of colonial domination. Today, they are not constructed as sovereign states as they remain subject to the authority of the countries into which they have been partially incorporated, but in many cases they retain some degree of self-government as well as a series of political and social institutions through which they exercise their autonomy and express their collective identity. Indeed, some indigenous thinkers reject the notion of sovereignty entirely, arguing that it is a Western, colonialist idea (Perrin 2017). Instead, they argue for self-determination, self-government, and autonomy and work to exercise those practices without regard for whether national governments recognize them (Cornell 2015).

monarchs do not come to power by seizing control of a state (except in the case of military campaigns that result in the conquest and annexation of other lands). Typically, monarchs come to power via a hereditary transfer or are appointed the successor by the prior monarch. It is even possible to elect a monarch, which may be the most reasonable way to understand the selection of the Pope. Monarchies can also be constrained by other political forces, such as constitutions that restrict the monarch's power or the employment of democratic practices for legal decision-making. Such monarchies are called democratic or constitutional monarchies. If the monarch's power is extremely limited, such as in cases where he or she serves only as a ceremonial head of state, it may not be appropriate to think of the country as authoritarian in nature.

Oligarchies, in contrast, are governments run by a small group of people, such as wealthy business elites. Some people consider South Africa under the apartheid system to have been an oligarchy, since the White citizens who held all the political power made up just 10 to 20 percent of the population (depending on the year). **Aristocracies** can be seen as a type of oligarchy. These are governments where a hereditary ruling class has authority, with a hereditary monarch at the top of the power structure but with some power devolved to the nobility. England between the signing of the Magna Carta in 1215 and the expansion of democratic power in the early 1900s is a perfect example of this system. Similarly, **corporatism** is a system where political power is exercised by social groups such as familial clans, business networks, and industrial organizations. Corporatism was the organizing principle in many of the more urban areas in early modern Europe, such as the principalities that became Italy.

Systems of authoritarian rule can exist without any particular governing philosophy. Dictators or monarchs can simply govern as they choose, since there are no restraints on their power. However, many authoritarian countries do have governing philosophies that shape their practices. For example, **fascism** refers to an authoritarian system in which the group is elevated over the individual, ethnic nationalism (often racism) is prioritized, diversity and modernism are rejected, and dissent is suppressed (Eco 1995).

As noted above, authoritarian governments can be republics. This occurs when the government is bound to some legal system or set of rules that extend beyond the principles of one individual. For example, **theocracies** are countries governed by religious principles. While it is possible to have a democratic theocracy, the truest expression of theocracy involves a government that conflates religious and political authority. For example, both the Vatican and Iran have religious leaders elected by religious figures.

Communism is a form of government based on the common ownership of property (the means of production) and state control of the economy (Marx and Engels [1848] 1906). In its original formulation, the theory of communism predicted that the transition to a communist regime would entail a period of central control, which would subsequently be followed by a period where political power and control were no longer needed. This latter stage has not been reached by any communist country. It is important to note that **socialism** is a much broader concept than communism, focusing more specifically on economic arrangements. Both philosophies provide for economic equality and collective ownership of the means of production, but socialism is compatible with democratic forms of government and does not imply the same kind of political control that communism does. Of course, there are other possible governing philosophies that can guide authoritarian leaders, but these examples are some of the most common.

Varieties of Democracy

Democracy refers to rule by the people. The simplest form of democracy is **direct democracy**, a system in which all citizens directly govern through some sort of majority vote. This system was practiced in classical Athens, where all adult male citizens (meaning they were born in Athens and were not slaves) were able to directly participate in state decision-making. Thousands of men—as much as a quarter of the male citizen population—would come to meetings of the Athenian Assembly to speak their minds and vote on proposals (Blackwell 2003). In most countries today, direct democracy would not be practical; there are simply too many people to be able to gather everyone together for a discussion. However, some smaller political entities, such as towns, continue to practice direct democracy. Countries or subnational units can also use ballot initiatives or referenda as a tool to bring an element of direct democracy into the political process.

Democratic countries today tend to be **representative democracies**, often called **democratic republics**. In such systems, people vote for representatives, and those representatives then govern in a democratic fashion. It is possible for some level of democracy to coexist with certain types of authoritarian rule. For example, democratic or constitutional monarchies retain a monarch alongside a system of democratic representation. Some theocracies also permit democratic governance over nonreligious areas of political and social life.

There are far more types of government that have existed in human history and human imagination than exist as typical forms today. One of the most common traditional forms of government is **tribalism**, a system in which government is organized by tribal loyalties and organizations. In this system, each tribe has its own process for selecting leaders, whether it is hereditary, democratic, strength-based, or derived from some other principle. The leaders of multiple tribes come together to decide issues of concern to the broader society. Tribalist societies typically have a traditional legal system. People's key loyalty remains to their tribe and tribal leaders rather than to any kind of national government, though a national government may exist. Map 5 details whether countries are best understood as dictatorships, monarchies, republics, or as having some other form of government.

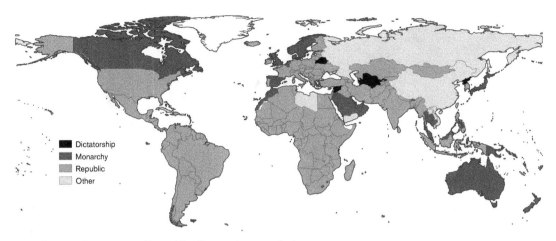

Map 5 Types of government (Central Intelligence Agency n.d.-a).

BRANCHES OF GOVERNMENT

There are three main branches of government, each of which has a different functional role in governing: the **legislative branch**, the **executive branch**, and the **judicial branch**. The legislative branch of government is responsible for making laws, though the exact procedures for doing so are specific to each legislative body. The executive branch is responsible for running the day-to-day operations of government and carrying out enforcement of the laws. Finally, the judicial branch, which includes the court system, is responsible for interpreting and applying the laws and resolving disputes. Not all countries are organized such that the three branches are separate entities. Where they are separate, we say there is **separation of powers**.

In countries with **constitutions**, the constitution lays out the structure of the government in terms of these three branches and the extent of separation of powers. Constitutions are thus documents that lay out the fundamental legal principles of a country, often including basic rights. They are generally written down and hard to change, or at least harder to change than legal codes. Most countries have constitutions, though they do not always abide by them. But not all do: England, for example, does not have a written constitution. Rather, its legal system is governed by a collection of various written documents, beginning with the Magna Carta, and common law traditions.

The judicial branch of government will be explored in more detail in chapter 6. In democratic countries, it is typically separate and independent from the other branches of government, but in authoritarian countries, it may be subject

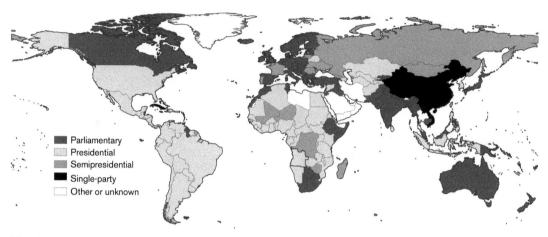

Map 6 Legislative-executive relations (Central Intelligence Agency n.d.-a).

to control by the executive branch. There is considerably more variation in the relationship between the legislative and executive branches of government. To understand this variation, there are three key questions we can ask (Siaroff 2003). First, is the chief representative of the government (often called the head of state) a different person than the official who runs the country (often called the head of government), or is this power vested in the same individual? Second, how are the heads of state and government selected? Third, is the head of government accountable to the legislature? Map 6 shows how countries are classified in terms of the relationship between their legislative and executive branches.

Countries like the United States have a **presidential system**. In this system, the head of state and the head of government are the same person, the president, who is elected by the people to his or her role and is not generally accountable to or removable by—barring something like impeachment proceedings—the legislature (Siaroff 2003). The presidential system is also found in much of Latin America and in the Philippines, due in large part to the colonialist influence of the United States in these countries (United Nations Development Programme n.d.). In presidential systems, there is full separation of powers between the legislative, executive, and judicial branches, and the executive may be from a different political party than the legislative majority. Cabinet ministers (called secretaries in the United States) are appointed by the president. While presidents can propose legislation and may have veto power over bills passed by the legislature, the legislature sets its own agenda. And while political parties can strongly encourage members to stick to the party line, their power to enforce party discipline is limited.

a variety of different goals for election systems, and they cannot all be equally maximized. These six goals, which will be explored in detail below, are:

- Proportionality of seats to votes
- Accountability of elected officials to voters
- Durability of government
- Victory of the Condorcet winner
- Interethnic and interreligious conciliation
- Minority officeholding

The first goal, **proportionality**, refers to the degree to which the proportion of legislative seats allocated to each political party as a result of a given election reflects the proportion of votes cast for that party in the election (Horowitz 2003; Reynolds, Reilly, and Ellis 2008). Electoral systems vary widely in the extent to which they achieve proportionality, and these differences are based largely but not entirely on whether the system involves a plurality/majority vote, relies on proportional representation, incorporates a mixture of these approaches, or does something else entirely.

The first of these approaches is used in the United States, where elections generally follow a **first-past-the-post voting** process. In this system, the person who receives the single largest number of votes, even if it is well short of a majority, wins the election (Reynolds, Reilly, and Ellis 2008). To clarify, a **majority** is 50 percent of votes plus one vote. If no one gets this percentage of votes, no one has achieved a majority, but the candidate with the highest number of votes has achieved a **plurality** of the votes. So, for example, if three candidates are running in an election, and candidate A gets 45 percent of the vote, candidate B gets 42 percent of the vote, and candidate C gets 13 percent of the vote, candidate A would win with 45 percent of the votes, a plurality, in a first-past-the-post system. In this system, individuals who would prefer to vote for a third party are generally unable to turn these preferences into electoral victory and thus are faced with a choice between either casting a "wasted" vote or voting for a less-preferred candidate from one of two major parties (Reynolds, Reilly, and Ellis 2008). First-past-the-post systems can be designed to require that the ultimate winner earn a majority of the votes by using multiple rounds of voting, including runoff elections featuring only two candidates (Reynolds, Reilly, and Ellis 2008), though runoff elections can reduce electoral participation.

In a **proportional representation voting** system, the goal is for the distribution of seats to parties after the election to closely resemble the distribution of votes cast for parties in the election (Reynolds, Reilly, and Ellis 2008). Typically in this system, voters vote for parties rather than individual candidates, and the results of the election determine how many representatives will come from each party. A proportional representation system can involve a single distribution of parties for the entire country, or it can involve multimember

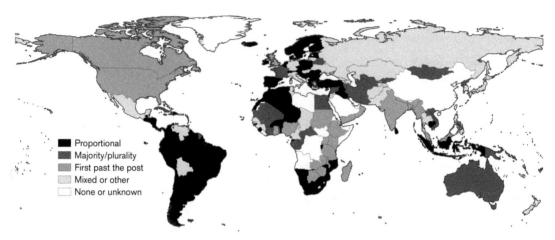

Map 7 Electoral systems as of 2004 (Reynolds, Reilly, and Ellis 2008).

districts in which a group of candidates is elected from a certain region or city and the parties are distributed proportionally among that group (Reynolds, Reilly, and Ellis 2008).

Mixed systems incorporate some elements of proportional representation and some elements of a plurality or majority system, for instance by allocating some seats according to each method. Such systems have been used by countries such as Bolivia, Hungary, Lesotho, Mexico, Italy, South Korea, Russia, and Japan. Some systems allow individuals to vote for more than one candidate, and there are other more complex systems. Map 7 shows the distribution of voting systems around the world. As of 2004, 36 percent of countries that directly elected a legislative body used some type of proportional representation, 24 percent used a first-past-the-post system, 22 percent used some other type of majority or plurality approach, 15 percent used a mixed system, and 3 percent used some other type of system (Reynolds, Reilly, and Ellis 2008).

In federalist systems, regional differences can be accommodated by allowing geographical subunits of the country, such as states or provinces, to make their own political decisions (often through subnational legislative bodies, such as state legislatures in the United States). Federalist legislative systems tend to have representatives from these subunits, who are generally elected without concern for proportionality. In the United States, for example, each state has two senators, regardless of the size of its population.

The second goal, **accountability**, refers to the extent to which elected officials are directly responsible to the voters, versus being responsible to some other set of people who control their access to elected office. In some electoral systems, individual elected representatives represent a given geographical district. Voters in that area then have the clear ability to retain or remove the representative at the next scheduled election. Representatives in such contexts often feel that they need to get to know the people who live in their districts and provide constituent services to them in order to retain their office. This type of accountability is promoted by systems in which voters vote for individual candidates rather than parties (Reynolds, Reilly, and Ellis 2008).

In other systems, especially those that use proportional representation in multimember districts, voters vote for political parties. These parties have the responsibility of choosing a list of candidates for office, so it is party officials who determine which individuals have the chance to stand for election. A system like this reduces the extent to which any given elected official can be held accountable to voters—though clearly the voters can still hold the entire party accountable.

One rare type of electoral system is the **electoral college** approach (Maskin and Sen 2017), in which elected officials are elected indirectly. Unlike the more typical process of direct elections, the electoral college approach involves the selection of electors who then elect the head of state or other officials. Both the United States and the Vatican use this approach. In the Vatican, the College of Cardinals gathers behind closed doors to elect the next Pope. In the United States, the electoral college was written into the Constitution because the Framers did not believe regular people could be trusted to elect the president (until 1913, this approach was also used to elect senators). Each state chooses its own method of selecting electors. While today, electors are generally expected to vote for the presidential candidate selected by the largest number of voters in their state, they originally acted as they wished. In most parliamentary countries, the parliament selects the prime minister, which in a sense is also a kind of indirect election (Reynolds, Reilly, and Ellis 2008). Officials who are elected indirectly can be understood as less accountable to the voters than those who are elected directly by the voters.

Where proportional representation is used to elect legislative bodies, there is a real risk that they will not be able to achieve **durable governments**. Horowitz's third goal, durability, refers to the extent to which a legislative body is able to govern in a stable fashion over the course of its normal term (Horowitz 2003). Durability is a problem in proportional systems because no one political party is very likely to obtain a majority of legislative seats and thus operational control of the legislative chamber. When no party holds a majority of the legislative seats, parties must negotiate a coalition in order to govern. Sometimes, this is impossible, and new elections must be called. Other times, coalitions are formed but remain unstable, facing difficulties in achieving legislative priorities and allowing small parties with atypical ideas to have an important impact on the way governing happens. When a coalition falls apart, new elections must be called. In systems with less proportionality, it is more likely that a single party will achieve a majority of the vote—unless there are significant regional differences in party preferences. When a single party does achieve a majority, it will generally be able to control the governing process and ensure a durable government throughout the standard electoral term.

Horowitz's fourth goal is the victory of the **Condorcet winner**. Named after the Marquis de Condorcet, an eighteenth-century political scientist (Maskin and Sen 2017), this term refers to the candidate who, when compared with all the other candidates, is preferred by more voters. Consider an election with three candidates, A, B, and C. If 46 percent of people prefer candidate A, 45 percent prefer candidate B, and 9 percent prefer candidate C, a first-past-the-post-style election would result in the election of candidate A. But what if all of candidate B's supporters think candidate C would be a good second choice, while the supporters of both candidate B and candidate C think candidate A is really terrible? A system based on the victory of the Condorcet winner would ensure that candidate C wins (Horowitz 2003).

This dilemma can be illustrated by looking at the results of the 2010 governor's race in the U.S. state of Maine. That race had a number of candidates, three of which were seen as serious contenders: Republican Paul LePage, Democrat Libby Mitchell, and independent Eliot Cutler. Among them, these three candidates split 92.3 percent of the vote, with the remainder going to other independent candidates or consisting of ballots without a selection for governor (Information Resource of Maine 2015). However, none of them got a majority of the votes cast. Le Page received 37.6 percent of the vote; Cutler, 35.9 percent; and Mitchell, 18.8 percent. LePage was thus declared the winner.

Since Cutler ran on a liberal platform, it is likely that many of Mitchell's supporters would have selected him as a second choice, had they been given the option to do so. If three quarters of the voters who cast their ballot for Mitchell had selected Cutler as a second choice, a Condorcet winner system would have resulted in Cutler winning the election when they were combined with the 35.9 percent of voters who voted for him initially. As a liberal candidate, his policies and platforms would have been quite different from the Republican LePage—and LePage, despite winning the plurality of the votes, was not the Condorcet winner.

There are a variety of ways to implement voting systems that seek to select the Condorcet winner. Usually, such systems involve a method called **instant-runoff** or **ranked-choice voting**, where voters rank the candidates in order of preference, though there are many variations on this method. In an **alternative voting** system, candidates with the lowest first-choice vote totals are eliminated from the pool, and their votes are reallocated to second-choice candidates until one candidate achieves over 50 percent of the vote (Reynolds, Reilly, and Ellis 2008). Such systems have been used in a number of countries, such as Australia, Fiji, Papua New Guinea, and Ireland, and they have now been adopted in Maine. There are other types of instant-runoff voting, such as the Borda count (used in Nauru), where voters rank multiple candidates, and choices lower in preference are assigned fractional vote totals; and Coombs voting, where candidates with the most last-choice votes are removed until a winner emerges (Pacuit 2011). Philosophers have even devised systems where voters would have the option to vote against a candidate they most dislike (Pacuit 2011). Note that while all of these methods are kinds of instant-runoff voting systems, they do not always produce exactly the same results.

Horowitz's fifth goal is interethnic and interreligious conciliation. In multi-ethnic and multireligious societies, there is often conflict and division between ethnic or religious groups. That conflict generally has political consequences, as different ethnic and religious groups tend to have different political priorities, and there is often a history of distrusting one another. Systems that encourage interethnic and interreligious conciliation are those that make it necessary for candidates and elected officials to work together across these divisions (Horowitz 2003) rather than those that reserve specific seats for members of minority groups.

Finally, the sixth goal we must consider is minority officeholding. The question here is whether members of minorities—including both minorities in a numerical sense and groups that have historically been denied access to political power, such as women—have access to political office. Countries concerned with this issue have developed various affirmative action and reserved-seat schemes to ensure minority officeholding and representation. For example, in India, a specific group of seats in the legislature is reserved for members of historically disadvantaged groups known as the Scheduled Castes and Scheduled Tribes. Only members of these groups may stand for election to one of these seats, guaranteeing that these groups will have electoral representation (Reynolds, Reilly, and Ellis 2008). At the local level, Indian legislatures also reserve seats for women. In proportional representation systems using party-constructed candidate lists, minority officeholding can be promoted through party practices or official policies of including more minorities (and/or women) on the lists of candidates (Reynolds, Reilly, and Ellis 2008). For example, in the late 1990s, Indonesia began strongly encouraging parties to ensure that at least 30 percent of candidates on their party lists were women, a practice that resulted in a significant increase in women elected to the legislature even without any enforcement mechanism (Reynolds, Reilly, and Ellis 2008). Of course, systems that specifically promote minority officeholding may be much less likely to achieve the goals of conciliation because both majority and minority groups may assume that the interests of minorities will be represented by those holding the reserved seats, and systems promoting conciliation may reduce minority officeholding (Horowitz 2003).

Given this complexity, how does a country choose an electoral system? In most cases, countries develop systems based on tradition, whether their own or that of another country, such as a colonial occupier or a neighbor (Reynolds, Reilly, and Ellis 2008). When one country adopts another country's model, however, it is not always good fit. When a country carefully considers what is best given its specific context, the design of its electoral system may seek to mitigate past conflicts. For example, a country with a history of oppressing particular ethnic groups may design an electoral system that ensures those groups will have the opportunity to hold power. But an electoral system cannot maximize all five of Horowitz's goals at once (Maskin and Sen 2017). Each national system, then, maximizes some goals at the expense of others—either intentionally or due to various accidents of history. Some countries try to mitigate this problem by employing complex mixed systems that seek to minimize the limitations of prior systems. Such systems may involve **bicameral** legislatures, or legislatures with two chambers, each elected according to a different process and principle (Reynolds, Reilly, and Ellis 2008; Weaver 2002). It is also possible to design an electoral system that simply makes it too hard for anyone to win. For example, the 1979 presidential elections in Nigeria required the winner to attain a plurality of votes nationally and 25 percent of the votes in at least two-thirds of all states (Horowitz 2003), a system so complicated that litigation was required to determine a winner. A system as complex as this could easily result in no one winning at all.

WHO VOTES?

Voting rates vary widely across the world, ranging from over 90 percent to below 40 percent of registered voters (International IDEA 2018b), as shown in map 8. (Turnout would be even lower in many countries if measured as a percentage of the voting-age population rather than as a percentage of those registered to vote, since many people who are eligible to vote are not registered.) Why does this variation occur? Research has found that electoral participation is highest in proportional representation systems and where elections are expected to be close (Reynolds, Reilly, and Ellis 2008). But perhaps the most important factors are the ease of electoral participation, the degree to which voters perceive the electoral system as fair, and whether voting is compulsory.

If access to voting is constrained or difficult, people will be less likely to participate, and thus the results of elections will not accurately reflect the real preferences of the population (Reynolds, Reilly, and Ellis 2008). There are wide variations in the way elections are scheduled. They may take place on a single day or over a longer period (Reynolds, Reilly, and Ellis 2008). Some countries schedule elections on ordinary workdays with limited voting hours, which makes it difficult for working people to get to polling places. Other countries make election day a national holiday or schedule elections on weekends. Some countries hold elections for president, national legislature, and other local races at the same time, while others schedule each separately. Some countries require voters to travel to a designated polling place, while others make it possible to vote remotely.

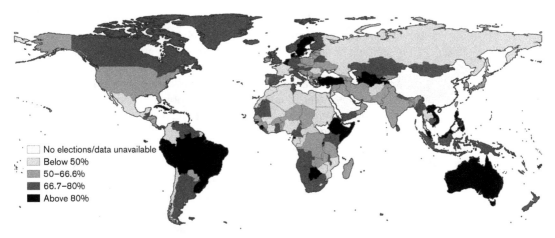

Map 8 Voter turnout in legislative elections (International IDEA 2018b).

Perceptions of fairness also influence electoral participation. When people do not believe that the election results will reflect popular preferences, or when electoral procedures are not transparent, participation is often reduced (Reynolds, Reilly, and Ellis 2008). In some countries, elections are held even though everyone knows the results will not matter. These countries hold elections because they want to be perceived as democracies, but they restrict electoral participation or fix electoral results to ensure the regime's desired outcome occurs. Electoral participation is often low in such countries. But electoral participation can be high even when people do not believe the system is fair or when results are fixed, such as in countries that require people to vote. Note that compulsory voting can also occur in places with free and fair elections. At various times, compulsory voting has been used in Australia, Belgium, Greece, and countries in Latin America, as well as in the period after the fall of the USSR in a number of former Soviet states (Reynolds, Reilly, and Ellis 2008). In Brazil, even eligible voters living outside the country are required to either vote or file a form justifying why they did not vote (Setor de Administração Federal Sul 2014). Voters in countries with compulsory elections may face various penalties for not voting, such as fines, imprisonment, or stigmatization, or the laws may simply require voting but not specify a penalty for failure to do so (International IDEA 2018a).

Calculations of voting rates are based on a determination of how many people are eligible to vote in a given country. Those who are not eligible to vote, such as small children, are excluded from the calculation. All countries have rules about who is eligible to vote, and they exclude different populations of people. Criteria used to limit access to voting in various times and places include citizenship, residency, age, sex, race or ethnicity, religion, literacy, and economic status. In addition, some countries automatically register people to vote, while others require individuals to actively register themselves.

In 87 percent of countries, the minimum voting age is eighteen (Electoral Knowledge Network 2018a). The youngest minimum voting age, sixteen, is policy in Austria, Argentina, Ecuador, Cuba, and Nicaragua; in Indonesia, people can vote at age seventeen. South Korea, Cameroon, Oman, and Malaysia have higher minimum voting ages of between nineteen and twenty-one. Until the twentieth century, women were generally prohibited from voting, and women's access to the polls expanded gradually over the years. Saudi Arabia extended the right to vote to women only in 2015, or the Islamic year 1435 (Kingdom of Saudi Arabia n.d.). Some countries also remove the right to vote from individuals as a punishment or due to employment in specific occupations, such as police or military work. For example, all but two U.S. states (Maine and Vermont) prohibit people convicted of certain crimes from voting, and these prohibitions extend well beyond the completion of any criminal sentences; in thirteen states, felons are permanently stripped of their right to vote (National Conference of State Legislators 2018).

Other than prohibitions on voting by young children, the most common voting restriction is that an individual must be a **citizen** of the country in which they seek to vote in order to be eligible, though some countries permit other kinds of residents to vote. So what does it mean to be a citizen? **Citizenship** is best understood as meaning that an individual belongs to a particular "political community" (Leydet 2017), which gives the person a legal status that entitles them to a bundle of rights and responsibilities that vary by country, as will be discussed in chapter 10. Most importantly, citizenship provides some protection to individuals, reducing "the risks associated with the absence of citizenship" (Findlay, Kuo, and Wei 2013:184).

Citizenship requirements vary greatly by country. Some of the main variations include whether citizenship is automatically granted to a child who is born in a country (this is known as birthright citizenship) or whether it must be transmitted by a child's parents; what individuals need to do to gain citizenship in a country (this process is called naturalization); under what circumstances individuals can lose their citizenship; and whether **dual citizenship**, holding citizenship in more than one country at a time, is permitted (United States Office of Personnel Management Investigations Service 2001). To illustrate the range of possibilities, let us consider several example countries around the world: Austria, Bahrain, Ghana, Israel, Mexico, Singapore, and the United States. The conflicts between different countries' policies can cause people to end up without citizenship anywhere, an issue that will be discussed in more detail in chapter 10.

- *Austria*   Children acquire citizenship at birth if the mother holds Austrian citizenship or if the father holds Austrian citizenship and either the parents are married or the father recognizes paternity within eight weeks of birth.

Dual citizenship is possible for individuals who were granted citizenship at birth, but not for others. To be naturalized, an individual must live in Austria legally and continuously for a decade without having been convicted of any criminal or severe administrative offenses or found to have links to any extremist or terrorist groups. The individual must also demonstrate the capacity to support themselves financially, whether through work or family-related support benefits, or be disabled. Additionally, they must demonstrate a "positive attitude towards the Republic of Austria," German language skills, and knowledge of Austrian history and government, though these standards are different for minors and those with disabilities. Austrian citizenship can be terminated if an individual acquires foreign citizenship, voluntarily serves in the military forces of another country, or "adversely affects the interests and reputation of the Republic of Austria" (Austrian Embassy in Washington n.d.; Sozialministerium and BM.I. n.d.).

- *Bahrain*   According to the 1963 Citizenship Act, children are given citizenship at birth if they are born in Bahrain to a father with Bahraini citizenship or born outside of Bahrain to a father with Bahraini citizenship who was born in Bahrain or whose father was born in Bahrain (European University Institute 2018). Children can be granted citizenship at birth through a Bahraini mother only if the father is unknown or stateless. Children born in Bahrain are granted Bahraini citizenship at birth if neither parent is known. Naturalization for men is possible after twenty-five years of continuous residence (fifteen for nationals of other Arabic countries) and demonstrated good conduct, command of Arabic, and property ownership; a man can then provide this citizenship to his wife and children. Women can also be naturalized by marrying Bahraini citizens. The monarch can also provide citizenship at will. Naturalized citizens cannot vote until ten years after their naturalization. Dual citizenship is generally not recognized but must be registered with the government. The government can revoke Bahraini citizenship at will and does so regularly, stripping affected individuals of their right to work, attend school, access medical care, and use government services (Bowler 2015). Female Bahraini citizens who marry foreigners lose their nationality unless they remain in Bahrain and request to maintain it (European University Institute 2018).

- *Ghana*   Children are granted Ghanaian citizenship at birth regardless of where they are born so long as at least one parent or grandparent holds Ghanaian citizenship at the time of birth. Children born in Ghana are also able to obtain citizenship if their parents are unknown. To be naturalized as a Ghanaian citizen, an individual must have lived in the country for at least five years, be of demonstrated good character, and be able to speak and understand an indigenous Ghanaian language. In addition, the individual must display the capacity to contribute to Ghana and have the intention of living there permanently (Government of Ghana 2018). These rules tend to discourage naturalization. However, they are eased for spouses of Ghanaian citizens. Ghanaians are able to maintain dual citizenship by application (Ghana Consolate General 2018). Citizenship may be revoked if it is found to have been granted on the basis of fraud or if a naturalized citizen has engaged in activities contrary to morality, public interest, or state security (Government of Ghana 2018).

- *Israel*   Children born to parents holding Israeli citizenship are citizens from birth. Children born stateless can apply for Israeli citizenship between ages eighteen and twenty-five, so long as they have lived in Israel for five consecutive years prior to the date of application. Under a doctrine known as the Right of Return, any Jewish person, along with their non-Jewish family members, is automatically eligible for citizenship as long as they can document their status as a Jew according to government religious standards and are not deemed to be "engaged in activities directed against the Jewish people" or to present a danger to public health or security. Naturalization is available at the discretion of the government to those who have lived in Israel for three of the past five years. Dual citizenship is permitted for those who have been citizens since birth and those who obtain citizenship through the Right of Return, but those applying for naturalization must renounce any other citizenship (State of Israel 2013). Citizenship can be revoked if it is found to have been granted under false pretenses, if the citizen leaves Israel for more than seven years and does not maintain a relationship with the country, or if the citizen has taken actions against the state (Herzog 2010).

- *Mexico*   Children born in Mexico are granted citizenship at birth if they are born in the territory of Mexico or if they are born abroad to at least one Mexican parent (Consulado General de México en El Paso 2018). Dual citizenship is permitted (Consulado General de México en El Paso 2018). Naturalization is permitted after at least five years of residency if the individual knows Spanish, is familiar with national history, and is "integrated into the national culture." A shorter period applies to those who are descendants or parents of Mexican citizens, are from a Latin American or Iberian country, marry a Mexican citizen, or have "rendered services or carried out outstanding works . . . that benefit the nation" (Secretaría de Servicios Parlamentarios 2012). Naturalized citizens can lose their citizenship if they accept titles of nobility from or serve other governments (Constitucion Politica de los Estados Unidos Mexicanos, art. 37).

- *Singapore*   Children born in Singapore are granted citizenship at birth unless neither parent is a citizen or the father is either an enemy citizen or a diplomat serving under a foreign power. Children born outside of Singapore to at least one Singaporean parent and registered within one year of birth are citizens from birth so long as the parent resided in Singapore for at least five years prior to the child's birth or for at least two of the five years immediately proceeding the birth, though prior to 2004 the father had to be a Singaporean citizen. Naturalization is permitted for those over twenty-one who have resided in Singapore for at least a decade, are of good character, speak one of the four national languages, and intend to live in Singapore permanently. The residency period is only two years for spouses of Singaporean citizens. Dual citizenship is permitted only for minors, who must then choose within twelve months of turning twenty-one whether to keep or renounce their Singaporean citizenship. Should they choose to keep it, they must renounce any other citizenship and take the Oath of Renunciation, Allegiance and Loyalty or their Singaporean citizenship will be revoked. Citizenship by naturalization may also be revoked if it is found to have been granted on the basis of fraud or mistake, or if the citizen has been disloyal, engaged in trade with or assisted an enemy in wartime, been convicted of a crime, carried out actions harmful to Singapore, or taken up residence outside of Singapore and failed to annually register (Constitution of the Republic of Singapore, art. 120–141).

- *United States* Birthright citizenship is granted to any child born in the territory of the United States. Children who are born abroad are able obtain citizenship through their parents if at least one parent is a U.S. citizen who previously lived in the United States for a minimum of five years, including two years after age fourteen. Naturalization is possible after five years of permanent residence, three years as a permanent resident and spouse of a citizen, or after completing military service. To be naturalized, an individual must pass a citizenship test and an English exam and go through a character interview. Dual citizenship is permitted. Citizenship can be revoked only on the basis of illegal or misleading information provided during naturalization, if a naturalized citizen is discharged from the military on other than honorable grounds, or if he or she joins certain terrorist or political groups within five years of naturalization (United States Citizenship and Immigration Services 2018).

Overall, 41 percent of countries worldwide provide for automatic, unconditional citizenship for children of citizens (this rule is known as *jus sanguinis*), even when those children are born abroad. Eighteen percent provide for automatic, unconditional citizenship for those born in the country (called *jus soli*), while an additional 23 percent provide this with conditions. *Jus soli* is more common in the Americas, where 83 percent of countries have the policy, than elsewhere in the world, though many countries do provide citizenship for children born on their territory who would otherwise be stateless. Sixty-four percent of countries permit dual citizenship (Bauböck, Honohan, and Vink 2018).

Some countries require voters to be resident in the country to vote, while others allow nonresident citizens to vote by absentee ballot or if they travel home in time for election day. For example, Cabo Verde permits nonresident citizens to vote as long as they are registered to vote and emigrated in the past five years; are providing for a child, spouse, or relative still living in Cabo Verde; are serving in a diplomatic or public service mission or are the spouse of such a person; or have visited Cabo Verde within the past three years. Cabo Verdeans abroad vote in three special electoral districts representing those living in Africa, the Americas, and the rest of the world, with two representatives each (Electoral Knowledge Network 2018b). In countries with territorial or colonial possessions, voters living in those areas may not have full national voting rights. For example, voters living in Puerto Rico can vote in elections at the local level, can elect a representative to the U.S. Congress (although that representative is a nonvoting member), and can vote in presidential primaries, but they cannot vote in the general election for president and do not have representation in the Electoral College.

Who Runs?

Many countries have age restrictions, linguistic requirements, or other criteria that must be met in order to stand for office. For example, in Kyrgyzstan, candidates for president must be at least thirty-five but no older than sixty-five, must demonstrate fluency in the Kyrgyz language, must personally deposit a sum of money equal to one thousand times the minimum monthly wage (to be returned only if they achieve a minimum percentage of the total presidential vote), and must obtain fifty thousand signatures on their nominating petitions, including signatures from each of eight regions of the country (Reynolds, Reilly, and Ellis 2008). These sorts of high barriers to entry greatly reduce the potential population from which candidates can be drawn. Even where restrictions do not exist, elected bodies may fail to represent the gender, age, class, religious, linguistic, and ethnic diversity of a society (Reynolds, Reilly, and Ellis 2008). Consider, for example, the number of women in elected office around the globe, as shown in map 9. The worldwide average for women in legislative bodies is 23.8 percent; only Rwanda, Cuba, and Bolivia have 50 percent or higher representation of women (Inter-Parliamentary Union 2018). Many countries, including Belize, Iran, Sri Lanka, and Haiti, continue to have legislative bodies that are less than 10 percent female. Even many supposedly modernized countries, like the United States, Korea, and Hungary, are well under the global average. Scholars argue that the continuing underrepresentation of women in electoral politics is shaped by many cultural, structural, and political factors, including the continuing presence of gendered barriers to women's electoral participation (Paxton and Hughes 2017).

There is also considerable global diversity in how elections are financed and what rules exist around campaign spending (Pinto-Duschinsky 2002). A majority of countries require some type of financial disclosure from candidates, and about half prohibit or limit the ability of candidates to raise

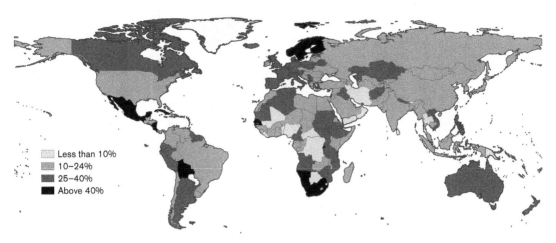

Map 9 Percent of legislators in lower or single legislative house, female (Inter-Parliamentary Union 2018)

campaign funds from foreign donors. Yet the majority of countries also provide free political television broadcasts and access to public subsidies for candidates. In the United States, the United Kingdom, and Italy, less than 5 percent of campaign spending comes from public funds; in Germany, France, Israel, Sweden, and Austria, more than half of campaign spending does (Pinto-Duschinsky 2002). Public financing can make standing for election much more feasible for low-income people. In many countries, the length of electoral campaigns is limited by law, in some cases to as little as a couple of weeks (in Japan and France), while in the United States, presidential campaigns can last for more than a year (Kurtzleben 2015).

CONCLUSION

Questions about campaign finance may seem far afield from core considerations of law and justice, but the outcomes of political campaigns lead to the government regimes that make decisions (at least in democratic states). Like the legal systems in place in a given country, the way state power is organized in that country has substantial impacts on the workings of law and justice.

The organization of state power in different countries around the world is varied and diverse. We find countries with authoritarian monarchies or dictatorships where regular people have no say in the running of government, and we find democracies with carefully considered electoral systems designed to encourage mass participation in decision-making and legislative bodies that are broadly representative of the country's social groups. Regardless, though, of the type of government, the system of legislative-executive relations, how elections work, and who votes and runs for office, governments enact laws and run administrative agencies. These laws and structures have consequences. They determine which actions are legal and which are illegal or criminal. They shape the practices and policies of law enforcement and determine the funding priorities for law enforcement agencies. They lay out proper court procedures and the rights of the accused. They maintain both the rules about and the mechanisms of punishment. They interface with international legal institutions and provide for (or violate) the legal, civil, and human rights of their residents. Thus, understanding the basic structure and function of governments is an important first step in developing knowledge of justice systems.

Crime and the Global World

CHAPTER GOALS

1. Understand explanations for differences in national crime rates.
2. Explain how crime is defined and measured.
3. Distinguish between different kinds of cross-border crime, including international crime, transnational crime, and terrorism.

Map 10 shows global intentional homicide rates (per 100,000 population) by country, using the most recent data provided to the United Nations Office on Drugs and Crime (UNDOC) between 2010 and 2015. UNDOC defines intentional homicide as "unlawful death purposefully inflicted on a person by another person" (Lemahieu and Me 2014:9). As the map makes clear, the differences between countries are quite large. Thirty-seven countries—ranging from Australia, Germany, and Japan to the Maldives, Tonga, and Brunei—recorded fewer than one intentional homicide per 100,000 population in the most recent available data year, while El Salvador recorded over 108 (more than one per 1,000 people), and Honduras, Venezuela, and the United States Virgin Islands record more than 50 (UNDOC n.d.). Differences are large even between neighboring countries—for example, the data shows Peru's homicide rate as

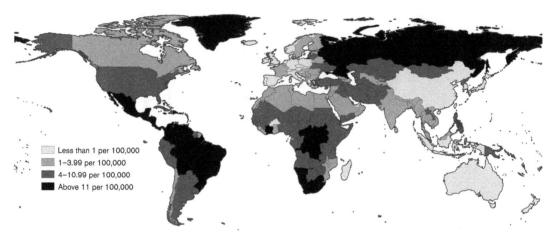

Less than 1 per 100,000
1–3.99 per 100,000
4–10.99 per 100,000
Above 11 per 100,000

Map 10 Homicide rate per 100,000 population (UNDOC n.d.).

7.2 per 100,000, while Brazil has a rate of 26.7 per 100,000, nearly four times higher. Why do these differences occur?

This chapter will examine variations in other types of crimes as well as homicide. But before getting to the data, the chapter will consider various explanations scholars have proposed for the differences we observe in crime rates. It will also explore the difficulties in measuring and comparing crime rates as well as differences in what types of actions and behaviors are considered criminal. Finally, the chapter will discuss crimes that cross borders, including international crimes like genocide, transnational crimes like trafficking in goods and people, and terrorism.

WHY DO CRIME RATES VARY?

As map 10 shows, crime rates vary considerably among countries. Scholars cite numerous factors that might impact and shape these differences. As noted in chapter 1, both culture and structure can shape outcomes such as crime rates. Cultural factors, including national cultures, local or regional cultures, and subcultures, shape people's views about what sort of (potentially criminal) behavior might be acceptable or excusable in which kinds of circumstances or contexts. Structural factors, including economic inequality, social and community structures, and aspects of the legal system, also influence the circumstances in which criminal activities may occur.

Cultural Explanations for Crime

Many commentators like to point to cultural factors when seeking to explain why crime rates vary. There are various cultural factors that could shape differences in crime rates generally or in rates of particular crimes. For example, different countries have different cultural values around violence. In some cultures, violence is seen as an accepted and important way to solve problems; in others, people are expected to avoid violence if at all possible. It is clear that these differences have the potential to impact crime rates, particularly those of violent crime. This type of cultural explanation has been used by many to explain historical differences in rates of violence between the southern states and other parts of the United States. Scholars have argued that southern culture teaches young people that violence is appropriate and that it is important to use violence in defense of honor or personal safety (Ellison 1991). Some research has found support for this thesis, especially among older lifelong residents of the south (Ellison 1991), though other studies suggest that cultural explanations fade when structural factors are included in the model (Dixon and Lizotte 1987).

Culture can matter in other ways as well. If a location's cultural traditions emphasize following the rules and obeying authority, individuals raised there may be less likely to engage in illegal activity than they would be had they been socialized in a culture emphasizing individual autonomy and freethinking behavior. Some scholars have presented this type of cultural explanation in seeking to explain Japan's crime rate, arguing that cultural values around self-control, the importance of the group, and traditional duty, among other factors, reduce the likelihood that Japanese citizens will commit crimes (Komiya 1999). Religious and moral beliefs matter too. If a particular action is illegal *and* it is condemned by religious authorities, the religiously faithful might fear punishment both by secular authorities and by a higher power after death. On the other hand, if secular authorities prohibit actions that are religiously significant, religious individuals who are otherwise law-abiding may continue to engage in these practices and thus may be seen as criminals.

The preceding paragraphs may seem to suggest that countries or regions have one single culture, which is of course not often the case. Where it is not, conflicts between people with different cultural backgrounds and practices can sometimes lead to criminal activities. However, when communities develop strong, cohesive networks, these connections can reduce crime—unless, of course, those networks happen to be gangs or other criminal organizations.

The Impact of Economic and Social Factors on Crime

Some crime occurs in response to economic motivations. People who steal money or property may do so because they need (or believe they need) access to those economic resources to pay for food, shelter, clothing, medical care, or other necessities. Or they may steal to obtain goods they want but cannot afford, like brand-name sneakers, jewelry, or luxury cars. In the latter situation, individuals considering criminal activity may rationally consider the potential benefits of the crime in relation to the risks it presents and decide to carry out the crime if they perceive the benefits to outweigh the risks.

The degree to which opportunities for crime are available matters too. For example, cars with ignition locks, locked doors, and steering column locks are much harder to steal than unlocked cars with older starter technologies (Clarke and Harris 1992), and it is much harder to steal condoms from the pharmacy when they are locked up away from reach (Ashwood et al. 2011). Research in Europe, Pakistan, and Nigeria, among other countries, has found that unemployment can lead to crime, in part because it increases the free time individuals have available to commit crimes, but also because it creates economic distress, especially among low-wage workers (Altindag 2012; Gilliani, Rehman, and Gill 2009; Torrum and Abur 2014). A cross-national study of European countries found that higher levels of unemployment, particularly among low-education individuals, increased property crime rates (Altindag 2012).

Social disorganization theory makes some related claims. Social disorganization is used to describe communities that cannot effectively exercise social control over community members (Sampson and Groves 1989). For example, communities experiencing social disorganization may lack informal networks, like those among friends and extended family relations; formal networks, like collective participation in local organizations; and structured "collective supervision" in relation to community issues and problems. In particular, communities that lack effective mechanisms for supervising and controlling the behavior of young people are expected to have higher degrees of criminal activity. Scholars of social disorganization theory argue that communities with fewer economic resources, greater degrees of residential mobility, and higher degrees of urbanization, where members of diverse social groups live in proximity but have not built communal ties across their differences and where family ties are disrupted, will experience more social disorganization (Sampson and Groves 1989).

Crime can also be a more general response to economic conditions and to social or economic inequality. Scholars use the concept of **relative deprivation** to refer to situations in which there is a significant gap between what an individual has and what he or she believes she should have (Merton 1968). Relative deprivation is not simply a measure of poverty—people who are poor but who do not perceive others as having much more than they do will not experience relative deprivation, while upper-middle-class people who are friends with billionaires and believe they too deserve to be billionaires will experience a high degree of relative deprivation. Some research has found that relative deprivation is correlated with crime rates, especially rates of homicide but also of assault, robbery, and burglary, while poverty is much less related to crime (Kawachi, Kennedy, and Wilkinson 1999).

In some cases, individuals commit crime as a form of social protest. This can occur when individuals choose to engage in **civil disobedience** or actively refuse to comply with laws, rules, or orders as a form of resistance. But it can also occur due to a more generalized sense of injustice or deprivation (Ferrell 1996). For example, if a community of poor people is forced to move to make way for the development of luxury homes, and one of the individuals who have been displaced chooses to burglarize or vandalize the new homes, this would be a crime committed out of a sense of injustice.

Crime and the Legal System

A variety of aspects of the legal system can impact crime rates. First and foremost are laws themselves. It is law that makes something criminal—without a legal prohibition against it, even the most socially disfavored activity is not a crime, at least in legal systems that function in accordance with the rule of law. But as soon as an action becomes legally prohibited, it becomes a crime, irrespective of individuals' knowledge of the law (Neily 2017). There is cross-national variation in which actions are legally prohibited, a topic that will be discussed later in this chapter. It is not only the legal process of criminalization that impacts crime. Other laws matter too. For example, as will be discussed in chapter 5, countries have different levels of regulation of firearms and other weapons. While access to firearms may not impact the overall rate of violent crime, it does increase the rate of gun crime and thus the likelihood that crimes will result in fatalities (Altheimer 2008; Grinshteyn and Hemenway 2016). Of course, homicides can be carried out by means other than firearms, and there are considerable international differences in homicide mechanisms: 66 percent of homicides in the Americas are carried out by a firearm, while this figure is only 28 percent in Africa and Asia and less than 15 percent in the rest of the world (Lemahieu and Me 2014).

The types of **punishments** assessed for crimes may also impact the crime rate if those punishments have a deterrent effect or keep potential criminals away from opportunities to commit crimes. Specific punishments and punishment philosophies will be discussed in chapter 7, but it important to note here that harsher punishments do not necessarily reduce crime. Researchers who have examined the impact of so-called tough-on-crime policies have found competing evidence about their outcomes, with studies finding both that tougher sentencing policies modestly reduce crime (E. Chen 2008) and that such policies may increase the crime rate (Kovandzic, Sloan, and Vieraitis 2004; Lynch and Sabol 1997).

Another way that punishment policy may impact crime rates is through the actions of **vigilantes**. Vigilantes are individuals or groups without any formal crime-fighting authority who take it upon themselves to police their community and punish people they see as offenders. This typically occurs when vigilantes perceive the legal authorities as insufficient for or incapable of meeting the demands of crime-fighting. Vigilantes' activities are typically themselves criminal, as they involve actions like harassment, assault, unlawful imprisonment, and even homicide, so while the vigilantes may believe themselves to be fighting crime, they simultaneously increase it.

Law enforcement activities may also impact crime rates. Effective law enforcement, as will be discussed in chapter 5, can work to prevent crime as well as to find criminal offenders and put a stop to their ongoing criminal activities. But even well-resourced law enforcement may not be able to reduce crime if its activities are not directed appropriately. In addition, corruption within law enforcement and other government agencies can lead to increases in crime rates if law enforcement officers themselves engage in or tolerate crime.

HOW DO WE MEASURE CRIME?

Official crime statistics come from two main sources: government crime data as collected by law enforcement or other appropriate government agencies (which then may be forwarded to international agencies for compilation and comparison) and data collected via local, national, or international victimization surveys (Howard, Newman, and Pridemore 2000; van Dijk 2009). In addition, some researchers have collected self-reports of criminal activity by surveying individuals and asking if they have ever committed various criminal acts. As figure 4 suggests, there are a variety of ways in which these measures may not accurately reflect the actual amount of crime that occurs (UNDOC 2010). Some crimes are never reported or recorded. This includes so-called victimless crimes; circumstances in which victims are too scared or ashamed to come forward (even in anonymous victimization surveys) or do not have access to local police who will take their reports; and errors in data entry, interpretation, and management of statistics. Official crime statistics maintained by the police can also contain errors. The police may neglect to record crimes when victims report them, or they may record crimes that never occurred as part of a scheme to make themselves appear busier or due to corruption. More mundanely, the police can make data-entry errors, lose crime reports, or manage their data poorly, and national agencies responsible for aggregating data may accidentally leave out particular regions or lose track of some submitted data. Thus, not all crime that occurs becomes known to officials. Furthermore, some crime may not be detected even by victims. For example, a pedestrian may have their cell phone stolen by a pickpocket but assume that they themselves were responsible for losing it, never suspecting that a crime has occurred. Victims of white collar or corporate crimes are especially unlikely to know that they have been victimized, given the complexity of such crimes and the fact that they

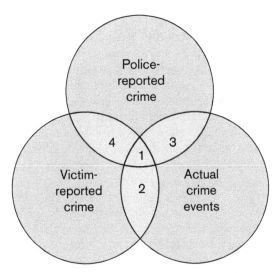

Figure 4 Collecting crime statistics (UNDOC 2010).

Note: the size of shapes in this diagram does not represent the actual magnitude of the categories described.

1: A crime occurs, is reported by the victim, and is recorded by the police.
2: A crime occurs and is reported by the victim, but the police do not record it.
3: A crime occurs and the victim does not report it, but it is recorded by the police.
4: An individual reports a crime and the police record it, but that crime never occurred.

tend to be impersonal in nature. Finally, sometimes people report crimes that never actually occurred, as part of an insurance fraud scheme, for example, and these crimes may be reflected in official statistics.

Beyond these errors, there are a variety of other reasons why it can be challenging to compare crime statistics across borders. For example, different countries collect data on different crimes, and even when countries collect data on the same type of crime, they may define that crime differently (Howard, Newman, and Pridemore 2000; Mosher, Miethe, and Hart 2011). Consider the crime of child abuse. In some societies, hitting a child with a belt may be a felony crime, while in others, it is seen as an acceptable way for parents to discipline their children and would therefore not be recorded in official crime statistics even if reported to the police. Even homicide does not necessarily have a standard definition. UNDOC's definition of homicide, discussed at the beginning of this chapter, focuses on unlawful and intentional killing. Police or judicial killings, killings committed in self-defense, killings occurring during armed conflicts, and accidental killings are all excluded from the standard UNDOC definition of intentional homicide, but some countries may include them in their national homicide data (Lemahieu and Me 2014). The crime definitions used in victimization surveys may not even match the official crime definitions in that country (van Dijk 2009). Later in this chapter, data will be presented to show how differently people from different parts of the world may think about the criminality of particular acts.

There are a variety of more technical and methodological issues with comparing crime data across countries. Even translation between languages or differences in dialects can introduce errors. Consider this (noncriminal) example: If you order chips in a fast-food joint in the United States, you'll get a bag of thinly sliced, prefried potatoes, or perhaps fried triangles of corn tortilla. Make the same order in the United Kingdom, and you will be served what Americans call French fries. Similarly, public schools in England require tuition payments and are not funded by taxes, while tax-funded schools are called state schools. In the United States and Scotland, the term "public school" refers to a tax-funded school. If such simple topics can introduce confusion between native speakers of the same language, imagine how difficult it can be to work across the hundreds of official languages in which crime reports are collected.

As noted above, there are many reasons why some crimes may not be recorded in the official crime statistics to begin with. Individuals may not report crimes when they do not trust the police or when police are not locally available and accessible. Those without formal legal status in a country, such as undocumented migrants and guest workers, may fear deportation if they report crimes. And some crimes, such as sex crimes, can be highly stigmatizing for victims, who may then choose not to report to protect their own reputations. Figure 5 shows the variation in estimated crime reporting rates among a small sample of countries for three crimes: physical assault, sexual assault, and robbery. Reporting rates range from over 80 percent to under 10 percent; figure 5 also shows how much the reporting rates vary between crimes even in a single country. Sexual assault is the crime most likely to have the lowest reporting rates, though Kyrgyzstan and South Africa do not fit this pattern. It is important to note, in reviewing this data and other data on crime rates presented throughout this chapter, that data is not available for many countries due to a lack of reliable or comparable data collection.

Police sometimes do not enter crimes into the official crime data collection system even if they do take a report, and of course they may refuse to take a report in the first place. When multiple offenses occur as part of the same crime—for instance, an assault followed by a car theft—they could be recorded as one crime or as multiple crimes. In addition, nations and even regions within nations may differ as to when they record crime data. Some law enforcement departments record crimes at the time they are reported; others record crimes only when a suspect has been identified and the case has been transferred to the prosecutor's office. It is worth noting that law enforcement agencies may be evaluated or funded on the basis of crime statistics, and this can influence their reporting and recording practices.

Research looking at the degree to which official crime statistics and the results of victimization surveys are correlated has had mixed findings, with stronger correlations resulting when analyses control for national differences in crime reporting rates (van Dijk 2009). Some studies have found no correlation at all between official and self-reported crime rates. Where correlations

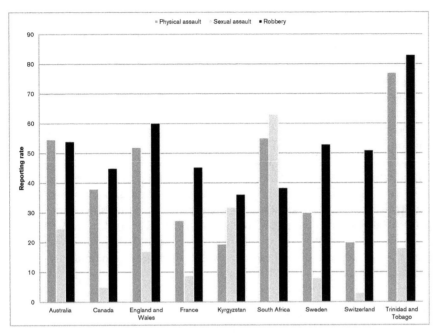

Figure 5 Variations in crime reporting rates, most recent data available, 2010–2015 (UNDOC 2018).

are found, they tend to be strongest for property crime. Analyses suggest that although official police crime statistics do reflect trends in crime rates, the discovery of trends will be delayed or lessened when relying on official statistics (van Dijk 2009). A final issue to be aware of is the overall variation in data quality, including limitations in both official statistics and victimization surveys, that is introduced by technological factors such as access to telephone and Internet service, whether data is recorded digitally or by hand on hard copy, and even whether the postal mail is reliable.

Historically, the most useful source of internationally comparable crime data is the International Crime Victims Survey (ICVS), which is administered in a number of languages to individuals residing in countries around the world, primarily in key urban areas. The ICVS has been administered in several waves—1989, 1992, 1996, 2000, 2004/2005, and in some countries more recently (ICVS 2018)—typically to a sample of one thousand people per country. However, since the most recent prepared statistics are from the 2004/2005 wave, this limits the ICVS's current utility (see, for instance, Lynch and Pridemore 2010). Each person who responds to the ICVS is asked to report the crimes experienced by members of his or her household during the preceding five years. This approach means that ICVS data suffers from several methodological limitations common to survey-based research, including memory lapses, discomfort with revealing sensitive information (such as sexual victimization), sample representativeness, and nonresponse bias (Howard, Newman, and Pridemore 2000), as well as impacts on the data from question wording, question order, and response options (Mosher, Miethe, and Hart 2011). Nonresponse bias may be a particular problem for the ICVS given that it relies on telephone-based data collection because rates of telephone ownership remain low in some countries.

The data on homicide presented at the beginning of this chapter, in comparison, comes from official UNDOC data. Homicide data suffers from fewer methodological limitations than other official crime data because it does not rely simply on law enforcement reports. It also takes into account vital statistics data collected by health officials, which includes mortality by cause. Not all countries have the infrastructure to collect and maintain such data, but in places where health departments are able to record mortality statistics, the reported homicide rate in vital statistics records tends to be somewhat higher than the rate reported in crime records (Howard, Newman, and Pridemore 2000).

How Do Crime Rates Vary?

As noted above, internationally comparable data on crime rates for offenses other than homicide is limited and problematic, especially in recent years. However, UNDOC has long administered the United Nations Surveys on Crime Trends and the Operations of Criminal Justice Systems, or UN-CTS (UNDOC 2018). This data is based on official national crime statistics but does include data on reporting rates for some countries. Figure 6 plots the rates of robbery, sexual assault, and physical assault as documented in the UN-CTS data for twenty-nine countries for which at least two of these three crime rates from between 2010 and 2015 are available (fifteen of the countries are missing one of the three rates). The data should be interpreted with caution, given the limited crime reporting rates shown in figure 5, but it does demonstrate the wide variation in crime rates across countries. In addition, it is clear that even if a country has a high rate of a particular crime (say, Canada's rate of physical assault), that does not mean rates of other crimes will also be high (Canada's rate of robbery is much lower than that in many other countries).

Individual researchers working on specific projects related to comparing crime rates have also developed useful studies. For example, an analysis of mass shootings worldwide found that between 1966 and 2012, ninety of the individuals who carried out these acts were Americans, meaning that Americans were responsible for 31 percent of all mass shootings (Fisher and Keller 2017). The second-highest number of mass shooters was found in the Philippines, where there were eighteen. If we adjust for population and look only at

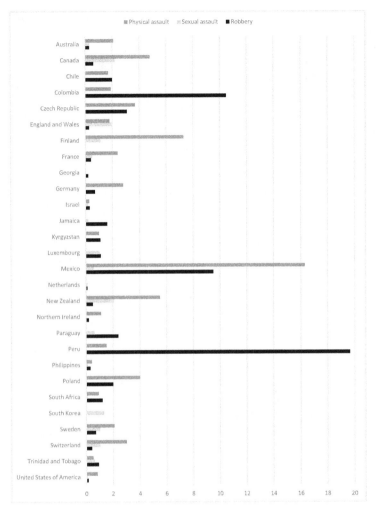

Figure 6 Percent of population victimized by various crimes in the past year, most recent data available, 2010–2015 (UN-CTS data; UNDOC 2018).

countries with populations above ten million, we find that Yemen had a higher rate of mass shooters, with forty per million population; in the United States, the rate was slightly under thirty per million population.

CRIMINALIZATION

An important factor that affects crime rates—one we tend not to think much about—is what is considered illegal in the first place. For a particular action to be criminal, it must first be defined as such under the law, a process known as **criminalization**. Most commonly, this occurs when a legislative body passes a law declaring that a particular action is criminal. However, in common law countries, it is possible for judges to determine that a particular act is criminal even if the legislature has not specifically laid this out in statute. Much of English and South African criminal law remains defined in this judicial fashion. For example, in South Africa, murder, rape, robbery, and other crimes remain uncodified and thus are criminalized by virtue of common law precedent (Department of Justice and Constitutional Development n.d.). There is generally no requirement that a person convicted of a crime must have been aware that their actions were criminal, but many countries follow legal principles that require statutes to be clear and unambiguous about which acts count as crimes.

In most instances, criminal statutes also specify the particular penalties or punishments to be assessed when they are violated. Punishment will be discussed in more detail in chapter 7, but it is worth considering how punishments for particular crimes can vary around the world. In particular, the type of punishment assessed, if any, tells us something about how serious that type of crime is seen to be in a given national context. Let's consider a few examples: possession of one gram (0.035 ounces) of marijuana, public urination, and assaulting a police officer.

In many parts of the world, possession of a small amount of marijuana for personal consumption no longer results in prosecution or penalty. Where marijuana possession remains a criminal matter, penalties range widely, from a small fine to a fine of more than $40,000 or up to ten years in prison. For possession of larger amounts, countries such as Singapore and Saudi Arabia can impose the death penalty (R. Jones n.d.). Similarly, public urination is not illegal in some places, such as in some German cities, though new paint technology that reflects urine back at the urinator might make doing so less than enticing (Noack 2015). Other cities in Germany, and other countries around the world, impose fines, which can range from the equivalent of $2 to over $400. Community service or cleaning up the urine are also potential penalties (Grimm n.d.). In the United States, public urination could land you on the sex offender registry (Carey, Tofte, and Fellner 2007). Punishments for assaulting a police officer tend to be more severe, ranging from a few months in prison in countries like the United Kingdom, Iran, and Israel or a few years in prison in Canada and Japan to as many as fifteen to twenty-five years in prison in the United States if the police officer sustains so much as a minor injury (Yanick n.d.).

As these examples show, all countries consider some crimes more severe than others. To some extent, countries agree on the relative severity of certain crimes—all countries discussed in the examples above, for instance, see public urination as less severe of a crime than assaulting a police officer. Many studies have found substantial cross-national agreement on the rankings of severe crimes. But this agreement is not universal.

Table 2 Comparing crime severity in the United States and Kuwait

Act	United States	Kuwait
Killing a spouse during an argument	1	6
Kidnapping a woman to rape her	2	4
Stabbing a spouse with a knife during an argument	3	8
Committing a forcible rape	4	2
Killing a child in one's care while driving under the influence of alcohol	5	10
Intending to injure another person by throwing a stone and accidentally killing them	**6**	**25**
Forcing a women into prostitution	7	3
Robbing a store with a gun	8	12
Selling illegal drugs	9	11
Throwing burning liquid in someone else's face and causing scarring	10	15
Burglarizing a neighbor's home	11	14
Setting fire to a warehouse	12	21
Stealing things worth about $100	**13**	**28**
Selling company secrets to another company	**14**	**31**
Forging an official document	**15**	**29**
Bribing a government official to win a business contract	16	23
Loaning money at a high interest rate	**17**	**30**
Using drugs	18	20
Committing perjury	19	19
Forging a check	20	27
Operating a public gambling house	21	16
Accidently shooting a person while hunting	**22**	**35**
A young person stealing an automobile	**23**	**37**
An employee taking a car as a bribe	24	32
A company executive falsely advertising the quality of a product	25	26
An individual falsely advertising prices	26	34
A pharmacist selling drugs for an abortion	27	23
A doctor performing an illegal abortion	28	26
A woman engaging in prostitution	**29**	**7**
An individual accusing a woman of adultery without adequate proof	30	17
A married man committing adultery	**31**	**5**
A married woman committing adultery	**32**	**1**
An individual insulting someone's honor in front of others	33	33
A man engaging in homosexuality	**34**	**9**
A woman having an illegal abortion	35	22
Someone abandoning religion and espousing atheism	36	13
An unmarried man having sex	**37**	**18**

SOURCE: Evans and Scott 1984.

A classic research study provides one of the best examples we have for examining cross-cultural differences in views of crime seriousness (Evans and Scott 1984). The authors asked college students in Kuwait and the United States to rank a list of seventeen punishments from most to least severe. The list of punishments included no penalty, reprimand, probation, fines, prison sentences of various terms, whipping, banishment, amputation, and two different kinds of death sentences. The Kuwaiti and American students ranked the punishments similarly. The researchers then asked the students to assign punishments to a list of thirty-seven criminal offenses. Using data from the first stage of the study, the researchers were able to rank the offenses by severity according to the typical punishment assessed. So what did the researchers find?

Table 2 shows the rankings the researchers produced in their study. Offenses for which the average ranking—out of thirty-seven, with one being the most serious and thirty-seven being the least serious—differed between the United States and Kuwait by more than ten places are highlighted in bold type. One notable finding is that the U.S. students seemed to think that stealing was very bad, even when the items were of low value, while the Kuwaitis considered stealing a less serious offense than having sex outside of marriage. In fact, Islamic law classifies crimes into three categories: *ta'zir*, *qisas*, and *hudud* (Baderin [2006] 2017). *Ta'zir* crimes are those not specifically outlined in the Qur'an and those that are mentioned in the Qur'an but not assigned a specified punishment. In contrast, *qisas* and *hudud* crimes and their penalties are specified in the Qur'an (Baderin [2006] 2017). *Qisas* crimes, also known as *jinayat* crimes, include murder and other crimes that result in bodily injury, which under Islamic law are punished by the paying of restitution (*diya*, or blood money) or by retaliatory acts (Baderin [2006] 2017). *Hudud* crimes are other specified crimes, including robbery, adultery, and acts of sex outside of marriage, that have specified punishments, such as amputation or execution, in the Qur'an (Baderin [2006] 2017). Thus, it is likely that exposure to Islamic law shaped at least some of the Kuwaiti students' responses in this study.

Decriminalization

Just as acts can be made criminal by the legislature, they can also be removed from the criminal code through a process of **legalization** or **decriminalization**. Legalization occurs when something that was previously illegal is made legal. For example, when marijuana is legalized, that means it can be legitimately bought, owned, and sold. When something is legalized, it can also be regulated. So, for example, cigarettes may be legal, but they are also taxed, and many countries require them to carry a health warning label and/or prohibit selling them to children. Decriminalization does not result in full legality, but it removes the offense from the realm of criminal law and instead treats it as an administrative violation. In other words, if marijuana is decriminalized, someone caught with it will

The Portuguese Drug Strategy

In 1999, 44 percent of convicted prison inmates in Portugal were imprisoned for drug offenses (Instituto Português da Droga e da Toxicodependência 2000). Portugal had the highest rate of HIV infection in the European Union (Ferreira 2017). And so the nation decided to try a radical new experiment in decriminalizing drug use and possession. The new policy was implemented by Prime Minister Antonio Gutieres, who later became United Nations Secretary-General, in November 2000 (República Portuguesa 2000).

As noted elsewhere in chapter 4, drug decriminalization means that drug use remains illegal but that it will be treated as an administrative violation rather than a matter for the criminal courts. Thus, in post-2000 Portugal, individuals possessing quantities of drugs considered reasonable for personal use can be subjected to a warning or a small fine imposed by a Commission for Dissuasions of Drug Addiction, which must include members with both legal and medical or social services backgrounds (Greenwald 2009). The commission can also wave the fine contingent on the drug user seeking medical treatment. Some other sanctions are also permitted, including the suspension of professional licenses and travel abroad. Selling or trafficking in drugs or providing them to children continue to be treated as criminal offenses (Greenwald 2009). Notably, the Portuguese law applies to *all* drugs, including so-called hard drugs like heroin.

The new law immediately brought about a considerable decrease in criminal charges for personal use and possession of drugs, from around two thousand cases a year to less than five hundred (Greenwald 2009). This change happened without any accompanying increase in drug usage; by some measures, drug use has decreased. More individuals are seeking drug treatment, while HIV diagnoses and opiate-related deaths have fallen (Greenwald 2009). The most recent findings show that while the number of individuals seeking drug rehabilitation treatment has increased somewhat, it remains lower than before the policy was enacted; drug-related crimes and deaths remain at lower levels; fewer HIV-positive individuals are using drugs; and judicial costs have been reduced (Félix, Portugal, and Tavares 2017). Consumption of drugs may not have decreased notably, but the secondary consequences of drug use have been reduced. The policy remains popular among Portuguese people and has not resulted in some of the negative effects people predicted, such as drug tourism and increased usage (Greenwald 2009).

One country Portugal is often compared to is the Netherlands. There, small amounts of marijuana for personal use are permitted, and coffee shops can sell small amounts of marijuana so long as they are permitted to do so by their local municipality and do not advertise or cause a nuisance. Only legal residents of the Netherlands aged eighteen or over can visit these shops. Individuals who grow marijuana plants may have the plants seized and can be subject to eviction, but so long as they do not have more than five plants, they will not be criminally charged (Government of the Netherlands n.d.).

The European Union consensus on drug policy is that it must deal with the global reality of drug trafficking, emphasize both supply reduction and demand reduction, and be evidence-based (EMCDDA n.d.-a). Thus, the experiences of countries like Portugal become an important part of the evidence other countries can use in designing policies grounded in data. For example, Italy, Latvia, and Spain have decriminalized drug possession for personal use (EMCDDA n.d.-b). But it is also important to note that most countries treat different

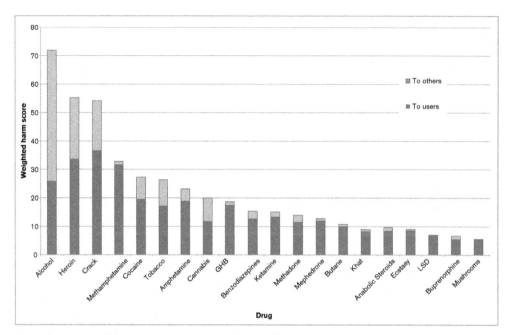

CS 4.1 Figure a Overall harm of various drugs (Nutt, King, and Phillips 2010).

kinds of intoxicating substances differently. Most countries claim that these decisions about criminalization and legalization are made on the basis of harm, but the evidence suggests other motivations may be important. One way to examine this issue is to look at research on the relative harms caused by users of various drugs to themselves and others. Researchers in the United Kingdom (Nutt, King, and Phillips 2010) examined twenty different substances, as shown in CS 4.1 figure a, to determine the harms they caused in a variety of categories: mortality; illness, injury, or other health-related harms; dependence or addiction; functional impairment; damage to property and other economic costs; crime; damage to family and other personal relationships; and harm to the environment, the community, and the global world.

They found that while heroin, crack, and methamphetamines are most harmful to *the individual user,* alcohol has the highest costs to others and the highest overall costs—and yet alcohol remains completely legal in much of the world. CS 4.1 map a, provides details on the minimum legal drinking age in countries around the world—note that in some countries, the youngest legal drinkers are permitted to purchase alcohol only for off-premises consumption; in some, they are allowed to drink only in licensed drinking establishments; in some, they are restricted to low-alcohol beverages; and in others, once an individual reaches the minimum drinking age, all kinds of alcohol consumption are permitted (World Health Organization 2014). There are some countries that do ban alcohol completely. Meanwhile, drugs that are commonly illegal or heavily restricted, like ecstasy, LSD, buprenorphine, and mushrooms, have far fewer harms than alcohol does (Nutt, King, and Phillips 2010). Thus, it is clear that

CS 4.1 Map a Minimum legal drinking age by country (World Health Organization 2014).

relative harm is not the key factor in shaping national decisions about criminalization and legalization. Portugal, then, presents a unique case for considering the concept of criminalization due to its choice to develop a policy ban based specifically on harm reduction.

not be charged with a crime for possession, but he or she may still be fined (like getting a parking ticket). In the realm of drug policy in particular, **depenalization** is more common than decriminalization or legalization. Under a regime of depenalization, drug possession would still be considered a crime, but users would not be put in prison for using drugs. However, drug possession could still result in an arrest and various noncustodial penalties.

CROSS-BORDER CRIME

Most of the crime we have considered so far in this chapter is **domestic crime**, which is crime that occurs within the borders of a given country. Some crime does not stay within one country, however, and we call this **cross-border crime**. Cross-border crime is typically categorized into two main types: international crime and transnational crime.

International Crime

International crime refers to actions that are defined as crimes under international law. Some of these crimes cross borders; others do not but are still classified as international crimes because they are crimes under international law. Current international law (International Criminal Court, Assembly of States Parties, Review Conference 2010) defines four specific types of international crime:

- **Genocide**, which encompasses acts undertaken with the intent to eradicate a national, ethnic, racial, or religious group. Acts of genocide include killing or physically or mentally harming members of a specific group, preventing births within a group, transferring children outside of a group, and otherwise imposing conditions designed to "physically destroy" a group.
- **Crimes against humanity**, which include a variety of actions undertaken on a widespread or systematic basis against civilian populations, such as murder, enslavement, deportation, deprivation of liberty, torture, sexual violence, persecution, and other intentional acts designed to inflict suffering or injury.
- **War crimes**, which are large-scale or officially sanctioned violations of standard international agreements as to proper conduct during war, especially the Geneva Convention of 1949. War crimes include willful killing; the willful infliction of suffering, torture, or biological experiments; wanton or unnecessary destruction of property; compelling prisoners of war to fight in a hostile power's armed forces; taking hostages; willful deprivation of the right to trial for prisoners of war; intentional attacks against civilian targets or peacekeeping forces; the use of poison or gas weapons; and conscription of children under the age of fifteen, along with a variety of other specifically prohibited actions.
- **Crimes of aggression**, which is the use of armed forces to invade or annex another country's territory or the bombardment or blockade of another country in such a manner as to attack the sovereignty, territorial integrity, or political independence of that country.

These four international crimes are very different from ordinary criminal acts. They are all crimes of a widespread nature that inflict suffering and destruction on a considerable population and are carried out in a systematic way, often based on orders or plans from government or military officials. Furthermore, their existence is cause for international concern, even among countries unaffected by or uninvolved with the suffering. Thus, international crimes are subject to the jurisdiction of the International Criminal Court (which will be discussed in chapter 10), though individual nations can still choose to prosecute them.

Transnational Crime

Transnational crime, in contrast, refers to any crime that occurs across national boundaries. This includes crimes as simple as crossing a border from one country to another to commit a robbery or a kidnapping and as complex as a scheme carried out by a coalition of hackers around the world to steal money from multinational banking corporations. While transnational crimes can be committed by a single person working alone, analysts and law enforcement personnel tend to focus more attention on transnational organized crimes, such as money laundering, cybercrime, and trafficking in humans, endangered animals, and objects like drugs, weapons, body parts, or art (Schneider 2017). Clearly, there are many different types of transnational crimes, more than can be fully explored within the limits of this book, but a few examples of specific types will outline some of the issues important to understanding crimes that cross borders.

Trafficking in People and Body Parts

One of the types of transnational crime that gets a lot of attention is **human trafficking**. This term refers to the practice of transporting people across borders illegally. Human trafficking occurs for many reasons, and not all of its so-called victims are being trafficked against their will. For example, economic migrants who wish to move to wealthy countries for work often pay smugglers (called coyotes in some Spanish-speaking areas of the Americas) to move them across borders illegally. Migrants voluntarily contract with smugglers because the smugglers provide access to knowledge, transportation, contacts, and documents that can ease the trip. However, because their work is illegal, smugglers are able to take advantage of migrants, such as by charging exploitative fees and allowing migrants to die in their care, without fear that migrants will report them to the legal authorities.

Of course, much human trafficking is not so voluntary, even among economic migrants. Traffickers prey on people who are desperate to make a better life for their families, offering them transport to wealthy countries and a job that will pay enough to support their relatives back home. But when those desperate people sign up, they often end up trapped in situations that are not unlike slavery. The traffickers take away their passports, require them to work very long hours in deplorable conditions, and confiscate their pay under the guise of reimbursement for transportation, job placement, food, and housing. They can work for years without making money to send home and without a way to return to their families—and traffickers may threaten to harm victims' relatives if they try to leave or report the abuse. Victims of labor trafficking can be found working many jobs in wealthy countries, including as farm laborers, in meat processing plants, as domestic workers in homes and hotels, in factories, as nail care or massage technicians, in restaurants, and even as door-to-door salespeople.

It is impossible to obtain good data on the extent of human trafficking given its underground nature and the reluctance or inability of victims to come forward. Estimates of the number of people victimized worldwide go as high as over ten million, but very few of these victims are ever officially identified

(Weitzer 2014). While commentators, government officials, and antitrafficking activists worry that human trafficking is a rapidly growing problem, evidence suggests that trends in trafficking vary considerably by country. Data collected in 2006 from sixty-one countries found that 66 percent of trafficked people were women, 22 percent were children, and 12 percent were men (Chawla, Me, and le Pichon 2009), though as stated earlier, many victims of trafficking, particularly forced laborers working in private settings, are not detected. Trafficked people may be moved to a neighboring country, or they may end up halfway around the world. Victims from nonneighboring countries are particularly likely to be found in the United States, Mexico, South Africa, Finland, and a number of Middle Eastern countries (Chawla, Me, and le Pichon 2009).

Sex trafficking is the form of human trafficking that many people are most concerned with. While sex trafficking is a real social problem, the majority of human trafficking victims are engaged in other kinds of forced labor, and researchers estimate that forced sex work accounts for only about 11 percent of labor trafficking (Weitzer 2014). Young people selling sex, even far from home, may be voluntary migrants who choose to engage in sex work, even if they do so because they can find few other opportunities to earn money. However, other research has found that the majority of victims of human trafficking have been subject to sexual exploitation (Chawla, Me, and le Pichon 2009), which suggests that victims of labor trafficking who work in homes, factories, and other settings may also experience sexual violence.

Combating human trafficking can be very difficult. It requires law enforcement and other agencies from multiple countries to work together to prevent, detect, and prosecute crime, and many difficulties can emerge during such efforts, including differences of opinion about what constitutes a significant crime problem, varying standards of evidence collection, political and moral conflicts about appropriate punishment, and resource shortages that impede investigations and prevention efforts. One of the reasons why responding to and combating human trafficking is particularly difficult is that the victims are often themselves criminalized as "illegal immigrants," meaning that they are subject to deportation without due process when legal authorities discover their status. Thus, immigration regimes play an important role in making it possible for human traffickers to continue to exploit their victims. A more effective response to human trafficking would focus instead on protecting workers of all types from exploitation and mistreatment and would criminalize the traffickers rather than their victims (Chuang 2017). If victims of human trafficking knew that they could trust the legal authorities to ensure they were paid fairly for their work, had adequate food and housing, and would not risk deportation, they would be more likely to come forward, and it would be much more feasible to locate and prosecute traffickers.

Trafficking more generally refers to illegal trade, particularly when it crosses borders, and such illegal trade comprises a notable part of the global economy.

Estimates of the global percentage of **gross domestic product**, or GDP (the total value of all goods produced and services provided in an economy in a given year), that can be attributed to trafficking range from 2 percent to over 33 percent (Storti and De Grauwe 2012). The largest contributor to this figure is drugs, but counterfeit goods, gems, firearms, and other items also play a large role. One type of trafficking that is difficult to figure into these estimates is the illegal organ trade.

Profit drives trafficking in organs, just as it does other forms of trafficking. The reason organ trafficking is so lucrative for traffickers is that there is a global shortage of legally obtained organs. In some cases, those desperate for organs travel overseas to seek surgery in countries like China and Pakistan, where it is easier to obtain organs from poor people or executed prisoners (this is called transplant tourism); in other cases, organ "donors" from poor countries like Moldova are transported prior to surgery (Budiani-Saberi and Delmonico 2008). In addition, body parts that can be stored outside the body for longer periods, such as corneas, skin, heart valves, pituitary glands, and bone, are harvested from the corpses of the poor and sold on the black market (Watters 2014). Kidney trafficking is particularly common, as kidneys can be harvested from live donors and thousands of people worldwide need new kidneys (Shimazono 2007). Wealthy individuals suffering from kidney disease will pay as much as $160,000 to obtain a kidney that will allow them to stay alive. Researchers estimate that about 10 percent of global organ transplantation is the result of organ trafficking or transplant tourism (Delmonico 2008).

While some trafficked organs are obtained from dead bodies, desperately poor living donors are common (Lundin 2010). It is not only people in poor countries who are taken advantage of in organ trafficking cases. For example, one notable case, uncovered in 2009, involved Levy-Izhak Rosenbaum, a rabbi in Brooklyn, New York, who had been trading in kidneys for a decade. He purchased kidneys from poor people living in Israel—a modern country with good health care—and sold them to Americans who needed them (Richburg 2009). Recipients of the transplants he arranged testified on his behalf at his sentencing hearing and sent letters of support to the judge hearing the case, who sentenced him to federal prison for two and a half years (Watters 2014).

The lower standards and black market nature of illegal organ transplants result in higher rates of complications, such as transmission of HIV and hepatitis, for recipients (Shimazono 2007). Black market donors also experience considerable negative impacts. While it is possible to live a long and healthy life with only one kidney, doing so requires appropriate medical follow-up and care. The impoverished individuals from whom kidneys are obtained do not receive such care, and thus they often end up with conditions that limit their ability to do the hard physical labor from which they earned money prior to selling an organ (Jafar 2009). The money they make from selling the kidney, which may be as little as a sixth of what a trafficker or broker charges for the organ (Fan 2014), does not last long, and so people who sell their kidneys often end up worse off economically than they were before the transaction occurred (Budiani-Saberi and Delmonico 2008; Shimazono 2007).

The global community has attempted to reduce organ trafficking through the development of the 2008 Istanbul Declaration on Organ Trafficking and Transplant Tourism, which sought to prohibit organ trafficking, transplant tourism, and the commercial sale of organs (Delmonico 2008). But these crimes continue. Experts on organ transplantation argue that reducing the prevalence of these offenses will require expanding access to legal organs for transplant, reducing the occurrence of kidney disease and other medical conditions leading to the need for organs (Jafar 2009), and further enhancements in global regulatory frameworks (Kelly 2013; Pattinson 2008).

Piracy and Cybercrime

Cross-border crime can also include acts that do not involve trafficking goods or people across borders. For instance, consider **piracy**, or the actions pirates take against ships at sea. The classic pirate of myth and history climbs aboard a ship loaded with gold or other valuable goods and steals everything to enrich himself or his sponsors (they were typically male). Until the seventeenth century, such actions were generally considered acceptable, and governments themselves encouraged and profited from acts of piracy, especially during military conflicts (Andreas and Nadelmann 2006). However, the emergence of new forms of international legal regulation and cooperation in the late seventeenth century changed things, as did the extraordinary growth of the British Navy and other seafaring military forces. Countries began to move away from sponsoring piracy, and naval forces began to use their military might to deter pirates from operating from nearby harbors. Some operations continued, especially during wartime, until the mid-1800s. In 1856, several European countries signed an international treaty abolishing state-sponsored piracy, but the United States did not participate, arguing that it needed to engage in piracy to sustain its naval forces (Andreas and Nadelmann 2006). Ultimately, international rules against piracy were codified in the 1958 Convention on the High Seas, which transformed all acts of piracy into cross-border crimes.

Yet pirates continue to operate. Today, the actions of pirates take a somewhat different form. Instead of boarding a ship and making off with the loot, pirates seek to make their money by exploiting marine insurance policies. Like cars, houses, and other property, seafaring ships are insured—and because today's ships are large, expensive, filled with valuable goods, and staffed with large crews, they are insured for hundreds of thousands or even millions of dollars. Thus, pirates hijack ships and hold them for ransom, often in the six-figure range, seeking payouts from marine insurance companies (Raffaele 2007). When pirates seize control of boats that are not heavily insured, the national governments whose flag the ships fly or the countries where the crews are citizens face pressure to intervene militarily to rescue the hostages. Professional hostage negotiators are often called in to negotiate the release of hostages and to try to reduce the financial demands of the pirates (Raffaele 2007).

At the end of the first decade of the 2000s, an epidemic of marine piracy took place off the coast of Somalia. Pirates attacked ships of all sizes, from small pleasure boats (Gettleman 2011) to large cargo ships with multinational crews (Verini 2015). The problem reached such proportions that the United Nations Security Council authorized the use of military force in the region (Verini 2015). Somali piracy has since been reduced, but piracy remains a worldwide issue. According to the International Maritime Bureau Piracy Reporting Centre, a project of the International Chamber of Commerce, nearly two hundred incidents of piracy occur around the world each year, and the most piracy-prone areas today are South and Southeast Asia, the East African coast, the Red Sea and the Gulf of Aden between Yemen and Somalia, and to a lesser extent certain areas of South America and the Caribbean (International Chamber of Commerce n.d.). The International Maritime Bureau broadcasts the information it collects to ships around the world so they can seek to avoid navigating themselves right into pirate-infested waters (Raffaele 2007).

Today, we also use the term piracy to refer to the theft of intellectual or online property, one of many types of cybercrime that also occur across borders. There are many forms of cross-border cybercrime, such as the coordinated hacking of government infrastructure by foreign powers or terrorists, the infiltration of financial institutions to steal money or identities, the theft of virtual property accumulated in video games and online worlds, and the export of films to regions in which they are not for sale (Lastowka 2010). The techniques of cybercrime have even been adopted by government security and military forces; one example of this was the development of the Stuxnet computer virus, which interfered with the operation of an Iranian nuclear facility (Broadhurst 2017). McAfee, a computer security company, estimates that cybercrime costs the world between $445 billion and $608 billion a year (J. Lewis 2018).

Due to the speed at which technology and technological capacities change and develop, cross-border cybercrime is constantly evolving new forms, practices, and techniques, making it difficult to combat. For example, cybercrime experts note that the increased Internet connectivity of cars and home technology products (like thermostats, smart speakers, and kitchen appliances) will open up new possibilities for cybercrime attacks (Broadhurst 2017), and the use of electronic pollbooks and voting machines makes elections more vulnerable to hacking by foreign interlopers. A 2003 United Nations treaty, the Convention on Transnational Organized Crime, and other related treaties were the first steps in creating international law against cybercrime activities (Broadhurst 2017), but responses often require coordination among countries that may not be allies. The difficulties of cross-border law enforcement and international legal responses will be discussed in chapters 5 and 10.

Terrorism

Terrorism can also be a form of transnational crime when it occurs across borders, though many acts of terrorism are domestic rather than transnational. For example, when the Tsarnaev brothers bombed the Boston marathon in 2013 or when the National Liberation Army carried out several bombings in Colombia in 2017, those were acts of domestic terrorism. In those incidents, people already living in a given country carried out terrorist acts against other members of the same country. For an act to be considered transnational terrorism, it needs to cross borders.

So what is terrorism? Well, that depends on who is asking. Parties in a conflict rarely define actors on their side of the conflict as terrorists, preferring instead to label their opponents as such (Turk 2004). For instance, governments create lists of officially designated terrorist organizations featuring groups with opposing political views. These same groups may be seen by citizens, especially citizens from certain opposition groups, as liberators.

Terrorism, then, can best be defined as the calculated use (or threat) of violence against civilians to further policy or ideological goals. This means, first of all, that terrorism must be intended and planned to achieve some kind of end. The goal may not be clearly articulated in a way that makes sense to others, but terrorists intend to bring about some kind of change in policy, further their ideological or religious beliefs, or change the balance of power, and they decide on actions based on these goals. Second of all, terrorism uses violence, whether actual or threatened. Organized nonviolent actions may be disruptive, but they do not constitute terrorism. Finally, terrorism is carried out against civilians. Actions targeting only military personnel are better understood as acts of war than as acts of terrorism.

Acts of terrorism also vary in terms of the type of actor carrying them out and the degree of selectivity in their target. Terrorism can be carried out by so-called lone wolf actors, who are inspired to commit acts of terror but have not coordinated with anyone else, or by small or large organized groups (Turk 2004). When organized groups carry out acts of terror, they may be part of or sponsored by a government (this is called state terrorism), or they may be disconnected from any governmental power. Their targets can be specific individuals; categorical targets, as when terrorists target members of particular religious, ethnic, or social groups; or they can be indiscriminate, targeting any member of the general population who happens to be in the wrong place at the wrong time (Goodwin 2006).

The extent to which countries experience terrorism or the threat of terrorism varies widely. Taking into account both domestic and cross-border

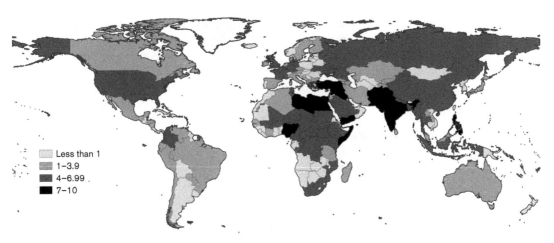

Map 11 Global impact of terrorism (Institute for Economics and Peace 2017).

terrorism, the Global Terrorism Index is an annual report on the impact of terrorism around the world as well as the most deadly incidents in the past year (Institute for Economics and Peace 2017). According to the Global Terrorism Index, an incident is terroristic in nature when it involves "the threatened or actual use of illegal force and violence by a non-state actor to attain a political, economic, religious, or social goal through fear, coercion, or intimidation," and furthermore must be intentional and must involve violence or the threat of violence against people or property (Institute for Economics and Peace 2017:6). Map 11 is a visualization of the Global Terrorism Index data for 2016. This data shows that 75 percent of all deaths from terrorism in that year occurred in five countries—Iraq, Afghanistan, Syria, Nigeria, and Pakistan—and four of those countries are also on the list of where the twenty most deadly individual incidents of terrorism in 2016 occurred, along with South Sudan, the Central African Republic, and France. In contrast, thirty countries are rated as having a terrorism index score of zero, indicating they experienced no impact from terrorism in 2016. Note that the Global Terrorism Index specifically excludes acts of state terrorism—the results might look different had they been included.

CONCLUSION

Crime occurs everywhere in the world, but not in exactly the same ways. As this chapter has shown, people in different countries or regions define and understand crime differently—and they measure it differently, too. That makes it extremely difficult for international criminologists to effectively compare crime rates cross-nationally and come to an understanding of how and why crime differs around the world. Yet it is clear that the rates of different crimes vary from country to country. Sometimes, as with firearm-related homicides, it is easy for analysts to come up with an explanation for these differences—in that case, the vastly greater availability of firearms in the United States explains why there are a disproportionately large number of firearm-related homicides in that country (which will be discussed in chapter 5). Similarly, differences between countries' drug criminalization policies explain much of the cross-national variation in drug crime rates. Other times, however, it is much harder to understand what is going on. Criminologists have developed a wide variety of theories for why crime rates may vary, including those based on cultural, economic, or structural factors. Without better data, of course, analysts cannot be certain which of these theories are the most useful for explaining the differences we observe.

Acts of crime are not limited to those that occur within the borders of a given country. Cross-border crimes include international crime—genocide, war crimes, crimes against humanity, and crimes of aggression—as well as transnational crimes, like human trafficking, piracy, and transnational terrorism. The growth of cybercrime means there are always new forms of cross-border crime to pay attention to.

Most people wish to live in a world with less crime, though they offer varying solutions for reducing it, including increasing law enforcement and punishment, reducing criminalization (as Portugal has done), and combating the structural inequality and injustice that can give rise to crime. The next chapter will consider the structure and role of law enforcement organizations at both the domestic and international levels, as these are generally assumed to have the primary responsibility for detecting, investigating, and preventing crime.

Law Enforcement

CHAPTER GOALS

1. Evaluate the different ways in which national law enforcement systems can be organized.
2. Understand cross-national variations in policing practices, such as styles of policing, weapons policies, and police training and qualifications.
3. Be able to explain the differences between police and military power.
4. Become familiar with mechanisms for international police cooperation.

What do you think of when you imagine police work? Perhaps you picture someone in a neat dark-blue uniform handcuffing a suspect or driving in a marked squad car with lights flashing and sirens blaring to chase down a vehicle speeding on the highway. Perhaps you imagine people in colorful and distinct uniforms, like the Royal Canadian Mounted Police or the Pontifical Swiss Guard that polices the Vatican, standing guard near important national monuments. Perhaps you imagine an undercover officer wearing a wire and working a club while a crew listens on a monitor from a trailer outside, or perhaps you think of underpaid and poorly trained personnel in a rural area struggling without resources to keep the peace. But police work is even more diverse than these examples might suggest. In Italy, for example, a highly trained unit of police is responsible for ferreting out fraudulent olive oil by performing their own taste tests (DePalma 2016). And in China, at the height of the policy permitting couples to have only one child, public officials called "granny police" went door to door to ensure that women in their neighborhoods were using contraception effectively (Liu and Chang 2006). These personnel may not have officially been classified as police, but they were engaging in police work.

So what are **police**? We might define them as people authorized by a group or a government to regulate behavior and engage in social control internal to a population, and to do so in part through the use or threat of physical force (Bayley 1990). Let's consider the parts of this definition. First of all, police have authorization to engage in policing. They are generally seen as **legitimate**, meaning that there is a consensus that they have the right to exercise power and have not usurped it. Of course, there are circumstances in which policing is carried out by an occupying force or some other body seen as illegitimate, but in such cases it still tends to be clear that the police themselves have the authority and standing to engage in policing. Second, the responsibility of police is to encourage compliance with legal norms of behavior and to respond when such compliance does not occur. Importantly, though, police exercise such responsibility within the population they are charged with policing. As will be discussed below, this focus on the internal is one of the main ways we can distinguish police from military forces, who occupy and patrol other, external populations. Finally, police do their work in part through the use or threat of physical force. While societies differ in the type and extent of physical force they permit police to use, the fact remains that police can carry out operations using force to achieve their social control goals.

Almost all societies today have some body of personnel that meets this definition of policing. However, that body of personnel does not always resemble what we might imagine when we think of the word *police*. Instead, policing might be undertaken by a military body called in at times of need, or by vigilantes charged with carrying out acts of revenge. And the development of formal, specialized police forces is relatively recent in our collective history.

THE HISTORY OF LAW ENFORCEMENT

Historically, policing—such as it existed—was a local responsibility. Groups of local people gathered when needed to accost a suspected criminal or keep order in a time of chaos. These groups were much like what we would now call militias. Guilds of tradespeople similarly developed collective forces to protect their interests.

One way of understanding certain traditional systems for providing protection and law enforcement is **feudalism**. Feudalism is a system of reciprocal obligation. As practiced historically, this system involved lords who owned land tended by vassals and owed those vassals protection, and in return vassals owed their service and some portion of the fruits of their labor to the lord. When a militia-like force needed to be raised, the lord was responsible for mobilizing and directing a group of vassals to do the work. Similarly, lords owed their loyalty to the monarch, who would call on them when he or she needed to raise a military force.

As countries began to develop standing armies (in the 1600s in Europe; far earlier in China), those armies were able to serve a policing function when called on. Monarchs were especially interested in the ability to deploy their armies to put down rebellions (Mears 1969), as this allowed them to avoid having to rely on the lords. Some combination of military forces and traditional community response has remained the source of policing in rural areas even today in some parts of the world. Some countries, such as Britain, developed a system of private security officers—constables working under the supervision of local judicial personnel—who were generally compensated from fines and restitution paid by the criminals they apprehended, much like bounty hunters or debt collectors would be today.

The first "modern" police force was created in 1667 in Paris, which was then the largest city in Europe. Policing spread rapidly to the rest of the country, and by 1699 all major French cities had Lieutenant-Generals of Police, and provincial authorities were establishing police control of outlying areas (Bayley 1975). But other parts of Europe, along with North America, were slower to develop modern police forces. The Metropolitan Police of London, for example, appeared in 1829, replacing a system of constables that had emerged centuries earlier and bore only a passing resemblance to modern police (Emsley 2014). Germany, Italy, the United States, and other countries also began developing police forces in the 1800s. Figures 7 and 8 show examples of police in two difference contexts around 1900.

Defining Modern Policing

Modern police can be differentiated from earlier forms of policing in terms of several characteristics: they are public, specialized, and professional, as shown in figure 9. When we say they are public, we mean that they are controlled and funded by the government. As will be discussed below, this governmental control and funding can occur at a local, regional, or national level or a combination of any of these three. In contrast, private police are those controlled and funded by nongovernmental entities, such as security guards working for a housing development (Yarwood 2007). When we say they are specialized, we mean that they focus their work on policing specifically. Historically, police forces have often been responsible for a variety of activities other than policing. For example, French and Prussian police in the eighteenth century managed

Figure 7 Chinese police circa 1900 (Judkins 2015, photographer unknown).

Figure 8 New York City Police Information Bureau circa 1908 (Bain News Service 1908).

tasks like health inspections, food supply maintenance, and the issuance of building permits alongside their policing functions (Bayley 1990). When we say they are professionalized, that means they are specifically trained for their work as police and that they are part of organizational bureaucracies with specific rules and guidelines for managing their work.

The fact that modern police are public, specialized, and professional does not mean that other kinds of policing work has disappeared. Private police, for

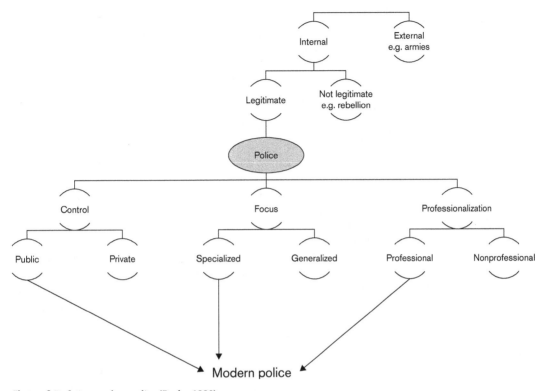

Figure 9 Defining modern police (Bayley 1990).

example, are a growing presence in many parts of the world. While good data on private police is hard to find, a 2011 report on seventy countries found that there were 1.81 times as many private police as public police in those countries (Florquin 2011). Australia, South Africa, and the United States all employed more than twice the number of private police as they did public police, and in Guatemala, India, and Honduras, there were over four times more private police as public police.

Similarly, vigilantes and community militias continue to exercise many law enforcement functions in various parts of the world, especially areas not well served by modern police. Even countries with functioning modern police experience vigilantism. For example, Florida's "Stand Your Ground" law empowers individuals to use deadly force to prevent the commission of a forcible felony, even if there is no threat of bodily harm (Florida Legislature 2018). In the seven years after the law was enacted in 2005, almost two hundred criminal defendants claimed Stand Your Ground defenses, and fewer than 30 percent of them were convicted of crimes (S. Martin 2013). Stand Your Ground cases have involved events such as the shooting of unarmed people, the shooting of people who were fleeing the scene of an incident or who were already on the ground, and even the shooting of a bear, for crimes as minor as pounding on a car and setting off its alarm or stealing a jet ski.

What We Expect of Police

In evaluating modern police forces, what we expect most from them is that they will successfully prevent and detect crime and improve our public safety (Bayley 1990), as well as provide public reassurance and emergency services (Yarwood 2007). A key concern in comparing police forces is their efficacy or effectiveness in carrying out these tasks—in other words, the extent to which they are able to reduce the occurrence of crime as well as the percentage of crimes that they are able to solve. But as shown in chapter 4, such data is hard to come by. Crime data is subject to error, as people may be reluctant to report crimes to police and police departments may have incentives to alter crime statistics to suit the funding and accountability schemes they are subject to. Given this level of error, how can we trust measures of clearance that are supposed to show what percentage of crimes have been solved? To further complicate things, most people would prefer the police to prevent crime before it happens rather than solving it after the fact, but how could we tell if this is occurring?

Beyond these basic functions, there are many other things we expect from police (Bayley 1990). We expect them to follow the laws of their jurisdiction, both in terms of the rules and regulations governing their professional behavior and in terms of the legal provisions all people are subject to. People tend to expect that police officers will not go around committing crimes and getting away with them, that they will comply with tax regulations, and that they will follow the rules about proper treatment of suspects. Beyond rules and laws, people also tend to expect that police officers will behave in morally appropriate ways, act with integrity, and show sympathy and concern for victims of crime. For example, most people would be upset if they reported a crime to the police and then found a photo of the interaction on a police officer's social media page. We also expect police to treat people equitably. At a departmental level, we expect police organizations to be open to public scrutiny and to be involved in their communities.

The United Nations has, since 1979, had a Code of Conduct for Law Enforcement Officials, which lays out basic global standards for police work (UN Code of Conduct for Law Enforcement Officials 1979). This code requires police to respect human rights, use force only when necessary, keep confidences, and provide medical treatment when needed. It prohibits corruption as well as the use of torture and cruel, inhuman, or degrading treatment. A thirty-page handbook lays out further details on these standards, including what they mean for law enforcement practices such as investigation and arrest as well as how police should treat suspects, victims, and other individuals (Centre for Human Rights 1997).

What We Do Not Expect

Of course, many police officers and police organizations worldwide do not live up to these expectations and standards. There are a variety of reasons why. As will be discussed below, many law enforcement agencies have very limited funding and thus cannot afford to fulfill their obligations fully. In authoritarian countries, the government may in fact require that police behave in ways that violate human rights and the public trust. And even in the absence of such orders, police departments or individual police officers may act on their own to violate human rights, engage in violence against civilians, or do other things that violate global police standards. For example, they may engage in the use of excessive or otherwise inappropriate force, sexual coercion, discriminatory treatment, corruption, or a variety of other activities that involve mistreatment or differential treatment of individuals or groups.

Police in most countries do use force as part of their legitimate work, as noted above. However, the use of *excessive* force, especially when it results in civilian death or permanent disability, is also widespread. Globally comparative scholarship on the use of excessive force is limited, in part due to the fact that there is no agreement on what constitutes excessive force (Belur 2010). Despite these data limitations, we do know that people in many countries perceive the police to be more likely to use excessive force against minority or disadvantaged populations (Belur 2010). There are a variety of explanations for such behavior, including political, economic, cultural, and social contexts that encourage it; organizational factors that protect and promote police misbehavior or enable corruption (to be discussed below); and the existence of particular individual police officers who have a high propensity to violence (Belur 2010) or have substance use problems (Ovuga and Madrama 2006).

In addition to force, police officers may use coercion to compel sex acts from individuals. Sex workers and sexual minority populations are especially likely to be targeted in such cases, particularly where sex work, same-sex sexual activity, and gender nonconformity remain criminalized or socially stigmatized. The vulnerability of sex workers to sexual coercion has been documented in many countries, such as Russia (Odinokova et al. 2014), Serbia (Rhodes et al. 2008), and South Africa (Fick 2006).

Another way in which police may not live up to expectations is in their treatment of crime victims. Police may fail to respond to reports of crime or requests for protection, or they may blame victims for their own victimization. This is especially common in response to reports of sexual violence, as police have often disbelieved and disregarded such reports in countries around the world (Du Mont and White 2007). Even when reports are taken, police may handle evidence carelessly or neglect to follow up, actions that can make it difficult to investigate, try, and convict offenders. As a result, global data suggests that even when victims report sexual assault to the police, a minority of cases result in charges and even fewer result in convictions (Du Mont and White 2007). However, it is important to note that in some countries, protocols around the response to sexual assault reports are changing in ways that may promote more appropriate police behavior, including greater involvement of medical personnel in the evidence-collection process and enhanced training of officers.

The treatment of both sex workers and victims of sexual assault illustrates the fact that police may act in ways that are discriminatory toward certain categories of people. To clarify, if police do not take *any* reports of crime seriously, that is a form of dereliction of duty, but it is not discriminatory. But if police take reports of some kinds of assault seriously but do not take reports of sexual assault seriously, then their behavior discriminates against victims of sexual assault. Police discriminate in many ways, and discriminatory behavior is nothing new. For example, research has documented discriminatory and unequal treatment of Indian Muslims by British colonial forces in the early 1900s (Noor 2010), and police in the United States have discriminated against Black and other non-White populations since modern police forces were first formed (R. Kennedy 1997). One of the ways in which such discrimination occurs is the practice of racial profiling.

The practice of **racial profiling** occurs when police use the racial, ethnic, or religious appearance of individuals to determine whom to question, arrest, or investigate in the absence of any specific information suggesting those individuals have committed a crime (Harris 2002). Such practices are common in countries around the world and have been documented by a variety of research methodologies. For example, one study conducted in Paris (Goris et al. 2009) involved observers who recorded police stops with cell phone cameras, documenting both the person stopped and others in the immediate vicinity. This study demonstrated that the police disproportionately stopped young men wearing what the authors called "youth culture" style and who appeared to be Black or Arab. In fact, Black and Arab individuals were between two and fifteen times more likely to be stopped than White individuals, depending on the specific location. Research has documented similar treatment of Roma and Arab individuals in Hungary (Pap 2009); Black, Latinx, and Arab individuals in the United States (Gross and Barnes 2002; Harris 1999; 2002); Tibetans in China (Tuttle 2015); those from the north of Nigeria who have traveled to other parts of the country (Ewulum and Oraegbunam 2014); and minorities in many other countries (see, e.g., De Schutter and Ringelheim 2008). It may not be surprising, then, to learn that minority youth in France perceive police activity as discriminatory (Goris et al. 2009)—a common perception among those from minority, disadvantaged, or oppressed communities around the world.

Police may also fall short of expectations due to corruption. Where police officers or police agencies are corrupt, they may purposefully engage in search and seizure in violation of laws and constitutional guidelines, whether as part of seeking convictions or to enrich themselves through the acquisition of others' property. This personal gain may involve the confiscation and resale of property, including contraband like drugs or weapons; the receipt of bribes; or the outright theft of cash. Corruption can also involve the falsification of testimony or police reports, or, most egregiously, sexual and physical violence committed by police officers.

According to Transparency International, a nongovernmental organization that measures people's perceptions of corruption in countries around the globe, New Zealand and Denmark rank as least corrupt, while Syria, South Sudan, and Somalia rank as most corrupt (Transparency International 2017). Transparency International's index is based on public corruption of all kinds, not just that involving law enforcement, but it does highlight the fact that the extent of corruption varies considerably from country to country.

Why does corruption within law enforcement organizations exist? Well, in many countries, there is very little enforcement that could detect corruption or punish those who engage in it. This is particularly true for law enforcement corruption, since police are typically those tasked with investigating criminal behavior. Police corruption experts argue that corruption can be tackled only by outside agencies (Ivkovic 2005). In addition, since many police departments and agencies are organized in a paramilitary fashion, group loyalty tends to be very high, and officers are unlikely to turn each other in even for illegal activities. Corruption is especially likely to occur in contexts in which police personnel receive low pay and meager benefits, as the incentive to increase personal resources through easily accessible illegal activity is quite high. In addition, political or other interference in the administration of law enforcement can exacerbate corruption, either by encouraging personnel to engage in corrupt activities or by creating a culture of disregard for legal standards (Punch 2009). As M. R. Haberfeld and Ibrahim Cerrah write, "Law enforcement serves the government and its purposes" (2008:8).

While most people would agree that the most extreme forms of police corruption—such as letting criminal suspects go free in return for large bribes or stealing and reselling illegal drugs—are a problem, some people argue that more minor forms of police corruption are not a big deal. After all, if a police officer looks the other way when a business that has been giving the police free coffee violates a local ordinance or lets a driver off the hook for driving five miles over the speed limit in return for US$20, who has really been harmed? But research shows that any level of law enforcement corruption has significant consequences. Corrupt police are police who are not fulfilling their obligations, who create arbitrary forms of justice that do not uphold the rule of law, and who reject guidelines and reforms designed to improve the quality of police work

(Ivkovic 2005). Police corruption reduces public trust (Punch 2009) and makes many people less likely to call the police when a crime has occurred or to cooperate in a police investigation. Police misbehavior other than corruption, such as the excessive use of force or the harassment of members of minority groups, can have similar effects. And police corruption can actually increase the amount of crime occurring in a society, especially organized crime (van Dijk 2007). When police personnel falsify reports, commit sexual assaults, or perpetrate violence without cause, they are engaging in criminal acts, even if they escape prosecution because law enforcement corruption is tolerated in their society.

CROSS-NATIONAL VARIATIONS IN POLICING PRACTICES

While modern police forces may have in common their status as public, their specialization, and their professionalism, they are diverse in many ways. Countries have developed very different police organizational structures. They have different levels of interaction and cooperation between police and military forces. Different police forces engage in very different styles of policing, which include variations in the use of force and require different levels of education and training. And, at the most basic level, they differ in size and resources.

A 2004 report estimated that globally we spend over US$220 billion a year (in 2004 dollars) on policing, about 62 percent of global spending on all aspects of criminal justice (Farrell and Clark 2004). The level of expenditure in individual countries varies considerably, ranging from less than US$50 a year per person in Japan, Belgium, Spain, and Malaysia, among other countries, to more than US$250 a year per person in Switzerland. This variation depends on a variety of factors, but the strength of the national economy and thus the amount of public funding available is the most important predictor of law enforcement spending. However, some countries (Belgium and Japan, for example) spend much less than would be predicted, while other countries (most notably the Bahamas and Israel) spend much more (Farrell and Clark 2004).

Similarly, there is extensive variation in the size of national police forces. While data shows a very strong relationship between the total population of a country and the total number of police personnel it employs, the per capita number of police personnel ranges from fewer than five to over one thousand (see map 12). The United Nations Office on Drugs and Crime (UNDOC), the international agency tasked with maintaining international statistics on police personnel, cautions that different countries' figures are not strictly comparable due to varying definitions of police and differences in police organizational structures. UNDOC asks that only public personnel "whose principal functions are the prevention, detection and investigation of crime and the apprehension of alleged offenders" be counted, excluding any support staff (UNDOC n.d.), but this still leaves room for considerable variation in who counts as

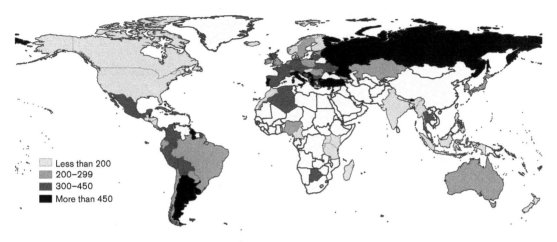

Less than 200
200–299
300–450
More than 450

Map 12 Police personnel per capita, 2010–2015 (UNDOC n.d.).

police, especially given the complex relationships between police and military forces, which will be discussed later in this chapter.

Organizational Structures

Before we consider what police forces do, we need to understand how they are structured. Countries differ in whether control of the police force is at local, regional, or national levels and also in the degree to which different parts of the police force coordinate their operations with one another (Bayley 1990; Varghese 2010). Table 3 details the most commonly used system for classifying the national organizational structures of police and identifies the position of several example countries in the system. So what are the terms experts use to describe police structures? The first distinction is between centralized and decentralized systems. In a **centralized police structure**, the national government exercises central control over all policing functions in the country. Centralized systems typically involve national funding of police work. For example, in France, the police forces are operationally controlled by the Ministry of the Interior, a cabinet-level department. In contrast, **decentralized police structures** are those where leadership and command do not come from the national government but instead are located in local police organizations. In many cases, decentralized systems also involve local funding of police work, though this is not a requirement for a system to be classified as decentralized.

The second distinction has to do with the extent to which multiple different police forces exist within a country, and if they do, the extent to which they coordinate their work. This is simplest to determine in countries with **single**

Table 3   Classification of police structures

Type of police structure	Dispersal of command	
	Centralized	Decentralized
Single	Saudi Arabia	Japan
	China	
	Sierra Leone	
	Turkey	
	Israel	
	Ireland	
	Ghana	
Multiple coordinated	France	Canada
	Russia	India
	Austria	Australia
	Vietnam	Germany
Multiple uncoordinated	Belgium	United States
	Italy	Brazil
	Spain	Mexico
	Switzerland	United Kingdom

SOURCES: Bayley 1990; Haberfeld and Cerrah 2008; Reichel 2007.

police structures, where there is one single police force covering all geographic areas of the country and dealing with all types of policing matters. In single systems, there is no need to work toward cooperation because the police are not divided into separate forces with different purposes or authority.

Where countries have multiple police forces, they may be coordinated or uncoordinated. In a country with a **multiple coordinated police structure**, there are multiple different police forces, and each has different areas of authority, whether broken down regionally or by type of policing activity. In a centralized multiple coordinated system, the central government will work to direct the activities of these different agencies. In a decentralized multiple coordinated system, the national government may play a very limited role, but there are still guidelines and structures for ensuring that different police agencies work together effectively. For example, in Canada, municipal (city) police, provincial police (like state police in the United States), aboriginal police, and the national-level Royal Canadian Mounted Police (RCMP) all engage in policing work. However, the RCMP provides coordination services, such as managing crime labs and information services, and also supplies contract policing services to many municipalities, meaning that it can also enforce provincial and local statutes, except in the provinces of Ontario and Quebec (Haberfeld and Cerrah 2008). Most importantly, though all of these police forces coexist, one force—whether it is the RCMP, the provincial police, or the local police—will have primary policing authority over any given location.

In a **multiple uncoordinated police structure**, there are different police forces with different areas of authority, but they have competing and overlapping jurisdiction. In the case of centralized multiple uncoordinated systems, this tends to mean that there are multiple competing national-level police forces. For example, in Italy, the Polizia di Stato (national police), the Arma dei Carabinieri (military police), and the Guardia di Finanza (finance, customs, tax, and treasury police) all coexist at the national level, and the Polizia di Stato and the Arma dei Carabinieri even have somewhat similar responsibilities (Barbagli and Sartori 2004). In the case of multiple uncoordinated decentralized systems, forces compete at all levels—local, regional, and national. The United States provides the perfect example of a multiple uncoordinated decentralized system.

Table 4 provides a list of law enforcement agencies at the national, state, and local levels in the United States, along with a small sampling of some of the more specialized police forces that exist. When looking at this list, it is easy to see how different agencies might come into conflict about whose responsibility a particular issue might be. Just to take one example, if a crime occurs on American Indian tribal lands, it may be under the jurisdiction of the FBI, the Bureau of Indian Affairs enforcement agents, or the tribal police, depending on the circumstances, and may require the involvement of other state or local agencies as well (Washburn 2006).

Perhaps the most interesting of all organizational structures is the decentralized single system. Commentators working from a theoretical perspective would argue that such a system is impossible (Varghese 2010)—how, after all, can you have both a single national command and a dispersed structure? But this is the system in place in Japan. Japan has a National Police Agency that is responsible for creating and implementing policies and standards for police work and is in charge of the training of all police personnel. Each prefecture (administrative region) has its own police agency, which is under local control, but all must follow the national policies (L. Parker 2001). Japanese police agencies maintain local substations, called *kōban,* permitting greater flexibility in response to local needs. Thus, Japan maintains a system of single control with decentralized command.

These different structures have important consequences for police work. In centralized systems, national governments can set clear standards and rules, and if they have the resources to do so, they can ensure that local police all across the country comply with those standards and rules. In contrast, in decentralized systems, like those in the United States and Mexico, the central government many have little or no authority over local police forces, who may then adopt wildly disparate practices.

Table 4   List of U.S. law enforcement agencies

National	Department of Justice agencies
	• Federal Bureau of Investigation (FBI)
	• Drug Enforcement Agency (DEA)
	• Bureau of Alcohol, Tobacco, and Firearms (ATF)
	• U.S. Marshals Service
	• Federal Bureau of Prisons
	Department of Homeland Security agencies
	• Customs and Border Protection (CBP)
	• Immigration and Customs Enforcement (ICE)
	• Federal Air Marshal Service
	• Secret Service
	• Coast Guard (peacetime operations only)
	• Homeland Security Investigations
	• Transportation Security Administration
	• Federal Protective Service
State	State police or highway patrol
	State bureaus of investigation
	Specialized state police
	• Departments of correction
	• Water police
	• Environmental conservation or fish/game wardens
	• Specialized facilities police
Local	County police/sheriffs
	Municipal police
	School police
	Campus police
	Airport police
	Port police
	Park police
Specialized Jurisdiction (examples)	Transit police
	Military police
	U.S. Capitol Police
	U.S. Mint Police
	U.S. Postal Inspection Service
	Tribal police
	Various federal agency police departments

Table 5   **Educational qualifications and training requirements for police in selected countries**

	Educational qualifications	**Police training**
China	High school diploma	1 year
Mexico	Typically no minimum	4.5 months on average
Sierra Leone	Equivalent of a high school diploma	6 months
Russia	High school diploma preferred	3–6 months
Turkey	Two years of college in a law enforcement program	Minimal additional
Israel	High school diploma	6 months
France	High school diploma	9–12 months
United States	Varies	Typically 3–6 months

SOURCE: Haberfeld and Cerrah 2008.

Police Training and Qualifications

There is considerable global variation in the educational qualifications and training requirements for police personnel, though most countries do require prospective police officers to be at least eighteen but younger than thirty (in some cases twenty-five), to live up to at least a minimal standard of ethical behavior (such as not having an extensive criminal record), and to pass some sort of qualification exam, which may include physical, intelligence, psychological, and/or health sections. To get a sense of the variation that exists around the world, consider the examples in table 5. In countries with multiple or uncoordinated systems, different police agencies may have markedly different requirements. For example, in the United States, many local police forces require only a high school diploma and three months at a regional police academy, but some have much more extensive requirements. The New York City Police Department requires a minimum of sixty college credits with at least a 2.0 GPA, followed by six months in the police academy. Note that many countries have additional requirements that police personnel must meet before they can be promoted to higher ranks. For example, in Brazil, police at some supervisory ranks must have an undergraduate degree in law.

Policing Styles

Police agencies around the world—and even within a given country—have different techniques for policing. The most important distinction is whether police emphasize reactive or proactive policing. Police agencies using **reactive**

policing wait for crimes to occur and then intervene to investigate, typically when called on by civilians. Such tactics tend to reduce police-civilian interaction and can reduce the cost of policing. In contrast, **proactive policing** involves police personnel actively looking for potential problems rather than waiting for problems to come to them. Proactive policing can involve activities as varied as setting up checkpoints, running undercover investigations, cultivating informants, and using crime data analysis and mapping. Rules and guidelines about undercover and covert police work are particularly worth considering—in some countries, such as the United States, these techniques are standard, whereas in Europe, courts tend to see them as invasions of privacy and as potentially violating other due process protections (Ross 2008). Regardless of which approach they use, police agencies can also vary in the intensity of policing they practice or the frequency of police actions and interactions with civilians.

There are many styles of police work, and criminologists who study law enforcement have generally grouped them into four main approaches to policing: traditional, intelligence-led, problem-oriented, and community-based. **Traditional policing** is the model of policing that was most common in the past. It is generally reactive in nature, with police personnel waiting for calls for service to come in and then responding. However, traditional policing can include some proactive elements, such as traffic enforcement, active surveillance of known trouble spots, or the use of confidential informants. More recently, technology like closed-circuit television cameras (CCTV) and speed or red-light cameras (Shahidulah 2014) have allowed agencies using traditional policing to engage in enforcement without waiting for civilian calls. Traditional policing notably involves little interaction with the community and little effort to prevent crime from occurring—the central emphasis is on catching offenders and turning them over to the justice system for punishment.

Intelligence-led policing is an approach in which police draw on the collection of information about crime to reduce or disrupt criminal offending and detect offenders (Ratcliffe 2008). Here, the law enforcement agency uses a data-driven process in which agency leadership makes decisions about crime control, tactics, and resource allocation proactively on the basis of intelligence and information about the operating environment. In particular, intelligence-led approaches tend to focus on the arrest of key criminal offenders and the active policing of known criminal hotspots. Alongside surveillance and data collection, new technological developments such as in-car access to criminal records, license-plate scanners, crime mapping, and predictive crime analysis greatly facilitate this style of police work (Shahidulah 2014). A similar but distinct approach has come to be known as Compstat (Ratcliffe 2008). In this approach, agency management makes decisions about strategy and priorities on the basis of crime data and holds local leadership accountable for changes in crime statistics in their area.

Like intelligence-led policing, **problem-oriented policing** is often seen as a more scientific approach to police work. In this approach, police agencies begin by identifying problems and then try to use evidence to understand how best to eliminate, reduce, or manage them (Bullock and Tilley 2003). Rather than simply relying on arrest and other police powers, police agencies subject their work to analysis to determine longer-term solutions, and police work is understood as encompassing a broader variety of issues affecting civilians. Such work requires significant modifications in the way police agencies operate, such as placing emphasis on longer-term planning and hiring staff skilled in research and data analysis. Problem-oriented policing is a proactive approach, but it is different from intelligence-led policing because of its emphasis on finding ways to reduce the occurrence of crime rather than on enforcement (Bullock and Tilley 2003). For example, a police agency using problem-oriented policing might direct drug users to treatment resources rather than arresting them, participate in summer and after-school programs for youth to help keep them out of trouble, actively evaluate homes and businesses to be sure windows and doors lock securely, and encourage the use of traffic-calming measures like curb bump-outs and raised crosswalks rather than speed cameras.

One interesting example of a problem-oriented policing approach is that of the German Ordnungsbehörde, best translated as Department of Order or Regulatory Agency. Personnel from this agency are responsible for enforcing laws and regulations about aspects of life as diverse as littering, riding a bicycle on the sidewalk, failing to shovel snow, and having a disorderly sidewalk sale (Kulish 2011). They are able to give warnings to those who are not following the rules, call on other government agencies to fix problems they detect, and issue small fines. They also work to keep government residency records up to date. This approach is in line with the original formulation of broken windows theory, a criminological model suggesting that people feel safer (and commit less crime) when police focus on maintaining public order (Wilson and Kelling 1982). Evidence to support the relationship between disorder and criminal offending is quite limited (Gau and Pratt 2010; Sampson and Raudenbush 1999), but it is clear that at least in some cases, people feel better about their neighborhoods or perceive them as safer when things are more orderly. So while the Ordnungsbehörde may not be proactively reducing the crime rate, its work improves Germans' perceptions of their surroundings. On the other hand, for those accustomed to living in more disorderly circumstances, the work of the Ordnungsbehörde might be perceived as an unwelcome intrusion that gets in the way of daily life. Similarly, some countries with Islamic legal systems employ religious or morality police to enforce dress code policies, rules against cross-gender socialization, and other religious edicts (BBC Monitoring 2016). While moderates may resent the activities of such police forces, religious conservatives value their role in ensuring conformity with strict interpretations of religious law.

Finally, **community policing** is an approach to law enforcement in which police agencies and personnel work closely with the community to build cooperative relationships. Community policing invites civilian input into law enforcement policy-making, encourages a broader view of police responsibilities to include tasks like resolving conflict and solving problems, and ensures that police personnel provide personalized service and get to know the communities in which they work (Cordner 2014). Police agencies that use community policing approaches tend to deploy personnel consistently to specific areas, encourage patrolling on foot, emphasize preventative work (especially with young people) rather than focusing on aggressive enforcement techniques, and refine their organizational structures to facilitate such processes (Cordner 2014). Community policing is generally seen as a proactive approach, but some people instead call it a coactive approach given the fact that it encourages action by police and the community together.

Advocates of community policing believe that such techniques will not only help police interact better with civilians in the community but also enable them to obtain more information from community members when needed to catch offenders and to more effectively reduce delinquency before it becomes a major problem. Research has found that community policing improves police-community relations and probably reduces neighborhood disorder, though the evidence about other impacts is more mixed (Cordner 2014). Some scholars argue that the idea of community policing relies on "the fundamental illusion of *the* community" (Brogden and Nijhar 2005:51), ignoring the fact that many societies are deeply divided as to what they want from their police, and leading to systems that continue to oppress or mistreat specific groups, such as young people, ethnic minorities, women, or the poor.

The Use of Force

Even beyond differences in the use of tactics like covert policing and other proactive strategies, police agencies differ in terms of their policies and practices around the use of force. Some police agencies heavily restrict the use of force, even limiting the number of police personnel who are permitted to carry firearms. Police in the United Kingdom, for example, do not generally carry firearms, with only a few officers authorized to carry them for special purposes, a standard designed to minimize the use of force (National Policing Improvement Agency 2011). These special units are deployed only when needed, and they must announce their presence when they arrive on scene if possible. Only 34 percent of police in Britain think they and their colleagues should be armed, a sizable minority would not want to carry a weapon even if asked to (Dodd 2017), and U.K. police receive considerable training in de-escalation techniques (Baker 2015).

In contrast, police agencies in other countries routinely use force, including levels of force considered excessive and inhumane by observers and non-

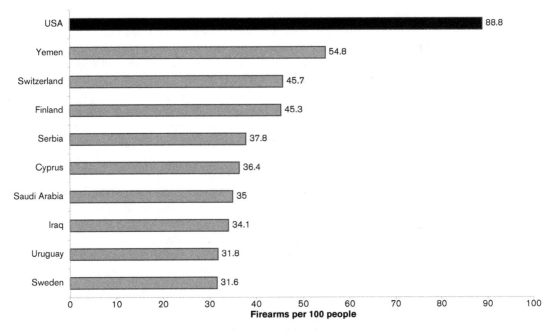

Figure 10 Firearms ownership, top ten countries (Berman et al. 2007).

governmental organizations (Human Rights Watch 2011). Police agencies also differ in their use of so-called less lethal weapons, like Tasers. These different policies and practices have real consequences for a civilian's chance of surviving an interaction with the police. In the United States, for example, over one thousand people were killed by police in 2016. In contrast, a fatal 2013 shooting in Iceland was the first in seventy-one years, and Finnish police fired a grand total of six bullets in that year (Lartey 2015).

Observers commenting on police weapons policies and use of force often point out that if criminals have guns, police need them to protect themselves and others. Thus, when considering police use of force, we must also think about civilian weapon ownership and regulation. The best global data on firearms ownership is from the 2007 Small Arms Survey (Berman et al. 2007), which compiled national registration figures, independent estimates, and statistical predictions to arrive at a measure of civilian gun ownership by country circa 2006 (excluding duty weapons used by police and military personnel). This data is clearly limited, and furthermore it is now well out of date. But since it is the best data available, journalists and academic analysts continue to rely on it. Figure 10 shows data for the countries with the top ten highest levels of civilian gun ownership. The data is reported in firearms per one hundred people. For example, in the United States, the Small Arms Survey found that there were 88.8 firearms per one hundred people. But this does not mean that 88 percent of people own firearms, as many people own more than one weapon. As of 2017, survey data in the United States showed that only 30 percent of adults owned a gun (Parker et al. 2017). Of those, 66 percent owned more than one gun, with 29 percent owning five or more.

Many factors affect the rate of firearm ownership in a country, including cultural views about weapons and violence and about the use of firearms for recreation or subsistence hunting. However, a central issue is the status of civilian weapons laws. In countries like the United States, gun regulation is very limited, and people in many parts of the country can obtain a weapon for almost any reason at one of the more than fifty thousand gun stores in the country without needing training or a permit (Carlsen and Chinoy 2018). Yemen is even more permissive, with no restriction on the purchase even of machine guns, though there are restrictions on the carrying of weapons in certain cities (S. Parker 2011). In contrast, other countries have very tight gun regulations, prohibiting most or all weapons except for authorized military and police personnel (in some cases, low-capacity hunting rifles may be more available). Of course, while some countries with extensive regulations (such as Japan, discussed below) are effective at limiting the availability of guns, others have been unable to stem the tide of illegal weapons. Mexico requires a background check and fingerprints before you are eligible to by a firearm at the one legal gun store in the country, located in Mexico City—but many people in Mexico obtain illegal guns on the black market (Carlsen and Chinoy 2018).

The case of Switzerland is worth special attention. All able-bodied Swiss men serve annual military duty from roughly age twenty to thirty (Swissinfo 2007), and when they first report for service they are issued a military rifle (DeVore 2017). These rifles are typically kept at home. However, a legal change in 2007 made it so that service members could no longer store their military ammunition at home (Swissinfo 2007)—and people cannot purchase ammunition for a gun they are not legally authorized to own (RS 514.51 1997). Furthermore, while hunting rifles can be obtained without a permit, permits are required for handguns and to carry a loaded gun in public, and military-style weapons are forbidden except for military use (DeVore 2017). Thus, despite relatively easy access to firearms for hunting and military purposes, the magnitude of gun ownership in Switzerland is only slightly more than half that in the United States. Similarly, Israel has a high rate of gun access due to the large number of active duty and reserve military personnel and security services workers, but unless you have a bona fide occupational or other documentable reason to own a firearm, you cannot obtain one. Gun owners also must have a gun safe and be able to safely operate the weapon, and they cannot buy more than a maximum number (usually fifty) of bullets at a time (Carlsen and Chinoy 2018). Israeli weapons regulation goes even further: individuals found with knives outside of the home must prove that they have a legitimate reason for

carrying them, so even campers are sometimes advised to avoid all but the most tiny and necessary knives (Bracha and Kamil 2016).

Japan provides an example of what countries with the most extensive levels of gun regulation look like. Japanese gun regulation has a long history, with recorded gun buybacks dating back to 1685 (Low 2017). Today, to acquire a gun permit in Japan, you must take a class and pass both written and shooting tests (with no more than 5 percent error) as well as document why you want to obtain the gun (handguns are prohibited). You also must pass mental health and drug tests and undergo an extensive background investigation, which extends as far as relatives and colleagues (Low 2017) and includes an examination of debt (Carlsen and Chinoy 2018). Before you acquire the gun, you must have a police inspection of your gun safe and separate locked ammunition storage (Carlsen and Chinoy 2018). After you acquire the gun, it must be inspected annually. Even police personnel are required to leave their weapons at the police station while off duty rather than carrying them (Low 2017). The Japanese case highlights many of the kinds of regulations countries choose from in establishing their gun control regimes, including the demonstration of need, training and testing, permitting and background checks, restrictions on the type of licenses, and safe storage requirements; other potential restrictions include waiting periods before purchase, limitations on carrying weapons in particular areas, and restrictions on the number of guns or the amount of ammunition that may be owned (Parker 2011). There are countries with even stricter regulations than Japan's. In Singapore, for instance, if one owns a gun for target practice, it must be kept at a gun club and not at home (Parker 2011). Countries with such regulations have low rates of civilian gun ownership and also tend to have low rates of officer-involved shootings.

Police-Military Relations

As noted above, the distinction between police and military work can be subtle—we say that police enforce social control internal to a population, whereas the military is deployed elsewhere. But in reality, these distinctions are not always so clear. For example, consider emergencies such as natural disasters or large-scale terror attacks. In circumstances like these in the United States, state governors often activate the National Guard, a military force, to help keep order and facilitate recovery efforts. The National Guard in such instances is acting as a police force, but it remains a military agency. So how can we better understand the relationships between policing and military work? Well, it helps to think of a continuum. On one end is what we call civil policing, where the military and the police are fully separate agencies with separate responsibilities. On the other is martial law, where the military has taken over and is in command of everyday life. Countries can move back and forth along this continuum as circumstances (and politics) change, but there are four basic models for police-military relations: civil policing, state policing, quasi-military policing, and martial law.

In the **civil policing** model, military and police forces have separate command and control structures and separate missions. The police are charged with maintaining order and responding to crime within the population, while the military defends society from external aggressors (Wright 2013). As Haberfeld and Cerrah write, "While the military is designated to fight the external enemy, the police face the enemy within. The problem with the concept, especially in the more democratic environments, is the definition of the enemy within. Similar to the terrorist in the cliché, 'one person's terrorist is another person's freedom fighter,' one's 'enemy within' is another person's family, friend, supplier of goods and services, symbolic figure, or just a plain hero" (2008:342).

This quote highlights the fact that even in a country using civil policing, the distinction between military and police action can be fuzzy. For example, in the United States, police carry out "wars" internal to the population, such as the War on Drugs. In doing so, they use military tools like sound cannons and paramilitary methods like SWAT raids to fight what the government defines as an enemy. But despite such procedures, the police are not a military force. Military forces like the National Guard can be called out in emergencies, but their deployments are (supposed to be) limited.

Countries like France rely on the **state policing** model. Here, there is some separation between the police and the military, but that separation is greatly reduced (Wright 2013). The police are at least partially responsible to the government offices in charge of military work—for instance, in France, one of the national police forces, the *gendarmerie*, is administratively responsible to both the Ministry of the Interior and the Ministry of Defense. This type of arrangement keeps police even more responsive to state interests and perceptions of threat than they might be in a civil police model, especially in systems of single or centralized control. Police forces using a state police model tend to use more military methods and tactics, including military-type deployment systems. The French *gendarmerie* even live in barracks, much as military personnel would.

Further along the continuum is the **quasi-military policing** model. In this model, the police and military share responsibilities (Wright 2013). While the police retain primary responsibility for preventing crime and enforcing law, they are also called on to enforce state security and pursue those enemies defined as "external." It is not uncommon in such systems for police and military personnel to move back and forth between forces (Wright 2013) and for police agencies to use paramilitary techniques and methods extensively. State interests and ideologies provide the central motivation for police actions, and in more authoritarian societies, quasi-military police may experience very limited legal constraints on their actions, which enables them to engage in human rights abuses and develop high levels of power and control over civilian life.

Such models were common in Communist countries in Eastern Europe as well as in many newly democratic countries emerging from authoritarian or colonial rule (Wright 2013).

Finally, **martial law** entails total control of policing functions by the military (Wright 2013). Rather than the police and the military being largely interchangeable, as in the quasi-military police model, the police become simply a branch of the military forces. Martial law in its most extreme forms is rare, as it remains useful for even authoritarian governments to maintain some limited separation between policing and military functions, but it often emerges in times of civil unrest in authoritarian and military-dominated countries.

Understanding Variation in the Armed Forces

While a full investigation into the structure, organization, tactics, and work of national armed forces is beyond the scope of this book, the close relationships between police and military work and agencies make a brief examination of the armed forces worthwhile. Globally in 2017, the world's nations spent over US$1.5 trillion on their military forces, which is an average of US$211 per person, or just over 2 percent of the world's gross domestic product (or GDP, a measure of all goods and services produced in an economy during a year); this supported 19.5 million active-duty troops and thousands more reservists and paramilitary forces in 2018 (International Institute for Strategic Studies 2018). Countries vary significantly in terms of their degree of militarism. Some countries employ few troops and spend little on their military forces, while for others, military spending makes up a significant proportion of the national budget and troop numbers are quite high. The countries with the highest number of active-duty troops are those with the largest populations: China, India, and the United States (International Institute for Strategic Studies 2018). However, per capita numbers, which are a much better way to explore exactly how focused a country is on military service, tell a different story. North Korea has the highest per capita number of active-duty troops at fifty per 1,000 population, followed by Eritrea at 40, Israel at 21, Brunei at 16, and Armenia at 15. In contrast, the United States has just over 4 active-duty troops per 1,000 population, the median country has just under 3, and China and India have less than 1.5 (International Institute for Strategic Studies 2018). The population of active-duty troops does not necessarily correlate with overall spending, as the most expensive portions of military budgets tend to be large-scale equipment like planes, aircraft carriers, submarines, and bombs.

There are many factors shaping countries' choices about military spending, structure, size, and responsibilities, including national geography and history, international trade, and various other elements of the cultural and political environment. However, we do know that military spending does not line up so closely with population. In 2017, five countries had military budgets over

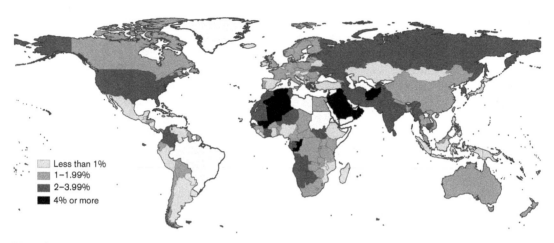

Map 13 Military spending as a percent of GDP (International Institute for Strategic Studies 2018).

US$50 billion: the United States, China, Saudi Arabia, India, and the United Kingdom. France, Japan, and Russia were close behind (International Institute for Strategic Studies 2018). The United States, with a budget of over US$600 billion, spent more than the next eleven countries combined. On a per capita basis, though, the United States is in fifth place at US$1,845 per person, after Saudi Arabia, Oman, Israel, and Kuwait, and just above Singapore. If we look at military spending as a percent of national GDP, we find that Oman, Saudi Arabia, Afghanistan, and Iraq all spend more than 10 percent of their GDP on the military, with Oman spending over 14 percent. In the Republic of the Congo, Algeria, and Israel, military spending makes up more than 5 percent of the GDP. In contrast, the United States spends 3.25 percent of its GDP on the military, and even China, ranked second in overall spending, comes in at only 1.27 percent (International Institute for Strategic Studies 2018).

The data in map 13 highlights the fact that while most of the world's countries do not spend all that much on their military forces, some countries invest intensively in their military capabilities. This tells us that countries differ in their perceptions of the role of the military, including when and why it should be deployed. In countries where the military has a very high degree of political power, including those that have martial law, the military tends to act to ensure that it continues to receive high levels of funding and personnel and will make its own decisions about when, where, and how to act. In other countries, the executive and/or legislative branches of government make decisions about military action. Some countries choose to deploy their armed forces only for self-defense or when called on by the international community to defend allies or participate in peacekeeping missions, while others pursue wars of aggression despite the fact that these became subject to International Criminal Court action in 2018 (as will be discussed in chapter 10).

Countries also differ in their procedures for staffing their military forces. Most commonly, countries either rely on individuals to voluntarily pursue military service (these are called volunteer forces, though troops in volunteer forces are typically paid for their work) or employ a system of mandatory service where all individuals of a certain age are required to serve a specified term in the military. However, some countries with mandatory conscription exempt women from service. Countries using conscription may also permit individuals to choose an alternative form of national service, usually in social services, maintenance, or public health work, especially if their religious beliefs make them opposed to military activities. In some countries with volunteer forces, a conscription or draft policy exists that permits the country to impose mandatory conscription in times of war, when a force buildup is needed. As of 2017, roughly forty countries had mandatory service policies and about thirty-five others had provisions for utilizing conscription in at least some circumstances (Central Intelligence Agency n.d.-c). Where the lines between police and military forces are more blurred, the existence of a conscription policy can also mean that individuals are conscripted into mandatory police service. Some countries also rely heavily on private contractors (much like the private police discussed above) to perform military services; such personnel are sometimes called **mercenaries**.

INTERNATIONAL POLICE COOPERATION

In our increasingly globalized world, police agencies face a growing need to work together across borders, whether to combat cross-border crime, locate suspects who have fled to other jurisdictions, or share knowledge (Andreas and Nadelmann 2006). This collaborative work has come to be known as international police cooperation. Such cooperation can involve, at the most basic level, temporary coalitions designed to track down fugitives, collaborate on investigations, and share police techniques or technologies. But it can also involve international policing organizations, like **Interpol**, or similar regional organizations, such as Europol in the European Union (Haberfeld and Cerrah 2008) and Afripol, an African organization created in 2017. Contrary to many fictionalized portrayals of Interpol, the organization does not directly engage in law enforcement but rather works to coordinate efforts and facilitate the sharing of data and skills across borders.

The organization today known as Interpol was founded in 1923 as the International Criminal Police Commission. At first, it was simply a way for police officials to work together on their own, and it had no enabling treaty or control by national governments (Deflem 2005). Today, it is an organization created by treaty that is further empowered to enter into its own agreements with countries and other international legal bodies (Interpol 2018a). Interpol is explicitly required to maintain political neutrality and therefore does not assist in law enforcement operations targeting political crimes, though it does assist in terrorism investigations, given the violence and harm such crimes can cause (Haberfeld and Cerrah 2008).

Interpol's most important role is to serve as a clearinghouse for information, providing support to and facilitating communication and cooperation among domestic law enforcement agencies. It has several main functions (Haberfeld and Cerrah 2008; Interpol 2018b):

1. Maintaining a global police communication system to facilitate secure, instant communications on a 24/7 basis and enabling the secure transmission of important law enforcement data and documents.
2. Providing and maintaining operational data services and databases, including databases of names, photographs, fingerprints, and DNA profiles of known criminals and wanted persons; stolen travel documents, vehicles, and works of art; firearms; nuclear material; and child sex abuse images.
3. Facilitating notices, which are alerts about or requests for assistance in resolving criminal activities. There are a variety of different types of notices, covering issues as diverse as locating missing persons, identifying unidentified bodies, warning member countries about known criminals, and providing information about criminal techniques. Red notices, which can be issued only based on domestic arrest warrants or judicial orders, seek the arrest of wanted persons wherever in the world they may be found.
4. Coordinating operational police support for cross-border work relating to issues such as locating fugitives, intelligence analysis, border management, terrorism, human trafficking, digital crime, and the smuggling of goods. The Command and Coordination Centre is available on request to facilitate crisis response and provide support teams to member countries. Interpol also supports investigations undertaken by the United Nations and the International Criminal Court (to be discussed in chapter 10).
5. Offering police training and development through actions such as sharing knowledge, skills, and best practices, establishing global standards, and providing training requested by member countries. This includes a series of labs working to expand global capabilities in forensics, policing strategies, digital technologies, and adaptive policing.

The governing structure of Interpol involves a number of elements (Interpol 2018a). The Interpol General Assembly, which has delegates from each member country, is the legislative body for Interpol, making policy, financial, and

CASE STUDY 5.1

Tracking the Pink Panthers

In 2013, a pair of jewelry thieves robbed a high-end store in London, making off with jewels worth more than US$30 million (Samuels 2010). While one of them escaped, the other was pursued by a security guard and arrested by a Scotland Yard (London Metropolitan Police) detective. The ensuing investigation uncovered evidence that the criminals were from Montenegro and were using fake Italian passports. In fact, they were part of an organized crime ring that had come to be known as the Pink Panthers, a name that references a series of comedic crime films beginning with the 1963 original *Pink Panther*, starring Peter Sellers as a bumbling French detective called Inspector Clouseau. The gang's exploits have been documented by the news media, in film, and even in a French comic book (*Gangs 1: Les Pink Panthers*).

When the Pink Panthers targeted a jewelry store, they used one of two standard techniques (Samuels 2010). In one, a well-dressed man with a concealed gun would enter as a customer, propping open the door for others who entered with tools for breaking display cases. In a matter of minutes, the group would leave with the loot. When this was not possible, they would ram store windows with a van or other heavy object and then descend as a group to empty the store. Getaway drivers would abandon—and sometimes burn—the vehicles used in the crime. In some instances, attractive young women were employed as lookouts, to case crime scenes in advance, or to manage local logistics.

The Pink Panthers are responsible for over US$500 million in theft globally (Skakavac, Skakavac, and Skakavac 2016) in crimes stretching back to 1993 and taking place in Europe, North America, Asia, and the Middle East. While no one was certain, investigating officers believed the gang originated in Serbia or Montenegro, had at least sixty but as many as several hundred members, and were highly professional. As of 2016, at least thirty so-called Panthers had been arrested, in several different countries. Their criminal acumen was such that it extended to dramatic, well-organized prison escapes (Agence France-Presse 2013; Samuels 2010).

There are scholars, particularly from the Balkan region, who believe this image of the Pink Panthers is overblown, that really the crimes attributed to the group have little more in common than a technique and are not part of some overarching network of criminals (Skakavac, Skakavac, and Skavavac 2016), and that other criminals not connected to the Pink Panthers have used similar tactics (Chambliss and Williams 2012). But a journalist who has interviewed Pink Panther associates has been told that the central network in the gang is a group of men who grew up together (Samuels 2010). It is also worth mentioning that criminal gangs like the Pink Panthers emerged in the Balkan region in large part due to the corruption, economic devastation, and political breakdown created by Slobodan Miloševic's presidency and the ensuing wars in the region. The Panthers had ties to government officials, with this corruption facilitating their activities, and strong economic and social motivations for their crimes. But they did not work alone—their spectacular crimes required accomplices, especially to turn the jewels they stole into the cash they desired (Chambliss and Williams 2012).

The effort to combat this enterprise was a global one. Interpol set up a special project to enable more effective sharing of data, including fingerprints and DNA, among countries investigating the group's crimes (Interpol 2018c). Dozens of police officers from as many as twenty different countries gathered for annual collaborative working meetings on approaches for policing the Pink Panthers. And the countries in which crimes were committed had to rely on other countries to apprehend the offenders (National Police Agency 2011). But this story also details the shortcomings of relying on international police cooperation: despite evidence that the Pink Panthers relied on Italian documents and phones and had committed crimes in Italy, investigators received little information or support from Italian police (Samuels 2010). And commentators have also noted that Interpol paid little attention to the accomplices laundering the stolen gems so they could be resold on the international diamond market (Chambliss and Williams 2012). Thus, the story of cross-border law enforcement cooperation in relation to the Pink Panthers may also be a story about "perpetuating the myth about the group" and making "it seem as if there is a rational and logical strategy to eradicating the criminal net-work" (Chambliss and Williams 2012:56), thus justifying international support for cross-border collaboration.

Interpol's official involvement ended in 2016, after several high-profile arrests of Pink Panther criminals in Spain, Japan (Interpol 2018c), and Croatia (Wight 2015), and Interpol officials believed that the group's activity had decreased (Wight 2015). But speculation about their continuing activities remains, such as in relation to a theft at Paris's Ritz Hotel in January 2018 (Allen, Boyle, and Davies 2018). In that case, three suspects were arrested and the stolen goods recovered. And even though Interpol is no longer staffing Project Pink Panther, its tools remain available to the French police investigating this crime, who may need to run fingerprints through international databases or issue a Red Notice for the arrest of one of the two suspects believed to have escaped the scene.

operational decisions. It also elects an Executive Committee of thirteen people, who must be from different countries and evenly distributed across the world, which is responsible for carrying out the decisions of the General Assembly. Day-to-day operations are managed by the General Secretariat, which functions as the Interpol civil service and is staffed by personnel from around the world. Its main offices are in Lyon, France, but it also runs seven regional offices and provides representatives to the United Nations, the European Union, and the African Union. In addition, each Interpol member country staffs a National Central Bureau, which serves as the official link between that country's law enforcement agencies and Interpol. Funding, which totaled US$156 million in 2017 (Interpol 2018a)—an amount well under the budget of a typical big-city police department—is provided by member countries. Almost all world nations are members, with the exception of some countries that are not fully recognized by the world community (such as Taiwan), several small Pacific island nations, and North Korea.

Domestic police agencies also increasingly engage in **transnational policing** (Andreas and Nadelmann 2006). Such work includes carrying out domestic police investigations of citizens who live abroad as well as creating police bureaus in other countries (international intelligence work, in contrast, tends to be classified as a military matter). For example, the United States Federal Bureau of Investigation has more than sixty official offices in countries around the world, enabling it to engage in operations nearly everywhere on the globe (Federal Bureau of Investigation n.d.), and China has posted officers in Italy, ostensibly to assist Chinese tourists (Yardley 2016). Even municipal police departments have gotten in on the transnational action—the New York City Police Department, for instance, has posted officers in thirteen cities outside the United States (Dienst et al. 2016).

CONCLUSION

This chapter has detailed a number of ways in which police forces around the world vary, as well as the ways in which they work together. It has not, of course, covered all of the different kinds of variation among and between police forces. If we think back to the beginning of the chapter and the examples of the Italian olive oil police and the Chinese granny police, we can wonder how many other unique police agencies may exist around the world. There are other kinds of variations that are also worth considering. For example, police agencies in some parts of the world, including the United States, have begun using body cameras—small devices attached to the police uniform that record the activity and interactions of police personnel. Supporters of body camera programs believe the devices are likely to reduce unnecessary use of force and the incidence of civilian complaints about police misbehavior. Opponents worry that they increase surveillance in heavily policed communities and may be misused in ways that facilitate police misbehavior. Body camera technology is still very new, and it will take several years to understand what the impacts of body camera programs are. Another factor that varies considerably around the world is the demographic diversity of police personnel. In some countries, police personnel are almost entirely male and tend to be drawn predominantly from particular ethnic or tribal groups. In such cases, police forces may be less responsive to the needs and issues of those with other backgrounds, such as women or ethnic minorities. Many countries are responding to this problem by seeking to diversify police recruitment and hiring.

There are many factors that influence the variations we observe in law enforcement policy and practice, and detailing all of them is beyond the scope of this chapter. But it is worth taking a moment to consider some of the factors that may matter. Of course, as discussed above, the type of government a country has can have a significant impact on the shape and structure of its law enforcement. Authoritarian, centralized governments will tend to have centralized control of their police forces and will be more likely to utilize quasi-military policing. In contrast, countries with a federalized structure or with autonomous regions will tend to have multiple police agencies working in different locations. Countries with mixed legal systems including both theocratic and civil or common law elements may have multiple police agencies, some concerned with religious offenses and others with nonreligious issues.

But government type is not the only factor that matters. National history is also very important. Countries that were colonized by an external power often found themselves with a police structure that had been imposed by the colonial rulers, and once that structure was implemented, countries typically continued to use it—even if it was not the best match for their current reality. Similarly, countries that have a tradition of military intervention in politics typically have closer police-military ties, even if they are today fully democratic in governance. And where multiple territories with different histories and traditions have been merged into one country, the likelihood of employing a multiple-agency police structure tends to be higher.

Police systems can, of course, change over time—just because something emerged at one point in history does not mean a country is stuck with it forever. Change may be slow to come to police agencies, but it does come. For example, globalization-related social change can result in the decentralization or multiplication of police agencies as countries seek to adapt to the new realities of global connectedness. These types of change also tend to increase police agencies' interest in multinational cooperation. The types of threats a country experiences can also shape its law enforcement agencies. For example, when serious threats are conceptualized as national issues, this tends to result in increased centralization and coordination among police agencies; where threats are seen as more particular or local, the country may assume local agencies can handle such issues on their own.

Understanding the structure and style of police work around the world helps us begin to comprehend the diversity of approaches to crime that are possible and to consider the kinds of systems that may work best in given circumstances or for dealing with particular kinds of problems. The police, of course, represent only the first step in the criminal justice system. As noted earlier in this chapter, we tend to believe that the primary functions of police center around preventing, detecting, and investigating crime. While police can detect and investigate crime on their own, their efforts are unlikely to result in much of an impact without the subsequent actions of the courts, which adjudicate offenses and mete out punishments. Thus, it is to courts we will turn next.

Resolving Disputes

CHAPTER GOALS

1. Understand the historical and contemporary variation in dispute resolution practices.
2. Be able to explain differences among the formal dispute resolution systems that are part of different families of law.
3. Become familiar with elements of trial practice, including legal personnel and elements of criminal procedure.
4. Evaluate the role of formal legal mechanisms for resolving different types of disputes.

In 2009, police in Nigeria held a goat under arrest for car theft. A vigilante group claimed that someone had stolen a car and then used witchcraft to transform themselves into that goat (BBC News 2009). The goat was released from custody after its owner came forward to claim it. But would it have been surprising had the goat been put on trial for its supposed crimes? Well, in historical perspective, not really. Medieval European history is filled with cases in which animals were tried for crimes—herds of pigs accused of murder (as shown in figure 11), mules accused of bestiality, and insects accused of causing famine. Courts carried out trials of these creatures and proclaimed sentences on them,

Figure 11 Trial of a sow and pigs at Lavegny (Chambers 1869:128).

often of death by hanging or by being burned alive, but sometimes lesser penalties, like a beating or a letter of reprimand (Simon 2014). Such practices might seem peculiar to us today, but they were essential to resolving disputes and addressing social problems in the contexts in which they were used.

What is a **dispute**? Legal scholar Sally Merry, in a classic article about disputes in a multiethnic housing project on the East Coast of the United States in the 1970s, writes that a "dispute is a disagreement which stems from the perception by an individual or group that rights have been infringed and is then raised into the public arena" (Merry 1979:899). Before a dispute is "raised into the public arena," it is a **grievance**, something that someone is upset about. When someone has a grievance, they often simply tolerate or ignore the issue that gave rise to it, what scholars call "lumping it" (Miller and Sarat 1980–81). When possible, they might choose to exit or avoid the context in which the grievance arose, for example by quitting a job or moving out of an apartment (Galanter 1983). But such approaches do not resolve the grievance or solve the problem; they simply provide people with a way to move forward despite its existence. If someone wants to solve the problem that gave rise to the grievance, they need to do something more, and thus a dispute arises.

All social animals have disputes. Just watch pigeons fight over a French fry on the sidewalk and that will be clear. For most animals, including humans, disputes are often settled by some kind of negotiation, threat of violence, or physical altercation. But as human societies—and the nature of their disputes—became more complex, the mechanisms we turned to as we sought resolutions of our disputes also became more complex. While many human disagreements are still settled with arguments, threats, or struggles, we now have access to a variety of dispute resolution processes, including informal means and formal methods of dispute resolution, such as courts (Galanter 1983).

Informal dispute resolution can involve negotiating directly with the person with whom one has a dispute, seeking a third party (such as a friend or relative) to mediate, or using more coercive methods (such as physical violence or threats) to get what one wants. Alternatively, people can choose formal dispute resolution mechanisms, including grievance procedures maintained by employers or other organizations, or the state-sanctioned procedures managed by courts. Research on dispute resolution has found that many factors affect the way people respond to disputes (Galanter 1983), including cultural factors (E. Hoffman 2003), people's feelings of competence or self-efficacy in managing the dispute, the type of dispute, and the accessibility of formal dispute resolution mechanisms (Merry 1979).

In this chapter, you will learn more about these formal dispute resolution mechanisms, both as they developed historically and as they exist today in different families of law around the world. You will also learn more about the workings of courts and trials in modern legal systems. As you begin reading, take a moment to think about the images you have of how formal dispute resolution—which, in most contemporary societies, takes place in courts— works. When you think about a court, what does it look like? What does it do? What kinds of people are present, and what are their roles? And when a dispute is resolved in a court, what is the outcome? Finally, which elements of the court process and system do you think will tend to be similar all around the world, and which will be more diverse?

DISPUTE RESOLUTION IN HISTORICAL PERSPECTIVE

Our historical knowledge about dispute resolution is limited, as we are dependent on the written record to tell us how disputes were settled in the past (aside, of course, from violent conflict—for that all we need are archeological finds involving smashed skulls or spear wounds). But even with this limitation, we know about a wide variety of historical techniques for resolving disputes.

Perhaps the most common historical methods of dispute resolution are various kinds of contests. These include duels and physical battles, whether to the death or to injury. They also include competitions in which disputants show off some skill (whether athletic, artistic, culinary, or something else) or battle to see who can host the largest feast or event for their village, with the victor winning the dispute. The contest as a means of dispute resolution continues to be used in contexts outside of the formal legal system all around the world, but its use in modern legal systems continued until rather recently. For example, the Tony–award winning musical *Hamilton* features several scenes in which disputes are settled with gun duels, including a depiction of the final moments of

Alexander Hamilton's life, when he is killed by Aaron Burr's bullet in 1804. In England, the use of duels as a formal legal tool came to an end after the court case *Ashford v. Thornton*. In this 1818 case, a man (Abraham Thornton) was put on trial for the brutal murder of a young girl (Mary Ashford) and was acquitted. As a 1488 statute permitted the close relatives of those who had been murdered to appeal not-guilty verdicts, the girl's brother, William Ashford, appealed. When asked to enter his plea, Thornton pled not guilty and demanded demand trial by combat—in other words, a duel (Riddell 1926). In such cases, the accused—or a paid fighter of his or her choice—would fight, with such weapons and protective gear as laid out in the statute, for a full day's time (Marke 1979). If the accused was defeated, he or she was hanged; if he or she survived to fight until dusk or defeated the opposing side, he or she was acquitted. As Ashford was neither physically fit nor a skilled fighter, he did not pick up arms, which resulted in Thornton's acquittal (Marke 1979). At the time of the trial, the 1488 statute had not been relied upon since at least 1638—although in that instance the actual duel had not been carried out (Marke 1979)—and many observers viewed trial by combat as a barbaric practice better left in the past. In the aftermath of *Ashford v. Thornton*, members of Parliament moved rapidly to disallow this practice, with a prohibition becoming law as the Appeal of Murder, etc. Act in July 1819 (Riddell 1926).

In many historical contexts, disputants may have been asked to present their dispute to a mediator or group of mediators, or to submit to a decision by a village or tribal leader, a council of elders, or some other body that would listen to the terms of the dispute and determine what should happen. We have detailed knowledge about several historical contexts in which such tribunals or hearings were used, including ancient Greece (specifically Athens), Viking-era Iceland, and Europe in the early Middle Ages. In ancient Athens, a panel of male citizens (those who had Athenian parents and who were not themselves enslaved) over thirty years of age served for renewable terms of one year (Carey 2012). Individuals were selected from this panel, often randomly, to serve as *dikastai* (Lanni 2006). Today, scholars often translate *dikastai* as jurors, but they were probably more analogous to nonprofessional (lay) judges (Carey 2012; Lanni 2006). A group of somewhere between 201 and 501 *dikastai* heard and decided on the outcome of cases, incorporating in their deliberations both the evidence presented and their prior knowledge of those involved in the case. A majority vote on guilt or innocence (and, depending on the offense, sentencing) determined the outcome of the case (Lanni 2006).

In Iceland, the Viking settlers developed a complicated legal system with a variety of complex rules that was maintained by the Lawspeaker, an elected official whose responsibility was to recite the body of law governing the populace as well as answer questions about it (Hadfield 2017). When a dispute arose, a group of thirty-six male householders heard the case and issued a decision. Given the lack of state structures like police and prisons, the courts had no capacity to

Figure 12 Old woman drowned at Ratcliff Highway (artist unknown; ca. 1780 and 1800.).

enforce the decision, so those who were aggrieved acted with their neighbors to carry it out, for example by obtaining compensation for a loss (Hadfield 2017). In severe cases, the accused might be declared by the court to be an outlaw. All citizens had the obligation to refuse food, shelter, or other support to an outlaw, who was banished from the country for a period of three years or permanently. In such circumstances, anyone was entitled to kill the outlaw on sight (Hadfield 2017).

Across Europe in the early Middle Ages, the process of determining guilt and innocence took place in a ceremony called **compurgation**. In this ceremony, a group of people gathered to swear an oath that the accused had not committed whatever offense he or she had been accused of committing (Kadri 2005). These oaths were administered in accordance with religious practice at the time, such that the faithful would believe false oaths would lead to their damnation. The processes also allowed for various countermeasures to enable false oaths, such as switching holy objects upon which an oath is to be sworn for those considered less sacred (Kadri 2005). The number of compurgators (oath-swearers) needed to support a claim of innocence varied across time and place, from just a handful to as many as six hundred (Carey 2012). In some cases, additional bodies of witnesses were required to enforce the rules of the compurgation ceremony.

But sometimes, compurgation was not enough, and the accused would be subjected to **trial by ordeal**. In this procedure, the accused would be given a physical test, the results of which were taken as a message from the divine power as to their guilt or innocence (Galanter 1983). For example, suspects might be asked to plunge their arm into boiling water to retrieve a trinket and then evaluated days later for evidence of healing; made to walk barefoot over heated iron implements; or bound with weights and immersed in water to determine if they floated or sank (floating tended to be seen as evidence of sin). The trial by ordeal re-emerged as a common approach in witchcraft trials and investigations through the 1700s (Currie 1968). For example, figure 12 shows the use of trial by ordeal in an English witchcraft trial in roughly 1800. Courts also used a procedure in which a suspected witch was pricked with a knife; if observers noted that she (accused witches were nearly always women) did not feel pain, she would be presumed guilty. In a strange twist on the ordeal, similar practices were used in trials seeking the nullification of marriage through the 1700s. Given that impotence provided grounds for an annulment, men could be subjected to tests of sexual performance to determine if an annulment would be granted (Hoffman 2009).

TYPES OF DISPUTES, TYPES OF LAW

In the modern world, most dispute resolution systems draw an important distinction between disputes that are a matter of **public law** and disputes that are a matter of **private law**. Public law is law governing matters involving the state, such as relations between different parts of the state, relations between the state and individuals, and constitutional and administrative matters. Private law is law governing relations between individuals or groups not directly involving the state. In many cases, it is easy to determine whether a given dispute would be a matter for public or private law. For example, if someone alleges that the government prevented her from voting, that would involve public law. Or if two homeowners argue about whose responsibility it is to pay for cutting down a dead tree that straddles their property line, that would involve private law.

But criminal matters are more complicated. If someone is murdered, is the murder a private dispute between the accused murderer and the victim's loved ones? Or is it a public matter because murder is a violation of public safety and security? Do we think differently if it is a different kind of crime? For instance, traffic violations like speeding or running a red light do not necessarily cause any private harm, so we might assume they are matters for public law because of the regulatory function of the state. Or we might consider offenses like trespassing or petty theft and argue that these are clearly offenses against an individual or business rather than the state. It is not as simple as saying that a particular act is illegal and thus involves relations with the state. For example, many societies make various types of employment discrimination illegal but do not tend to prosecute employers criminally for their failure to abide by equal opportunity guidelines. Instead, they use administrative regulations or sue in civil court to address this sort of problem.

As discussed in chapter 4, states criminalize certain acts and not others, and those acts that have been criminalized are those we see as crimes. But not all states treat crimes the same way in terms of the distinction between public and private law. In some states, almost all crime is addressed as a matter of public law, with state-appointed legal personnel investigating criminal matters and bringing legal actions against those assumed to be responsible. In other states, many crimes are considered matters for private law, with those harmed responsible for mounting a dispute.

Formal dispute resolution mechanisms, including modern courts, address both public and private law, but they may be treated differently or segregated into different courts. For example, many countries hear criminal matters in different courts or under different legal rules than noncriminal (civil) matters, or they may have special courts for administrative, family, inheritance, bankruptcy, or other specialized legal topics. A quick side note: the term "civil" can get very confusing when talking about comparative law, since it refers both to civil (code) law as a family of law and civil (noncriminal) law as a type of law that exists in all legal systems.

Within both criminal and civil law, there is an important distinction between **substantive law** and **procedural law**. Substantive law is law defining actual substance—rights, responsibilities, crimes, penalties, obligations, and remedies. Procedural law is law laying out the procedures that a given court or tribunal must follow and the way that its business is to be carried out. Substantive criminal law includes law governing categories of criminal acts, the potential sanctions available for each category of criminal acts, and what sorts of factors might make an individual not responsible for a crime (for instance, being too young). In civil law, substantive law might include your responsibility to ensure that your place of business is free of hazards, your right to seek employment without facing discrimination, and your obligation to financially support your spouse and children. Procedural law covers such issues as the rules of evidence (what can be presented to the court and what cannot); the roles of judges, juries, and lawyers; how and when cases can be appealed and to what bodies; how hearings are to be conducted; and even what font lawyers must use in documents submitted to the court. The rules of criminal and civil procedure are often quite different, even when addressing similar topics. For instance, criminal and civil courts in the same country often rely on different standards of proof and have different rules about what sorts of evidence must be turned over to the opposing side.

In most advanced-economy countries, civil legal matters make up a much larger proportion of court cases than do criminal legal matters. For example, in the U.S. federal court system in 2017, 18 percent of initial district court filings and 20 percent of courts of appeals filings, not including bankruptcies, were criminal (Administrative Office of the U.S. Courts 2017). In Japan's court system, 40.5 percent of all new court filings in 2016 were criminal (Saiko saibansho n.d.). Despite the overwhelming prevalence of civil matters, this chapter will focus more of its attention on criminal matters given the centrality of criminal justice issues to the overall themes of the book. In particular, in light of the coverage of crime and criminalization in chapter 4 and of punishment in chapter 6, this chapter will focus on criminal procedure, which varies widely between countries and among legal systems.

CONTEMPORARY DISPUTE RESOLUTION SYSTEMS

Formal dispute resolution systems vary widely around the world. Indeed, their characteristics are one of the elements that are foundational to the classification of countries' legal systems into families of law (as discussed in chapter 2). Thus, this section will detail the particular dispute resolution systems common to particular families of law. Note that, as is the case for families of law more generally, the dispute resolution systems discussed here are ideal types. In reality, each country has its own unique peculiarities, but the classification scheme laid out here highlights some of the key features of each system and the differences between them.

Dispute Resolution in Common Law

In common law countries, an adversarial system of trials is used. This is the system that will be most familiar to readers in the United States. As the name suggests, **adversarial trials** are based on two (or more) opposing sides fighting to win a case. In most cases, each side is represented by a lawyer. These lawyers present arguments in a competitive fashion, focusing on scoring points almost as if the case were a game or contest. While real common law cases are not nearly as entertaining as those we see on television or in movies, they are still more theatrical than cases in other legal systems. This is because they rely on dramatic elements like lawyers making speeches, witnesses giving emotional appeals, and dueling experts arguing about esoteric details. Furthermore, case strategies are a surprise not only to observers but also to the jury, the opposing side, and sometimes even the judge.

Aside from lawyers, common law courts also rely on judges and juries. A judge's role, in the common law court, is to make decisions of law—for example, what evidence is permissible in a case, or what sentence can be assigned for a given crime—and to act as a referee between the competing parties. This role is complicated by the fact that, as discussed in chapter 2, common law courts are tasked with applying not only laws encoded in statutes but also the complex precedent established by prior court cases. Juries consist of laypeople, not court employees, and their role is to determine questions of fact, such as whether the accused committed the crime, or who is responsible for a given injury. They do not participate in direct questioning of witnesses or lawyers during trials. Judges, however, can ask questions of witnesses or lawyers, but only in a limited capacity designed to clarify confusion, calm witnesses, save time, or prevent error (Hobgood 1981). This means that neither the judge nor the jury is involved in carrying out an investigation; rather, the investigation is done by the police or by the lawyers prior to the trial. As will be discussed later, the role of the jury has diminished somewhat in many common law jurisdictions, but it is still central to the ideal typical adversarial trial, particularly in criminal courts.

Witnesses who are called to testify in cases take oaths to tell the truth (here you can see the continuing influence of the compurgation ceremony discussed above), and should they fail to be truthful, they can be held criminally responsible for their lies—this is the crime of perjury. However, in most common law jurisdictions, defendants are not required to testify. In the United States, defendants and witnesses can "take the Fifth," or in other words, invoke their constitutional Fifth Amendment right against self-incrimination, to avoid revealing in court any details that might relate to their criminal responsibility, and judges and juries are expected to draw no conclusions about guilt from this invocation (though of course some do so anyway). In other common law jurisdictions, it may be permissible to draw conclusions when a defendant chooses not to testify, but the defendant still has the right to make this choice.

Many commentators argue that the primary goal in adversarial trials, given their competitive nature, is determining a winner. However, the vast majority of all cases brought to court in common law countries never go to trial: most cases are withdrawn, thrown out by the court, or result in a pretrial settlement or a plea bargain. While this trend is most pronounced in the United States, where over 90 percent of accused criminals plead guilty and therefore do not go to trial, it is clearly present in the United Kingdom and other common law jurisdictions as well: in the United Kingdom, about 70 percent of those accused of crimes plead guilty (C. Smith 2013). Well over 90 percent of civil cases in both countries never go to trial (Ministry of Justice 2014; National Center for State Courts 2015). This means, we might argue, that the goal of adversarial cases (perhaps not trials) is resolving the dispute efficiently, though as Merry (1979) points out, disputants may not come away from the process feeling that there has been a resolution.

One of the most notable aspects of the common law system is its reliance on precedent. This reliance means that a complex system of judicial review is required, as higher courts are empowered to review the decisions of lower courts on appeal to ensure they are in line with the accumulated body of precedent. The appeals process can be quite complex, with many layers of review taking many years to process (see figure 13 for examples of this complexity). Common law judicial systems also engage in judicial review to ensure that decisions comport with constitutional guidelines. Indeed, the act of judicial review may be the necessary last step in legislation becoming recognized as law, since the idea of precedent requires judicial interpretations.

In adversarial, common law courts, essential legal personnel include judges, juries, and lawyers. Of course, courts rely on quite an extensive variety of other personnel, such as support staff like clerks and transcriptionists, security staff, and administrative staff, but as important as these roles are to the proper functioning of courts and legal systems, understanding their work is not as necessary for understanding the differences and similarities between trial processes in different nations.

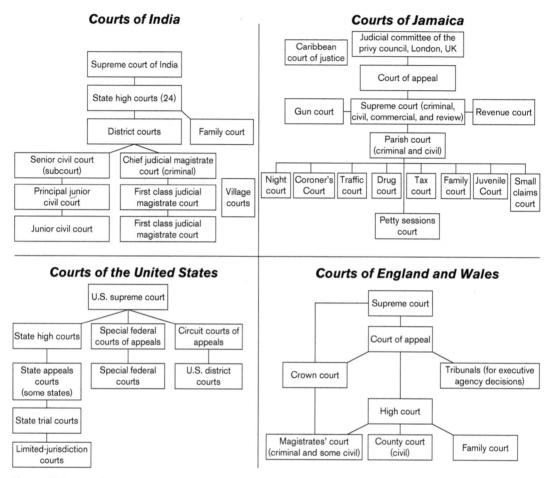

Figure 13 Common law court systems.

As noted above, judges in adversarial courts play the role of referee, making legal and procedural decisions in cases. They are part of an independent judicial branch of government and are typically educated much as any lawyer would be, with limited training specifically for the judicial role. In some cases, judges may not even have formal legal training. Selection and appointment procedures for judges vary considerably from country to country and even within countries.

In the United States, judges can be appointed or elected. Appointment procedures may involve direct appointment by the executive or appointment via a nominating committee procedure, typically followed by confirmation by the legislative branch of government. In some cases, they are then subject to a **retention election**, a procedure where voters determine whether to keep them in their position or reject them in favor of some future, as-yet-unnamed replacement. Judicial elections can be partisan or nonpartisan. Once judges are selected, they may be subject to reappointment or reelection after a term of years, permanent life tenure until they die or retire, or tenure until a mandatory retirement age. Federal judges are nominated by the president, subject to confirmation by the Senate, and have life tenure, but such procedures are less common for state judges—thirty-nine states use some form of election for judicial appointments (Brennan Center for Justice 2015). Judicial elections are extremely rare in other countries. The United Kingdom provides an example of a more typical judicial appointment process. First of all, potential judges must have several years of experience working in the legal profession to qualify. Then, they apply through a formal procedure requiring an application with a self-assessment and assessments by peers, a formal interview and presentation, and a written examination (Judicial Appointments Commission, n.d.). Commentators both within the United States and around the world frequently note that judicial elections may increase the degree to which judges consider political and ideological factors in making their decisions, thus reducing judicial impartiality (Liptak 2008).

Historically, the jury has been one of the most essential features of the adversarial trial, but the role of the jury has diminished notably in recent years. In part, this is due to a global decline in trials, as systems encourage disputes to be settled out of court, including by guilty pleas (Freshfields Bruckhaus Deringer LLP 2017). But even beyond the decline in trials, common law jurisdictions have moved away from a guaranteed right to a jury (Vidmar and Hans 2007). Juries are extremely rare in noncriminal courts in countries other than the United States (Hans 2008), and in some countries, jury trials' legitimacy has been undermined by high rates of reversal by appellate courts (Smith 2013). Some trial systems require juries to reach a unanimous verdict, while others permit supermajorities or even simple majorities. Juries also vary in size, with a global range from around six to as many as fifteen members. Finally, jury selection procedures are an additional source of variation. In the United States, lawyers for either side are permitted to challenge the seating of any potential juror either for cause (juror bias or incapacity) or by using **peremptory challenges**, which require no reason but are limited in number. Other adversarial systems tend to limit the ability of lawyers to object to potential jurors but do still provide for the ability to dismiss those with extreme bias. For example, a potential juror in a 2012 criminal case in the United Kingdom was dismissed from service after attesting to his "extreme prejudices against homosexuals and Black/foreign people" and noting that he "couldn't possibly be impartial if either appeared in court"—though he then "faced prosecution under the Contempt of Court act for failing to serve on a jury" (Telegraph Reporters 2012), as systems utilizing jury tend to require such service as a matter of law to ensure a sufficient jury pool.

In contrast to judges, juries in adversarial trial systems determine questions of fact. This means that they answer questions about criminal or civil responsibility but do not make decisions about trial procedure or appropriate legal standards. In rare cases, where juries feel the law would lead to a factual conclusion they feel is wrong or unjust, juries can make decisions that do not confirm to the facts so as to reach an outcome they feel is more appropriate (for example, where an individual is accused of an act that the jury does not believe should be illegal); in the United States, this is called **jury nullification**, and in the United Kingdom, **jury equity**. In some countries and for some kinds of cases, juries can also make recommendations about or determinations of **sanctions** or punishments, such as civil damages or criminal sentences, but judges more typically hold this responsibility, and even where juries can make such determinations, judges can often overrule them.

Adversarial trials depend heavily on the work of lawyers representing the two (or more) sides of the case. In civil trials, each side is typically represented by their own privately hired lawyer, though if one side cannot afford a lawyer or prefers not to hire one, that side may represent itself **pro se**. In criminal trials, a **prosecutor** brings the case and a **defense attorney** represents the defendant. In common law countries, prosecutors are most typically civil servants who work independently of the judiciary as part of the executive branch of government, though some countries permit victims or their families to hire private lawyers to prosecute cases when the state has declined to do so. Defense attorneys may be hired privately by the defendant, but many countries provide for legal representation at state expense for those who cannot afford a lawyer on their own (to be discussed further below). In a given country, lawyers tend to receive similar training and education regardless of which type of law they practice or what role they will play in the trial process, with their education focusing on precedential cases. However, legal education and training varies considerably across countries. For example, in the United States, lawyers must first complete a bachelor's degree and then earn a three-year juris doctor (JD) graduate degree. After this, they sit for a two- or three-day standardized bar examination in the state in which they intend to practice law, and they must take additional examinations to be licensed in other states. Most states do not require extensive practical training, and lawyers can practice any type of law as soon as they are licensed.

In contrast, the English system does not necessarily require legal education, as prospective lawyers can choose to train via apprenticeship. The majority do obtain law degrees, but the degree is at the undergraduate level. Lawyers must choose between two different legal career paths, that of the **barrister** or the **solicitor**. Solicitors, who work directly with clients, take a one-year postgraduate course and then complete a two-year apprenticeship at a low rate of pay. Barristers also complete a one-year training course, and then they undertake a year of practical training without pay. Only since 2004 have barristers been permitted direct client contact; before that, they accepted cases referred by solicitors. Since that change, the line between the work done by barristers and that done by solicitors has become less clear. However, as a general rule, solicitors are more focused on tasks involving direct client contact, including providing legal advice and services to clients, filing documents with the court, and serving documents on other parties. In contrast, barristers specialize in representing people or companies in court, and they also provide advice to solicitors about more complex legal matters (Bar Standards Board, n.d.; Chambers and Partners 2019).

Dispute Resolution in Civil Law

In contrast to the adversarial trial system used in common law countries, civil law countries feature inquisitorial trials. The term "inquisitorial" is not meant to recall the Spanish Inquisition or other torturous episodes. Rather, it denotes the extensive questioning that is the hallmark of inquisitorial trial procedures. In inquisitorial trials, the judicial process is structured as an investigatory proceeding, with much less of a distinction drawn between the pretrial and trial phases than would be the case in adversarial courts. The judge asks questions (including of the defendant) and plays a major role in steering the process of evidence-gathering.

Defendants in inquisitorial courts are typically required to testify, though they do not do so under oath and thus are not subject to perjury charges if their statements are untrue. During their testimony, they have the opportunity to explain things from their point of view, but they need not necessarily say anything about the crime itself. Defendants and their lawyers come to court with knowledge of the prosecution's case and the evidence against them. The lawyers in inquisitorial trials focus their efforts on suggesting questions, sources of evidence, and paths of inquiry rather than presenting a dramatic case in the courtroom and cross-examining witnesses. This means that lawyers in inquisitorial courts may focus less on winning and more on searching for the truth, which is supposed to be the court's main goal as well. A final note is that inquisitorial trials, as part of the civil law system, rely on written statutes and not on accumulated precedent from prior court decisions in making their determinations. Table 6 presents some key points of comparison between adversarial and inquisitorial trial systems. It is important to note that, as the case study on Amanda Knox later in this chapter shows, adversarial and inquisitorial trials are not simply opposites, and indeed, countries often borrow elements from both types of systems. Rather, the comparisons detailed in table 6 present a set of distinctions designed to make clear the foundations of the differences we can observe between the typical adversarial trial and the typical inquisitorial trial.

Table 6 Comparing adversarial and inquisitorial trials

Adversarial trials	Inquisitorial trials
Based on *precedent*	Based on *statute*
Central but diminishing role for jury, which determines questions of fact	Juries are very rare, though lay judges may participate
Contest between lawyers	Investigation into facts
Judges are independent professionals who determine questions of law	Judges are trained state appointees
Suspect has the right to silence	Suspect is expected to participate
Oral hearings are primary	Investigation is primary
Cases determine a winner	Cases seek to know what happened

In contrast to their prominent role in adversarial trials, juries are rarely found in inquisitorial trials, though some civil law countries do use them in certain (typically severe) criminal cases. Instead, professional judges decide issues of both law and fact in inquisitorial trials, often accompanied by nonprofessional (lay) judges. In many countries, judicial personnel, both professional and lay, sit in odd-numbered panels, so one individual does not make court decisions on his or her own. The fact that judges sit in panels may explain the vastly greater number of professional judicial personnel seen in non-common-law systems (see map 14). Judges in most civil law countries have special training for their roles and a career ladder within the judicial profession, with selection following similar rules as for other civil service positions, though judges on high courts may be political appointees. This civil service system means that judges tend to experience much less political pressure than do judges in systems that involve political appointment or election, such as the United States.

Lawyers play an important role in inquisitorial courts, though it is a different one from that in adversarial courts. Each side in a case in an inquisitorial court is represented by a lawyer, but the lawyers have less of a sense of personal winning and losing as their roles are primarily supportive and advisory. The specific practices surrounding defense and prosecution in criminal cases vary widely among civil law countries.

In most civil law countries, prospective lawyers study law as an undergraduate degree. This does not mean the study of law in civil law countries is somehow less advanced than in countries where legal study begins at the graduate level; rather, it reflects a more fundamental difference in the organization of higher education, in which specialization occurs earlier in the educational trajectory. Many students study law even if they do not intend to become lawyers or judges, though those who do wish to become legal professionals may be

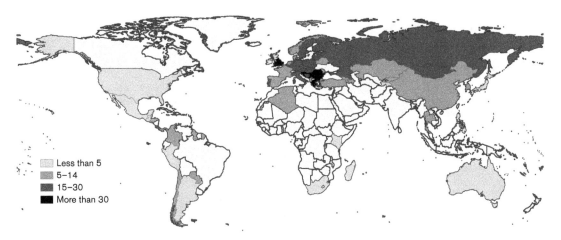

Map 14 Professional judges or magistrates per 100,000 population (UNDOC n.d.).

required to supplement their undergraduate law degree with a specialized one-year training program. Formal education and training is typically followed by a standardized national examination or an oral examination on a specified national curriculum as well as by an internship or apprenticeship. By the time they complete their studies, students will have chosen a specific career path as a lawyer, judge, civil servant, notary, or scholar, with little mobility likely between career paths. For example, French law students interested in a judicial career select this path during law school and serve a one-year apprenticeship following their graduation. After passing an examination, they are posted to small local courts, and they move up through the court hierarchy over the course of their careers, with rigorous civil service standards governing promotions. A quarter of judges in France are selected from among lawyers who move into the profession later on in their careers.

The legal profession in Japan provides an interesting example of a country in some ways very similar to most civil law systems, but with unique features. Japanese students interested in legal careers study law as undergraduates, but very few graduates will go on to work as lawyers (there are alternative pathways, such as tax law and document preparation, which provide a home for some of those who do not become lawyers). After college graduation, prospective lawyers must take a notoriously difficult national exam with failure rates as high as 50 percent (Tanikawa 2011), and there are limits on retaking the exam multiple times. Students who pass the exam take special one-year training courses that include both field and classroom elements at the Legal Training and Research Institute of Japan, which prepare them for career paths as prosecutors, civil advocates, criminal defense lawyers, civil judges, or criminal judges (Supreme

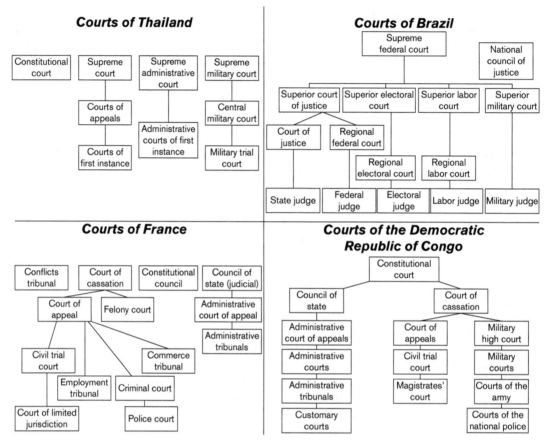

Figure 14 Civil law court systems.

Court of Japan 2006). Following a second examination, graduates can then begin their careers. These days, the national target is 3,000 new legal professionals per year (Tanikawa 2011) out of about 560,000 annual university graduates (Research Institute for Higher Education 2018).

Inquisitorial courts have a vastly reduced role in judicial review as compared to adversarial courts. However, there are legal issues requiring review, including appeals, constitutional issues, and within-government conflict. Civil law countries do have appeals processes in which parties to cases can seek review by higher courts, but in civil law countries appellate decisions do not serve as precedent and thus do not themselves make new law. Unlike appeals in common law countries, which tend to concern themselves with questions of law, civil law appeals are more likely to handle cases involving a wholesale review of the entire trial record and even the presentation of new evidence (M. Shapiro 1980). Many civil law countries have special constitutional courts tasked with reviewing proposed or new legislation to ensure that it abides by constitutional standards. These courts typically review legislation after it has been passed by the legislative body but before final enactment, and as is the case with appeals, the decisions of constitutional courts do not make new law. Rather, if the law is found unconstitutional, it can be struck down, and the legislature must go back to the drawing board, guided by the court's decision. Civil law countries also define separation of powers differently than do common law countries, with the effect of constraining the power of the judiciary over legislative and executive functions. Therefore, many civil law countries have special administrative personnel or executive or administrative courts to deal with legal issues that arise outside of the judiciary's jurisdiction. Examples of the ways in which constitutional and administrative courts fit into national court systems can be seen in figure 14.

Dispute Resolution in Theocratic Law

In countries with theocratic legal systems, it is religious belief and scripture that guide dispute resolution. This means that each set of beliefs and guidelines leads to a somewhat different set of dispute resolution practices stemming from those beliefs and guidelines. What theocratic systems have in common, beyond the fact that they are rooted in religious belief, is that they are governed by a set of principles. These rules are laid out in or have been developed based on the scriptural guidelines the faithful follow as having been revealed by the divine spirit or spirits of that religion. In addition, the judicial and legal authorities in theocratic systems tend to be clergy rather than secular judges and lawyers, and they may or may not have any additional training in law or dispute resolution. However, it is important to remember that hybrid legal systems are very common. Many countries have hybrid systems combining theocratic dispute resolution with one of the other types of dispute resolution discussed in this chapter, whether in a fully mixed system or one with dual courts where theocratic dispute resolution is used in some parts of the country or for certain types of disputes. What this means is that just because a country says it is theocratic does not mean all aspects of its dispute resolution procedures actually stem from the religious beliefs the government espouses.

Shari'a Courts

Today, Islamic law is the most common form of theocratic law we see in the world, and so we will focus more attention on it than on other forms of theocratic dispute resolution. Islamic law, or **Shari'a**, comes from the Islamic scriptures—the Qur'an, which is the foundational text of Islam, and other texts including sayings of the Prophet Muhammed and reports of his life and practices—as well as from legal interpretations of these texts made by Islamic scholars. Shari'a law lays out clear rules and standards for dispute resolution, including procedural rules for the hearing and adjudication of disputes as well as substantive guidance on the appropriate penalties for various criminal acts. While the practice of Shari'a law had faded under European colonialism, it has re-emerged in the postcolonial era, and some observers argue that its presence has continued to grow in recent decades.

In criminal disputes under Shari'a law, evidence must include confessions and/or testimony of a minimum number of respectable Muslim eyewitnesses. Other forms of evidence, like telephone records, DNA, or weapons, are not generally considered admissible in Shari'a courts. Similarly, in contract disputes, witnesses and oaths are much more important sources of evidence than even the written contract itself. Shari'a courts are presided over by a judge who is an expert in Islamic theology, and there is no jury. While some countries do permit disputants to bring lawyers to court, the role of lawyers is limited to an advisory one, with no possibility for cross-examination of witnesses. Indeed, in some Shari'a courts, disputants are required to represent themselves, or they may bring a male elder to help argue on their behalf. In many criminal cases (other than cases of specifically religious crimes), a prosecutor is not used, with the victim or the victim's family bringing the case to the court. If the judge is persuaded that a crime occurred, deference may be given to the victim in determining the desired outcome, such as punishment or restitution.

In modern Islamic states, traditional practices of Shari'a law tend to coexist with some written statutes, and judges are tasked with interpreting and applying both. However, Shari'a law, and especially the teachings of the Qur'an, is considered supreme. In some countries, though, the role of Shari'a law has diminished, and secular law is applied in most areas of the legal system other than religious crimes and family matters. Traditionally, the decisions of Islamic judges did not set precedent, but some countries have established appeals processes designed to standardize interpretations of Shari'a law. For example, Saudi Arabia has established some appeals courts, with final appeal to the king.

Other Theocratic Systems

Of course, Shari'a law is not the only type of theocratic law. Historically, many religions developed theocratic legal systems. For instance, in Great Britain, ecclesiastical courts heard cases related to issues of morality well into the 1800s and still have authority over disputes involving church property. Today, theocratic dispute resolution can still be found in various non-Muslim countries, including India, Israel, and the Vatican. India, for example, is a secular country, but it maintains religious courts for each significant religious group (except in the province of Goa). These courts have authority over marriage, divorce, adoption, and related issues and make decisions according to the religious principles of their respective faiths.

Similarly, Israel maintains a secular legal system alongside separate religious courts for Jews (the *beth din*), Muslims, Druze, and Christians. These courts generally hear disputes over family issues, such as marriages and divorces. *Beth din* also control conversions to Judaism, which means they play an important role in some citizenship decisions (as discussed in chapter 9), as well as other types of religious disputes both in Israel and around the world. The Vatican is a slightly different type of case, as it has a legal system in which city law is deeply intertwined with Catholic canon law. Judges and lawyers in the Vatican must be experts in canon law, and the Pope retains the right to overturn or revise the decisions of Vatican legal bodies (Cismas 2014). Catholics around the world, and particularly Catholic churches and clergy, are also subject to canon law and the decisions of canon courts.

Traditional Dispute Resolution Practices

While any country today with a functioning government has created some kind of formal court system charged with resolving disputes, traditional dispute resolution practices continue to be used alongside these formal courts in many parts of the world. In traditional dispute resolution—much as in the historical dispute resolution practices discussed at the beginning of this chapter—there is less of a sense that criminal acts should involve a different sort of dispute resolution than any other conflict or grievance. The goals of traditional dispute resolution are focused on the maintenance of social cohesion in the community rather than on seeking the truth or adjudicating a winner.

Specific traditional dispute resolution practices vary widely from community to community even within the same country. Most frequently, they take the form of some kind of mediation or hearing in front of religious figures, tribal leaders, or elders, who apply their accumulated wisdom and experience to helping the parties to the dispute come to a resolution. But as these practices tend to operate without written guidelines, it is also possible for traditional dispute resolution practices to enable leaders to simply do as they wish.

In recent years, organizations and courts in civil and common law countries have begun to look to traditional dispute resolution practices as a model for finding ways to resolve disputes without the formality and zero-sum nature of modern courts. These approaches have come to be called **restorative justice**. Restorative justice incorporates **mediation** between a victim and an offender, oriented toward repairing—to whatever extent possible—the harm the offender has done to the victim (Koss, Bachar, and Hopkins 2003) as well as to the broader community. This mediation typically takes place in a community setting where each involved party can bring supporters and a trained facilitator manages the interaction. Restorative justice approaches have become common

Traditional Courts in South Africa

In the contemporary world, traditional law is typically found as part of mixed legal systems that also utilize some other family of law. An example of such mixing is found in South Africa. South Africa's legal system is formed from a complex mixture of English common law and Dutch civil law as imposed by colonial powers alongside various traditional elements from the customs of indigenous tribal groups. But the balance between these different elements has changed over time.

Under the apartheid system, traditional courts were empowered to resolve disputes and hear cases involving certain types of crime, though only for those defined under law as "Black" (Koyana 2011). This empowerment entailed the creation of an "official" form of traditional law, which had previously been flexible, changing, and unwritten (Iyi 2016). When apartheid was abolished, the law regulating these courts—part of the Black Administration Act of 1927—was repealed, but certain portions were retained so as to perpetuate the function of traditional courts (Griffin 2017). In the modern period, more than seventeen million people—nearly a third of South Africans—live in areas where traditional courts are the most accessible venue for dispute resolution (Iyi 2016). Traditional courts also can provide access to justice at a lower cost and in local languages (Koyana 2011). However, the practices and decisions of traditional courts can come into conflict with the legal rights and procedures in formal courts, creating legal dilemmas for justice systems (Oomen 2005).

In 2008 and 2012, efforts were made to revise the governance of traditional courts, but both pieces of legislation were withdrawn due to the magnitude of public objection. The 2008 legislation would have forced members of tribal communities into traditional tribal courts even when they preferred to take their cases elsewhere, depriving them of legal representation and empowering tribal leaders to deny community members civil rights without the possibility of appeal (Griffin 2017). Advocates for these provisions believe that imposing elements of the adversarial system, such as legal representation, on traditional courts is unwarranted given the different dispute resolution processes used there and that doing so would "irrevocably change the very nature of conducting business in customary courts and rob the system of customary dispute resolution of many of its virtues" (Mokgoro 2002:24). Opponents argued that there was insufficient public consultation as the provisions were developed and that without careful attention to ensuring that traditional courts protected constitutional rights, individuals could face significant harm (Iyi 2016). In particular, traditional courts have severely limited women's participation. In many instances, women are prohibited from hearing cases or even presenting their own cases to the courts (Koyana 2011; Williams and Klusener 2013), though the reform legislation has sought to increase women's representation on tribal councils.

A new effort was introduced in 2017. The 2017 Traditional Courts Bill was developed through a process of consultation and is designed to retain traditional courts without limiting the rights of tribal community members. Individuals must consent to having their case heard in a traditional court (Griffin 2017). In particular, the new bill pays special attention to ensuring that women's rights are protected. While lawyers are still not permitted to practice in traditional courts, participants in cases can bring anyone they choose with them to provide assistance, much as is the practice in mediation and other forms of alternative dispute resolution (Griffin 2017). Additionally, the 2017 bill permits appeals when court procedures are not followed.

Many obstacles still remain, including a lack of individuals trained to understand and interpret traditional legal practices (Xueguan 2017). More importantly, the bill remains under consideration by the South African parliament over a year after its introduction. Critics on both sides continue to argue that the bill does not go far enough—on the one hand, it still does not provide all the procedural rights and protections of the noncustomary court system, while on the other, it does not hew closely enough to tradition to satisfy those committed to maintaining tribal practices.

The continuing debate about the role and practices of traditional courts in South Africa highlights just how difficult it is to navigate the complexities of mixed systems. In mixed systems, competing intellectual frameworks, models of justice, and sets of fundamental rights must be balanced as procedures are developed. For example, the South African case highlights conflicts between the right to perpetuate particular cultural traditions and the right to legal representation (Iyi 2016), as well as women's rights to serve in a presiding role in dispute resolution procedures and to be treated equally in relation to issues of marital relationships, child custody, and sexual violence (Williams and Klusener 2013). To Barbara Oomen (2005:23), these debates highlight "the predetermined mismatch between the fluidity of culture and the rigidity of law."

There are ways to preserve traditional dispute resolution practices without abandoning protections for legal rights and equal treatment. Incorporating legal protections for human rights and membership in regional human rights courts (to be discussed in chapter 10), reforming both formal and traditional legal systems to remove discriminatory provisions without fundamentally changing traditional cultural practices, and encouraging mass participation in rethinking norms and practices can all provide more acceptable and lasting mechanisms for change (Ndulo 2011).

in many settings dealing with young people, such as schools and youth courts, and some programs have tried using them on a voluntary basis for more serious adult crimes. The evidence suggests that for those who choose them, restorative justice approaches may provide a greater sense of closure and more opportunity for reparations than modern trials do (Koss, Bachar, and Hopkins 2003), but this evidence has been collected only in contexts where participating in the restorative justice process is voluntary.

Mediation can also be found in contexts that do not draw on restorative justice, where it is one of a variety of types of **alternative dispute resolution**, or ADR. ADR is a catchall phrase for any method of dispute resolution that takes place outside of formal courtroom **adjudication**. Another common type of ADR is **arbitration**, a process in which a third party hears about the dispute from those involved and issues a decision, often binding on the parties, but without a full courtroom process. While ADR processes often draw on mechanisms found in traditional dispute resolution, these mechanisms have been developed not due to their traditional role but rather to provide alternatives to the courts and to reduce caseloads.

Dispute Resolution under Authoritarianism

Authoritarian governments may permit for the existence of dispute resolution systems for managing the kinds of routine disputes that occur between people in everyday life, such as divorce cases or arguments about property ownership. In such cases, state interests are less likely to be implicated, and there is less opportunity for the dispute to morph into a challenge to state power. Where such systems exist, they generally mimic the procedures of civil law, follow religious guidelines, or maintain traditional practices. But not all authoritarian governments provide this sort of option, as any opportunity for disputing does bring with it the potential that grievances relevant to the state may be raised.

For other kinds of issues—any issue that involves the state, whether it be a criminal accusation, an argument over state policy, or an instance of activism—authoritarian states do not provide for true dispute resolution. They may entirely foreclose the expression of grievances, arranging for those who dissent or who are accused of crimes to be summarily imprisoned or executed or to simply disappear. Alternatively, many authoritarian states use **show trials**. Show trials are highly public trials that have at their base dramaturgical, political, and/or educational functions rather than a concern with finding the truth or resolving a dispute. They may be structured much as a trial would be in an adversarial, inquisitorial, or theocratic system, with the accused granted a lawyer and a hearing in front of a judge, but the result—including the sentence—is typically predetermined. It is important to remember that show trials coexist, in most authoritarian countries, with "regular" trial procedures free from predetermined outcomes. Most authoritarian countries wish to appear as if they adhere to global governance norms, and thus many are committed to maintaining the pretense of having real dispute resolution systems in which people can seek justice.

Lawyers and judges in authoritarian systems play somewhat different roles than they do in other types of countries. Most notably, the judiciary is not independent. It is subject to political control by a state apparatus that is able to interfere in judgments. In many cases, the prosecutor has more power than the judge, given that the prosecutor determines the charges and then, in a show trial environment, the judge is tasked with acting upon them. While defendants may be granted a lawyer, the lawyer's role in the courtroom and the defendant's ability to mount a defense are typically limited. Instead, the case is likely to focus on the presentation of evidence of guilt and then a sentencing hearing, where the lawyer may be permitted to present mitigation evidence. However, lawyers in authoritarian societies who defend those accused of political crimes or who deviate from the expected narrative may find themselves under surveillance or criminal investigation and may ultimately end up facing punishment for their work on their clients' behalf (Liu and Halliday 2016).

CRIMINAL PROCEDURE IN COMPARATIVE PERSPECTIVE

Now that we have covered the basic parameters of dispute resolution in different legal systems, we can dive deeper into some of the elements of criminal procedure. While it is easiest for comparative legal scholars to establish what the official rules are, it is important to remember that the official rules are not always the best guide to what really happens in any given country. Countries may not have the resources or capacities to enforce the rules and to guarantee rights, or they may choose to disobey their own legal guidelines. Nonetheless, it is worth discussing some of the key issues that arise in comparing criminal court systems.

Fairness and Impartiality

Most countries claim that their dispute resolution systems are fair, with impartial (unbiased) judges who assess each claim on its merits. In common law systems, juries are supposed to be impartial, while in civil law systems without juries, it would only be the judges whose impartiality matters. In authoritarian systems, no such principles of fairness can be assumed, and in traditional legal systems, those tasked with dispute resolution may have obvious biases toward their own tribe. Of course, all people have biases, so it may be unreasonable to expect that any tribunal is truly impartial. But in some cases, it is not even possible to determine what sort of bias may exist. For example, after the mass murder of judges by Colombian drug cartels, Colombia enacted a system in which judges remained behind one-way glass, had their voices electronically distorted, and were known only by numbers (Luna 2004). This system was designed to protect judges, but it surely could have enabled the introduction of biases that would be hard to detect.

The Presumption of Innocence

In the United States, those suspected of committing a crime are considered innocent until proven guilty beyond a reasonable doubt, a standard inherited from the British common law. Such a standard is found in many legal systems around the world. However, some legal scholars argue that in civil law systems, the presumption should more accurately be understood as a presumption of not-guilt, or perhaps as no presumption at all. What is the difference? Well, in inquisitorial courts, the fact that the investigation and the trial are so intertwined means that if there were truly no evidence to suggest guilt in a given case, the case ought to be closed. Of course, prosecutors in the United States are also supposed to drop cases if there is no evidence to support a conviction, so perhaps the systems are not as different as they might at first appear. In contrast, authoritarian courts may undertake proceedings with the presumption of guilt, as in the case of show trials.

One additional issue raised by the presumption of innocence is the issue of pretrial detention. In some cases, individuals are incarcerated while awaiting trial, sometimes for lengthy periods that can be as long or longer than the customary sentence for the crime they are accused of committing. In such cases, it can be difficult to understand how it is possible to claim that the presumption of innocence is operating. And these cases are not unusual. The International Centre for Prison Studies estimates that 2.5 million people worldwide are in pretrial detention at any given time, and in some countries, more than two thirds of people imprisoned have not yet stood trial (Walmsley 2014). Figures are over 20 percent in the United States, South Korea, and many European countries. In the Netherlands, for example, 47 percent of those imprisoned are awaiting trial.

Evidentiary Rules

All formal dispute resolution systems have a variety of rules about what sorts of evidence can be presented and under what conditions. For example, as noted above, Shari'a courts emphasize confessions and eyewitness statements and find other types of evidence (such as circumstantial evidence, which is evidence that supports facts underlying the case rather than directly demonstrating the guilt or innocence of the accused) much less important—if they permit them at all. Many countries prohibit evidence gathered through torture. The United States is generally considered to have the broadest set of protections, called the **exclusionary rule**, against the improper use of evidence. Under the exclusionary rule, evidence that has been collected in such a way as to violate the rights of a criminal suspect is not permitted in court, as it is "the fruit of the poisonous tree," in Supreme Court Justice Felix Frankfurter's words (*Nardone v. United States* 1939). However, there are a variety of exceptions to the exclusionary rule. First, it prohibits only evidence that has been illegally obtained by law enforcement or other state agents, not that obtained by a private person—a standard that has led to numerous legal debates about when informants are working for the state versus taking their own initiative. Second, evidence is excluded only if obtaining it violates a criminal defendant's rights, not if it violates the rights of third parties, and rights are limited for certain categories of people, such as noncitizens when evidence is obtained out of the country; people currently under criminal justice supervision (jail, prison, probation, parole, etc.); and border crossers. Finally, if a court determines that evidence gathered illegally would have been inevitably discovered later on through another (legal) search, it can be admitted.

The exclusionary rule is important in the United States legal system because of the decentralized nature of law enforcement (as discussed in chapter 5), which means there is no way to compel law enforcement agencies to respect the legal rights of suspects other than to provide a strong negative incentive such that if they do not follow the rules, a conviction may not be possible. In other countries, violations of suspects' rights are more apt to be dealt with through centralized discipline of law enforcement officers (or, in some cases, ignored). Courts in such circumstances use various kinds of balancing tests (Luna 2004) to determine whether to admit unlawfully obtained evidence, admitting it when the harm it may cause to justice seems lesser than the harm of excluding it. Balancing tests tend to mean that unlawfully obtained evidence is more likely to be included in cases of severe crimes; when the evidence is credible; and when the legal violation is accidental or technical rather than willfully abusive.

Confessions and Self-Incrimination

One key form of evidence is the confession, and legal systems vary considerably in terms of how much weight they give to confessions and how much protection they provide against self-incrimination (often called the right to silence). In most common and civil law countries, those who are arrested are read some kind of warning noting that they have the right to remain silent, such as the Miranda warning in the United States. In the United States, courts and judges are not permitted to make any conclusions from the fact that a suspect has elected to exercise this right to silence, though of course in reality some do. Furthermore, the plea bargaining process in the United States encourages many people to confess to spare themselves the hassle and expense of a trial, sometimes even when they are not actually guilty. Yet in the United States, the fact that suspects have the right to silence means that confessions are given considerable weight. When individuals confess due to coercion, deception, or other factors and later withdraw their confessions, the original confession is presented at trial, and jurors tend to be quite likely to believe it.

Other nations go much further than the United States does in protecting the right against self-incrimination by extending it to noncustody circumstances. For instance, in Germany, the right against self-incrimination extends to whenever there is danger of incrimination, not just when the accused is in official police custody. In addition, incrimination of family members is also covered (in the United States, only spouses have such protections), oaths to tell the truth are not administered, and the limits on deception in interrogations are more stringent. An even stronger protection against self-incrimination was found historically in *halakha* (Jewish religious law). While there are no courts today applying *halakha* to criminal matters, when such courts did exist, self-incrimination was strictly prohibited (Levine 2006). In other words, suspects could not be punished on the basis of a confession, no matter what.

In most countries, courts *can* draw inferences from a defendant's decision to remain silent. The right to silence may also be subject to various limitations. In France, for instance, the accused has the right to silence during investigations before the official beginning of the trial but can be compelled to speak at the trial itself. Remember, though, that inquisitorial courts typically do not require the swearing of oaths at trial, so perjury concerns do not apply to those who wish to lie to protect themselves. Thus, French suspects who speak at trial need not fear perjury charges.

More extreme examples of limitations on the right to silence are found in authoritarian countries, where the suspect must answer questions and typically may not consult a defense attorney until after the interrogation has ended. In some countries, torture is used to extract confessions. This occurs despite the fact that empirical evidence shows confessions extracted by torture are extremely unreliable—people experiencing torture will say whatever their torturers want to hear to make the pain stop (Scarry 1985). And this practice is not uncommon—the nongovernmental organization Amnesty International (2014), which fights to reduce torture, received reports of torture in 141 countries between January 2009 and May 2013. Given the importance of confession in Shari'a law, some Islamic jurists have interpreted the law as permitting deception, psychological pressure, and even limited physical force, and in practice, many countries operating under Shari'a law have used torture to extract confessions. However, Shari'a criminal procedure guidelines permit the accused, in some circumstances, to withdraw his or her confession at any time, even up until the moment before the sentence is to be carried out (Zakariyah 2010). If the confession is withdrawn, the sentence cannot go forward unless eyewitnesses are available.

The Right to Counsel

While court systems may claim that participants in dispute resolution processes have all kinds of rights, those claims are of limited value without a system for ensuring that they are protected. The main way that the rights of participants are protected is through their representation by counsel (another word for lawyers). Most common and civil law countries provide for some kind of right to counsel, while such a right is less likely to exist in other families of law. Under Shari'a law, for example, lawyers do not play an important role in trial proceedings, though participants may be permitted to bring an advisor, who may be a lawyer or a family member, with them.

But the fact that a dispute resolution process provides for the right to counsel does not tell us very much about how that right works in practice, as the right to counsel can mean many different things. For instance, does the right to counsel mean simply that the court will not prevent a participant in a dispute resolution process from bringing a lawyer with them, or does it mean that the state must provide and pay for the lawyer? If the state must provide a lawyer, is this only when asked, or is it the obligation of the state to provide a lawyer in all circumstances? What if the person to be represented by counsel objects to the lawyer who has been provided, or to having any lawyer at all—should the state still insist that it is in that individual's best interest to be represented? In criminal cases, at what juncture in the case must the lawyer be provided—upon questioning, upon arrest, or only when the trial is soon to begin? Must the lawyer be competent—or even awake during the trial? Can the court draw inferences about likely guilt or responsibility due to the presence of a lawyer? And finally, does this right extend to all kinds of disputes, or only to criminal cases, or only to the most severe accusations?

Countries that claim to protect the right to counsel can come to very different conclusions about these questions. Furthermore, while nearly all countries today articulate a right to counsel, the articulation of that right does not mean that everyone who must go to court does so while being represented by a lawyer. A United Nations survey of 105 countries at all levels of economic development found that there is wide variation in the extent to which counsel is provided, and in some cases recognition of the right to counsel is a very recent development (United Nations Development Programme 2016). Budgetary allocations for legal representation also vary widely, from as little as pennies per year per capita in Kazakhstan and Ghana to over US$34 per year per capita in Finland. Even among the wealthiest countries, a substantial portion of legal assistance is paid for by nongovernmental actors (United Nations Development Programme 2016). However, all countries that responded to the survey stated that the right to counsel in their court systems included representation in criminal courts.

Some countries provide for the right to counsel in only the most severe criminal cases. For example, Indonesia provides for lawyers for those who could be sentenced to death or to at least fifteen years in prison, and in Pakistan lawyers are provided only when a convicted person is appealing a sentence of death (Flores 2014). Where the right to counsel is guaranteed, some countries further obligate themselves to provide lawyers in specific types of cases. Those involving the potential sentence of death or where children or people with intellectual disabilities are accused of crimes are most likely to invoke such an obligation (United Nations Development Programme 2016). Furthermore, the right to counsel is much more likely to be enforced during trial than at pretrial stages or during an appeal. Even where state-funded legal representation is available, it may not cover the full cost of representation (United Nations Development Programme 2016).

A guaranteed right to counsel in noncriminal cases is much less common. While many governments make at least some provision for funding legal aid services for those who cannot afford lawyers, that aid may be severely limited, and only those who have the most meritorious cases or who are lucky may have access. However, some countries have made a stronger commitment to providing for the right to counsel in civil cases. The European Union Court of Human Rights has ruled that at least in some circumstances, lawyers must be provided for litigants in noncriminal cases (*Airey v. Ireland* 1979). Brazil has an extensive system of legal aid centers, which provide both legal representation and access to social services, while Ireland provides legal aid for civil, family, and refugee cases (Flores 2014). In contrast, while nonprofit legal services organizations exist throughout the United States, their limited funding means they can provide only limited representation of clients. Individuals facing civil lawsuits, litigating family disputes like those involving divorce or child custody, or who are at risk of deportation by immigration authorities must find their own lawyer if they are to be represented by counsel. Most countries that do not provide for the provision of counsel, though, do still guarantee the right of those involved in litigation to bring their own privately hired lawyers into court. It is common for countries to use some kind of means test before providing a lawyer, such as limiting a monthly or yearly income, a maximum asset limit, or both, or using sliding scales to assess fees. These limits are much more prevalent in the cases of noncriminal legal aid, but some countries enforce them in criminal contexts as well.

Where individuals without financial resources do not have guaranteed access to noncriminal legal aid, one alternative is for them to hire private lawyers on a **contingency fee** basis. In these cases, lawyers get paid a proportion of the money they recover for their clients (and do not get paid if they do not recover any money). This method of funding lawsuits is especially common in the United States; it is less common in many other countries, since the United States is one of the few countries in which the loser in a lawsuit is not expected to contribute to or cover the legal fees for the other side. Where fees are paid by the loser, the court typically determines what the loser must pay. Such systems may encourage those who are filing suits to have more reasonable expectations about their winnings, but they also lessen access to the legal system for many.

There are a variety of models for providing access to counsel. In some countries, governments pay for lawyers who specialize in providing counsel to those who cannot otherwise afford it. In others, private lawyers are assigned to take on cases, either as part of a systematic process or as needed. Alternatively, states can contract with private organizations to run programs providing access to counsel (United Nations Development Programme 2016). Over 40 percent of the nations that responded to the United Nations survey mentioned above use combinations of two or more of these systems.

Other Factors

There are a variety of other elements of criminal procedure that vary across nations. Indeed, if this entire book consisted of nothing but a discussion of comparative criminal procedure, it would still not contain enough pages to cover everything legal scholars consider important.

The Trials of Amanda Knox

How different are adversarial and inquisitorial systems really? The case of Amanda Knox, a young college student from the United States who was tried for murder while studying abroad in Italy, gave many court-watchers in both countries the chance to understand in much more detail how their countries' respective court and trial systems diverged. This case captivated news-watchers around the world due to its attractive young protagonist.

In 2007, Amanda Knox was a college student at the University of Washington studying abroad in Perugia, Italy. She, her Italian boyfriend Raffaele Sollecito, and another man were arrested for the murder and sexual assault of her British roommate, Meredith Kercher. Each of the three suspects entered a plea of innocence, with Knox and Sollecito arguing that they had not been in Knox and Kercher's apartment, where the crime took place, on the night of the murder (Bassiouni 2014). They were convicted in 2009 and sentenced to more than twenty years in prison, based in large part on the testimony of witnesses who had seen them in the neighborhood and on the fact that their DNA was found on several items, including a knife ultimately determined *not* to have been the murder weapon. Knox filed an appeal, and in 2011 the Appeals Court of Assizes in Perugia acquitted her of murder based on a reassessment of the evidence but upheld a conviction for slander that was imposed after she accused another man of committing the murder. In 2013, the prosecution filed an appeal to the Court of Cassation, the highest criminal appeals court in Italy. It sent the case to the Appeals Court of Assizes in Florence for reconsideration, and in 2014 this court reinstated Knox's murder conviction (Head 2014). However, by this time Knox had returned to the United States, so she was con-

victed in absentia. This new conviction was further appealed to the Court of Cassation, which acquitted Knox in 2015.

Confused yet? Well, there are several important differences in criminal procedure and court process between Italy and the United States that might explain why. First of all, in the United States, the principle of double jeopardy means that the same individual cannot be tried twice for the same offense, and thus prosecutors are prohibited from appealing acquittals. In Italy, no such principle applies, and prosecutors are free to appeal (Bassiouni 2014). Because of the potential for a long sequence of such appeals and retrials, commentators on the Italian justice system argue that criminal cases are never "satisfyingly, convincingly resolved"; instead, people debate the guilt or innocence of the accused for many years (T. Jones 2011). Civil and criminal trials can also proceed through the court system together (Mirabella 2012), such that evidence that would not be permissible in a criminal case but that is part of a related civil case may be presented to the single panel of judges hearing both matters.

Furthermore, the Italian justice system is profoundly overloaded. The Court of Cassation hears over 80,000 appeals per year—in comparison, the U.S. Supreme Court hears fewer than 150—and, on average, it takes almost five years to conclude a criminal case in Italy (Moody and Landucci 2012). Italian courts do not provide for plea bargains, so they have no mechanisms to speed up cases and lighten their loads. In addition, Italian prosecutors are required to prosecute all cases that come to them—only judges can dismiss cases (Mirabella 2012).

Another reason why the Knox case, and Italian criminal justice in general, can be confusing is that, as legal scholar John Head argues, legal reforms in Italy have involved "transplanting" elements of the common law adversarial process into an entrenched civil law system (Head 2014). Italy's 1930 Code of Criminal Procedure enshrined a classic inquisitorial process. Lawyers were not even permitted to directly question witnesses—all questions had to be asked by the judge (Head 2014). The reform process, which began in the 1980s and was heavily inspired by the U.S. legal system (Mirabella 2012), introduced a second judge to supervise pretrial procedure so that investigations could be formally separated from trials, ensuring that trial judges would not have undue familiarity with the evidence and that prosecutors are no longer part of the judiciary.

However, the complexity of these changes means that legal observers may have difficulty understanding how the mixed system works in practice. For example, despite the adversarial features of cases, judges still evaluate evidence holistically, meaning that an accused person can be found guilty based on a volume of circumstantial evidence even when much of the evidence, taken piece by piece, is suspicious (Duncan 2017). Other elements of the inquisitorial system that have been retained include judicial questioning of witnesses during trial as well as the lack of oaths, which in common law courts open defendants to the potential of a perjury charge if they are not truthful (Mirabella 2012). This hybrid model also highlights the different implicit goals in adversarial and inquisitorial trials. Inquisitorial trial procedure is designed to seek the truth of whatever events the trial is investigating and pursuing. While adversarial trials are also concerned with truth, they are fundamentally organized around the idea of a contest or competition, one occurring based on a series of rules and principles established to ensure a level playing field for both sides. Thinking about it this way, it is clear why the exclusionary rule would make sense in an adversarial context, and the new Italian hybrid system indeed incorpo-

rates elements of the exclusionary rule. Yet the emphasis on fact finding that is central to the inquisitorial system remains, and thus even some evidence that is formally excluded may be seen by the judges (Mirabella 2012).

Many American viewers thus followed the case due to their perception that a young American woman was being mistreated by a court system that did not provide appropriate legal protections, such as a prohibition on double jeopardy and a strong exclusionary rule. The fact that juries in U.S. courts are not asked to explain the basis for their verdicts while judges in Italy must do so also contributed to American viewers' sense of discomfort with the outcome of the trials (Mirabella 2012). Moreover, Knox signed several confessions, confessions she later argued were false and coerced, and this outraged American court-watchers, though it is important to note here that false confessions are far more common in the U.S. justice system than most people realize (Crane, Nirider, and Drizin 2016; Starr 2013). As legal scholar Julia Mirabella (2012) argues, Americans may have contrasted their idealized views about American justice with the reality of the Italian system, ignoring what actually goes on in U.S. courts and insisting that to be considered just, the Italian system should directly replicate American procedures. Such discourses are further intensified by Americans' lack of education about the trial procedures routinely found in other countries, including a common unfounded belief that inquisitorial systems rely on torture or other violations of rights in order to seek convictions.

In contrast, Italian viewers watched because they saw a suspect who did not follow the rules of their society. Knox did not dress, express emotions, manage her sexuality, or interact with the legal authorities in the ways Italians would expect of a young woman. Indeed, the Italian news media frequently showcased what they saw as outrageous courtroom fashion choices, such as an oversized

T-shirt reading "All You Need Is Love," which American viewers might think understandable (if ill-advised) on a young defendant (Duncan 2017). Stories also focused on Knox's sexual and social behavior, highlighting her personal liberation in ways that contrasted it starkly with the conservative culture in Perugia (Duncan 2017). To Italian viewers, accustomed to the complex, hybrid process and lengthy trials that characterize their system, what was unique about the Amanda Knox case was its exotic, foreign suspect—while to American viewers, the suspect was a person they could relate to, and nothing else about the case made sense.

To put a final spin on this case, in January 2019, the European Court of Human Rights held that Amanda Knox had not been granted a fair trial (N. Chan 2019). In particular, it held that she was denied legal assistance and was not provided with access to a translator in addition to not being fully informed of the nature of the charges she faced. Amanda Knox had also alleged that the Italian police had violated a provision of the European Human Rights Convention prohibiting torture, but the European Court of Human Rights determined that there was insufficient evidence to support this allegation. The court ordered Italy to pay Amanda Knox nearly US$20,000 in compensation for the damages and costs she experienced. The saga should now be at its end, over a decade after it began.

A few additional elements are worth mentioning:

- Statutes of limitations, or guidelines on how long after a criminal offense occurs a suspect can be put on trial;
- Speedy trial rules, or guidelines on how long the accused can be asked to wait after being charged and before his or her trial concludes;
- The conditions under which criminal convictions can be appealed, either by someone who has been convicted or by the prosecution;
- Whether someone who has been tried for a crime and found not guilty can be tried again, also known as double jeopardy; and
- Whether it is permissible to put an individual on trial for an act that was not legally a crime at the time it was committed but that was later criminalized (the impropriety of doing this is one of the principles of fairness in criminal procedure that has the widest agreement around the world).

CONCLUSION

This chapter has highlighted many of the differences we can find in the way formal dispute resolution systems work across countries. But studying those differences may not answer our most fundamental question: What, in the end, do courts accomplish in their role managing dispute resolution? Sometimes, not much. In Merry's (1979) study of the multiethnic urban housing project,

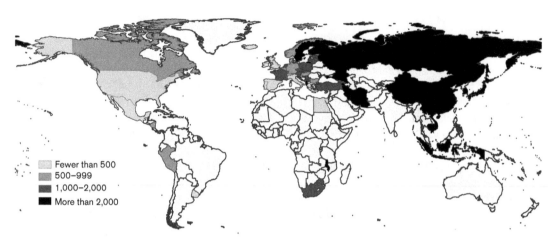

Map 15 People per lawyer, most recent data available, 2005–2010 (Michelson 2018).

mentioned earlier in this chapter, she found that courts sometimes function more as a mechanism enabling harassment by those who cannot or will not resolve their disputes with violence rather than as a real way to resolve disputes. This is in large part due to the fact that court processes force all disputes into the narrow parameters created by procedural and substantive law, which does not leave room to engage with the full range of emotional issues a dispute may entail. Thus, even those who pursue the court process and get a just result may feel that their voice was erased by the proceedings.

Given these limitations, why do people choose to use courts to resolve their disputes? Well, in our complex modern society, especially where the parties to a dispute do not have overlapping social ties and connections to other social institutions that might help them work things out, courts may be the only option available. And they tend to be the best option in certain circumstances, such as when public accountability is desired and when disputes touch on aspects of law or government policy. Scholarship on the legal profession has found that the volume of legal work in a society is related to its level of economic development, the complexity of the local legal system (with more lawyers needed in common law countries than in civil law ones), and the availability of nonlegal or extralegal forms of dispute resolution and social control (Rueschemeyer 1987).

Some scholars and commentators have argued that these explanations do not go far enough and that additional factors shaping the turn to litigation include litigious culture, as will be discussed in chapter 11, and the presence of lawyers (who, it might be argued, can manufacture demand for more lawyers). This line of argument tends to especially focus on the high number of lawyers available in the United States in comparison with certain other advanced economies, such as Japan. In 2010, the most recent year for which data is available,

Figure 15 Adolf Eichmann stands as he is sentenced to death, December 15, 1961 (Israel Government Print Office 1961).

there were 4,427 people per lawyer in Japan, while in the United States, the figure was 297 (map 15 shows the number of people per lawyer in countries around the world). However, the number of lawyers per capita does not necessarily correlate with litigation rates (Ramseyer and Rasmusen 2010), and as discussed above, in some countries, like Japan, some legal tasks are performed by legally trained personnel who are not classified as lawyers, limiting the comparability of this data.

The narrow nature of conventional dispute resolution processes becomes even more clear when confronted with grievances of the most enormous magnitude, such as genocide (defined in chapter 4). To take one example, consider the trial of Adolf Eichmann. Eichmann was a Nazi official who was personally responsible for managing the deportation of Jewish and Roma people from across Europe to the death camps during the Holocaust. After the end of World War II, Eichmann escaped to Argentina, where he lived under an assumed name until he was abducted by the Mossad (the Israeli foreign intelligence agency) and brought back to stand trial in Israel. His trial in 1961, shown in figure 15, is commonly claimed to have been the first in the world to be shown on television, and it provided a spectacle worthy of the medium. Over one hundred witnesses testified, while Eichmann spent the trial in a glass booth with two guards due to the risk of an attempt on his life. At the trial's conclusion, Eichmann was found guilty. After his hanging, he was cremated, and his ashes were scattered at sea.

Despite the magnitude of evidence of Eichmann's guilt, commentators agree that the trial had many of the elements of a show trial, as it was constructed for dramaturgical and cathartic purposes rather than the search for the truth. But they disagree about what the implications of this fact are. Hannah Arendt, who covered the trial for the *New Yorker,* argued that the "purpose of a trial is to render justice, and nothing else; even the noblest of ulterior purposes . . . can only detract from the law's main business: to weigh the charges brought against the accused, to render judgement, and to mete out due punishment" (Arendt 1963:253), and in this light, Arendt considered the Eichmann trial "seriously impaired" (274) due to its focus on providing world lessons rather than rendering justice. In contrast, legal scholar Lawrence Douglas argues that genocide trials play an important role in providing a space for survivors to testify to their experiences and as a place for the creation of an official historical narrative (Douglas 2005). He agrees with Arendt that trials like Eichmann's may serve political purposes, but says that despite their flaws, and as long as they attend to procedural norms, such trials can "become a powerful forum for understanding and commemorating traumatic history" (Douglas 2005:182). What this scholarly argument highlights is exactly how limited legal proceedings are in cases like Eichmann's, cases where the magnitude of the harm done vastly outstrips the capacity of courts and states to dispense justice.

In more recent times, new approaches to justice have been developed in postgenocide societies that attempt to resolve these limitations. Under the umbrella of **transitional justice**, these approaches emphasize individual dignity, acknowledge and redress harms, and work to prevent future atrocities (International Center for Transitional Justice 2018). Transitional justice mechanisms include a combination of criminal prosecution, fact-finding commissions, reparations, and political and legal reform, incorporating broad participation by marginalized and excluded groups. But as valuable as these approaches are, they may still fall short, as formal dispute resolutions mechanisms always may when confronted with crimes of such magnitude.

And of course, it is not only in cases of genocide that courts fall short. Think about the drawing at the very beginning of this chapter, the one of a pig and her piglets on trial. This pig family was blamed for murdering and eating a child in 1457 (Chambers 1869). The mother pig was executed, though the piglets were spared due to their youth and an absence of evidence of their involvement. Perhaps the neighbors were relieved that the marauding pig would not be back for more. But did the court process in this case really resolve the dispute? Well, the grieving human family did not get their child back, and there is no evidence that the court case even convinced the pig's owner to build better fences to prevent events like this from recurring. Instead, what this court case may have done was provide the village with a chance for vengeance and a sense of justice—subjects at the core of chapter 7's discussion of punishment.

Punishment and Social Control

CHAPTER GOALS

1. Understand the different goals and motivations for punishment and be able to infer which goals and motivations are likely to have shaped particular punishment systems.
2. Become familiar with the historical development of and modern variation in punishment practices.
3. Evaluate different factors shaping punishment and sentencing policy cross-nationally.

In a prison in Bangkok, Thailand, prisoners were once sealed into a rattan ball lined with nails (Thuan 2017), as shown in figure 16. The ball was then given to elephants for their afternoon recreation. Until the Bangkok Corrections Museum closed, around 2015, visitors could see a model of this punishment device on display. What led Thai correctional authorities to develop this unique punishment? Undoubtedly, the availability of elephants had something to do with it, but of course that explanation is incomplete—elephants roam many countries in Asia and Africa without taking on a role as soccer-playing tormenters.

We use the term **"punishment"** to refer to a wide variety of actions, including those within as well as outside the legal system, designed to provide penalties in response to

Figure 16 Thai "elephant ball" punishment
(illustration by Sam Art, 2018).

perceived wrongdoing by others. Thus, giving a kindergartener a time-out for screaming too loudly is a punishment, just as is a long prison sentence or being assigned to serve as an elephant's soccer ball. Sometimes, people refer to punishments as **sanctions**.

In this chapter, you will learn about various types of punishment that have been used at different points in history and in different places around the world. You will also learn about some of the many reasons why this variation occurs. As you begin reading, take a moment to think about the system of punishment in the country you are most familiar with. How does punishment in this country compare to punishment in other countries? Is it harsh and punitive, or is it focused on helping people avoid crime in the future? Which types of penalties are most common? What do you think most people in this country believe is the goal or purpose of punishment? And why do you think this country has the type of punishment system it does?

WHY DO SOCIETIES PUNISH?

If you ask someone why societies develop punishment systems, most people would say that punishment exists to reduce wrongdoing—in other words, that we punish to prevent or stop people from doing things that we as a society would prefer that they not do. The wrongdoing that punishment is designed to limit includes crime, but it can also include many other types of wrongs,

Table 7   Types of social control

	Direct	Indirect
Formal	Police presence in a public park that causes drug dealers to take their business elsewhere.	Not drinking in your dorm room with the door closed because you understand it is against the rules on your college campus.
Informal	Getting a new pair of jeans after all your friends told you your old pair was out of style.	Washing your hands when you use the bathroom, even though no one else is there.

ranging from social faux pas to acts seen as contrary to religious or moral guidelines.

In a broader sense, social scientists call efforts to ensure compliance and conformity with values, norms, and rules of behavior **social control**. Punishment meted out by a legal system is part of the system of **formal social control**, which is social control that comes from the law or other codes of rules and regulations. In contrast, **informal social control** is social control maintained outside of rules and regulations through social norms, stigma, and other elements of social life. Social control can be direct or indirect. **Direct social control** is maintained by obvious or overt power. For example, when you are driving on the highway and see a police cruiser's blinking lights, you most likely slow down immediately to comply with a speed limit you were probably ignoring just seconds before. **Indirect social control** involves the internalization of norms or expectations for behavior, so that compliance occurs even in the absence of any clear mechanism of enforcement. Table 7 provides examples of these types of social control.

While all punishment is part of a system of social control designed to reduce the likelihood that people will engage in wrongdoing, punishments can be designed to achieve a variety of different goals and purposes, often more than one at the same time. Among the goals and justifications of punishments and punishment systems are:

1. Deterrence and crime control
2. Revenge and retribution
3. Rehabilitation
4. Reconciliation

Deterrence and Crime Control

When people talk about legal punishment, they most often use the language of **deterrence**. Deterrence entails getting someone not to do something because they fear the consequences of that act. To understand deterrence on the most basic level, think about why you do not put your hand down on a stove burner;

you avoid doing so because you know that the burner is very hot and would burn you, and you do not want to experience that consequence. Many punishments are designed with the idea of deterrence in mind. Lawmakers and others who design punishment systems create penalties that they believe will make potential offenders think twice about carrying out an act of wrongdoing. Deterrence-based policies can focus on deterring people in general from engaging in wrongdoing, but they can also be more focused, as in systems where punishments are designed to reduce the likelihood that someone will become a repeat offender.

For a punishment to have a deterrent effect, the potential wrongdoer must perceive the cost of that punishment as worse than the benefits they might gain from committing the offense. For example, imagine you are looking for a parking spot for the afternoon and have a choice between a place you could safely but illegally park for free near your destination or a parking lot a few blocks away that charges $10 an hour to park. If you could park in the illegal spot and risk a fine of $25, you might very well take the spot and risk the fine. It might even be less than what you would have paid to park in the lot! But what if you faced having your car towed? Or the loss of your driver's license? Or a prison sentence? However, those same sentences might not seem so bad if you were stealing money to pay for lifesaving medical treatment for your small child.

What these examples highlight is that while more severe punishments do have a stronger deterrent effect, severity is not everything. In fact, punishments may be more likely to deter when they are *certain* than when they are *severe* (D. Kennedy 2009; Kleiman 2009). If a potential offender believes that the likelihood that he or she will ever be caught is low, then the severity of the punishment may not matter. But a certain punishment, even if that punishment is relatively light, can present a much bigger deterrent—especially if the punishment is likely to be carried out soon after the offense. A third element that shapes the deterrent effects of punishments is salience, or the extent to which potential offenders are conscious of the punishment they face. Without this consciousness, severity and certainty can have no effect at all. Authorities sometimes work to increase both salience and certainty by using **surveillance**, or close and constant monitoring of people or spaces. Examples of surveillance include video monitoring, GPS tracking, logging the websites people visit, and telephone wiretaps, all practices law enforcement agencies—and sometimes private actors—use in various countries to keep watch over targeted individuals or entire populations. It is important to note here that surveillance—and social control more broadly—are not used only to deter or respond to crime. They are also used as tools of repression by many societies. A more detailed exploration of surveillance is beyond the scope of this text, though its role as a tool of social control and repression will be further discussed in chapter 9.

Even a punishment scheme designed to take full advantage of certainty, salience, and severity may not have a deterrent effect, however. This is because not all offenses and offenders are equally deterrable. Many potential offenders feel invincible, while others assume some kind of punishment will be inevitable. In both cases, potential punishments are not likely to reshape behavior. In addition, deterrence can work only when potential offenders think carefully about the cost-benefit tradeoffs implied by their plans. If offenders are impulsive or if they are offending for emotional reasons like revenge, deterrence may not work.

In circumstances where deterrence is less effective or where there are difficulties in creating a punishment policy likely to deter offenses (such as where law enforcement resources make it hard to raise the certainty of punishment), policymakers may instead turn to **incapacitation**. Incapacitation refers to punishments that are carried out simply to prevent offenders from committing future offenses, such as extremely long prison sentences or the death penalty. While such punishments might seem very severe, they are severe not because the severity might discourage other offenders but rather because the severity simply keeps the offender away from the opportunity to reoffend. When incapacitation takes the form of very long prison sentences, it is sometimes called **warehousing**.

Revenge and Retribution

In other cases, policymakers' arguments about punishment do not focus on the goal of reducing crime. Instead, they focus on the fact that offenders need to suffer for what they have done. At its most fundamental level, such punishment comes from an act of revenge. **Revenge** is typically carried out by the victim of an offense or his or her family and friends. It is not about justice but rather about the direct, personal infliction of harm or injury on an offender, which may or may not be in proportion to the volume of harm the victim suffered.

In some circumstances, acts of revenge are carried out by vigilantes, actors without legal authority who take it upon themselves to inflict suffering on those they perceive as offenders. **Vigilantes** are sometimes then themselves subject to legally authorized punishment, as many societies prefer that punishments be determined with due process and legal authorization. But in other circumstances, revenge is an acceptable way to deal with victimization. Some Islamic legal systems permit revenge on behalf of victims by their family members. An interesting example can be found in the history of Iceland between the tenth and thirteenth centuries (Hadfield 2017). Early Iceland did have courts to hear disputes, but they did not have police. While victims were permitted to carry out acts of revenge without waiting for a court's decision, those who did so might themselves be considered offenders, so in most cases people took their disputes to court. The court would issue a decision awarding the right to collect compensation or inflict other consequences, and people would call on their neighbors for help in carrying out the punishment. The courts could even declare someone an outlaw, which in its most extreme version required the complainant to kill the individual who had been so declared. What is important to note about this Icelandic system is that despite the room for revenge, it was still governed by a set of legal rules and norms that people generally followed—it was not just a free-for-all.

Retribution is closely related to revenge. The difference is that rather than stemming from an individual, emotional response to an offense, retribution is a societal response to offenses, ideally meted out by a rational, impartial judge on the basis of commonly understood standards. One way to think about the difference between revenge and retribution is to see retribution as, in Andrew Oldenquist's words, "sanitized revenge" (1988:474). According to Oldenquist, sanitizing revenge, and thus converting it to retribution, requires meeting several key conditions:

- Punishments must be determined and imposed by officials who are not closely connected to the victim;
- Punishments must be predictable and consistent across comparable circumstances;
- Punishments must be determined with due process and with some emotional distance from the circumstances of the offense;
- Punishments must be determined and imposed in a ritualistic fashion that makes clear that they come from a communal (rather than individual) source; and
- Knowledge of procedures and potential sanctions must be available to the public.

While architects of retributive punishment schemes may hope that the punishments they design will have a deterrent effect, they would proceed with the punishment even if they knew it would deter no one—because the fundamental goal is to mete out justice rather than to reduce crime.

Rehabilitation

While **rehabilitation**, or a process of restoring someone to health and normal life, may not seem like a punishment, this is exactly how many societies have historically handled offenses. Like deterrence, rehabilitation is designed to reduce crime, but in this case it does so by fixing the problems that might have made people likely to commit offenses in the first place rather than by making people scared of the potential consequences of their actions. When punishment systems emphasize rehabilitation, they do so because policymakers believe that offenses occur because the people who commit them are broken or sick and that these conditions can be remedied. It is worth noting that some rehabilitative sanctions can also have a deterrent effect—for example, some drug users may seek to avoid getting sentenced to mandatory treatment.

Perhaps we are most used to thinking about mental health treatment as a form of rehabilitation. Some people commit offenses due to mental illnesses that reduce their impulse control, create anger problems, or cause them to misperceive social interactions. When these offenders are provided with therapy and/or medication, their mental health conditions may diminish or resolve, making them much less likely to commit the same offense in the future. Thus, rehabilitative programs emphasizing mental health treatment, especially psychiatric hospitalization, are common. Substance abuse treatment, including drug and alcohol rehabilitation and the provision of medications like opioid antagonists, works similarly. In many parts of the world, including the United States, some individuals are found to be unable to stand trial due to their mental health status and are subjected to rehabilitative treatments even before trial that are aimed at restoring them to a condition suitable for prosecution.

Rehabilitative systems draw on many different kinds of remedies beyond those related to mental health, though not all of these remedies are used by every rehabilitative system. Offenders may experience other kinds of health problems, such as neurological conditions, hormone imbalances, or severe pain, that spur them to commit crime and that can be reduced or resolved through proper medical care. In some cases, offenders may commit offenses simply to try to receive treatment for medical conditions—stealing medications, for example—and proper care might reduce the incentive to commit these crimes in the first place. In the United States, people have even gone as far as robbing banks in hopes of obtaining medical care in prison that that they could not afford outside (O'Rourke 2019).

In many systems, the provision of social services, education, and training are also seen as rehabilitative. Such systems view offenses as stemming from lack of resources or opportunities. As a result, they may help offenders find suitable housing or provide job training or adult education to help them develop the skills to find employment. For people who take a retributive view of punishment, providing housing and education to offenders often seems unjust—why give those who have offended against society such benefits? But research in the United States finds that prison inmates who receive appropriate education are less likely to reoffend in the future (Davis et al. 2013; Kim and Clark 2013). Similarly, homeless ex-offenders who are provided with housing and support services are less likely to reoffend (Lutze, Rosky, and Hamilton 2013), as are ex-offenders who are able to access decent employment (Uggen and Staff 2001).

In theocratic or autocratic systems, reeducation or indoctrination camps may be seen as a rehabilitative punishment. Individuals who commit offenses may be seen as political traitors who need to relearn the political and moral standards of the community. For example, in the 1970s, the Vietnamese government imprisoned many former military personnel as well as people who had worked with the American forces in reeducation camps in which they were subject to political indoctrination and forced labor. Such camps typically use extremely harsh treatments and violate human rights in pursuit of their ideological goals. Those who violate religious norms in theocratic countries may similarly be subject to efforts to restore "proper" religious thought and behavior. One might view the practice of exorcism as a kind of religious rehabilitative punishment—people have even died during exorcisms, but those around them often see the exorcism as necessary to restore their friend or relative to proper spiritual health by ridding them of demons (Friedkin 2016).

Reconciliation

A final approach to punishment is one focused on reconciling the offender with his or her community. For those concerned with **reconciliation**, the problem with an offense is not so much the wrongdoing itself but rather the pain it causes to victims and the rift it opens in the community or between community members and the offender. In many traditional legal systems, there is little or no differentiation between crime and other types of acts resulting in physical or financial injury, and thus reconciliation is the most common response to wrongs. There are a variety of approaches to reconciliation. Some focus on victim compensation, often through a system of fines. Historically, some societies would permit victims or their relatives to take offenders as slaves until they worked off their debt to the family. Offenders might be required to provide a victim's family with livestock or to throw a feast for the community. Other reconciliation-based approaches emphasize apologies and community service.

Restorative justice is a reconciliation-based approach that has become more common in contemporary societies. The Youth Restoration Project, a group working to implement restorative justice practices in educational settings, defines restorative justice as

> the subset of restorative practices that is utilized after a harmful behavior has taken place. It emphasizes restitution for those who have been harmed and reintegration of those who have caused harm. It is unlike conventional justice systems, which are concerned with establishing guilt or innocence and then meting out punishment, ignoring the needs of victims and leading to high recidivism rates. Restorative Justice interrupts this cycle of crime and retribution by focusing on repairing, to the extent possible, the harms that have occurred, and including all those most affected by an offense in its resolution. Restorative justice holds offenders accountable for their actions, provides restitution to victims and strengthens communities. (Youth Restoration Project 2016)

Typically, restorative justice approaches to punishment involve victims, offenders, and community members coming together to talk about the impact that a given wrongdoing has had on them. Victims are able to have a voice in shaping the response to the wrongdoing they have experienced, ensuring that victims' needs and experiences remain central to the process. Restorative justice

Transitional Justice in Rwanda

BY CARSE RAMOS

Transitional justice, commonly abbreviated as TJ, is a term used broadly to describe a framework and set of mechanisms that are put into place after political transition or mass atrocities, such as genocide, war, or extreme oppression, to help a society come to terms with its past. The term was coined by Ruti Teitel in 1991 in response to rapid and extreme political changes in the Soviet Union and Latin America (Teitel 2000; 2010), but the roots of modern TJ can be traced back to the Nuremberg Trials following the end World War II (Arthur 2009; Teitel 2003). TJ emerged as a named framework based on the idea that formal court procedures alone could not sufficiently address the needs of victims and communities after periods of extreme violence and sociopolitical change. The International Center for Transitional Justice, the foremost international organization working in the area, has stated that "[t]ransitional justice refers to the ways countries emerging from periods of conflict and repression address large-scale or systematic human rights violations so numerous and so serious that the normal justice system will not be able to provide an adequate response" (International Center for Transitional Justice 2018). Conceptualizations of what this should look like, however, differ widely. Nonetheless, TJ frameworks are generally understood as incorporating a variety of legal, quasi-legal, and depending on the source, nonlegal components (see, e.g., Minow 1998).

At its core are legal mechanisms—international tribunals, national courts, and traditional legal or dispute resolution bodies—and quasi-legal mechanisms, such as truth and reconciliation commissions and reparations schemes, which sometimes incorporate full or partial amnesty, or a pardon for past wrongs. Some take a wider view, incorporating fully nonlegal measures, such as formal apologies and memorialization projects (see, e.g., Hinton 2010; International Center for Transitional Justice 2018; Roht-Arriaza and Mariecurrena 2006). Disputes also emerged early on about what the breadth and scope of transitional justice should be and to what sorts of situations the framework should apply. Interpretations continue to vary widely (Clark 2008).

Transitional justice makes for an interesting topic of study, not only because of its purported victim-centered focus but also because in designing an attempt to "deal with the past," a society might employ several mechanisms, operating according to differing and sometimes contradictory justice logics. International tribunals and courts typically serve a retributive, or punitive, function, whereas traditional justice mechanisms, truth commissions, and reparations schemes typically claim to operate on a more restorative model, focusing on community healing and rebuilding, through "a process of active participation in which the wider community deliberates over past crimes, giving center stage to both victim and offender in a process which seeks to bestow dignity and empowerment upon victims, with special emphasis placed upon contextual factors" (Quinn 2004:404). Memorialization projects serve a symbolic, yet important, function.

While transitional justice schemes exist and have existed all over the world, perhaps one of the most well known was that which was implemented in Rwanda after the 1994 genocide. Between April and July 1994, upward of one million Tutsis and moderate Hutus were massacred by Hutu extremists. The genocide began in the capital, sparked by the death of then President Juvénal Habyarimana, when his plane was shot down as it approached Kigali airport. The

Rwandan government blamed the RPF rebels for killing the president and violating the ceasefire agreement, and violence broke out almost immediately. The Rwandan genocide has been called the best-organized genocide of the twentieth century. According to a placard at the Kigali Genocide Memorial, the plane went down at 8:23 P.M "By 9:15 P.M, roadblocks had been constructed throughout Kigali and houses were being searched. Shooting began to be heard within an hour." Execution lists had been prepared and distributed in advance. Over the next one hundred days, genocidal violence spread rapidly throughout the country.

In the aftermath of such devastation, the country was faced with the onerous task of "dealing with the past" and moving forward. One of the primary routes through which Rwanda has proceeded has been through extensive focus on memorialization through annual commemoration events, a wide array of memorial centers and sites, the preservation of mass graves, and the development of educational programming. Photographs and information on several of these memorial sites can be found at the Through a Glass Darkly Project website (Meierhenrich 2010). Another has been through multiple levels of legal and quasi-legal proceedings. After the genocide, the country, including the judicial system, was in shambles. Most of the infrastructure had been destroyed, and Amnesty International estimated there were ten lawyers left in the country (Corey and Joireman 2004). On the other hand, there were roughly 120,000 people waiting in jail to be tried. By 1996, the courts were beginning to pick up speed, but it was estimated at the time that it would take over two hundred years to work through the caseload. In response, the Rwandan government developed a three-pronged system incorporating the International Criminal Tribunal for Rwanda (ICTR), which was responsible for

adjudicating the highest-level offenders; the domestic or classical courts; and *gacaca,* a quasi-traditional judicial mechanism. Beginning in 2003, tens of thousands of prisoners were provisionally released, conditional upon their appearance in front of *gacaca.* Over the course of its lifetime, the ICTR indicted ninety-five individuals; by contrast, nearly two million people went through the *gacaca* system by the time it wrapped up in 2012.

Gacaca was a singular phenomenon. Loosely derived from a word meaning "on the grass" in the Kinyarwanda language, the name, credited to Filip Reyntjens, is descriptive of where many of these proceedings were held (Reyntjens 1990). Proponents hoped that *gacaca,* which lay somewhere between court system and truth commission, would be able to expedite the processing of cases and encourage community participation by providing an alternate, more "local" means of adjudication and encouraging witness testimony. During *gacaca* sessions, community members gathered, together with a panel of *inyangamugayo,* a term meaning "persons of integrity" that is used in reference to community elders and was subsequently applied to *gacaca* judges. Individuals could accuse one another, ask questions, and act as witnesses, providing corroborating information or contradicting testimony given. No lawyers were allowed to participate in their professional capacity. This less formal setup allowed for a more discursive process, where details about what had happened to loved ones were laid bare and, at times, apologies were given—not unlike the functioning of a truth and reconciliation commission. At the end of each case, however, the judges would levy a verdict and punishment, most frequently jail time. In this way, these sessions also functioned as quasi-courts, which generated a great deal of criticism over due process concerns. Discussions surrounding *gacaca*'s intended function have also highlighted disagreement about whether it is a retributive or restorative mechanism (Corey and Joireman 2004; Daly 2002; Waldorf 2008).

Despite its unique format, *gacaca* is most frequently described as a traditional justice mechanism, as it is considered by many to be a "new" and revamped version of a traditional Rwandan dispute resolution system that was used previously for matters involving property (see, e.g., Clark 2007). Its history and "traditional" status, however, have been contested. Bert Ingelaere, for example, has argued that *gacaca* is the quintessential example of an "invented tradition," a concept developed by Eric Hobsbawm and Terrance Ranger to refer to a set of practices that purport to establish continuity with the past but are actually "responses to novel situations which take the form of reference to old situations, or which establish their own past by quasi-obligatory repetition" (Hobsbawm and Ranger 1983:2). To this end, critical voices maintain that that the new *gacaca* was designed, loosely based on a traditional mechanism, to establish and maintain social control throughout the country (see, e.g., Burnet 2011; Ingelaere 2009; 2016; Thomson 2011).

Gacaca, and the Rwandan transitional justice framework as a whole, represent but one of many transitional justice efforts that have taken place across the world on nearly every continent. Other notable examples include the South African Truth and Reconciliation Commission, which was put into place following the end of apartheid (see, e.g., Truth and Reconciliation Commission 2018; Richard Wilson 2001); the truth and reconciliation bodies established after the fall of dictatorial regimes in Latin America (see, e.g., Hayner 2001; Laplante and Theidon 2007); the victim reparations program recently established in Colombia as part of the peace accord between the Colombian government and FARC rebel group (International Center for Transitional Justice 2019); and various approaches being explored by communities in Northern Ireland to deal with violence leading up to and following the Good Friday Agreement (see, e.g., Aiken 2010; Cambell and Ní Aoláin 2002; Kilmurray 2017; Northern Ireland Human Rights Commission 2013). While debates continue within the field over how universal or local transitional justice is and should be, it is important to observe that a given scheme and its component mechanisms will vary and look quite different in every situation and in each society (McEvoy 2012).

programs are usually consent-based and voluntary. This means that both the victim and the offender must agree to participate in order for the restorative justice process to begin, though there are some adjudication and punishment systems based on restorative justice principles that have moved away from this principle of voluntariness (for example, in postgenocide societies). Restorative justice approaches are used in a variety of contexts and in response to a variety of types of offenses, such as genocide (Waldorf 2008), criminal sexual assault (Koss, Bachar, and Hopkins 2003), and school misbehavior (Fronius et al. 2016). While additional sanctions, such as monetary fines, may be incorporated into restorative justice practices (Criminal Justice Policy Group 2000), these sanctions are designed to restore—as much as possible—the victim to his or her pre-offense state rather than to deter offending or inflict suffering on the offender.

HOW HAS PUNISHMENT CHANGED OVER TIME?

Today, many people see prison as the default punishment, assuming that in most cases it makes sense to confine those convicted of crimes for a term of years in proportion to the seriousness of the offense or the threat of potential reoffense. But prison is a relatively recent innovation as punishments go. Running prisons requires the financial capital to build and maintain a facility, a bureaucracy to manage and staff it, and a system for determining when it is appropriate to release prisoners. Thus, the first facilities resembling modern prisons did not develop until the 1700s in England. One of the first theorists of the prison, Jeremy Bentham, developed a model prison he called the **panopticon** (Bentham 1843). In the panopticon, prisoners live in cells organized around a central guard tower, which is lit with a bright light. This means that prisoners are always visible to guards, though prisoners cannot tell when the guards are actually looking at them. The system of surveillance at the core of the panopticon was, in Bentham's construction, designed to ensure that prisoners learn to control their own behavior. (You can see modern echoes of this design, shown in figure 17, in all kinds of facilities where people want to be able to engage in surveillance, from hospital wards to call-center cubicles.)

Before the development of the prison, some societies had constructed dungeons. Dungeons typically had one or more small cells and were located either in the basement of fortified castles or in remote areas far from any other structure. They were usually accessible only through heavy, locked doors or through small trapdoors in the ceiling. Typically, political or religious prisoners would be housed in dungeons for long periods, in some cases until they died. But dungeons were not a typical punishment for ordinary crimes.

In premodern times, societies used a variety of other potential punishments. In some cases, forced labor of various kinds, such as enslavement or military conscription, was used as a form of punishment, though wealthier people could often avoid this fate through their ability to pay a fine or sign over their property. More often, punishments took a bodily form. Criminals might be subjected to public humiliation by being locked in stocks in the town square, where passersby could pelt them with jeers or rotten fruit, or they might be shunned. They might be flogged or paddled, or they might be subjected to bodily mutilation, such as branding, tattooing, or amputation. In some cases, torture was used, but torture is better understood as part of the investigatory or court process rather than as part of the punishment process.

In cases of more severe crimes, and in the absence of a prison system, societies sought ways to incapacitate the offender and remove the potential for them to reoffend. This might be accomplished by exiling them, or it might be accomplished by executing them. Execution could be undertaken by various means, such as hanging, burning at the stake, stoning, crushing, poisoning, the use of weapons, or through even more gruesome methods. For example, one

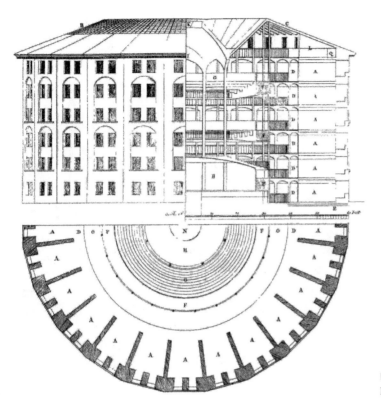

Figure 17 Jeremy Bentham's panopticon (Bentham 1843:172–73).

punishment used in medieval Europe was drawing and quartering. In this punishment, each of a person's limbs was tied to a horse, and the four horses were sent off in different directions, tearing the limbs from the body (Foucault 1977). In many cases, other forms of bodily harm occurred before or during the execution, and the corpse may have been desecrated or prohibited from being buried after the execution.

Many of the forms of punishment discussed so far are still used in various societies, but in altered form. For example, executions still occur in many countries, including the United States, but they tend to take a more clinical and impersonal form. This change perhaps began with the invention of the guillotine, which was first used in 1792 in France. Guillotines used a sharp blade to behead a person instantly without the risk of gruesome scenes of suffocation (as can be the case with hanging) or torture. They were used throughout the French Revolution—for instance, to execute Queen Marie Antoinette, as shown in figure 18—and up until the 1970s in France. Unlike with prior execution methods, the executioner could act at some distance from the condemned and did not need to dirty his hands in carrying out the execution—but the

Figure 18 The execution of Marie
Antoinette (Monnet 1794).

guillotine remained, like hanging and other more traditional methods of execution, an occasion for public spectacle. Hundreds or thousands of onlookers would arrive to observe executions, which often were accompanied by picnics and public festivities.

According to social theorist Michel Foucault (1977), older methods of punishment were primarily focused on punishing the body, while newer methods are focused on punishing the soul and subjecting it to discipline. This development can be clearly seen in contrasting a punishment like drawing and quartering to a punishment like the guillotine. While both result in the death of the condemned, in the former the death is excruciating and protracted, while the guillotine provides an instantaneous and (theoretically) painless death. Thus the punishment provided by the guillotine is not bodily pain but rather the deprivation of life as an abstract phenomenon. Furthermore, as Foucault notes, modern punishment began to move out of the public sphere, with executions gradually withdrawing behind prison walls and prison itself growing in importance as a form of punishment. As he argues, the prison was invented as form of punishment that involved not only "the deprivation of liberty" but also the "transformation of individuals" into disciplined souls (Foucault 1977:233).

WHAT TYPES OF PUNISHMENT DO SOCIETIES USE?

In the contemporary world, punishment practices continue to vary among countries. Among the most common types of punishment are imprisonment, control-in-freedom (restrictions on movement other than imprisonment), fines, corporal punishment, and capital punishment. Some countries also frequently use warnings or suspended sentences. When such sanctions are used, individuals are left with a criminal record, but they are not immediately punished so long as they stay out of trouble for a specified period of time. Not all countries use all of these types of punishments, but most use more than one type. And the balance between these different types varies considerably from country to country (Villé, Zvekic, and Klaus 1997). For example, in Japan, fines are extremely common, with prison sentences and death sentences much less common. In Singapore, almost all sentences involve imprisonment, corporal punishment, or capital punishment, depending on the severity of the crime. In Slovenia and Kazakhstan, over half of sanctions imposed are warnings or suspended sentences, whereas in Korea, Lithuania, and the Czech Republic, control-in-freedom sentences are the most common. Figure 19 details the different distribution of sanction types found in the United States, Germany, and the Netherlands. As you can see, even in countries we might consider to have fairly similar economic, moral, and cultural perspectives, sentencing practices can be very different (Subramanian and Shames 2013).

Prisons

Early prisons, such as Bentham's panopticon, typically required prisoners to maintain silence as they pursued religious redemption or performed physical labor. By the early 1900s, prisons began moving to a model more heavily emphasizing work as a context for rehabilitation and a way to demonstrate prisoners' readiness for the outside world. Today, despite the fact that prisons can be found in nearly every country, imprisonment practices vary widely across national contexts. Some focus on warehousing prisoners. Maximum-security facilities in the United States, for instance, may keep prisoners locked in solitary confinement for as many as twenty-three hours a day, or more if the prison is on lockdown. Other prisons are designed to mimic the outside world, providing prisoners with educational and rehabilitative opportunities to enhance their chances for successful lives after release.

Simply knowing that a prison is designed to emphasize warehousing or to promote rehabilitation is not enough to predict how it operates. For example,

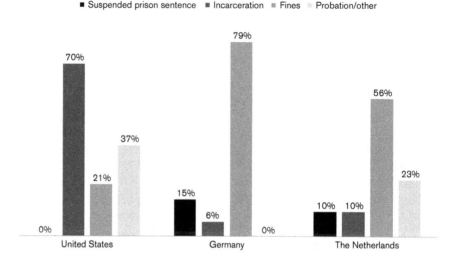

Figure 19 Comparative sentencing practices (Subramanian and Shames 2013:9).

contrast the warehousing model familiar in the United States to the warehousing model found in South American countries like Bolivia and Colombia. There, prisons are designed simply to prevent escape. Prison guards concentrate on fortifying the walls, but inside, prisoners run everything. Such prisons have complex internal economies, with sleeping space available to rent, food available to purchase from restaurants and stalls run by inmates, and markets for consumer goods and drugs. Visitors are often permitted to move freely inside the prison, and women who are imprisoned can raise their children behind the walls.

Prisons vary widely in terms of standards for humane treatment of prisoners. In some countries, such as China, the United States, and Iran, solitary confinement is common; in many European countries, such practices are seen as human rights violations. Indeed, European countries sometimes refuse to extradite accused criminals to the United States because of concerns about the treatment of inmates or the possibility of a death sentence. Prisons in many countries engage in torture or mistreatment of inmates. Until 2013, for example, prisoners in Thailand with long-term or life sentences could expect to have metal shackles welded onto their legs (Benko 2015a).

Work models remain common in prisons around the world. In some countries, prisoners are a source of slave labor. In others, work assignments may be optional, and prisoners who take them on can receive compensation. Compensation levels vary, from token payments redeemable for goods at a prison commissary to real wages equivalent to what someone in a similar job might earn outside prison walls. In the latter case, prisoners may be provided with the

Figure 20 Prison overcrowding at the California Institution for Men (California Department of Corrections and Rehabilitation 2006).

means to save for their post-release life and required to pay compensation to the victims of their crimes. Prisoners in some countries are provided with food and other necessities, while in other cases they are required to pay for food, personal hygiene items, clothing, and even the cost of their own **incarceration**. Countries—and even prisons within a given country—vary considerably in terms of the access they provide to hygiene and sanitation facilities, exercise, outdoor space, medical care, reading material, contact with the outside world, visitors, and rehabilitative services.

Prisons are frequently overcrowded. Overcrowding can contribute to the spread of disease and to other social problems within the prison walls, such as violence. The impact of overcrowding may be different depending on the design of the prison. For example, in prisons with separate cells designed to hold one or two prisoners, overcrowding may mean that more prisoners are housed in each cell than the cell is really capable of holding, or that some prisoners end up sleeping in hallways or communal areas. In cells with dormitories, it is often possible to squeeze additional beds and bodies into the space, though often at a cost in terms of noise and hygiene. Figure 20 shows overcrowding at the California Institution for Men, a state prison, in August 2006. This overcrowding was part of the basis for *Brown v. Plata* (2010), a United States Supreme Court case that compelled the California prison system to release some inmates because overcrowding had reached inhumane levels. Yet the United States,

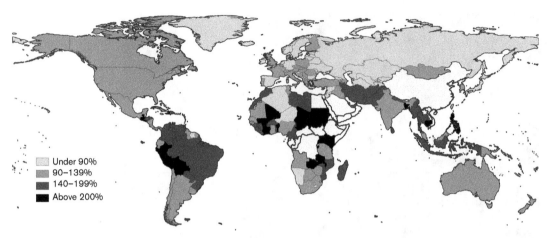

Map 16 Prison occupancy rates (Institute for Criminal Policy Research n.d.).

with prisons filled to a nationwide average of 103 percent of capacity, is far from the worst offender. Many other countries' prison systems hold two or more times the number of inmates they were designed for (Institute for Criminal Policy Research n.d.), as shown in map 16.

One way that some countries reduce prison populations is through the use of **parole** or early release. In both cases, a prisoner is released before the end of their sentence, though in cases where prisoners are paroled, they remain subject to continued supervision by the criminal justice system to ensure they comply with specified terms. These terms may include avoiding future infractions or contact with others who have committed crimes (including relatives), living in designated areas and maintaining appropriate housing, holding down a job, participating in rehabilitative programs, and paying restitution to victims. Parole and early release can also be used to incentivize good behavior for those who are in prison, with days or years removed from the sentence in exchange for following rules, staying out of trouble, or completing educational or rehabilitative programs within prison.

Control-in-Freedom

Control-in-freedom refers to a set of punishment options in which individuals are not restricted to prison but are still subject to monitoring and control by criminal justice authorities. This includes sentences of house arrest or probation, as well as mandatory treatment programs. **Probation** refers to a system in which offenders are subjected to monitoring for a period of time to ensure that their behavior meets specified standards. Typically, individuals on probation are

CASE STUDY 7.2

Prisons and Punishment in Norway

What comes to mind when you think of a prison? For people in most of the developed world, the image is probably one of locked metal bars, handcuffs and shackles, and distinctive prison uniforms, with anything sharp or dangerous locked away and constant surveillance by guards, who control inmates' every move. But this is not what prisons look like in Norway.

Even maximum-security facilities in Norway are designed to emphasize rehabilitation and reduce psychological stress and interpersonal conflict (Benko 2015b). Their design incorporates access to nature and the outdoors, even including

wooded areas within prison walls (or borders, in the case of a prison on an island). While strict security is maintained, officers do not use the overt techniques common in other countries, instead focusing on ongoing interaction with inmates in close quarters, roles for which personnel are thoroughly prepared by a three-year training program (James 2013). Inside prisons, routines and facilities are designed to replicate the outside world, with inmates able to access and use ordinary kitchen tools, walk by themselves between buildings, and wear their own clothing (Benko 2015b). Vocational training, addiction treatment, mental health services, and other rehabilitative

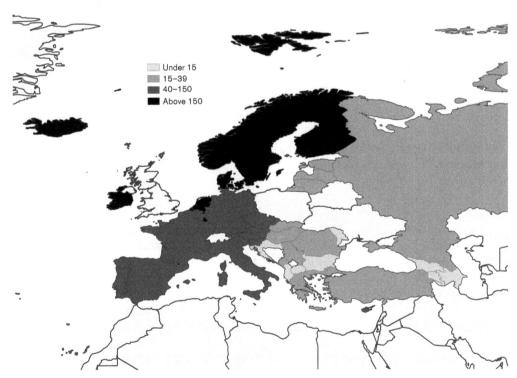

CS 7.2 Map a Daily spending per inmate, in 2014 U.S. dollars (Aebi, Tiago, and Burkhardt 2017).

CS 7.2 Table a   Two-year recidivism rates in selected countries

Country	Data year	Reconviction rate
Denmark	2005	29%
Finland	2005	36%
Iceland	2005	27%
Netherlands	2007	48%
Norway	2005	20%
Singapore	2011	27%
Sweden	2005	43%
United States	2005–2010	36%
Northern Ireland (United Kingdom)	2005	47%

SOURCE: Fazel and Wolf 2015.

programs are provided, and inmates have regular work assignments for which they are paid wages, albeit at a below-market level. At lower-security facilities, inmates may be permitted to visit relatives or to work outside the prison (James 2013). It is important to note that this unique system is not merely a reflection of Norwegian culture. Many Norwegian prison inmates are immigrants, most from Eastern Europe, the Middle East, and Africa, and many do not even speak Norwegian.

Norway does spend quite a bit more per inmate than many other countries do (as shown in CS 7.2 map a)—an average of over US$450 a day in 2014—though it incarcerates far fewer inmates as a percentage of its population than do many other countries (Aebi, Tiago, and Burkhardt 2017; Benko 2015b). Comparable data for the United States shows spending of about US$90 a day per inmate in 2015, while Canada spent US$215 a day per inmate in 2014 (Statistics Canada 2016).

When inmates are released, the Norwegian Correctional Service works to ensure that they have housing and employment ready for them on the outside (Benko 2015b), and they continue to have access to the social services available to all Norwegians, including health care. As CS 7.2 table a shows, within two years of their release, about 20 percent of Norwegian prison inmates are convicted of a new crime, while 36 percent of inmates released from U.S. prisons are reconvicted in that two-year span (Fazel and Wolf 2015). In part because of these differences, some state prison officials in the United States are beginning to think seriously about what their prison systems might be able to learn from Norway's (Slater 2017).

Anders Breivik is a Norwegian prison inmate who might be considered the worst of the worst. In July 2011, he killed seventy-seven people. First, he blew up a car in Oslo, which killed eight. Then, on the island of Utøya, he shot sixty-nine people, most attending a youth camp. The youngest victim was fourteen. He did not regret his actions; he regarded them as necessary given his extremist racist and anti-Muslim views, as detailed in a 1,500-page manifesto he posted online in advance of his crime (Lewis and Cowell 2012).

In countries that routinely use capital punishment, Breivik would almost certainly have faced execution. But Norway does not use the death penalty. Nor does it use life sentences. Less than one hundred prisoners in Norway are sentenced to "preventative detention," which permits authorities to keep them locked up beyond the twenty-one-year maximum sentence if they continue to present a risk to society (*BBC News* 2016a).

In the United States, if Breivik avoided a sentence of death due to a plea bargain or because the state in which the crime was committed does not use the death penalty, he would have been sentenced to a supermax prison in which he would have been kept in solitary confinement. But Norway does not offer such options, so Breivik could not be sentenced to solitary confinement.

The correctional authorities in Norway, however, concluded that he was a threat to other prisoners, especially given his extremist views, and thus needed to be housed separately. They provided him with a three-room cell, furnished with exercise and media equipment and a personal fridge (Libell 2016), and he was offered access to hired companions to provide socialization. However, Breivik sued, claiming that solitary confinement, strip searches, and limits on communication with the outside world constituted torture and harmed his mental health. In 2016, a Norwegian judge found that Breivik's treatment violated the European Commission on Human Rights' prohibition on "inhuman or degrading treatment or punishment." He was awarded legal fees, and the judge also ordered the correctional authorities to reduce his isolation, though she did not grant his demand for reduced restrictions on communication (Libell 2016).

The Breivik case highlights several of the distinct features of the Norwegian prison system: its emphasis on the dignity and fair treatment of the imprisoned and on rehabilitation, and its goal of providing prisoners with an environment as close as possible to that in the outside world. When most prisoners will leave prison after twenty-one years or less, the goal of facilitating their adjustment to nonprison life makes sense. In Breivik's case, though, the prison system is faced with an unusual set of issues—how do you achieve such goals for a prisoner who is unlikely to ever be released?

expected not only to refrain from criminal activity but also to comply with a set of additional behavioral requirements, which vary by jurisdiction and by offender but may include curfews, holding down a job, prohibitions against spending time with those who have committed crimes in the past, screening for substance abuse (including legal substances), frequent check-ins with probation staff, and prohibitions on leaving the jurisdiction without permission. Those who violate the terms of their probation supervision may face additional sanctions, including being sent to prison. Probation is a very common sentence in the United States; in 2013, 1,605 of every 100,000 adults in the United States were under probation supervision, though the rate varies considerably by state, with Ohio, Rhode Island, and Idaho having the highest rates and New Hampshire, Utah, Nevada, and West Virginia using probation at a rate closer to that of many European countries (Alper, Corda, and Reitz 2016). Turkey, with 1,212 people under probation supervision per 100,000 adults, has practices similar to those of many U.S. states, but the European average was only 297 per 100,000 adults (Corda and Phelps 2017).

House arrest has many elements in common with probation, though it carries the additional condition that offenders are prohibited from leaving their homes. Sentences of house arrest typically include exceptions for court dates and necessary medical treatment, and in some cases offenders are permitted to continue to work but not to go anywhere else other than work and home. There are a variety of mandated treatment programs that also might be considered control-in-freedom punishments. Most commonly, these include drug and psychiatric treatment programs that provide the offender with some freedom to continue to live a normal life but require attendance at program sessions and compliance with specific behavioral rules, such as avoiding the use of intoxicating substances.

In modern societies, control-in-freedom punishments are often regulated through the use of electronic monitoring systems, such as ankle bracelets with GPS trackers or ignition locks requiring those convicted of driving under the influence to undertake a Breathalyzer test before starting their car. Such practices, often referred to as **electronic monitoring**, or EM, have become widespread and often co-occur alongside more traditional control-in-freedom punishments such as probation and house arrest. EM can be deployed in a variety of ways, such as to track the movements of an offender, prevent certain behaviors (such as driving drunk), ensure compliance with curfews, and prohibit offenders from visiting specified areas (Nellis, Beyens, and Kamnski 2013). Supporters of EM approaches argue that they are less expensive than incarceration and permit greater control and surveillance of offenders than traditional approaches. Opponents argue that EM expands the scope of penal control in society, for instance by allowing it to intrude into the home, and that it allows for the privatization and monetization of sanctions when private companies are contracted to provide devices and monitoring technologies (Nellis, Beyens, and Kamnski 2013). Such companies may in turn charge fees to those who are monitored; offenders who cannot afford the fees may have to "choose" the alternative of imprisonment. Today, EM is used in countries on all inhabited continents, though technological and financial considerations keep it out of reach of some countries (Paterson 2013). Private companies providing monitoring services have a global reach, with contracts in countries on multiple continents (Paterson 2013).

The function of these sorts of punishments is complex. Many advocates of control-in-freedom argue that such sanctions reduce costs, increase freedom, and provide greater opportunities for rehabilitation and reconciliation that imprisonment does. However, some commentators argue that the many conditions that control-in-freedom imposes actually serve to inhibit possibilities for rehabilitation and reconciliation, and that instead these sorts of punishments are best seen as ways to increase control without having to find room in the prison system for more offenders. In fact, the function of control-in-freedom punishments may depend on the details of how they are implemented. Probation or mandated treatment that is accompanied by substantial social services support such as medical care, supported housing, and job placement and that does not revoke offenders into prison at every opportunity may indeed promote rehabilitation; probation programs that provide little support and frequently result in terms of incarceration clearly do not.

Financial and Other Sanctions

In many countries, **fines** are used as punishment. These fines may go to the government, or offenders may be required to pay victim compensation.

In many countries, specific fines are set by statute based on offense characteristics and do not vary based on offenders' ability to pay. But there is an alternative to this system: the **day fine**. Day fines are calculated to ensure that offenders are treated similarly regardless of their existing resources, so that those with more resources pay higher fines. Instead of a statute setting the dollar amount of the fine, a day fine statute will set out a specific number of days' worth of disposable income as the appropriate fine. Then, each offender's disposable income is calculated and multiplied by the number of days set out in statute to determine the fine that will be assessed. Day fines are most commonly used in Scandinavian countries, but they can be found elsewhere as well. In Finland, for example, day fines are used for traffic tickets, sometimes resulting in fines of over €100,000 for speeding by very wealthy drivers.

We typically think of punishment as occurring only as a response to criminal acts, but punishment is part of civil law as well. When individuals are adjudicated as responsible for a tort, or civil injury, the courts can assess various kinds of penalties. Some of these penalties are compensatory, or designed to remedy the injury or harm that has been suffered. For example, if you cause a car accident, you might be required to pay for damage to the victim's car, the costs of medical care, and lost wages while she is out of work recovering from her injuries. **Compensatory damages** are probably not best understood as punishments. In contrast, **punitive damages** can be assessed in the course of civil litigation and are best understood as punishments. Punitive damages are assessed over and above the amount of any compensatory damages in those court systems that permit them, typically but not only common law systems.

Societies use a variety of other nonbodily punishments. For example, various systems of warnings and suspended sentences may be used, in which no immediate punishment is carried out but offenders must avoid future offenses or risk more significant punishment. Some societies use mandatory community service as a punishment. Others withdraw various civil rights. For example, offenders in many U.S. states lose their right to vote, either temporarily or permanently, and they may lose the licenses that permit them to practice their profession.

Corporal Punishment

Corporal punishment refers to punishment on the body, not including execution. As of June 2017, fifty-two countries have prohibited corporal punishment in all settings (including home, schools, penal institutions, and as a sentence for a crime), while thirty-four permit sentences of corporal punishment. The remaining countries permit corporal punishment in some contexts, most typically childcare and home settings, but do not permit sentences of corporal punishment.

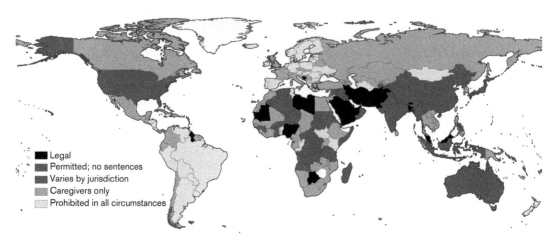

Map 17 Corporal punishment laws (Global Initiative to End All Corporal Punishment of Children 2017).

As used today, corporal punishment most frequently takes the form of flogging, caning, whipping, or amputation. In Malaysia and Singapore, for example, criminal offenders can be sentenced to a specified number of strokes of a rattan cane. This cane is of a designated diameter and is designed to be painful and leave marks. However, caning sentences are carried out under the supervision of a doctor, and offenders are supposed to be healthy at the time of the caning. Caning in Singapore came to the attention of the global community in 1994, when Michael Fay, an American eighteen-year-old, was subjected to four strokes of the cane for vandalism and theft of street signs.

Some countries prohibit the imposition of corporal punishment as a sentence in the criminal justice system but do permit caregivers to administer it. But countries' definitions of "caregivers" vary; some limit corporal punishment to the home, while others permit day-care providers and schools to use it or allow it within prisons. The data presented in map 17 reflects what countries say they do; reality may vary.

The Qur'an specifies amputation as punishment in particular circumstances. Amputation of the hand is prescribed when an adult steals an object of some value from a secured location, though there are some exceptions, such as if the act is committed during times of famine. More severe offenses may result in sentences of cross-amputation (removal of the right hand and left foot), and repeat offenses may result in additional amputations. Qur'anic amputation sentences are carried out in countries with theocratic Shari'a legal systems, such as Saudi Arabia and Iran. It is important to note that in many cases, proper anesthetic is used and follow-up medical care is provided, as the judicial authorities seek to distinguish these sentences from acts of torture.

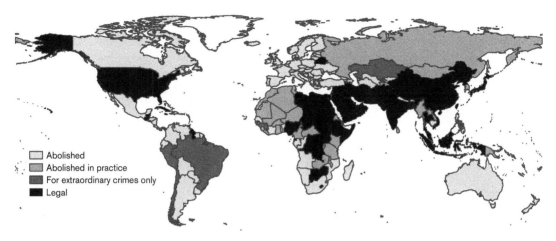

Map 18 Legal status of capital punishment, 2017 (Amnesty International 2017).

Capital Punishment

Capital punishment refers to sentences resulting in death. While capital punishment was once a common punishment for the most severe and even for moderately severe crimes all around the globe, it has become increasingly rare in the modern world. Today, 104 countries have abolished the use of the death penalty for all crimes (Amnesty International 2017). An additional 30 have abolished it in practice, meaning there are still capital punishment statutes on the books but no executions have been carried out in the past decade, and 7 retain the death penalty only for extraordinary crimes (such as crimes against humanity or military offenses). That means there are only 57 countries remaining where the death penalty is an available punishment for ordinary crimes, as shown in map 18, though countries vary as to the types of offenses that qualify for sentences of death. In some countries, like the United States, only murder qualifies; in others, death sentences can be imposed for much less severe offenses, like selling drugs or being a repeat offender as a thief.

There were over one thousand executions globally in 2017 (Amnesty International 2018b). Just over half the recorded executions—not including those in China and Vietnam, countries that do not provide specific figures—took place in Iran, as shown in table 8. Together with Saudi Arabia, Iraq, and Pakistan, these countries account for 84 percent of executions globally (Amnesty International 2018b), and the number of executions carried out is falling in many of the countries that do still use capital punishment. However, many more people are sentenced to death than are actually executed—in some cases, the

Table 8   Top ten global users of the death penalty, 2017

Country	Executions	Sentences of death
China+	1000s	unknown
Iran+	507	unknown
Vietnam+	unknown	35
Iraq+	125	65
Pakistan+	60	200
Egypt+	35	402
Somalia	24	24
United States	23	41
Jordan+	15	10
Singapore	8	15

+ Refers to countries in which the documented number is a minimum and there are likely additional executions and death sentences.

SOURCE: Amnesty International 2018b.

sentences are commuted or reduced on appeal, and in other cases, the condemned die of other causes before their executions can be carried out.

Capital punishment used to be one of the most common forms of punishment globally, but its use has declined markedly. As recently as 1997, Amnesty International (2017) recorded 40 countries carrying out executions, while in 2017, only 23 did, and the number of countries that have legally abolished the death penalty rose from 64 to 104 over the same period. Given this global move away from capital punishment, what explains the fact that some countries continue to use it?

Well, there are a variety of explanations. In the case of countries with Islamic legal systems, the system of law prescribed in the Qur'an requires that execution be used as a sentence, so it would not be possible for such countries to move away from capital punishment without some deeper changes in their justice systems to incorporate other sources of authority beyond the Qur'an. In many other countries, capital punishment is maintained because people believe that it has a deterrent effect or that it offers the most profound level of retribution. Note that these are beliefs about punishment, not empirical facts—evidence suggests that the deterrent effect of the death penalty is limited, particularly in jurisdictions where it is used sparingly. Similarly, people may favor the death penalty because it presents the opportunity for permanent incapacitation, but life sentences without the possibility of parole can similarly prevent future crimes. Historically, executions may have been easier and less expensive than other forms of punishment, and this is still the case in some countries that lack modern correctional facilities. But in modern countries with due process rights, such as the United States, executions are far more expensive than imprisonment. For example, a study in Nebraska found that the average death-eligible prosecution in the state cost nearly $1.5 million more than it would have cost to prosecute and imprison the same person under a life-without-parole sentence (Goss, Strain, and Blalock 2016). Findings from other states are similar.

Sociologists David Greenberg and Valarie West conducted a statistical analysis designed to determine how countries that continue to use capital punishment differ from those that do not. They found that homicide rates and national population are not predictors of whether or not a country will use capital punishment (Greenberg and West 2008). However, countries are more likely to use capital punishment when they imprison more criminals, provide for fewer political rights, are less economically developed, and have lower rates of literacy. Capital punishment is more likely in countries with common law legal systems and less likely in countries governed by leftist but not socialist governments. As far as the effect of religion, Christian and Hindu countries are less likely to use capital punishment, but this effect is due to the fact that such countries tend to protect political rights more (Greenberg and West 2008). Similarly, countries with larger Muslim populations are more likely to use capital punishment, but Greenberg and West argue that this effect is found because of the lack of political rights in such countries.

Executions can be carried out in a variety of different ways. Among the most widely used are hanging and shooting (often by a firing squad). Poisonous gas, lethal injection, and electrocution are also used. In the United States, lethal injection is used for most executions, but some states have provisions for other methods as alternatives. Countries with Islamic legal systems often use stoning or beheading.

Associated Press reporter Anwar Faruqi (2000) describes the scene of a beheading in Saudi Arabia as follows:

> Policemen clear a public square of traffic and lay out a thick blue plastic sheet about 16 feet by 16 feet on the asphalt. The condemned, who has been given tranquilizers, is led from a police car dressed in his own clothing. His eyes are covered with cotton pads, bound in plaster and finally covered with a black cloth. Barefoot, with feet shackled and hands cuffed behind his back, the prisoner is led by a police officer to the center of the sheet and made to kneel. An Interior Ministry official reads out the prisoner's name and crime before a crowd of witnesses. A soldier hands a long, curved sword to the executioner. He approaches the prisoner from behind and jabs him with the tip of the sword in the back so that the prisoner instinctively raises his head. It usually takes just one swing of the sword to sever the head, often sending it flying about three feet. Paramedics bring the head to a doctor, who uses a gloved hand to stop the fountain of blood spurting from the neck. The doctor sews the head back on, and the body is wrapped in the blue plastic sheet and taken away in an ambulance.

This Saudi execution, like most executions in historical periods, is structured as a public spectacle. Indeed, its public nature is presumably seen as enhancing its deterrent effect. But in many countries today, executions are no longer public. As Foucault points out, countries have sought to "ensur[e] that the execution should cease to be a spectacle, and remain a strange secret between the law and those it condemns" (Foucault 1977:15). Today, in the United States, people can witness executions, but the number of witness is limited, and only specific people, such as lawyers and family members, are permitted to observe.

In contrast, some countries have truly secret executions. This is often because executions are being used as a tool of state terrorism. For example, during Argentina's Guerra Sucia, or Dirty War (1974–83), thousands of people were disappeared by the government to secret locations, where they were often killed. Their bodies were not returned to their families, so it was never possible to prove what happened to them. These people, who were usually alleged political dissidents or ideological opponents of the governing regime, have come to be called *los desaparecidos.* The military government used this tactic to try to silence the opposition. Similar techniques are sometimes used by national intelligence services, proceeding outside of the normal court system, to assassinate individuals who are thought to be spies or enemies of the state.

But secret executions are not used only as tools of state terrorism. In Japan, for example, executions have long been secret, and only recently has some information about the execution system been made public (Mail Foreign Service 2010). The condemned themselves are notified of their execution only about an hour before it is set to take place, and their families are given no advance notice—they find out only after the execution has occurred. The argument in the past has been that releasing information about executions and sentences of death would stigmatize the families of those condemned in a society where honor and shame are very important culturally. However, the Justice Ministry began to release the names and crimes of those who had been sentenced to death in 2007. And in 2010, journalists were permitted their first glimpse into the execution chambers, where the condemned die by hanging (Mail Foreign Service 2010). Some experts believe this secrecy explains why support for the death penalty in Japan remains so much higher than in most other developed countries (the United States being the only other exception).

In China, some executions are public and others are secret, which contributes to the country's ability to conceal the total number of executions from international observers and human rights groups. Some executions in China are carried out in mobile execution vans, which use lethal injection (and can record video footage of the executions, if desired).

WHAT FACTORS SHAPE NATIONAL DIFFERENCES IN PUNISHMENT PRACTICES?

Cross-national differences in punishment practices can be shaped by a variety of factors, including different views of the severity of crime, legal culture and

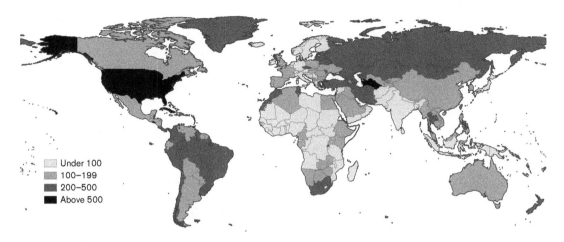

Map 19 Incarceration rate per 100,000 population (Institute for Criminal Policy Research n.d.).

national values, the goals and justifications of punishment emphasized in each country, and policymakers' beliefs about the causes of crime and the consequences of punishment. It is important to note that empirical findings about the relationship between sentencing practices and crime rates are unclear. For example, an analysis of sentencing in the United States, Finland, and Germany from the 1960s through the early 1990s found that violent crime rates more than doubled in all three countries, while imprisonment rates skyrocketed in the United States, declined significantly in Finland, and declined slightly in Germany (Tonry and Frase 2001). As you can see in map 19, the proportion of the population that countries incarcerate varies widely, from over 600 people per 100,000 in the United States and the Seychelles to less than 20 per 100,000 in Comoros, the Faeroe Islands, the Central African Republic, and Guinea-Bissau (Institute for Criminal Policy Research n.d.).

Most countries seek to treat like cases alike and different cases differently. Countries with mandatory sentencing schemes treat like offenses the same but cannot take into account differences in offenders' biographies or circumstances. In contrast, truly discretionary sentencing can respond effectively to differences in circumstance but may produce wide disparities in the treatment of similar offenses, including disparities that are discriminatory in nature.

Countries also tend to value proportionality in sentencing, meaning that sentences for crimes seen as severe should be harsher than punishments for crimes that are not so severe. Countries clearly differ in their views of which punishments are acceptable, as some countries use capital or corporal punishment while others have banned such practices. But despite these differences, people do tend to have somewhat similar views of punishment severity. For instance, a study asking people in Kuwait and the United States to rank the severity of seventeen different types of punishments, ranging from no penalty or a reprimand to life imprisonment, stoning, and amputation, found that respondents from both countries ranked the punishments similarly (Evans and Scott 1984).

However, when asked to apply those punishments to a list of thirty-seven different offenses (some of which were likely not considered criminal by all respondents), the researchers found substantial cross-cultural disagreement. For example, the Kuwaiti respondents viewed adultery among married women as the most severe offense, worse than murder, kidnapping, or assault, and also ranked adultery by men, false accusations of adultery, prostitution, same-sex sexual relations, and apostasy as much worse than did respondents from the United States. In contrast, the U.S. respondents ranked theft, accidental killings, and fraud as much worse than did the Kuwaitis (Evans and Scott 1984). There was some agreement—both groups of respondents ranked crimes like rape, selling illegal drugs, and perjury similarly—but this study highlights the fact that countries do not all agree on which crimes should be seen as severe and which should be considered more minor. This disagreement inevitably shapes the cross-national differences in punishment practices that we observe.

Different countries' punishment systems emphasize different combinations of goals and justifications for punishment, and these differences have implications for the types of punishment those countries will choose. A system based on deterrence, for example, must ensure that punishment is certain, that potential offenders are aware of the punishment they face, and that punishment is at least somewhat unpleasant. In contrast, a system emphasizing rehabilitation need not worry about whether potential offenders are aware of the punishment they face or if punishment is unpleasant—they simply need to ensure that offenders are sentenced to rehabilitative programs that work. For incapacitation, none of these factors matter—it matters only that offenders are kept away from society for as long as the threat of future offenses remains. This means that systems emphasizing incapacitation will choose long sentences (or execution). In contrast, systems emphasizing rehabilitation or restoration aim to return offenders to society as people who can participate in it, often suggesting shorter prison sentences or less use of imprisonment.

Policymakers' beliefs about the causes of crime and the consequences of punishment also shape punishment practices. It is important to note here that these beliefs need not be accurate—it is what policymakers believe that matters to the structure of the system more than what is actually true. For example, if policymakers tend to believe that crime occurs as a result of "bad people," they will be more likely to support punishment policies that emphasize incapacitation. Therefore, in the United States, life imprisonment (and capital punishment) remains common. Both policymakers and the public frequently argue that sentences should be longer and tougher across many categories of crime. Such attitudes reflect a philosophy of incapacitation and deterrence.

In contrast, if policymakers believe that crime occurs because of social, economic, or mental health conditions, they will be more likely to believe that rehabilitative interventions can make a big difference in reducing future criminal acts. Some countries are much more likely to use fines or community service, perhaps because of a deeper commitment to reconciliation, while others hope the sanctions they emphasize will serve as a strong deterrent. Many countries use much shorter sentences than does the United States—as noted earlier in this chapter, in Norway, sentences cannot exceed twenty-one years, and similar limits are found in other Scandinavian countries. In Finland, very short sentences are common, and even people sentenced to life tend to be released in less than fifteen years (Houseman 2010). Such practices may reflect the belief that short sentences provide correctional authorities with the opportunity to assess inmates' needs and connect them to the appropriate rehabilitative services, such as drug treatment, without transforming them into "hardened" criminals. Shorter sentences may also be more feasible in countries that maintain sufficient personnel to provide post-release supervision. In contrast, in Germany, policymakers have moved away from short sentences (Tonry 2011). The German philosophy is that during a sentence of less than six months, there is insufficient time to make real progress in rehabilitating an offender, but there is ample time to disrupt individuals' connections to employment, education, and family, so the sentence may do more harm than good.

Even within a given country, sentencing practices can be quite complex. While most countries have sentencing guidelines laying out the particular types and lengths of sentences that are appropriate for given crimes, many countries provide for a special phase of the trial in which sentencing is discussed, with prosecutors able to present evidence about the severity of the crime and the potential for the defendant to reoffend, and the defense able to present evidence of regret, contributions to the community, or factors that might explain the offense. In some countries, procedural rules are less strict during the sentencing phase. At the conclusion of the sentencing phase, judges (or in some cases juries) make sentencing decisions. There is often, but not always, substantial latitude for judges to deviate from sentencing guidelines. And the guidelines themselves may specify adjustments to sentences for various reasons, for example lengthening prison sentences for repeat offenses or reducing them based on age or gender.

For example, in Russia, life sentences are permitted only for men who were over eighteen at the time of the offense and under sixty-five at the time of sentencing; women can never be given life sentences. Similarly, in Singapore, men over fifty and women of any age cannot be sentenced to caning. In many countries that employ capital punishment, only adults can be sentenced to death.

Of course, these rules relating to age require countries to decide who counts as an adult, and the results of this decision vary across countries, as can be seen in map 20. Countries often have two different sets of age guidelines, one

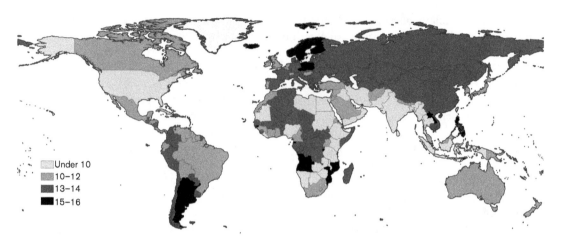

Map 20 Minimum age of criminal responsibility (Child Rights International Network 2017).

determining who can be tried and sentenced as an adult and one setting a minimum age below which individuals cannot be held criminally responsible. Some countries provide ages as young as seven or have no minimum age at which individuals can be considered criminally responsible, while in others the minimum age is sixteen. This question can be contentious. Under United Nations guidelines, the minimum age of criminal responsibility should be no lower than twelve, while Islamic law sets the age at the onset of puberty. In Pakistan in 2012, the Ministry of Law and Justice blocked an effort by the Ministry of Human Rights to change the law to comply with United Nations guidelines, arguing that "a child in our subcontinent starts understanding nature and consequences of his/her conduct much earlier than a child in the west specially because of general poverty, hot climate, exotic and spicy food," which result in earlier maturation (Crilly 2012).

CONCLUSION

As you have seen, there is great diversity in punishment practices across the world. Countries vary in their understandings of the goals and purposes of punishment, as well as in the types and severity of sanctions they impose. Variations can be extensive even within the borders of a single country. Different regions within a country may impose different kinds of punishments. Punishment practices thus reflect legal culture and national values. Discrimination and inequality can also shape punishment practices, as the wealthy or politically favored may be given lighter or less unpleasant punishments than the poor, politically disfavored, or religiously or racially oppressed. Punishments are in some cases different for women and men and are often different for children than for adults.

These variations occur for many reasons, both cultural and structural. Punishment practices reflect countries' values—perhaps shared values, or perhaps those of the governing regime. Where social control and conformity are valued, more severe punishments, including those that are stigmatizing and those that have the greatest capacity to incapacitate, are likely to be common. Where the human rights or dignity of the offender are seen as important, punishment will focus on rehabilitation or reconciliation. Structural factors shaping punishment practices include the financial resources available for carrying out sentences and the availability of government bureaucracies necessary for performing punishment. For example, control-in-freedom sentences require personnel to supervise those under sentence; rehabilitative programs can be expensive; and elephant soccer, as discussed at the beginning of this chapter, clearly requires a local population of cooperative elephants.

What almost all countries agree on is that they seek to use their punishment system to reduce crime. But they do not agree on what crimes they most seek to reduce or on how best to solve the crime problem. Yet the global variation in practices can be an asset to those looking to develop new responses to crime. By considering different practices in different national contexts, it may be possible to determine which practices are most effective in reaching specific goals—be they reducing overall crime rates, reducing recidivism, ensuring human rights, or engaging in retribution.

Family Law

CHAPTER GOALS

1. Become familiar with cross-national differences in laws relating to marriage, divorce, child custody, and reproduction.
2. Be able to explain how family law regulations can maintain or reduce gender inequality in societies.
3. Understand the continuing influence of religion on secular legal systems.

In Jiangsu Province, a coastal region of China north of Shanghai, couples seeking a divorce have been given multiple-choice quizzes by local officials in an attempt to screen out couples with a chance of reconciling, though the authorities walked back this policy after extensive criticism (Kuo 2018). In Jersey, an island territory in the English Channel, a Facebook chat was used to contemplate changes to the current divorce law, which requires couples to be married for three years before they can seek a divorce (State of Jersey 2018). A Philippine woman in Queens, New York, hopes that a new law will finally permit her to divorce the husband she left a decade ago (Fung 2018). In Italy, a man was granted a divorce after he alleged that his wife was possessed by the devil (TheLocal 2017). And a sixteen-year-old boy from a Bangladeshi village has illegally married four times, divorcing three of his young wives shortly after each wedding (Sabuj 2018). These stories are not just fodder for the gossip pages—they are starting points for a deep consideration of legal structures that shape and regulate everyday life.

Scholars of comparative law and justice have historically been less likely to focus on family law than to focus on many of the other areas of law covered in this book. While anthropologists may have studied family forms along with their focus on other elements of culture, legal scholars positioned family as "too cultural" and thus not a proper area of study for lawyers (Mandal and Dhawan 2016). Family law's association with the private, the noneconomic, and the female surely influences its omission from the canon of comparative legal study. Where scholars of comparative law do study family law, they have tended to reinforce Western-centric views, focusing on legal transformation projects designed to align the practices of countries in the global south with European notions (Mandal and Dhawan 2016), though some more recent scholarship has begun to address this gap (Nicola 2010).

But today, the study of family law in comparative context is of growing importance in our globalized world. Because of increased migration and global connection, new kinds of family law issues have arisen, and issues that used to be rare have become commonplace (Stark [2005] 2016). For example, consider the Sean Goldman case discussed in chapter 1—an understanding of comparative family law, particularly the different child custody regimes of Brazil and the United States, is necessary for puzzling through the complex issues cross-border child abduction can raise. Increased global population flows have led to a wide variety of family law questions, such as how to deal with the migration of polygamous families to countries that do not recognize multiple marriages, how to regulate intercountry adoption, and how to manage noncustodial parents' obligation to provide child support when their children live in a different country. A body of family-related international law, such as the Hague Abduction Convention, discussed in chapter 1, has developed to deal with some of these issues (Stark [2005] 2016; Sutherland 2012), though a more detailed discussion of this body of law is beyond the scope of this book. Family law also has profound relevance in discussions of legal rights (Nicola 2010), an issue to be discussed in chapter 9.

The creation of family law regimes initially occurred as part of a process by which the state extended its authority over more aspects of life (Mandal and Dhawan 2016), including matters that had historically been private or community concerns. Thus, the study of family law highlights law's importance in regulating and shaping private life. The study of comparative family law is also important because it provides a way to examine the continuing influence of religion on law, even in countries with formally secular legal systems. In some countries with secular legal systems, family law matters continue to be left in the hands of religious authorities. In others, religious belief continues to dictate some aspects of secular law. The most obvious examples of areas of law where religion continues to have a profound influence are same-sex marriage and abortion. Legal prohibitions on both acts stem from the beliefs of certain religious groups—for example, the Catholic Church. And these prohibitions then shape the legal rights of people who are of other faiths, or of no faith at all.

Even where the impact of religion has faded, conflicts may emerge between religious and secular approaches to family-related issues (Sutherland 2012). For example, in the United States, religious officials (clergy) are empowered to perform marriage ceremonies that fulfill both religious and secular marriage requirements. However, the same privilege does not extend to divorce. The Jewish religion requires additional steps beyond those of secular divorce in order for a couple to be religiously divorced, as will be discussed later in this chapter. Thus, a Jewish couple seeking a divorce will likely wish to obtain one from the religious authorities—but doing so does not then grant them a legal divorce. Some countries address this by empowering religious communities to regulate marriage and divorce according to their own particular rules or through the creation of other legal processes, such as England's treatment of the *beth din*, or Jewish religious court, as an arbitration tribunal (Estin 2009).

These examples make clear the profound complexity of family law regimes and the important impact they can have on people's lives. Indeed, the body of family law in a country shapes legally permissible avenues of union formation (marriage or alternatives) and dissolution (such as divorce) as well as childbearing and fertility control. Family law also has important consequences for property rights and inheritance, though those topics will be touched on only briefly in this chapter.

WHAT IS A FAMILY?

The first task in the study of comparative family law is determining what constitutes a family. Families may be defined biologically, economically (including based on coresidence), or in terms of felt and claimed relationships of choice (Sierra and Alviar 2015). Biological definitions of family focus on biological parent-child relations, though they do allow for legal kinship ties such as those created through marriage or formal adoption. Economic definitions of family posit that families are those groups of people who live together and provide for one another. And affective definitions suggest that families are those who are bound together by love ties. Countries use different combinations of these definitions in shaping what issues and relationships will be covered by family law.

In fact, the question "What is a family?" is even more complex than these three sets of definitions suggest. It raises all kinds of interesting lines of inquiry. How distant, for instance, may relationships be? Are your fourth cousins family? How many people must a family include? Is a couple without children a family? What about a group of siblings living together without parents or children? Can a group of people with no legal relationship—say a same-sex couple in a jurisdiction where such relationships are not legally recognized who are bringing up a foster child—count as a family? Do families need to live under the same roof? In other words, are you still a member of your family of origin if you move out of the house and across the country? What if you get married and have children of your own, are you still part of your parents' family then?

While many of the family law issues to be discussed in this chapter concern rules about entering into or terminating family relationships, the legal question of what constitutes a family can itself be legally significant. Consider the United States Supreme Court case *Moore v. City of East Cleveland* (1977). In 1966, East Cleveland enacted a housing ordinance regulating the combinations of people who could occupy individual housing units. It stated that a housing unit could be occupied only by a married couple (or single parent) and their dependent children, along with only one parent of the spouses and only one child of the spouses with a child of his or her own. Violations of this ordinance could be punished with a maximum of six months in prison or a US$1,000 fine for *each day* of the prohibited living arrangements. Inez Moore was living in violation of this ordinance. She lived with her unmarried son, his son (her grandson), and another grandson with different parents. Upon conviction for violating the ordinance, Ms. Moore was sentenced to five days in jail and a US$25 fine. She took her case to the United States Supreme Court, which held in a 5–4 ruling that we have the right to live in extended family arrangements of our choice.

However, it remains legal to limit the right of *unrelated* individuals to live together, a provision many U.S. municipalities use to try to prevent groups of college students from sharing apartments. Thus, being able to prove that, under the relevant legal definitions, a household actually constitutes a family is important for the ability to maintain stable residential ties. This case provides just one example of a reason why governments seek to regulate who counts as a family—to regulate residential arrangements. Governments also regulate families to control property distribution, sexual behavior, and procreation, and to avoid responsibility for the care of children, the elderly, and others unable to care for themselves, who, but for the intervention of families, might leave the state responsible for care.

FORMING A FAMILY

When people think about forming a family, there are two central processes they tend to consider. They think about marriage or other ways of forming a union between partners in a relationship. They also think about the process of acquiring children, be it through the standard biological process of procreation, the legal process of adoption, or the use of assisted reproductive technology. Law plays a role in all of these processes of family formation.

Marriage and Union Formation

Marriage is the most common legal process through which people form a legal family relationship. Typically, marriages are formed through a contractual process in which both parties to a marriage sign an agreement to be married to one another. These contracts are then registered with the appropriate legal authorities. The use of contracts to solemnize marriages is not a new thing—Jewish and Muslim marriages, for example, have used this approach for centuries—and they can be administered by secular or religious authorities, depending on local legal rules. These contracts are usually legally standardized, and all people marrying in a given jurisdiction use the same marriage contract. The process has become so standardized in some places that individuals may not even realize that they are entering into a contract when they get married. It is possible to alter the default contract in some jurisdictions. Islamic marriage contracts can be customized to the particular couple, a procedure that enables couples to modernize the terms of their marriages. For example, a couple might include a provision preventing the husband from taking additional wives or ensuring that the wife will have equal access to divorce and child custody (Weisbrod 1999). In three U.S. states (Louisiana, Arizona, and Arkansas), an alternative form of marriage contract called **covenant marriage** is available. Covenant marriage compels premarital counseling and restricts access to divorce by requiring the couple to attempt to reconcile and mandating a two-year waiting period prior to divorce unless specific conditions are met (Spaht 2005), most notably physical or sexual abuse of a spouse or child, adultery, or felony conviction.

There are other approaches to marriage besides the contract. Many common law jurisdictions offer an alternative marriage procedure called **common law marriage**. Recognition of a common law marriage requires that a couple see themselves as, and hold themselves out to their community as, spouses and that they have lived together for some period of time (Sutherland 2012). The fact that this system is called *common law* marriage points to its historical roots as a type of marriage recognized in countries with common law legal systems. However, in many contemporary common law countries, such as Scotland, and in most U.S. states, common law marriages are no longer recognized (Sutherland 2012). Similar systems have been adopted in some countries without common law legal systems. For example, common law marriages are recognized under Colombian law (Sierra and Alviar 2015). Even where common law marriage exists, however, partners may not be entitled to the same rights as they would if their marriage were registered (Perelli-Harris and Gassen 2012), and either partner can deny the existence of the marriage.

In some societies, traditional marriage procedures required nothing more than a ceremony of some kind, and where traditional law remains, it may legally recognize such marriages. A couple's statement that the partners consider themselves to be married may also be sufficient. In some parts of the world, most notably Kyrgyzstan, marriage still occurs via kidnapping. Sometimes, these kidnappings are consensual, with a young woman agreeing to be kidnapped by her prospective husband to escape an arranged marriage or as a kind of elopement. This was typical of marriages by kidnapping in former times, when most marriages were arranged by parents without their children's consent. However, marriages by kidnapping carried out without the consent of the woman or her parents have become more common recently. Estimates are that as many as 50 percent of marriages in Kyrgyzstan take place through kidnapping, and of those, the majority are nonconsensual (Kleinbach and Salimjanova 2007). This is illegal, and contrary to the majority Islamic faith, but it is rarely prosecuted, and when it is the man usually gets only a small fine.

Most countries have some legal restrictions on who can get married. The Kyrgyz example points to one area with which such restrictions might be concerned, the question of consent. Countries vary in terms of whether the individuals to be married must themselves give consent and whether parental consent is required. In some countries, parental consent is required for minors to marry, while adults are permitted to consent for themselves. In others, minors are simply prohibited from marrying. While many countries hold that marriages performed before the minimum age of marriage are simply invalid, there are other approaches. For example, India and Pakistan prohibit child marriages and criminalize parents who arrange them but do not invalidate the marriages themselves (Stark [2005] 2016)—meaning that young children can grow up to find out that they were married years ago. Under common law, children could be married so long as they had reached puberty (Weisbrod 1999), which is the standard in Shari'a law (though some areas have traditions of marrying younger children). Most common law jurisdictions have modernized their approach to marriage, creating legal provisions that set out minimum ages. In the majority of countries today, people must be at least eighteen before they can marry without parental consent, and some countries have older minimum ages. However, some countries set a lower minimum age for girls than for boys. Throughout much of the world, people are getting married later, and they are more likely to be able to choose their own spouses than they were in earlier generations (Rashad, Osman, and Roudi-Fahimi 2005).

Another set of restrictions on marriage concerns **consanguinity**, literally "blood relations." All societies have some prohibitions on sexual relations and childbearing—and thus marriage—for those who are considered to be too closely related. The most common restrictions prohibit siblings from marrying and parents from marrying their children; countries may also prohibit uncles and aunts from marrying their nieces or nephews and may restrict the marriage of first cousins, especially double first cousins (individuals who share the same grandparents on both sides due to being descended from pairs of first cousins). However, consanguineous marriages remain common in some countries—40 to 50 percent of marriages in Sudan, Libya, and Saudi Arabia are between first cousins (Rashad, Osman, and Roudi-Fahimi 2005). Marriage may also be prohibited for those who have previously been divorced.

Marriage laws also set out the number of people an individual can be married to. **Polygamous** or **plural marriages** are those where one person marries multiple spouses, as opposed to monogamous ones, which involve a single pair of marriage partners. Polyandry refers to marriages where one wife marries multiple husbands, while polygyny refers to marriages where one husband marries multiple wives. Polyandrous marriages are much rarer than polygynous marriages, with the most notable polyandrous cultural practices being found in Tibet (Stark [2005] 2016). Some countries not only prohibit polygamous marriages but also criminalize them, prosecuting those who enter into or solemnize them. Polygamists are even barred from legal admission as immigrants or visitors to the United States (Estin 2009). In contrast, polygyny is legally permissible in many Muslim countries, as men under Shari'a law can marry up to four wives (though they are generally supposed to have the consent of the first wife and to maintain a separate household for each wife). Polygyny is also practiced in other religious communities, including breakaway Mormon fundamentalist groups in the United States, though such marriages are not legally recognized, nor are they recognized by the Mormon authorities. The term "polyamory" refers to the practice of engaging openly and without deception in multiple romantic or sexual relationships at a time, but outside of the circumstances noted above, countries do not legally recognize such relationships.

Finally, as shown in map 21, many countries regulate the sex or gender of marital partners. **Sex** refers to the biological characteristics that make someone male or female (or intersex), such as genitals and chromosomes. **Gender** refers to the social roles and personal identities of individuals. Countries can use sex, gender, or both in crafting marriage restrictions. While under traditional law, some societies recognized various types of same-sex or same-gender relationships, modern legal recognition of such unions is a recent phenomenon. In the year 2000, the Netherlands became the first country in the world to legally recognize same-sex marriages; as of this writing, nearly thirty countries worldwide recognize such marriages, and additional countries provide a type of legal recognition short of marriage.

If a couple is legally permitted to marry, some traditions and legal systems impose additional obstacles before the marriage can be solemnized. These can range from mandatory premarital counseling or blood tests for genetic or sexually transmitted diseases to required financial gifts from one family to another, such as **bride prices** and **dowries**. More unusual requirements can be

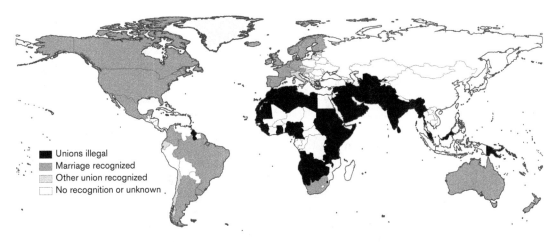

Map 21 Legal recognition of same-sex marriage (Carroll and Mendos 2017; Yi 2017).

found: in West Java, Indonesia, a protocol requires couples to provide a minimum of ten trees in order to legally marry (Reuters 2009).

A bride price is a payment from the groom or the groom's family to the bride's family to compensate them for the loss of her household labor. Islamic marriage contracts require a form of bride price, though today it is more typically provided to the bride or set aside to be paid to her in the case of a divorce. Bride prices remain common in Islamic countries, rural China, Thailand, and some parts of Africa and tend to be found in areas where polygyny is practiced (S. Anderson 2007). Where bride prices are provided, they tend to consist of the equivalent of a year's income or a number of livestock animals.

A **dowry** is a payment from the bride's family to the groom or his family, which sometimes takes the form of money or property brought by the bride into the marriage itself. Even if the payment goes to the couple, it is generally expected by societies that use dowries that the husband will take control of the couple's property during the marriage, and providing a dowry would typically mean a daughter was no longer entitled to any inheritance she might have otherwise received. Dowries remain particularly common in South Asia, despite laws that have been passed against the practice, and in some parts of the Arab world. The value of dowries tends to be higher than that of bride prices; estimates suggest that the average dowry is more than twice the average bride price (S. Anderson 2007). In Egypt, some dowry costs are paid in advance, while others are saved to be paid in case of divorce. Grooms and their families are also responsible for many other costs, including gifts of jewelry and the majority of expenses related to housing, furniture, and other necessities for the new household (Rashad, Osman, and Roudi-Fahimi 2005). Costs have become so high in the United Arab Emirates that the government created a marriage fund to provide grants to low-income men on the condition that they marry Emirati women (Rashad, Osman, and Roudi-Fahimi 2005). Traditionally in China, both bride price and dowry payments are exchanged, with the dowry sometimes constituting the return of some percentage of the bride price (S. Anderson 2007).

Another economic tool used in the context of marriage is the **prenuptial agreement**. This is a contract signed prior to entering into a marriage that lays out the distribution of property in the case of divorce. In prior eras, they were common only among the very wealthy, but their use has spread due to the increased average age at marriage in many countries and thus the greater likelihood that marital partners will have acquired property or wealth prior to marriage. However, prenuptial agreements are not enforceable in all jurisdictions.

Once people have entered into a marriage, their new status can have many impacts on their lives, particularly for women. Many countries provide for additional legal rights upon marriage (Perelli-Harris and Gassen 2012). These include financial rights, such as the right to file joint income taxes, the opportunity to qualify for certain tax benefits, the ability to provide health insurance to a partner, and the obligation to provide for an unemployed partner; childbearing benefits, such as the right to use reproductive technology (discussed below) and to jointly adopt; and other legal rights, such as the ability to sponsor a partner for immigration and citizenship and the right to make legal decisions for an incapacitated partner.

We often focus on the legal and economic benefits of marriage, but marriage can have costs as well. The common law doctrine of **coverture** meant that married women ceased to exist as individual legal persons. Their rights, property, and identity were subsumed under that of their husband, who had substantial authority over them—men could determine where their wives could live, hold their wives captive in the household, and even physically punish them, so long as the punishment did not cause permanent injury (Hasday 2000). When a man was married to a woman, he could not be convicted of raping her, no matter the circumstances of the sexual assault, as marriage was seen as providing for irrevocable and universal consent to sexual activity (Hasday 2000). Similar standards can be found in many countries using legal systems other than common law. While some of these countries have moved in the direction of gender equality, especially in terms of criminalizing physical assault by spouses, marital rape remains fully legal in many parts of the world, with over a third of the world's population living in such countries (M. Anderson 2016). Where it has been criminalized, prosecution may require special circumstances, such as unusual brutality or a formal legal separation of the spouses at the time of the crime.

In some countries, low-income individuals may lose access to social insurance benefits upon marriage. In others, married women are not permitted to claim child tax deductions and other work-related benefits unless their husbands are disabled or unemployed (Rashad, Osman, and Roudi-Fahimi 2005). In many countries, all of a woman's property passes to her husband upon marriage, and she no longer retains any control over it. In countries with patriarchal regimes, women's decision-making may be reduced or eliminated upon marriage. Women may need their husbands' permission if they wish to seek employment or education, use birth control or get an abortion, or simply leave the house. Saudi Arabia has been a key example of such a system. It is currently in the process of reducing the extent of male control over women—previously, women needed male guardians' permission for such activities as driving, traveling abroad, and obtaining official documents. While these restrictions have been removed, the guardianship system remains in place, restricting women's ability to make many legal decisions for themselves (Coker 2018; Public's Radio 2019). As will be discussed later in this chapter, women may even lose the right to their names upon marriage.

Marriage, at least monogamous marriage, brings with it the expectation of sexual fidelity. Violations of this norm have been addressed via various legal regimes. In some countries, adultery has been treated as a severe criminal offense, punishable by death. In others, adultery is treated as a private wrong, with the husband of a wife who has engaged in adultery entitled to kill or claim compensation from whichever man slept with his wife (Weinstein 1986). Today, traces of this past remain in jurisdictions that permit the aggrieved spouse to sue the third party they deem responsible for the adulterous act, as in the 2010 case in which a North Carolina woman sued *American Idol* winner Fantasia for having an affair with the woman's husband (McMillian 2012). Such provisions have rarely punished men who engaged in sex outside of marriage, so long as their partners were not themselves married women, as the violation of adultery was generally understood as a violation against the proprietary interest of a man in his wife. While many countries have decriminalized adultery—at least thirty-five did so between 1947 and 2005 alone (Frank, Camp, and Boutcher 2010)—it remains grounds for fault-based divorce (to be discussed later in this chapter) in most of them. And in some countries today, adultery can result in criminal charges. It is considered among the most serious of criminal offenses under Shari'a law. In countries such as Iran and Saudi Arabia, adulterers can be put to death, though the evidentiary rules of Shari'a courts would require either a confession or four witnesses to the act. In India, men who have sexual relations with married women without the consent of their husbands are subject to prison terms, but the women are not subject to punishment (Malhotra and Malhotra 2012). In some U.S. states, adultery remains criminalized but is only lightly punished. For example, in Rhode Island, acts of adultery can result in a US$500 fine (Rhode Island General Laws § 11–6-2), which means that during divorce proceedings, spouses accused of adultery can exercise their right against self-incrimination and refuse to testify about the accusations.

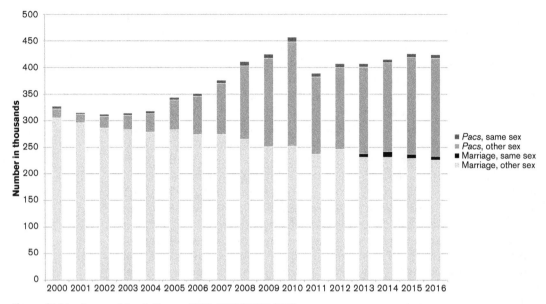

Figure 21 Marriages and *Pacs* in France, 2000–2016 (INSEE 2018).

As noted above, marriages supply people with various rights, and it is possible to split some of them off, creating legal recognition schemes for relationships that fall short of marriage itself. Civil unions provide couples with some of the rights of marriage, while domestic partnerships have even fewer rights but do grant some legal recognition to a relationship. The areas in which the greatest number of legal differences between marriages and other forms of legal recognition tend to be found are taxes, immigration benefits, and regulations relating to child custody, assisted reproductive technology, and adoption.

In the Netherlands, such unions are called registered partnerships and provide nearly all the legal benefits of marriage. In France, these are called *pactes civils de solidarité,* or *Pacs. Pacs* provide for fewer legal rights than do marriages. Partners in a *Pacs* do not have access to survivor benefits in pension systems, face restrictions on joint property ownership that affect property distribution upon union dissolution, and do not automatically have joint custody over children (Perelli-Harris and Gassen 2012). The creation of some of these systems was spurred by countries' desires to provide some legal recognition but not full legal marriage to same-sex couples. In some countries, only same-sex couples are eligible to enter into such unions, while male-female couples must enter into marriages, but in others, these union types are available to all couples. France's *Pacs* are available to both same-sex and male-female couples. As figure 21 shows, *Pacs* have become very popular among other-sex (male-female) couples since their introduction, while marriages have declined in popularity. Contrary to the fears of some commentators, it does not seem that same-sex marriage rates have impacted other-sex marriage rates. Rather, couples are choosing *Pacs* for their own personal reasons.

Nonmarital cohabitation by male-female couples remains illegal in some countries, as all sexual activity outside of marriage is considered criminal in such countries, a form of adultery. Even countries such as Italy, Germany, and Norway prohibited it until the late 1960s or early 1970s (Perelli-Harris and Gassen 2012). However, in recent years, nonmarital cohabitation—and the choice to remain single—have become more common in many parts of the world, reducing the stigma of such arrangements (Sutherland 2012). In some cases, individuals choose to marry within a religious community and do not obtain a legal marriage in the jurisdiction in which they live. Such a strategy may also be utilized by individuals whose religious traditions encourage polygamous marriages but who live in jurisdictions where such marriages are illegal. These couples will typically be treated as any cohabiting couple would be in that jurisdiction, as a religious marriage that does not conform to civil marriage rules is not considered valid (Estin 2009).

The Legal Status of Children

The most significant legal question around the creation of the parent-child relationship is when that relationship is legally recognized. For children born into a marriage or registered union involving both of their biological parents, this is a simple question. But in other cases, it can be more complex.

Adoption refers to the legal creation of a relationship between a child and one or more adults who are not the biological parents of that child. Not all countries provide for legal adoption: for instance, under Shari'a law, adoption is not permissible (Pollack et al. 2004). However, this does not mean Muslim societies abandon parentless children. Rather, the maintenance of such children is a communal responsibility, and they are supported through a type of long-term foster care in which the child does not become a full member of the new family and has no rights of inheritance, but the new family does take on responsibility for and authority over the child (Pollack et al. 2004). In Catholic canon law, adoption was traditionally prohibited (Witte 2003). Historically, and still today in many parts of the world, adoption is undertaken primarily by close relatives. This is often quite informal and may not be legally sanctioned but does result in the child having a home.

The development of the legal concept of adoption comes from the development of property rights rather than from a historical concern about orphans. In traditional societies, especially where only males could inherit property, families without heirs could adopt in order to pass on their land. Such a system was used in classical Rome (Pollack et al. 2004), where the typical adoptee was

Marriage, Children, and Surnames

For many people born and raised in the United States, the idea that most women take their husband's surname upon marriage—and that children are given their father's surname even if their mother has chosen not to change her name—is taken for granted. Indeed, recent research in the United States shows that, at least among men with lower educational attainment, women who do not change their names upon marriage are seen as less committed wives, though no such pattern of views is observed among women or highly educated men (Shafer 2017). And data from 2004 shows that 94 percent of married women in the United States have the same surname as their husband (Gooding and Kreider 2010). But such practices are far from universal. Rates of name changing in the United States are lower among young women; women who are Latina, Asian, or Native American, and to a lesser extent among Black women; and women with graduate degrees (Gooding and Kreider 2010). Interestingly, data suggests that same-sex married couples are less likely to share a common last name than are male-female married couples (Emens 2007), and countries greatly vary in their marital naming practices. Some countries require name changes, others largely forbid them, and many end up somewhere in between.

Common law did not require women to change their names upon marriage and in fact permitted people wide latitude to determine their names by choice (Emens 2007), but countries such as the United States implemented many legal provisions that made it extremely difficult for women to retain their birth names. For example, some states prohibited married women from registering to vote or obtaining a driver's license if they did not take their husband's name (Goldin and Shim 2004). Such rules were gradually elimi-

nated following a series of court cases in the 1970s, though many local officials still act as if women's names are required to change at marriage (Emens 2007). Empirical data from the United States shows that women became more likely to keep their birth names in the years after these legal changes, but between 1990 and 2000, the likelihood that women would keep their birth names declined (Goldin and Shim 2004). This data also shows that more highly educated women are more likely to keep their birth names (Goldin and Shim 2004).

There are a variety of alternative naming practices used in countries and cultures around the world. Japanese law requires that married couples share a surname, though it is just as permissible for a husband to take his wife's name as it is for a wife to take her husband's, a requirement that was reaffirmed by the courts as recently as 2015 (Judgment Concerning Article 750 of the Civil Code and Article 13 of the Constitution 2015). The practice of husbands changing their names is long-standing, particularly in cases where a man marries into a family that has only daughters (Emens 2007), but it remains very rare—96 percent of couples use the man's name (Judgment Concerning Article 750 of the Civil Code and Article 13 of the Constitution 2015). The current Japanese practice is starkly different than it was 150 years ago, when women retained their birth surnames (MacClintock 2010). Switzerland has similar requirements, though men who wish to take their wife's surname need special permission (MacClintock 2010).

Unlike common law jurisdictions, which have a history of permissiveness about name changes, civil law has no presumption of individual choice in naming, and indeed many civil law countries have strict rules about both surnames and given names. In France, marital name changes are forbidden, and in Quebec a name change is possible only after five years of continuous use of the new name (MacClintock 2010). In fact, naming rules are so strict in some countries that children may be given first names only from designated lists of approved names or parents must seek official approval of names before they can be recorded (Israel 2010). Women are also likely to keep their birth names upon marriage in China and South Korea as well as in Spanish- and Portuguese-speaking countries (United Kingdom General Secretariat 2006). While retaining birth names can be a mark of gender egalitarianism, it is not necessarily. Instead, it may simply mean that a country values encoded knowledge about one's connection to one's family of birth more than it values encoded knowledge about women's marital connections.

Countries vary in terms of the surnames given to children as well. In some civil law countries, such as Switzerland, children born to unmarried parents cannot receive the father's surname; in other countries, children born to unmarried parents can be given the father's surname only if paternity has been established (Perelli-Harris and Gassen 2012). In the Netherlands, the default option is for such children to be given the mother's surname, though couples can opt out (Emens 2007). The practice in many Spanish- and Portuguese-speaking countries is to give children both parents' last names as part of their surname (Emens 2007). So as to avoid names of extraordinary length, only one of each parent's dual names is typically passed on to the next generation, though some people may use four or more surnames.

Icelandic surnames are **patronymics** or **matronymics**, names formed out of the first name of a parent with a prefix or suffix indicating the relationship (Emens 2007). For example, the full name of the performing artist Björk is Björk Guðmundsdóttir, as her father's first name was Guðmundur. Islamic tradition suggests that women are supposed to keep their birth names, but in some cases Muslim women do take their husband's name. For example, Turkey requires women to take their husband's surname upon marriage (MacClintock 2010). Muslim women in societies where women typically do change their names may conform to local custom. However, countries more strictly conforming to Shari'a law do not require women to change their names (United Kingdom General Secretariat 2006). Surnames as such may or may not be used in such countries. Where they are not, individuals instead may be given several generations of patronymics.

Many Slavic countries also use patronymics; in some, women take their husband's patronymic as a new surname but change the ending to indicate a feminine gender (United Kingdom General Secretariat 2006). For example, if Stefan Novak and Jelena Kalinovski marry, Jelena's marital name might be Jelena Novaka. Suffixes vary depending on the details of the local language. Similar patterns are found in other countries, including Greece. A variation on this practice is found among Turkish Cypriots, where surnames are typically individuals' father's names and women replace their father's name with their husband's name upon marriage (United Kingdom General Secretariat 2006). For example, if Ahmet Ersoy and Sibel Özer marry, Sibel would become known as Sibel Ahmet.

As this brief survey of naming practices and laws demonstrates, there is considerable variation in the regimes governing names in countries around the world. This variation highlights some of what makes comparative family law so interesting. One of the reasons many commentators—and marital partners themselves—give for marital name changes is the importance of creating a unified family unit with a shared surname. Yet many societies see no need for such a practice, instead using names to emphasize connection to an individual's family of origin. Such practices are most obvious among those who use patronymics or matronymics, but they can be seen elsewhere as well. There are even still societies where surnames of any kind remain rare (United Kingdom General Secretariat 2006). Especially notable are the countries in which women commonly change their names but do so in a way that results in a surname somewhat different from their husband's, such as adopting a feminized patronymic or using the husband's first name as a surname. In these cases, it is clear that marital name changes are not about the creation of a unified family name but rather about the creation of a new legal identity for women that places them as part of their husband or their husband's family, thus reaffirming gendered inequalities in those societies.

an adult. In these circumstances, adoption was explicitly not about ensuring a home for a child. In some times and places, adoption was used as a way to increase the domestic labor force of a farm, household, or workshop by acquiring employees such as agricultural laborers, domestic workers, or apprentices in trades in the form of adopted children. The novel, movie, and television series *Anne of Green Gables* tells the story of this kind of adoption.

Legitimate children are those whose parents were married at the time at which the pregnancy became known; **illegitimate** children are those born into unsanctioned relationships, such as those between unmarried parents. In many contexts, children can be legitimated if the parents of the child later marry, though such a remedy is not feasible in cases of adultery (Witte 2003). Some societies, particularly those that trace lineage through the mother, do not have this concept. Both church law and common law in Europe and the Americas prohibited the use of adoption to legitimate an illegitimate child; in the United States, parents were not even required to support the illegitimate children they produced (Witte 2003).

Until relatively recently—as recently as the 1980s in some parts of Europe—laws held that only children born into marital unions were entitled to inherit property or names (Perelli-Harris and Gassen 2012) and to pass on property to their own spouses and children (Witte 2003). Illegitimate children have also faced prohibitions on service in many professions, ordination as clergy, and membership in social associations. Due to the increased rate of births out of wedlock around the world (as shown in figure 22), the legal hardships resulting from illegitimacy have declined in many countries in recent years (Sutherland 2012), as have social stigmas. However, illegitimate children in some parts of the world continue to face hurdles. Under Jewish religious law, the descendants of *mamzerim* (illegitimate children born either out of incest or adultery specifically) continue to be considered *mamzerim*, even over multiple generations. Unlike under common law and canon law, *mamzerim* face no restrictions on their names and no limit on their ability to inherit, but they are forbidden to

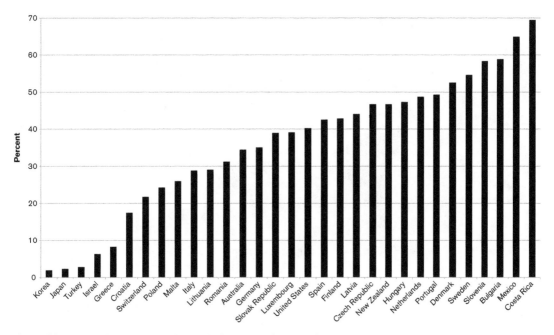

Figure 22 Percent of births outside of marriage by country (OECD n.d.-a).

marry Jews unless those Jews are also *mamzerim* or converts. Legitimacy status can also affect individuals' citizenship status. For example, children born outside the United States to mothers with United States citizenship or to married fathers with United States citizenship automatically become citizens at birth so long as the mother lived in the United States for at least one year. In contrast, children born to unmarried fathers with United States citizenship where the mothers are not United States citizens do not automatically get United States citizenship. Their fathers must actively choose to acknowledge paternity, or it must be proven in court, in order for them to obtain citizenship (Cornell Law School n.d.).

Regulating Reproduction

Both governments and individuals may seek to control, limit, or encourage reproduction. The regulation of reproduction provides a useful site for thinking about the interaction of state and individual interests. For example, a country experiencing overpopulation, as China was in the 1970s, might impose limits on the number of children individuals could have. In China, these limits came to be known as the One-Child Policy. This policy, which has since been relaxed, limited couples to one child, though many exceptions were given, such

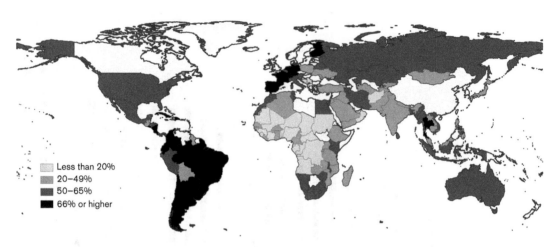

Map 22 Contraceptive prevalence, modern methods only, most recent post-2010 data available (United Nations 2018).

as to rural people, ethnic minorities, and those whose first child was female or disabled. Considerable fines were imposed on those who did not abide by the limits, and women were required to have IUDs implanted or undergo steriliza-tion procedures to prevent additional births. In contrast, countries experienc-ing population declines might adopt policies designed to encourage more births, such as limiting access to contraception, subsidizing access to assisted reproductive technology, and paying stipends to parents who have more than a specified number of children. But neither restrictions on childbearing nor state policies encouraging births respect individuals' choices and rights to control their own fertility and bodies. Countries that respect reproductive autonomy permit individuals to access services like contraception but do not impose them on people who do not want to use them.

While the United Nations has declared access to contraception to be a human right (Center for Reproductive Rights 2010), access to contraceptive technologies varies across the globe. In some countries, contraceptives such as the birth control pill are available over the counter and national health insur-ance pays for long-acting, reversible contraceptives like IUDs, while in others, women may face obstacles to obtaining contraceptives. In the Philippines, for example, many hormonal and implantable contraceptives were illegal until 2017 (AFP-JIJI 2017). Even where contraceptives are available, they may be so expensive as to be out of reach of some women, especially where national health insurance coverage for contraception is not available. Social stigma and opposition to contraception from the community or from sexual partners can limit women's access to contraception. And in some countries, unmarried women face particular difficulties in accessing contraception (Sedgh, Ashford, and Hussain 2016). Thus, as map 22 shows, contraceptive usage rates remain very low in many countries, even under 10 percent (United Nations 2018). It is worth noting that while clinical trials for male contraceptives have been promising, countries have generally focused their attention on women in attempts to regulate reproduction, leaving men to act as they please.

Access to abortion is also an important part of discussions about the control of reproduction, especially as it represents one of the legal sites in which the continuing influence of religion on secular legal systems is most clear. In part, this is due to the fact that there are no scientific or empirical markers for when life begins. While science can determine if a heart is beating, it cannot determine if a heartbeat is sufficient to indicate that life has begun. Thus, we turn to our own religious or moral codes to determine when life begins. Depending on your perspective, life may begin at conception; at implantation; at quickening, or the point in a pregnancy at which fetal movement is first detectable by a pregnant woman, usually between fifteen to twenty weeks; at the point of fetal viability; at birth; or at some time after birth when a child is officially given a name. Even frameworks that sound empirically valid, like fetal viability, do not have clear indicators. For instance, neonatologists—doctors specializing in treating newborns—agree that infants born at less than twenty-two weeks' gestation are unlikely to survive, while those born at twenty-seven weeks' gestation or more have a high survival rate. But for pregnancy durations of between twenty-three and twenty-six weeks, neonatologists do not agree on viability (Kaempf et al. 2006). This discussion is further compounded by the fact that doctors can only estimate when a pregnancy began, based on indicators like the date of the last menstrual period or observations of an ultrasound (Committee on Obstetric Practice 2017).

Historically, abortion would not have been subject to legal regulation, as the primary technologies available to end a pregnancy (as well as to serve as contraceptives) were herbal medicines known primarily to female midwives and healers (Riddle 1991). In fact, even infanticide—the killing of a live-born infant—was legal in some contexts; in others, it was somewhat decriminalized in comparison to killings of those beyond the infant life stage (Damme 1978). Beginning in the early and mid-1800s, countries sought to regulate or even entirely prohibit access to abortion. The nature and extent of these regulations varies, including restrictions on when during a pregnancy abortions may be performed, what medical techniques may be utilized, and what reasons are considered legitimate grounds for seeking an abortion.

Some countries prohibit abortion entirely. According to 2017 data collected by the Guttmacher Institute, there are no exceptions to laws banning abortions in twenty-six countries. An additional thirty-eight countries permit abortions only to save the pregnant woman's life. Until 2018, this included Ireland, which recently removed the constitutional grounds for such restrictions by referendum (McDonald, Graham-Harrison, and Baker 2018). Prior to this referendum, abortion restrictions in Ireland were so severe that permission to terminate a pregnancy sometimes came too late to save a dying pregnant woman. Now, abortions are permitted in Ireland early in pregnancy for any reason and later in pregnancy when there are risks to the life or health of the pregnant woman or the fetus is not viable (Health [Regulation of Termination of Pregnancy] Act 2018). Today, about seventy-five countries permit abortion for a broad array of reasons (Singh et al. 2018). Where abortion is permitted for reasons beyond a threat to the pregnant woman's life, exceptions for her physical health, for cases of rape or incest, or where there is a significant fetal abnormality or the fetus is not viable are the most common. Other countries add exceptions for the pregnant woman's mental health or when the pregnancy would present socioeconomic difficulties. Where abortion is permitted to protect the pregnant woman's physical health, some countries consider only very significant health risks, while in others this grounds will cover most circumstances, as abortion is much safer medically than giving birth (Raymond and Grimes 2012). Restrictions may also be placed on the time period during the pregnancy during which abortions are permitted. Even countries that broadly permit abortion may impose time limits that are so early that many women have not yet been able to confirm that they are pregnant; other countries allow abortion until the point of fetal viability. Finally, countries may restrict the types of procedures medical providers are allowed to perform.

Where abortion is legal, it still may not be accessible. Countries, or regions within them, may impose substantial restrictions, such as multiday waiting periods, spousal or parental notification or consent rules, or requirements that women seek permission from medical ethics panels at hospitals. These restrictions can prevent women from accessing abortions. For example, in Turkey, abortion remains broadly legal up until the tenth week of pregnancy, but in 2015, only three of thirty-seven state hospitals in Istanbul were willing to perform the procedure (Letsch 2015). In the United States, so-called TRAP (targeted regulation of abortion providers) laws in many states have made it nearly impossible for doctors to keep clinics providing abortions open in those states, leaving most counties with no abortion providers. Countries may also choose to exclude abortion coverage from national or private health insurance schemes, leaving the procedure out of financial reach for most women (Singh et al. 2018).

People who experience obstacles on the road to biological reproduction may wish to employ assisted reproductive technology. This includes sperm or egg donation, in vitro fertilization, and gestational surrogacy. There is a wide variation in the regulation and availability of such reproductive technologies. For example, gestational surrogacy may be prohibited, permitted only when the surrogate uses a donor egg, permitted only for altruistic reasons (where the surrogate is not compensated), or permitted with little regulation (Sutherland 2012). Most reproductive technology is seen as unacceptable by the Catholic Church, and thus access may be heavily restricted in countries where the

Catholic Church continues to have a considerable impact. In contrast, countries with declining populations may encourage or subsidize the use of assisted reproductive technologies to facilitate higher birth rates.

ENDING FAMILY RELATIONSHIPS

Family law regimes also govern the circumstances under which family relationships may be terminated. Most notably, marriages may be terminated by divorce in countries in which this is legal. Marriages may also end with the death of one of the marital partners, and this can have legal consequences for the surviving partner. In addition, many countries have legal procedures governing the circumstances in which parents may lose the right to raise their children.

Ending Unions

In considering marriage termination, the first legal question is whether divorce is possible. Today, most countries have provisions permitting divorce. However, the Philippines (unless the parties are Muslim or one is a foreign citizen) as well as Malta do not allow divorce at all, and in some other countries, access to divorce is extremely recent. In Ireland, divorce did not become legal until 1995 (Htun and Weldon 2011), and in Chile, it was not legalized until 2005 (Rohter 2005). Even after legalization, Ireland maintains an onerous divorce process (Holmquist 2015). After a year of marital problems, spouses may seek a legal separation. They then must be separated for at least three more years before a divorce can occur. Note that the countries with the most restricted access to divorce tend to be predominantly Catholic countries, given the Catholic Church's strong prohibitions on divorce.

Where divorce is legal, it may be heavily restricted as to reason and circumstance. Fault-based divorce is divorce that is permitted based on allegations of specific wrongs. The most common circumstances in which fault-based divorces are permitted are adultery and the inability to bear children. Deception at the time of marriage, including the concealment of medical conditions, can also be a reason, as can a woman's disobedience to her husband or certain types of spousal abuse. Some religious faiths permit divorce if a spouse converts to another faith. In some countries that allow polygamy, wives may be permitted a divorce if they disapprove of or are damaged by their husband's taking of an additional wife.

Historically under common law, divorce was extremely difficult to obtain, even on the limited grounds for which it was permitted—mostly cruelty, desertion, or adultery. Marital rape, as well as physical abuse that did not cause permanent injury, were insufficient to claim cruelty (Hasday 2000). This regime even prohibited marital partners from recovering in suits against one another due to the doctrine of coverture, which treated the couple as a single legal person (Hasday 2000). In sixteenth- through eighteenth-century England, women were able to file for a nullification of marriage (not quite a divorce, but with the same effect) or a legal separation on the basis of adultery, life-threatening cruelty, or a husband's impotence preventing consummation of the marriage (S. Hoffman 2009). Men could gain full divorces on the basis of wives' adultery. Notably, men in some cases could defend themselves against charges of impotence by performing public acts of masturbation or having sex with a paid sex worker in view of the court (S. Hoffman 2009). Knowledge of infertility or impotence at the time of marriage usually voids those conditions as grounds for a divorce—or else marriages of the elderly would be impossible. It has occasionally been suggested by those who believe the sole purpose of marriage is procreation that such marriages be prohibited (Weisbrod 1999).

In some cases, a wide variety of causes provide grounds for divorce. For instance, the traditional legal system of the Ifugao, an indigenous group in the Philippines, had a long list of conditions under which divorce was permitted, ranging from adultery and refusal to engage in sexual activity to bad omens and insults from the in-laws (Barton 1919). Occasionally, divorce systems also provide for circumstances under which a normally permissible divorce would not be permitted. Under traditional Chinese law (not relevant to today's China), a man could not divorce his wife if she had observed traditional mourning rituals for his parents for three years, if she had no family to return to, or if he had been poor when the marriage commenced but was now wealthy (Weisbrod 1999).

A fault-based divorce system remained in place in the state of New York until 2010. It permitted divorce on the grounds of adultery, cruel and inhumane treatment, or abandonment (DiFonzo and Stern 2007). Couples who wanted to divorce but could not find adequate grounds were known to hire models to pose for photographs in a hotel room with the husband so that adultery could be claimed. Beginning in 1967, the law did permit for an alternative to fault-based divorce in which couples separated for two years (later reduced to one) and then petitioned the court to transform the separation into a divorce (DiFonzo and Stern 2007). However, this procedure required both spouses to participate—if neither spouse would move out of the house, a separation would be impossible. Other U.S. states and many Western countries developed systems of no-fault or consent-based divorce earlier, typically between the 1960s and 1980s. These systems permit people to seek divorces without alleging specific grounds, such that they can split up if they are unhappy in the marriage.

In some contexts, important gender differences in access to divorce remain, particularly in theocratic and traditional legal systems. Men in such systems typically have much easier access to divorce, as they may be able to obtain a divorce through a no-fault system (perhaps with the requirement to undergo mediation or a period of trial separation first), while women may have to demonstrate fault on the part of their husband. Islamic and Jewish religious law provide examples of such systems. Obviously, same-sex marriages that end in divorce do not exhibit these kinds of gender differences.

Under Islamic law, a man can divorce his wife with no restrictions, but a woman typically must get her husband's consent to divorce and then give up claims to a marriage payment she would otherwise be entitled to upon divorce (Estin 2009) or else demonstrate fault-based grounds for divorce. Yet these restrictive rules have not done much to limit the divorce rate. Today in Saudi Arabia, which strictly follows Shari'a law, more than 40 percent of marriages end in divorce, and the number of divorces has continued to grow (Saudi Gazette 2018).

The situation under Jewish law is similar in that it privileges men's access to divorce over women's. In order for a Jewish divorce to be valid, the man must grant his wife a *get*, a legal document releasing her from the marriage contract, and she must accept it. If both parties agree to the divorce, this is a simple procedure. If a man wishes to divorce and his wife will not accept the get, a rabbinic court can grant him special dispensation to remarry anyway. However, if a woman wishes to divorce and her husband will not grant her a *get*, she cannot remarry in accordance with Jewish law (Capell 1998; S. Weiss 2009). Rabbinic courts are increasingly willing to use coercive means to encourage men to provide *gets*, especially in cases where a woman presents certain acceptable grounds, such as her husband's refusal to engage in sexual relations or his infertility (S. Weiss 2009). These courts have some latitude to make their own decisions in accordance with religious law, so while some will support a woman seeking divorce due to her husband's adultery or abusive behavior, others will not. If a man will not grant the *get* even after the religious court has ordered it and engaged in coercion to encourage his compliance, the divorce does not occur (S. Weiss 2009). Such a wife is known as an *agunah*, or chained woman, and is not permitted to remarry in accordance with Jewish law. Any future children she bears will be, as discussed above, *mamzerim* (Capell 1998). Under New York state law, couples married in a Jewish religious ceremony must remove all barriers to remarriage under religious law in order to be granted a secular (civil) divorce, but most other jurisdictions have no such provision, and in Israel, all divorces are governed by the relevant religious law (Capell 1998).

Divorced people may experience considerable social stigma in those parts of the world that disapprove of divorce, and divorce has consequences for child custody, to be discussed below. There may be financial consequences to divorce. Where a woman entered a marriage with a dowry, it may be returned to her upon divorce. The marriage gift or other financial resources spelled out in Islamic marriage contracts are also due upon divorce (Rashad, Osman, and Roudi-Fahimi 2005), though in practice this does not always occur. Husbands—or in more egalitarian contexts, the higher-earning spouse—may be required to pay **alimony** either temporarily or permanently after a divorce. Alimony refers to payments of spousal maintenance designed to ensure an adequate standard of living for a divorced individual. Historically, alimony was required in fault-based divorces where the husband (who was higher-earning) was at fault so as to ensure that the wife did not unduly suffer after the divorce (Garrison 2011). The emergence of no-fault divorce transformed the alimony system. Today, in many countries, alimony is available only for a limited time to enable a spouse who has been out of the workforce to get back on his or her feet (Garrison 2011).

The right to remarriage may be limited in various ways. For example, Kohanim, members of the hereditary class of priests in Judaism, are prohibited from marrying divorced women. Many legal systems require a waiting period after a divorce before remarriage is permitted. Historically, this requirement was designed to allow for the proper determination of paternity for any children, though today the availability of paternity testing by DNA reduces the value of such procedures. In Islam, the waiting period (*iddah*) is three months, and during this period a divorced couple may get back together without having to remarry (Awal 2012). Some countries may have shorter waiting periods designed to provide an opportunity to appeal the divorce.

Annulment is an alternative method of ending a marriage, though technically obtaining an annulment requires an indication that the marriage never should have been considered valid in the first place. Suitable grounds include deception or fraud at the time of marriage, marriages that are invalid due to age or other factors, or the discovery of a disqualifying condition such impotence, discussed above. The annulment procedure has often been used in Catholic contexts to allow for the equivalent of a divorce when suitable grounds can be found. For example, in Chile prior to the legalization of divorce, some couples would deliberately introduce errors into their marriage documents so they could seek an annulment later if they wanted to end the marriage (Rohter 2005).

Another alternative method for ending marriages without a divorce is the temporary marriage. This is a marriage with an expiration date built in. It is a practice among some Shi'ite Muslims (Rashad, Osman, and Roudi-Fahimi 2005) in Iran and other Shi'ite areas. No divorce is necessary to end the relationship, though a male marital partner in a temporary marriage may end the marriage early with a payment. The man bears parental responsibility for any children resulting from the union. Women in temporary marriages are more free to work and leave the home than they would be in regular marriages. Notably, temporary marriages can be used to provide access to sex that would otherwise be considered illegal nonmarital sex under Shari'a law. As in the case of temporary marriages, ending other kinds of nonmarital unions (like domestic partnerships and *Pacs*) is typically simpler than is seeking a divorce (Perelli-Harris and Gassen 2012), though those in nonregistered unions may be unable to draw on legal resources to help them disentangle their relationships. In cases of nonmarital unions, surviving partners may not have the same rights to stay in the joint home, inherit property, or receive survivorship benefits from pensions as they would have were they married (Perelli-Harris and Gassen 2012).

Finally, unions can be ended through the death of one of the partners. While this requires no legal recognition, it can have important legal consequences for the surviving partner. For example, some cultures impose mourning rituals on people who have lost spouses that can result in severe restrictions, such as confinement to the home, limited nutrition, and specific clothing requirements. Such restrictions are more likely to be imposed on women, who may also lose access to their property and be prevented from remarrying.

Two examples highlight how profound the impact of widowhood can be for women. In some regions of India, the traditional expectation for widowed women was that they would throw themselves—alive—onto their husband's funeral pyre, where they would burn alive (Bracey 2006). This practice, called *suttee* or *sati*, has long been illegal, though it does still occasionally occur. Such practices have been found in other parts of the world as well. Levirate marriage is another practice that impacts women's lives upon widowhood. In levirate marriage, a woman's marriage extends beyond the death of her husband if she has not given birth to sons and is transferred to her husband's brother. This practice was once common in many parts of the world, as it provided a mechanism for addressing inheritance issues in societies where women could not inherit. Today, it remains a practice in some tribal areas in Africa and Asia. Levirate marriage is also a traditional Jewish custom, where it is known as *yibbum*. Today, however, it is rarely practiced; instead, observant Jews are more likely to engage in a ritual renunciation of this marital obligation. The same type of practice can be used to marry a widower to his wife's sister, in which case it is called sororate marriage.

Child Custody and Parental Rights

Custody is the legal term for control over a child. There are two primary components to custody, **physical custody** (with whom the child will live) and **legal custody** (who is empowered to make decisions about the child). Both physical and legal custody can be shared among multiple adults or can be granted to only one adult, and these two types of custody may or may not coincide. For example, one parent could have physical custody while both share legal custody. Parents who do not have physical custody may or may not have legal custody and may or may not have the legal right to visitation with the child.

For situations in which all known legal parents live with their children, custody determinations do not enter the legal context. But in cases of divorce or where children were born to parents who are not in a union with one another, custody can become a legal question, especially if the parents cannot come to an agreement among themselves. Different countries have different legal standards for determining custody. In some countries, specific legal standards are used, while in others, courts are charged with determining what would be in the best interests of a child. Courts may also require or recommend mediation or other alternative dispute resolution processes in an attempt to encourage parents to come to a nonjudicial agreement about child custody (Blair and Weiner 2005).

The standard assumption that fathers should be awarded custody was longstanding in many countries. In Taiwan through the 1990s, over 80 percent of all child custody cases resulted in custodial fathers (H. Liu 2001). This may be surprising to people in Western countries today, given the cultural presumption that women are superior caregivers, but it was rooted in the stigmatization of women as single parents. No one expected a single father to be a competent caregiver in regimes where fathers were preferred custodial parents. Rather, the assumption was that a single father would remarry or otherwise find a suitable woman to care for the children for which he was responsible.

Under Shari'a law, a mother is entitled to physical custody of young children, though fathers retain legal custody (Blair and Weiner 2005), and physical custody is transferred to fathers as the children grow older (Ebrahimi 2005). Countries use different specific age standards to determine custody. A mother's remarriage often causes the termination of custody, which then may be awarded to the father or to another suitable relative (Ebrahimi 2005). In Nigeria, different regimes govern custody in civil and traditional courts, with civil courts presuming custodial mothers and traditional courts presuming custodial fathers (Blair and Weiner 2005). As noted in chapter 2, Aztec law awarded custody of girls to their mothers and boys to their fathers. Older children are typically given a say in their custody arrangements. In Iran, girls over age nine and boys over age fifteen make their own determinations of where to live (Blair and Weiner 2005). In Germany, children over age fourteen have a say in custody hearings, while in Japan the age is fifteen (Blair and Weiner 2005).

Today, many countries, including Taiwan, but not those countries using Shari'a law, have moved to a "best interests of the child" standard. As there is no objective way to evaluate a child's best interests, this standard may not require gender-equal treatment of parents so much as providing space for judicial discretion. For instance, in Taiwan, within three years of the legal change to a "best interests of the child" standard, over 70 percent of custody cases resulted in custodial mothers (H. Liu 2001). Fathers' rights activists point to statistics such as these to argue that family law is biased in favor of women. But what research on child custody cases instead suggests is that a bias toward maternal custody "tie[s] women more tightly to their stereotyped social role" (H. Liu 2001:218), reinforcing the assumption that children are the defining feature of women's (and only women's) lives. Judicial discretion may also provide a license to discriminate on the basis of socially disfavored characteristics. Courts may make custody decisions based on the religious beliefs of parents

(Blair and Weiner 2005) or refuse to award custody to parents who are in same-sex relationships. There is considerable worldwide variation in the extent to which single parents are provided with full parental rights (Perelli-Harris and Gassen 2012). Where parents are unmarried, fathers may face additional obstacles in demonstrating paternity (Perelli-Harris and Gassen 2012; Sutherland 2012).

Parents may lose custody of their children in circumstances other than a divorce, such as in cases where government officials determine that parents are abusing or neglecting their children or in other cases where the state declares parents unfit. Terminations of custody or of parental rights have been used in countries like the United States and Australia to remove indigenous children from their families so they could be forcibly assimilated into White society and trained for low-wage work (Buti 2004), or in cases where parents are deemed enemies of the state. Under Shari'a law, children can be removed from their parents' custody if the parents behave immorally. This might include engaging in alcoholism or drug use, gambling, maintaining unclean living conditions, converting to a non-Muslim faith, or being involved in criminal activity. Custody can also be lost if a parent becomes insane or contracts a terminal illness (Ebrahimi 2005). Removal of custody and termination of parental rights requires the state to have some kind of child welfare system with the resources and authority to act, which is not always the case.

A final question concerns parents' responsibilities for children they do not have custody of. In many countries, children are entitled by law to maintain their standard of living, even if a parent no longer lives with them. Thus, non-custodial parents, especially if they are earning more money than custodial parents, may be required to pay child support or child maintenance. The responsibility to pay may end when the child is in his or her teens, or it may extend through young adulthood (especially if the child stays in school). Even where such payments are required, they may not be made, as enforcement can be weak. Child support payments are less important in countries with extensive social safety nets, given that safety nets provide for basic needs and a sufficient standard of living.

CONCLUSION

For much of human history, the regulation of marriage and children was left to local communities, tribes, and religious groups, even well after national governments asserted control over many other areas of life. Today, governments have created legal regimes for governing marriage, childbearing, and childrearing, but even in secular countries, these issues tend to retain a religious feel (Htun and Weldon 2011). One might argue that family law is, then, the last bastion of theocratic law.

In India, there are separate family and inheritance law regimes for each major religious group, though couples can choose to register their marriage as nonreligious (D. Smith 2005). When couples get divorced, the terms of their divorce are governed by the type of marriage they entered into—meaning that two similarly situated divorced women of different religions would be legally entitled to different levels of postdivorce financial support from their former husbands, simply because of their faith at the time of marriage (Khory 2005). Even some U.S. states have legal provisions allowing members of certain religious groups to practice alterations in the general marital rules, such as a New York law providing for slight differences in marital solemnization for Quakers (Estin 2009). Some countries erect obstacles to those seeking marriages outside religious supervision. For example, in England, those marrying in the Church of England can simultaneously hold their civil and religious marriage ceremony, while members of minority faiths must hold separate ceremonies (Estin 2009). In Israel, those who do not meet the requirements to marry according to some formal religious body must travel outside the country to solemnize their marriage, though it is then recognized by the Israeli government upon their return (Lubell 2013).

Religious beliefs may themselves be an element of traditional culture, though culture extends far beyond religion. Other elements of traditional cultural practices may also impact family law regimes. For example, countries may establish formal laws prohibiting spousal abuse or permitting divorce where abuse occurs. Yet the efficacy of such laws will depend greatly on what sorts of acts people view as abusive. While worldwide disapproval of intimate partner violence has been increasing alongside the increased presence of national legal policies addressing it (Pierotti 2013), women living in countries where legal provisions exist to protect them from intimate partner violence will not avail themselves of such protections if they and their communities believe men's violence is justified. An international survey asked individuals in twenty-six countries whether a man would be justified in hitting his wife "(1) if she goes out without telling him, (2) if she neglects the children, (3) if she argues with him, (4) if she refuses to have sex with him, and (5) if she burns the food" (Pierotti 2013:248). While over 80 percent of respondents in the Dominican Republic, Armenia, Benin, and the Philippines rejected all of these potential justifications for violence, in Ethiopia, Mali, Uganda, and Jordan more than 70 percent of people believed a man would be justified in engaging in violence in at least one of these circumstances, despite the fact that all of these countries have policies addressing intimate partner violence or violence against women more generally (Pierotti 2013).

One analysis of sex discrimination in family law as of 2005, which looked at legal provisions such as minimum marital age, spousal obligations, rules about adultery, and the legal consequences of divorce, found that the most unequal countries were Egypt and Saudi Arabia, with Algeria, Bangladesh, Iran, Jordan,

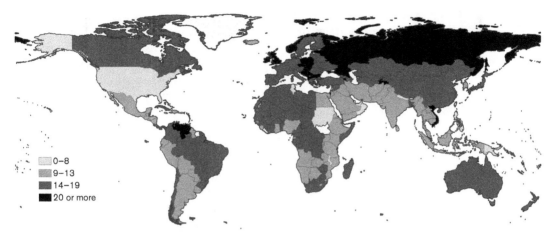

Map 23 Weeks of paid maternity leave in law, 2013 (Addati, Cassirer, and Glichrist 2014).

Malaysia, and Pakistan close behind; all of these countries use Shari'a law to regulate family matters (Htun and Weldon 2011). These findings highlight the fact that examining family law is a key site for understanding the extent of gender inequality and discrimination in a society. The tentacles of such inequality and discrimination extend outward from the family context to other areas of life. For example, gendered inequality in child carework has consequences not only for family life but also for women's opportunities to achieve economic independence. And employment rights and social insurance benefits have important consequences for gendered inequality in carework. One policy that impacts carework and employment is parental leave policy, which varies greatly around the world. Countries differ in terms of how long their guaranteed parental leaves are, whether they are paid, and whether they are available only to women or to all parents.

As map 23 shows, most countries offer paid maternity leave, though it is important to note that even in countries with maternity leave policies, individuals who work in the informal economy, who are self-employed, or who are otherwise outside the bounds of the regulation may not have access to these benefits. Of the 186 countries for which policies are known, only the United States, Papua New Guinea, and the Philippines do not have laws mandating paid maternity leave, and the average country mandates fifteen weeks of paid leave (Addati, Cassirer, and Glichrist 2014). Paid paternity leave is much less common, with only 40 percent of countries mandating any leave and an average paid leave of less than one week (Addati, Cassirer, and Glichrist 2014). An additional 18 percent of countries offer longer periods of parental leave, which may extend as long as a year or more in certain countries, primarily in Europe (Addati, Cassirer, and Glichrist 2014). Countries similarly differ in the provisions they make for the care of the elderly or others who may need assistance. Some countries provide social insurance benefits for this purpose, including subsidized institutional or home-based care and public old-age pensions, while others leave care primarily in the hands of individuals and their families (Anderson and Hussey 2000). In China, where children have traditionally been responsible for caring for their parents in old age, a law has even been passed allowing parents to sue their adult children for neglect (Schiavenza 2013).

Thinking about these sorts of policies more broadly, we can see that in some countries, caregiving is seen as the responsibility of families. Relatives, particularly women, are expected to care for children, the elderly, and others needing care, generally without monetary compensation or even the guarantee that they will be able to schedule employment hours around their caregiving obligations. In countries that have policies such as guaranteed parental leave and social insurance to provide for the needs of the elderly, the obligation to provide for care of society's most vulnerable is seen as an obligation of the government. It is not that relatives abandon their loved ones in such countries. Rather, provisions such as paid leave, compensation for caregivers, and state pensions ensure that people will not fall through the cracks and that caregiving responsibilities will not lead to economic ruin. In such countries, access to resources like food, housing, and health care may be understood as legal rights rather than family responsibilities, and thus it is to the question of legal rights that we turn next.

Legal Rights

CHAPTER GOALS

1. Be able to explain what civil and human rights are.
2. Understand how law can work to both maintain and reduce inequality.
3. Become familiar with ways that countries seek to protect various legal rights and with ways they balance competing rights.
4. Understand the debate between proponents of natural law and those of positive law.

In Bojayá, a town in the district of Chocó, Colombia, in 2002, in the midst of an armed conflict that had begun decades earlier, a bomb killed seventy-nine people who had sought refuge from the conflict in a local church (Pont, Ángel, and Dávila 2018). The affected community was primarily Afro-Colombian and indigenous. It was not until 2017, after the victim's bodies were exhumed, that a full accounting of the event could be made. The exhumation of these bodies was part of a national process of reconciliation carried out in the wake of peace talks between the government and the main opposition group, the Revolutionary Armed Forces of Colombia (Fuerzas Armadas Revolucionarias de Colombia, or FARC), that resulted in a cease-fire agreement in 2016 (Felter and

Renwick 2017). This exhumation, and the rituals and investigations surrounding it, were public events, and indeed the survivors and the families of the victims were exposed to a great deal of public attention that intruded on the privacy they sought as they mourned.

Yet the massacre and the reconciliation process of which the exhumation was part were matters of intense public concern, given the duration and magnitude of Colombia's armed conflict and the tens of thousands of people who were kidnapped, injured, or killed during the course of the hostilities (Felter and Renwick 2017). Thus, journalists obviously sought to witness the exhumations and funeral rites and to write about what they saw, activities ordinarily considered central to speech and press freedoms. But an organization called the Committee for the Rights of the Bojayá Victims issued a protocol requesting that outsiders, including journalists and scholars, refrain from recording or interviewing during the exhumation process and related events; that the committee have the authority to approve or reject material for publication; and that the committee itself be primarily responsible for maintaining an appropriate photographic record (Pont, Ángel, and Dávila 2018). While this protocol did not have the official force of law, it was based on a legal provision establishing the right to privacy in cemeteries and funeral homes, and the committee that crafted it represented the interests of the affected ethnic minority community.

The massacre clearly represents the violation of human rights—seventy-nine people who were not combatants in any conflict lost their lives, and their bodies were buried without the opportunity for traditional funeral rites. The protocol drafted by the committee sought to protect the survivors and the victims' families from further violations of rights, particularly of their right to privacy. But it is possible to argue that the protection of that right, important as it may have been as part of the reconciliation process, created in turn a new set of rights violations: violations of freedom of expression and of the press that had the effect of limiting access to historical truth of concern to the broader population (Pont, Ángel, and Dávila 2018).

What the Bojayá case shows is that understanding legal rights is not simple. Even in cases that seem clear-cut—people were massacred, and that is a violation of human rights—there can be complexities as governments and local populations seek to balance competing rights. This chapter, then, will explore legal rights of various kinds, including the rights to privacy, expression, conscience, and subsistence, as well as violations of those rights. It will also consider how law is related to equality and inequality. Finally, it will consider whether rights can be understood as universal or whether they stem from the more particular decisions of individual countries.

WHAT ARE LEGAL RIGHTS?

Legal rights are entitlements in law to be able to take certain actions or to be protected in certain ways (Donnelly 2013). Depending on the context, legal rights can be conceived of on individual or communal/group levels. Classically, **civil rights** are individual rights to equal treatment in the public sphere, such as the right to own property and the right to fair trials (Cmiel 2004). **Political rights**, which were once conceived of separately but today are generally lumped in with civil rights, include the rights to vote, hold office, and otherwise participate in political and civic life (Cmiel 2004). **Human rights** include a broader set of economic, social, and cultural rights, such as those to economic subsistence, health, and cultural practices (Cmiel 2004). They also include the right to self-determination by indigenous peoples (Perrin 2017; as discussed in chapter 3) and the ability for minority cultural groups to maintain their cultural and linguistic practices (Epps and Graham 2011). This last construction of human rights has been more popular among African, Asian, and Latin American countries than among those in Europe (Cmiel 2004). More broadly, human rights are the rights one has by virtue of being a human (Donnelly 2013), while civil rights are rights one has as a member (especially a citizen) of a particular political entity (Arendt 1951).

Legal rights include both **positive rights** and **negative rights**. Positive rights are rights that require a government to do something, such as provide access to economic subsistence or health care, and that may thus be out of reach of the most economically marginal countries. Negative rights are rights that require a government to avoid doing something, such as engaging in torture or acting to prevent people from voting (Epps and Graham 2011). In addition, while human rights are understood as universal, that does not mean that *all rights* are always held equally by all people (Nickel 2014). For example, rights related to political participation are typically linked to citizenship. There are also circumstances where particular rights may be linked to or unavailable based on particular social positions, such as rights for children, the elderly, or indigenous people. For example, we do not expect the right to vote to be available to those in elementary school. And in many societies that consider education a basic right, that right extends only to a certain age.

Finally, many people believe that it is acceptable to terminate certain rights for those who have engaged in crimes or other misdeeds. Thus, the right to free movement does not extend to those who are imprisoned. Those who have been convicted of crimes may lose a variety of other rights as well, depending on local laws, such as rights to freedom of expression, personal privacy, and participation in civic life. For instance, some countries deny at least some individuals convicted of crimes the right to vote (Ewald and Rottinghaus 2009), a practice referred to disenfranchisement. In the United States, which has one of the broadest disenfranchisement practices in the world (Ewald and Rottinghaus 2009), only two states never take away individuals' right to vote upon criminal conviction, while twelve prohibit even some people who have completed all of the terms of their punishment from voting (Chung 2018). In some countries, those who have been convicted of crimes may be subjected to forced labor without compensation, a practice that represents a further diminishment of their human rights.

It has become common for commentators to assume that the development of human rights discourses has occurred as part of the unavoidable march of human progress. But in reality, the situation is more complex. Many of the rights we assume to be inherent in modern governments today developed as part of other processes that had little to do with rights per se. For example, human rights scholar Samuel Moyn (2010) argues that the idea of religious freedom emerged in response to sectarian conflicts rather than as a commitment to religious rights and that labor law in many countries has been more about protecting economic welfare than economic rights. Nonetheless, today all of these kinds of issues are understood to belong under the umbrella of legal rights.

In 1948, the United Nations issued a foundational document laying out its vision for human rights in the world, the United Nations Universal Declaration of Human Rights, or UNDHR (Universal Declaration of Human Rights 1948). Its thirty articles cover rights as diverse as freedom from slavery and torture, freedom to marry, freedom of movement, freedom of religion, freedom of association, and the rights to education and leisure. This chapter will discuss a number of the rights enumerated in the UNDHR. However, it is important to note that in the six decades since the UNDHR was issued, change in terms of world protection of the rights it enumerates has been slight. There is little global consensus about which rights should be protected or even whether human rights ought to be among countries' highest priorities. For example, in July 2018, Philippine president Rodrigo Duterte argued in his State of the Nation Address to lawmakers that protecting human rights was not important given ongoing problems with drug trafficking in his country. "Your concern is human rights. Mine is human lives," Duterte said (Villamor 2018).

The Most Severe Violations

According to Amnesty International (2018a), the Philippines has engaged in numerous abuses of human rights in recent years. Amnesty alleges that police forces and other groups supported by the government have carried out extrajudicial killings of thousands of people alleged to have committed drug offenses, as many as thirty-two in a single day. The national government has denied such a campaign, but as Duterte's statement above suggests, it has also not taken steps to stop the killings. Amnesty also alleges that journalists, human rights activists, and others speaking against these violations have faced murder or arrest. In addition, allegations of torture have been lodged against certain police groups (Amnesty International 2018a).

These allegations are examples of some of the worst kinds of human rights abuses engaged in by governments, and when people talk about working to protect human rights they often mean working to prevent these types of abuses—like the Bojayá massacre. There is broad international agreement that torture and governmentally sponsored campaigns of murder, sexual assault, and similar abuses are violations of human rights, and these types of abuses are among those criminalized in international law (as discussed in chapters 4 and 10). Indeed, 164 countries are state parties to the United Nations Convention against Torture and Other Cruel, Inhuman or Degrading Treatment or Punishment, and an additional 7 are signatories (United Nations Office of the High Commissioner for Human Rights 2014). While there are 26 countries that have not signed, including Oman, Iran, Tanzania, Zimbabwe, North Korea, Myanmar, and Malaysia, many of the countries Amnesty International and Human Rights Watch allege to have engaged in considerable abuses in recent years—including Syria, Libya, and the Philippines—have signed (Amnesty International 2018a; Human Rights Watch 2017).

It is clear that despite the broad international agreement against torture and other severe human rights abuses, countries continue to engage in these violations. Some, like the Philippines, argue that other priorities must come before human rights. Others, like those that have not signed the Convention against Torture, have not joined this international agreement. Still others argue that the actions they take should not be understood as torture and are instead appropriate punishments for criminal activity, be they the amputations Saudi Arabia uses as punishment, Singapore's practice of caning (see chapter 7), or the practice in the United States of separating migrant children from their parents (Cumming-Bruce 2018).

LEGAL RIGHTS: A TOUR

The legal rights being violated by the severe abuses discussed above are among the most fundamental rights—the rights to be free from arbitrary arrest, physical harm, sexual violence, and murder. But there are many other kinds of legal rights that are worth learning about. While one chapter cannot possibly cover all types of legal rights, this brief tour of rights will consider the rights to privacy, expression, freedom of conscience, and subsistence. Those rights more specifically relevant to the criminal justice system, such as due process and the rule of law, have been covered in earlier chapters.

The Right to Privacy

There are two main types of privacy, **physical privacy** and **informational privacy**. Physical privacy relates to privacy in and of one's body and one's personal space or property. The right to physical privacy includes protections against trespassing and unreasonable searches, unwanted bodily touching or invasion of one's body, and photo or video surveillance. Some people argue that bodily privacy also includes the right to dress as one wishes, such as by covering one's hair or wearing a face veil (Syed 2017), and to make other choices about one's body, such as hairstyles and body modifications like tattoos and piercings. Others argue that such choices are better understood as religious, cultural, or political statements and as such that their regulation should be considered a matter of speech regulation, to be discussed below (Michaels 2018). Informational privacy refers to the ability to keep private information about oneself, such as financial, medical, and voting records, and to be free from Internet surveillance, GPS tracking, and other similar techniques of information and data collection. The survivors and victims' families after the Bojayá massacre were concerned with both kinds of privacy. They sought physical privacy in wanting to avoid photo and video recording of their loved ones' bodies and of their own participation in funeral rites, and they sought informational privacy in wanting to avoid unapproved narratives of their experiences and traumas becoming part of the public record (Pont, Ángel, and Dávila 2018)

Physical Privacy and Sexual Autonomy

One area of physical privacy that deserves special attention is that of sexual activity (Hagan, Sheppele, and Tyler 2013). The right to privacy in sexual activity would suggest that, so long as sex acts are carried out in private spaces by consenting adults, they should not be a matter for government concern. But sexual activity raises questions not only of privacy rights but of other kinds of rights as well. The idea of a right to autonomy or self-determination would suggest that our bodies are our own to control and use as we wish, including for sexual activity. And sexual activity is also implicated in discussions of equality—do people of different genders, sexual orientations, and other identities have equal rights to decide what kinds of sexual behavior to engage in and with whom they wish to engage in those behaviors?

On the other hand, governments can make arguments against these rights, coming from the perspective that sexual activity needs state regulation for moral, public health, or other reasons. Such restrictions concern a wide variety of aspects of sexual activity, including regulations around appropriate sexual partners, specific sex acts, commercial sex work, consent, and other areas. Historically, such restrictions have been primarily concerned with sexual activity as the procreative act; today, countries are more likely to conceive of sexual activity as a matter of individual choice (Frank, Camp, and Boutcher 2010). Indeed, in a 2017 case concerning a fifty-year-old woman whose ability to engage in sexual activity had been impaired by a botched medical procedure, the European Court of Human Rights held that the ability to engage in sexual life is an important right (S. Chan 2017).

Among the most common restrictions on sexual activity are those prohibiting incest and regulating sex based on marital status and age. Chapter 8 discusses some of these issues, especially as pertain to marriage, in more detail. All societies have an incest taboo, which has generally been encoded in law, but there are considerable variations as to which relationships violate this taboo. Sex outside of marriage is illegal in many countries with Shari'a legal systems; in other countries, sex between two unmarried people, or between a married man and an unmarried woman, is legal, while sex involving a married woman is not. Nearly all countries have set a minimum age for consent to sexual activity, though this age may be different for males and females and it may be different for same-sex sexual activity than it is for heterosexual sexual activity (Waites 2005). Historically, these minimum ages were set around the time of puberty, but they have been increased in modern times due to changing social expectations around adolescence (Bullough 2004). Some countries where sex outside of marriage is illegal do not have minimum ages of consent for sexual activity separate from their regulations around marriage (Waites 2005). Another common set of restrictions concerns same-sex sexual activity—as of 2018, 37 percent of countries maintained laws criminalizing some forms of same-sex sexual activity (Carroll and Mendos 2017). The criminalization of sexual activity between men is more common than the criminalization of sexual activity between women.

Countries may also restrict particular types of sexual activity, such as prostitution, pornography, stripping, and other commercial sex work; sodomy; or even masturbation. Indeed, sodomy was illegal in thirteen U.S. states until the 2003 *Lawrence v. Texas* Supreme Court decision, and four of those states criminalized heterosexual sodomy. Countries may require disclosure of HIV status or other sexually transmitted diseases prior to the initiation of sex (Hagan, Sheppele, and Tyler 2013). A newer form of regulation involves what has come to be known as "affirmative consent," or the requirement that individuals actively consent to sexual activity before it begins. Such rules have been implemented in Sweden, Germany, and California and are under consideration in other jurisdictions (Clark-Flory 2018; Grinberg 2018).

Finally, countries regulate access to contraception. On the one hand, countries may restrict access to contraception as part of an effort to control women's sexuality or in an attempt to increase birth rates. Without access to contraception, women cannot have equal rights to sexual activity (S. Davies 2010). Indeed, access to contraception is relevant to both sexual activity and health rights for women (health rights will be discussed below). On the other hand, countries may impose the use of contraceptives such as IUDs or even forced sterilization out of eugenic concerns or a desire to reduce the birth rate, such as in China under the One-Child Policy. Both forced contraceptive usage and limitations on access to contraceptives do not respect individuals' rights to sexual autonomy, especially those of women.

Informational Privacy

The right to informational privacy can include both protection from the government and protection from third parties. For example, consider the right to privacy at work. In the United States, employers are legally permitted to use a vast array of technologies to monitor employees' activities. These include scanning the content of emails, tracking keystrokes, maintaining copies of chat logs and phone call recordings, capturing screen shots of employee devices at frequent intervals, and remote monitoring of devices (Determann and Sprague 2011). Employers may require employees to use company-provided devices with GPS monitoring turned on even when they are not on work time, or they may require employees to install monitoring software on personal devices such that it can capture nonwork activities. While not all of these tactics are common, the majority of employers monitor at least some of what their employees do online. It would be illegal for the United States government to carry out such activities without a search warrant, but employers are permitted to do so except where specific state or federal laws prohibit a particular practice (Determann and Sprague 2011). And wherever employees may have an expectation of privacy at work, employers can simply notify employees that they are using monitoring technologies and thus overcome that expectation (Determann and Sprague 2011).

In contrast, while employers in Europe have access to the same technologies, employees in Europe have more robust privacy rights. The European Union charter specifically protects privacy, including informational privacy, while the right to privacy in the United States is not specifically articulated in the Constitution (Determann and Sprague 2011). Employers who wish to monitor employee communications and Internet usage must seek voluntary consent from employees and cannot coerce this consent (Determann and Sprague 2011). European countries have strict data protection laws giving individuals control over their personal data. Even where a company has reason to believe crimes are being committed, this does not give them the right to engage in pervasive monitoring of employee activity (Determann and Sprague 2011).

In fact, European data protection rules go even further than that. A European Court of Justice ruling in 2014 held that Internet users had the "right to be forgotten." In other words, users can request that search engines remove links to pages detailing information about them, and search engines must comply unless there are public interest reasons to preserve the links, such as in the case of news articles or information that is professional rather than personal (Reputation VIP 2018). The greatest proportion of removal requests come from people seeking to have their personal addresses removed, with large numbers of people also seeking the removal of material that is damaging to their reputation, of negative reviews, and of information about past employment terminations (Reputation VIP 2018). This right does not require web services to delete

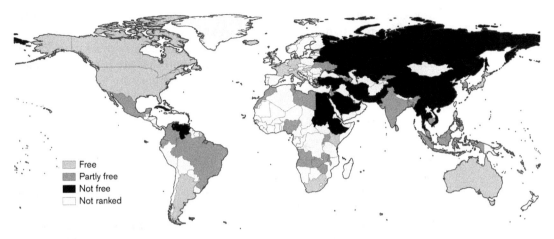

Map 24 Internet freedom (Freedom House 2017).

webpages themselves, just search engine links to them. Similar procedures are available in some other countries, such as Argentina, India, and South Korea, but in the United States they are generally considered to be a violation of freedom of speech and freedom of the press (to be discussed below).

In 2018, the European Union adopted the General Data Protection Regulation (GDPR), which further extends data privacy in Europe. The GDPR requires companies to delete individuals' personal data upon request, permits individuals to prohibit certain uses of their data, and mandates the notification within seventy-two hours of people whose data might have been compromised due to data breaches. Companies that do not comply can be assessed multimillion-euro fines (Jaffe and Hautala 2018). Companies have to get parental consent to retain personal data for those under sixteen. And the data that is considered "personal" under the GDPR is not limited to private financial, medical, or ID information—it includes cookies, IP addresses, and location trackers. The provisions of the GDPR are applied to all companies that do business with EU citizens, even if the companies are based elsewhere, though protections do not extend to those outside the EU (Jaffe and Hautala 2018).

Freedom House, a global organization, conducts an annual survey that gathers data about access to the Internet, legal control over Internet companies, legal censorship of Internet content, robustness of online news media, and surveillance of and repercussions from online activity. Thus, it is really best understood as a hybrid measure of online and information privacy and of freedom of speech. According to Freedom House, China, Syria, and Ethiopia are the worst countries in the world in terms of Internet freedom (Freedom House 2017), as shown in map 24. For example, in China, Internet users have been detained for comments made on chat programs; news websites must be licensed, and user-generated news is limited; online activists have been sentenced to multi-year prison terms; the national government cuts off access to many global services and filters or blocks content it finds objectionable, with no grounds for appeal; and Internet companies (including cybercafes) are expected to track user activities and provide information to law enforcement.

The Right to Expression

The example of China highlights the limits many countries place on speech and other forms of expression (such as art and music). In China and other authoritarian countries, criticizing the government or advocating for policies the government does not approve of can be illegal. But even among countries with a commitment to legal rights, policies about the regulation of speech can vary greatly. In most countries, the right to freedom of expression is balanced with some other competing principles. These include things ranging from the right to be forgotten (as discussed above) to limits on speech that might be considered obscene (such as pornography) or hateful, and from a prohibition on inciting a riot to rules about criticizing the government. In many countries, commercial or corporate speech is regulated more strictly than private, individual speech. In particular, companies may be prohibited from issuing advertisements that make false claims or from advertising certain kinds of harmful products. The case of the Bojayá massacre provides another example, where the right to privacy and to communal self-determination had to be balanced with freedom of expression.

One way to think about some of these competing principles is to consider the balance between the right to freedom of expression and the right to be free of discrimination and hate. Countries differ in terms of where to draw this line. Most countries consider incitements to violence to be outside the bounds of free speech, as such statements begin to take on the nature of an attempted crime. Some countries consider hate speech, especially in its more extreme forms, to be almost an incitement to violence and thus ban it on those terms. In Germany, Austria, Switzerland, and France, genocide denial is illegal. Germany, for instance, holds that freedom of expression does not extend to "false statements of fact" (Lewy 2014:10) and is particularly concerned with Holocaust denial given its association with acts of hate. Turkey goes in the opposite direction, prohibiting reference to the Armenian genocide its predecessor state, the Ottoman Empire, perpetuated (Lewy 2014). But other countries do not regulate hate speech, viewing it as an individual opinion that people are permitted to express (Rønning 2016) and holding that the government cannot regulate what constitutes truth (Lewy 2014).

When regulating obscenity, a number of countries use a type of "community standards" test in which the model "average person" is used to determine if the community would find the material to have any redeeming (artistic, scientific, literary, political, etc.) value. The community may be a national one or specific to the local area in which a supposedly obscene work is displayed (Boyce 2018). Such an approach leads to wildly different standards in different countries. For example, in Canada, violence and degrading or dehumanizing treatment in a sexual context are considered obscene, while in India sexualized content involving Mahatma Gandhi is (Boyce 2018). Japan uses a different approach, regulating images of procreative sexual activity more heavily than other types. Where the government has extensive control over the Internet, including the ability to block people in the country from viewing materials from outside that country, these restrictions may have an impact—but generally the global nature of the Internet means that people are able access material their government might believe to be obscene (Boyce 2018). This means that the regulation of obscenity is rarely able to achieve its goal of protecting morals and instead often becomes simply a tool for criminalizing cultural producers.

A final example of competing principles has to do with the regulation of **defamation**, or statements that cause harm to one's reputation. Slander and libel are types of defamation; slander refers to instances of spoken statements, and libel to instances of written ones. Countries take very different approaches to these issues, with the United States and England representing two of these approaches. In fact, the approach taken by the United States is so different from that taken in some other countries that U.S. courts are largely forbidden from enforcing libel judgments from other countries (Johnson 2017). The United States and England do share some commonalities. In both, a true statement is not considered defamatory, distributors (like booksellers) are not liable for defamation so long as they were unaware of the defamatory nature of the content, defamation cases require that the statements be made to someone other than the person alleging defamation, and there are certain types of statements—particularly those about criminal activity and professional standards—that are more readily considered defamation (Johnson 2017).

However, it is here that the similarities end. In England, defamation law places the burden of proof on the defendant (Johnson 2017). This means that those accused of defamation must demonstrate that they did not engage in defamatory practices (for example, by demonstrating that the published statements were true or that they were an honest opinion). In contrast, in the United States, the burden of proof is on the plaintiff, requiring the plaintiff to prove that defamation occurred (Johnson 2017). Prior to 2013, those wishing to obtain a judgment of libel would often take their cases to the British courts even if they had no reasonable ties to the United Kingdom (Johnson 2017) as the English courts were more plaintiff-friendly in terms of burden of proof and the extent to which plaintiffs were required to demonstrate actual malice in order to collect damages. A 2013 reform limited this practice and made other changes, protecting scholarship and material in the public interest and requiring those claiming to have been libeled to demonstrate serious harm (*BBC News* 2013). In some countries, criticisms of the government or rulers can be treated as a kind of criminal defamation, as noted in the discussion of lèse-majesté in chapter 2.

As noted in chapter 3, many countries also regulate the kinds of speech that can be used as part of a political campaign. On the most severe end, such restrictions can limit the number and types of political parties that are permitted to participate in a campaign. Other restrictions might impact election financing, where candidates or parties can speak to voters or post signs, and whether political polls can ask questions designed to suggest untrue things about candidates. Some countries regulate political advertising, limiting how long before an election advertisements may be published or broadcast and what kinds of claims candidates and parties can make about their opponents.

Countries may also limit rights around public protest. In authoritarian countries, public protest is heavily restricted, and people may need government permission for any large gathering—including, in some cases, family celebrations and weddings. But even in countries with some commitment to freedom of expression, the right to protest is often balanced with some other concerns, such as the maintenance of public order. In such cases, protestors may be required to seek permits or may be restricted to certain areas. Such limits can be consistent with a commitment to freedom of expression so long as they are applied in an issue-neutral way (e.g., demonstrations in favor of government policy are treated the same as those opposed to government policy) and maintain real opportunities for people to express their views in public.

Press freedom is an important part of freedom of expression. Where press freedom is not protected, it is difficult for anyone to scrutinize government activities or learn about what is going on in their country. Countries that restrict press freedom may require advance approval from censors before news pieces can be published or shared; may pull broadcast or publishing licenses if publications do not comply with official or unofficial content guidelines; and may even arrest or murder journalists or their sources (Carlsson 2016). Current threats to press freedom have become more complex, as some countries—including Russia—have embarked on disinformation campaigns designed to drown out the real news by planting incorrect stories and spreading them on social media. It is important to note that in many countries, the main news stations (such as the United Kingdom's BBC, Qatar's Al Jazeera, and Venezuela's Venezolana de Televisión) are state owned, controlled, or funded. Such state control can and does coexist with a commitment to press freedom, but it can also be used to limit criticism of the government.

Another type of speech regulation involves language policy. Countries may designate official languages in which government business is done; when they do so, they may choose to incorporate or to exclude languages spoken by minority populations. Some countries designate only one official language, while others designate two, three, or many. For instance, India has twenty-two official languages (Department of Official Language 2015). Where official languages are designated, those who speak alternative languages may be prohibited from using these languages to conduct official business or from having their children learn them in school. Other countries, including the United States, do not designate an official language.

Beyond the designation of official languages, countries may regulate language in additional ways. For example, France maintains a body, the Académie Française, with the responsibility of regulating and managing the development and change of the French language. This body is a conservative one, seeking especially to limit the introduction of loanwords from other languages by creating official French equivalents (Estival and Pennycook 2011). Similar policies are found in other Francophone countries. For example, Canada has established official French equivalents for English terms like "tweeting" in the social media context—the French term is *gazouiller* (Translation Bureau 2015). The province of Quebec has established a number of other restrictive language policies, limiting individuals' ability to educate their children in English to only those parents educated in Canada in English; ensuring that businesses post their signs and advertisements in French; and ensuring the right of all consumers to be served in French (Schmid, Zepa, and Snipe 2004). Similar policies are found in Latvia in response to the era of Soviet domination, requiring that signage be posted in Latvian, that higher education be conducted in Latvian, and even that individuals' names be spelled according to the conventions of Latvian regardless of their language of origin (Schmid, Zepa, and Snipe 2004). While some of these restrictions have been slightly relaxed, especially around the Québécois signage policy, both regions continue to work hard to ensure the prominence of their preferred languages.

The Right to Conscience

While the right to expression concerns protections for what one says, publishes, or otherwise outwardly expresses, the right to conscience concerns protections for one's beliefs. This protection may extend to those actions required by one's beliefs. The right to conscience can involve any kind of belief, be it a political ideology, a moral position, or a tenet of religious faith. For example, the question of whether there is a right to conscience might come up in contexts where individuals are asked to swear loyalty oaths before taking on public employment, conscientiously object to the military draft, or seek to avoid educational programs that teach views they find objectionable. However, the right to conscience is discussed most often in the context of religion.

Clearly, some countries do not protect freedom of religious conscience. Theocratic governments that enshrine official religions in law rarely provide full equality for those of minority religious faiths and may require at least some adherence to elements of the official religion. According to the Pew Research Center, about half of all countries have experienced recent increases in government restrictions on religion, and in 2016 twenty-five countries heavily restricted freedom of religion (Kishi 2018). Twenty six percent of countries worldwide have laws against blasphemy, or speech insulting religion, while 13 percent have laws penalizing apostasy, or the abandonment of one's faith (Theodorou 2016), policies limiting both the right to religious conscience and the right to expression. The countries with the greatest restrictions on religion in 2016 were China, Iran, Indonesia, the Maldives, Malaysia, and Russia. In Iran, the Maldives, and Malaysia, the official religion is Islam, and in Russia it is the Russian Orthodox Church, and government restrictions on religion support the dominance of official doctrines of these faiths. Indonesia does not have an official religion but recognizes only six faiths and largely requires individuals to affiliate with one of them, as will be discussed below. Officially, China guarantees freedom of religion within the context of a formally atheist state. However, religious groups must be registered with the government, have official permission to establish registered sites for religious rituals, and report their clergy to the government (Wang 2017). The government officially recognizes national Buddhist, Taoist, Muslim, Protestant, and Catholic organizations. Unrecognized religions may be tolerated, or their activities and facilities may be shut down (Buckley 2016). Where the government determines that a particular religion is a serious threat, as it has with Falun Gong, it can designate them as "evil cults" and prosecute adherents (Wang 2017).

Note, however, that not all countries with an official religion are truly theocratic. For example, Costa Rica, England, and Denmark all have official state churches. Secular countries—those without official religions—may still provide state support for particular faiths, or they may have a legal separation between church and state. There are also countries that do not have official legal restrictions based on religion but have significant social hostilities, such as acts of vandalism or hate crimes, that can impact the extent to which individuals feel fully free to practice their religion (Kishi 2018).

The question of religious freedom is separate from the question of establishment of an official state religion, and it has two component parts. One the one hand, there is the question of whether one has the freedom to practice one's religion as one chooses (the free exercise of religion). On the other, there is the question of whether one has freedom *from* religion, or the ability to avoid being forced to practice religion or forced to experience and engage with religious content. Countries with official religions, at least those that are not theocracies, may protect the free exercise of religion, but they are unlikely to protect freedom from religion. Truly secular countries may protect the free exercise of religion and provide for freedom from religion, or they may provide for freedom from religion without protecting the free exercise of religion, such as in contexts where public displays of religious belief are prohibited.

Legal protections for freedom of religious conscience do require countries to wade into the thorny question of what constitutes religion. Some countries permit individuals to claim whatever religious beliefs they choose, while others permit only specific faiths to count as religions. In Indonesia, the constitution notes religious belief as a foundational tenet of the country and recognizes six faiths: Islam, Catholicism, Protestantism, Buddhism, Hinduism, and Confucianism (Colbran 2010). While other religions are not illegal per se, individuals do not have freedom of religious conscience. Each religion can establish its own principles of belief, and activities that do not coincide with these can be prohibited. In addition, individuals are expected to indicate a religion on their national identity cards, a situation that obviously creates difficulties for atheists, other people who do not adhere to a religious faith, and those who follow traditional animistic religions (Colbran 2010).

The issue of determining what constitutes a religion can be illuminated by considering the case of Pastafarianism. Pastafarianism emerged in the United States in 2005, when Bobby Henderson wrote a letter in opposition to intelligent design curricula in public schools that did not provide instruction about evolution. In his letter, he laid out a body of theology that includes the obligation to wear pirate uniforms and colanders, a weekly religious observance incorporating a spaghetti dinner and beer, and the belief that the world was created by the Flying Spaghetti Monster. Since the emergence of Pastafarianism, courts and government bodies in a number of countries have struggled to determine whether or not it counts as a religion, applying legal tests ranging from the presence of "dogmas" (Deutsche Welle 2017) to the sincerity of belief (Blevins 2016). In New Zealand, Pastafarian clergy have the right to conduct weddings (Hanson 2016), while courts and government bodies in the United States have come to different decisions about the status of the religion. Some states permit individuals to take their driver's license photos wearing a colander as religious headgear (Mosbergen 2015), as shown in figure 23, while others prohibit this practice (Woods 2017). A U.S. federal court has held that a Nebraska prisoner who is a Pastafarian does not have the right to religious accommodations while in prison (Matas 2016). None of these cases were cases about religious accommodations per se. Rather, all turned on the question of whether Pastafarianism is a religion or simply a well-done satire piece.

Where any degree of free exercise of religion is permitted, the activities and practices of a minority religious faith may come into conflict with those of the majority. Countries vary in terms of the extent to which they provide accommodations for such conflicts, exempting individuals from standard laws or expectations based on religious belief. For example, members of certain religious groups may object to portions of the compulsory education system, leading them to seek exemptions for their children from certain course content, to place their children in alternative schools with different curricula, or to remove their children from formal education entirely. Such decisions may be facilitated by the educational authorities, or they may be considered grounds for charges of child abuse or neglect. A more extreme example is the Jain religious practice called *sallekhana* or *santhara.* In this practice, an elderly or terminally ill

Figure 23 A Pastafarian in his religious headgear (Dennis van Zuijlekom, CC BY-SA 2.0).

individual—usually an ascetic monk but sometimes a common person who no longer has family responsibilities—stops eating or drinking and dies. Jains believe in reincarnation, and the *santhara* practice is supposed to release an individual from the cycle of reincarnation. In 2015, the Rajasthan High Court ruled that this practice was a criminal form of suicide (Felder 2015). Upon hearing arguments that *santhara* was an essential religious practice, the Indian Supreme Court stayed the Rajasthan High Court's decision. In 2018, the Supreme Court ruled that the practice of passive euthanasia was legal so long as the individual's family consented and doctors agreed that the person would not survive their illness (Barnett 2018), thus permitting Jains to continue to engage in *santhara* in at least some circumstances.

Many countries have designated days of rest during the week when government offices, schools, and sometimes even stores are required to close. Even in secular countries, the choice of which day is the day of rest is typically based on religious belief, and state holidays may be based on the religious calendar. So, for instance, countries with majority-Christian populations typically designate Sunday as the day of rest; in majority-Muslim countries it is Friday; and Jews observe their day of rest from shortly before sundown on Friday to shortly after sundown on Saturday. This creates a conflict for those who practice a minority religion, as they may need to seek accommodation of an alternate schedule for religious observance. Where laws require businesses to be closed on the official day of rest, this can cause additional challenges. For example, a Jewish business in a Christian country may be required to close Friday evening and Saturday

Intellectual and Academic Freedom in Qatar

BY GEOFF HARKNESS

Many Americans presume that rights such as freedom of speech, the autonomy to gather and protest, and the liberty to read anything they please are inalienable. In part, the belief that such rights are universal stems from their enshrinement within the United States' laws and founding documents, but also arises out of a culture that largely supports freedoms of expression. This is not, however, the way all nations or governments view such matters.

Take Qatar, for example, a small, petroleum-rich country located on the Arabian Peninsula. With a population of about 2.7 million, 90 percent of whom are expatriates, Qatar is an autocratic state ruled by Shari'a law, the Islamic code of conduct that sets standards for everything from crime to culinary matters. Among Qataris, there is widespread backing for Wahhabism, one of the most conservative interpretations of Islam (Katzman 2017; Welchman 2012).

Qatar's laws restrict freedoms related to personal expression in ways that many Americans would find extreme. For example, in 2011, the government arrested literature student Mohammed al-Ajami, who was charged with inciting to overthrow the Qatari leadership and insulting the emir, both illegal under the state penal code (Miles 2012). Al-Ajami's crime? He wrote a poem that some found offensive.

Al-Ajami's trial served as a microcosm of Qatar's byzantine legal system, where court sessions may be held in secret, defense attorneys are sometimes privy to little information, and tribal leaders may have jurisdiction over outcomes (Amnesty International 2015; Hall 2018; Khedr 2016). Al-Ajami's hearing included testimony from three government-employed poetry experts, who unsurprisingly found in favor of their employer (Miles 2012). In 2012, a judge sentenced al-Ajami to life in prison. Although international outcry led to the poet's eventual pardon in 2016, his case illustrates the Qatari government's legal stance on individual expression (*BBC News* 2016c).

State censorship in Qatar can be overt. Customs agents supposedly examine every book and magazine that passes through the country, searching for objectionable content. Those deemed questionable are flagged and forwarded to the Ministry of Culture and Sports for review. This is particularly arduous for colleges, universities, and libraries, which order printed materials frequently and sometimes experience long delays. On other occasions, books simply disappear into the ether, failing to reach their destination without explanation from the Ministry. Art and photography tomes are the most likely to go missing, but it can happen to any title.

Magazines like *Esquire* and *Sports Illustrated* are sold in watered-down versions published exclusively for Middle Eastern markets. Even these do not escape government intervention. It is not unusual to purchase a magazine in Qatar only to discover entire pages removed or images redacted with a magic marker.

The Ministry of Culture also edits most movies that play in Qatar. The government censors can be as arbitrary as they are harsh, quick to take scissors to any scene that might remotely offend. Films that feature nudity and curse words are cut, but also removed are nonsexual scenes that take place in a bedroom, religious content, anti-Muslim sentiments, and any hint of homosexuality. (Violence is unproblematic and rarely nixed.) Because of this, R-rated movies that play in Qatari movie theaters are often significantly shorter than their uncensored counterparts. A ninety-minute feature might screen at just over an hour.

Survey data of Qataris finds widespread public support for state censorship of films, television, and music (Martin, Martins, and Wood 2016). If anything, Qataris believe the government is not doing enough. There is strong sentiment that American cinema, with its supposed emphasis on secularism and sexuality, is morally destructive to viewers. Those who disagree with the government have little recourse—unauthorized public protests are against the law.

Qatar heavily filters the Internet, too. Pornography is banned, but some religious and political content is also inaccessible, as are most sites and stories that have to do with dating and sexuality. Even seemingly innocuous news items are prohibited at times. In 2014, the government passed sweeping cyber laws that criminalized online content deemed harmful to Qatar's social order or personally insulting to someone. What was considered harmful or insulting, however, was not defined under the new crime statutes. Those with Internet access are told to assume the Qatari government is monitoring everything they do online.

Qatar's overt surveillance and censorship are especially problematic for the largely Western and Western-trained academics who work in Qatari colleges and universities. The nation's most prominent postsecondary educational institutions are branch campuses of elite Western entities, such as Northwestern, Carnegie Mellon, Georgetown, and Cornell, each of which reportedly are paid between US$42 and US$122 million per year to operate satellite outlets in Qatar's capital, Doha (N. Anderson 2016). While these establishments ostensibly enjoy complete academic and curricular autonomy, studies and media reports find otherwise.

Geoff Harkness and Peggy Levitt (2017) argue that intellectual and academic freedom are core expectations for Western and Western-trained scholars, liberties that directly conflict with Qatar's restrictive social, political, and legal climate. Qatar operates under an employment scheme, formerly known as *kafala*, that allows employers and the government to exercise near total control over expatriates, be they low-wage construction laborers or college professors. Under this system, foreigners are not allowed to quit their jobs, seek employment elsewhere, file a workplace complaint, or leave the country without written permission from their employer. In response to international criticism, Qatar has eliminated the word *kafala* and revamped its regulations for expatriate workers. Historically, however, Qatar's labor laws have included unofficial workarounds that render many legal changes moot.

Restrictive labor regulations, combined with a host of laws that explicitly forbid freedom of expression, lead to college campuses staffed by self-censoring faculty members who are careful about everything they say and do in the classroom (Romanowski and Nasser 2010). While these educators supposedly enjoy intellectual and academic freedom, as expatriates, they are required to obey the country's laws and regulations. A single complaint about a reading, film, discussion, email, social media post, or even gesture could lead to arrest and conviction. Becoming ensnared in Qatar's legal system might mean anything from imprisonment to corporal punishment to deportation.

Adding to the complications, Qatar's laws are written in Arabic, and official translations are nonexistent. Representatives of foreign embassies are typically barred from visiting arrestees until after an interrogation has taken place, and criminal defendants are not guaranteed the right to an attorney. It is standard procedure for the government to forbid people from leaving Qatar while legal matters are pending, including outstanding loans or even bounced checks. In his book, *The Glass Palace*, Nasser Beydoun chronicles being "held hostage" in Qatar for nearly two years following a business deal that turned sour (Beydoun and Baum 2012).

Although the Qatari leadership has been slower to censure academics than its neighbor the United Arab Emirates (which has deported several Western scholars for their teaching and research topics), it has demonstrated a willingness to do so. For example, Kristina Bogos was a graduate student at Georgetown University in Qatar who intended to study the conditions of the low-wage migrant workers that comprise the majority of Qatar's population. She flew to Doha, where she was detained at the airport and denied entry. The Qatari government eventually rejected her student visa application. As is common for Western branch campuses funded by repressive regimes, Georgetown was largely silent on the issue. In an op-ed for the *New York Times,* Bogos (2016) castigated the university for its unwillingness "to call out the suppression of critical speech. . . . The transactional relationships that underpin these American universities' campuses [in] Qatar subvert the very academic freedom they're supposed to promote."

As Western colleges and universities continue to expand to new areas of the globe, tensions between authoritarian governments and faculty trained to expect intellectual and academic freedom are likely to persist. It remains to be seen if educators' desire for autonomy in pedagogy and research will eventually surmount the will of conservative governments backed by wealth and the rule of law.

for religious reasons *and* Sunday for legal reasons, while Christian business are able to work a six-day week.

Another example is objection to military service. Members of a variety of religious faiths, including Buddhists, Quakers, Jains, and Jehovah's Witnesses, have pacifist beliefs that may include refusal to participate in military service. Countries with compulsory military service often accommodate this practice by providing for alternative service. Until 2018, South Korea did not provide such accommodations, instead imprisoning those who refused to serve for religious reasons (Sang-Hun 2018). The number of those imprisoned for this offense since 1953 is more than nineteen thousand, mostly Jehovah's Witnesses, and some have been tortured. In June 2018, the South Korean Constitutional Court ordered the creation of alternative service pathways for such conscientious objectors, putting an end to the practice of jailing them (Sang-Hun 2018), a decision later upheld by the South Korean Supreme Court (Marotta 2018).

The Right to Subsistence

The right to subsistence refers to individuals' rights to maintain the minimum necessities of life that allow them to survive (sometimes called social welfare), such as food, housing, and health care. In some countries, citizens are guaranteed the ability to access a minimum standard of living. In others, they are not, either because the government has insufficient resources to provide that standard to everyone or because the country does not see doing so as a government

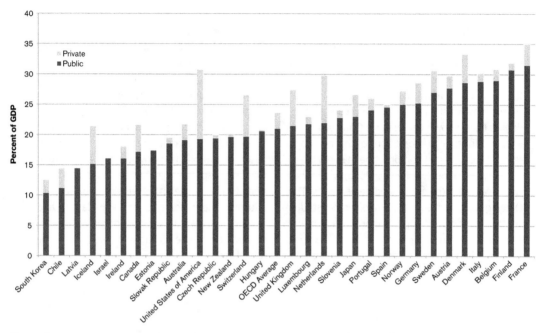

Figure 24 Public and private social expenditure as a percent of GDP, OECD countries, most recent data available, 2013–2016 (OECD 2016).

responsibility. Where the government does provide social welfare benefits, it may do so through the direct provision of goods and services, like government food programs, heath clinics, and public housing, or it may provide a basic income to everyone (universal basic income) or to those without other sources of support.

Even those countries commonly referred to as "developed" vary considerably in the extent of such spending, as shown in figure 24. Among OECD countries—a group of relatively well-off countries that work together on certain economic issues—social expenditures including cash, in-kind benefits, and other spending on low-income households, health care, the elderly or young, the unemployed, those with disabilities, and other similar social purposes varies from 12 to 35 percent of GDP. In most countries, the vast majority of such spending comes from public sources, whether national or local governments, while in the United States over a third comes from private sources, like charities.

Thinking about the right to subsistence raises a number of other issues. For example, consider property rights. In some countries, property rights have strong legal protection, including protection for property owners to use their property in whatever way they see fit. In others, people have very little ability to protect their property from government **takings**, and the government has considerable power to regulate the uses of property. In a general sense, the question here is how countries balance property rights with other kinds of rights or concerns. So, for example, a country that is more concerned with the right to subsistence than with property rights might take away property from the rich when wealth has become too concentrated and use it to ensure subsistence for the poor. Or a country concerned with environmental degradation might prohibit property owners from engaging in polluting enterprises on the land they own. Some countries permit government takings of property only for public purposes, such as to build a highway or school, while others allow takings of property for commercial development that will not benefit the public. And when the government takes property, some countries require compensation for that taking, while others do not. One of the most interesting cases is China. Despite a long history of public takings, including a period when private property ownership was entirely abolished, today in China individuals cannot be forcibly removed from property they own. However, developers can terminate access to utilities like power and water, and they can build new highways right up to the doorsteps of a house, hoping to constructively evict occupants by making their lives unpleasant. This has resulted in several circumstances in which roads were built around houses while people still lived in them, with the asphalt coming right up to the front door (Ward 2012).

Another way in which governments extract money from people is through taxes. Taxes are different from takings in that taxes are applied to the whole population (or at least the whole population able to pay them) while takings are of specific property. Taxes can be **progressive**, where those with higher incomes pay a larger proportion of their income in taxes, or **regressive**, where those with higher incomes pay a smaller proportion of their income in taxes. Sales taxes tend to be regressive, because poorer people spend a larger proportion of their income on taxable goods. Some countries also have wealth taxes, requiring people with a certain amount of wealth to pay a small percentage of it in taxes every year. Tax rates are highly variable (Schanz n.d.), with some European countries collecting well over 35 percent of the average family's income in taxes, while other countries collect under 25 percent (the United States is somewhere in the middle).

Related to the right to subsistence is the right to economic initiative, including the right to create businesses and to contract for employment as one chooses. Governments typically implement regulations around many aspects of work life that could be seen as interfering with the right to contract but that are designed to protect workers' rights, such as regulations around workplace privacy, discussed earlier in this chapter. Such regulations may also include limits on working hours and requirements for minimum standards around working conditions. Some countries have created such limits but impose them only on some workers, most notably children but at times women as well.

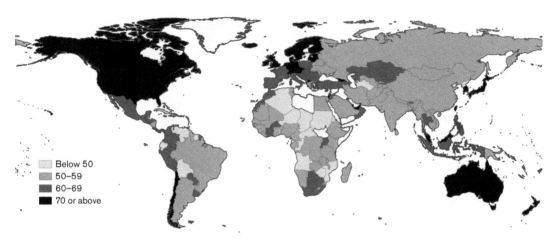

Map 25 Heritage Foundation economic freedom index, 2018 (Heritage Foundation 2018).

When limited working hours are imposed on child workers, the idea is to ensure that children are not exploited such that they cannot attend school, though some commentators argue that such limits may prevent children from earning sufficient money to subsist. Limitations on women's work historically arose from the same concerns about exploitation but today are more likely to be a way to maintain gender inequality in earnings. A more contemporary form of work regulation involves the "right to disconnect." France passed a right to disconnect law that, since 2016, has required employers with more than fifty employees to negotiate policies permitting those employees to ignore their digital devices and email outside of work hours (Agence France-Presse 2016). New York City proposed similar legislation in 2018 (Wolfe 2018).

The Heritage Foundation, a politically conservative think tank based in the United States that advocates for free enterprise and limited government, has for many years produced the Economic Freedom Index. This global measure is designed to indicate the extent to which a given country permits free movement of goods, labor, and capital and avoids regulating workers, production, investment, and consumption. It is based on a complex set of indicators, including measures of property rights, government integrity, taxes, government spending, extent of economic regulation, and open markets. Thus, the index takes into consideration some of the economic rights discussed above, along with other factors. While not all countries are covered by the index due to data limitations, the 2018 index—as shown in map 25—positions North Korea, Venezuela, and Cuba as the least economically free, while New Zealand, Singapore, and Hong Kong are considered the most economically free.

Countries may also maintain minimum wage standards and mandate a certain number of vacation or sick days. While cross-national comparisons of minimum wage are complicated by different costs of living in different countries, including differential provision of subsidized social benefits such as health care and higher education, the Organisation for Economic Co-operation and Development (OECD) has produced a measure using a calculation called Purchasing Power Parity that attempts to control for at least some of these differences (OECD n.d.-b). It finds that the 2016 minimum wage in member countries ranged from over US$11 an hour in France, Australia, and Luxembourg to less than US$2 an hour in Russia and Mexico, with the United States at US$7.9 an hour. A global analysis found that the average country mandates a minimum of eight days of paid leave per year, with a quarter of countries mandating more than twenty-four days a year, and that 69 percent of countries require a minimum of five paid sick days per year (World Bank 2018b). The only countries with *no* mandatory paid leave are the United States, the Gambia, the Marshall Islands, Micronesia, Palau, and Tonga, though of course some other countries may not enforce their leave legislation. Some European countries go so far as to create legal incentives to encourage employees to take all of their guaranteed vacation time (Ray, Sanes, and Schmitt 2013).

The right to subsistence additionally includes the right to health care, as one may be unable to survive without medical treatment. The right to health care raises many interesting questions (S. Davies 2010; Weale 2008). For example, do people have the right to all types of medical care they might wish to access, no matter how expensive or effective? Or should the government provide access to some very minimal standard of care only? Is this right a right to health, or merely a right to access health care? Most commonly, countries that think of health care as a right provide universal health insurance to all citizens or residents. They may do this through single-payer health care systems, like those in Canada and the United Kingdom, where all health care is paid for by the government. Or they may provide a backup health plan for everyone who does not receive health insurance through an employer, union, or other entity, like in Germany. Given the cost of health care, countries do find it necessary to impose some kinds of reasonable limits on the care provided, especially where certain treatments are very expensive and not very effective (Weale 2008).

Health care can of course be quite costly, though it is important to note that countries spending more on health care do not necessarily have better outcomes. For example, the United States spends considerably more money on health care than other countries. In 2016, it spent over ten thousand United States dollars per person on health care, 30 percent more than the next high-spending country, Switzerland, and over twice the average spending of comparable countries like Canada, Australia, Japan, and the United Kingdom (Sawyer and Cox 2018). Yet the United States does not get much from this high spending. It has higher health-related death rates and rates of disability, more hospital admissions for chronic disease, higher rates of maternal and infant mortality, more medical errors, and longer waiting periods to see a doctor than the average comparable country (Chen, Oster, and Williams 2016; Montange and Martin 2017; Sawyer 2017), though of course less developed countries often fare far worse.

LAW AND EQUALITY

The discussion of the right to subsistence, and many of the other rights detailed above, highlights the ways in which law shapes equality and inequality in societies. The general assumption under the rule of law is that equals are to be treated equally, but this doctrine does not tell us who counts as equal. Historically in many countries, for example, women and men were not considered legally equal, and this was consistent with the rule of law because it corresponded with fundamental assumptions about gender and worth. Today, most developed countries at least claim that men and women are equal, and thus the rule of law would imply that they should have equal legal status as well. But the lived legal reality may not conform to this expectation. In considering legal processes for seeking equality, it is also important to understand the difference between **formal equality** and **substantive equality**. Formal equality refers to equal treatment, while substantive equality refers to equality of outcomes or results. So, for example, a regime of formal gender equality would ensure that men and women have equal opportunities to apply for and be interviewed for jobs, while a regime of substantive equality would expect that men and women be hired at equal rates and paid equivalent salaries.

Law does not necessarily set out to ensure equality. Indeed, law can create inequalities between different groups of people. Consider regulations setting out minimum ages for voting, drinking, or driving—these are policies that create inequality based on age between different groups of people. Some of the laws mentioned above, such as those imposing stricter restrictions on working hours or sex outside of marriage for women or those prohibiting same-sex sexual activity, are also examples of law creating inequality. Law can also fail to remediate existing inequalities. If discrimination or long-standing arrangements of inequality exist and laws are not made to prohibit such discrimination or to counteract these long-standing arrangements, the inequalities are likely to continue.

On the other hand, law *can* work to reduce or eliminate inequalities. For example, countries can create laws that prohibit companies from paying workers differently depending on race or sex. Such laws may not go as far as actually eliminating differential pay, but they are a step toward reducing it. Iceland has implemented legal changes seeking to go further. These changes, enforced beginning in 2018, require that men and women doing the same work for the same employer be paid equal wages and otherwise be treated the same in the workplace (Ministry of Social Affairs 2018; Government of Iceland n.d.). While many countries have such laws, Iceland's innovation is to require organizations with at least twenty-five employees to proactively obtain certification to prove their compliance with the law. To obtain certification, employers contract with external auditors who review their wage policies in accordance with the ÍST 85 Standard, a body of regulations that instructs employers on classifying employees in terms of job requirements, skills, and performance, and ensuring that gender is not used as part of this evaluation. Organizations that do not comply can be fined the equivalent of more than US$400 per day (Ministry of Social Affairs 2018; Government of Iceland n.d.).

The Icelandic equal-pay initiative is an attempt to go beyond formal equality and achieve substantive equality in pay for men and women. There are a variety of other approaches countries have used in their attempts to seek substantive equality. Sometimes, seeking substantive equality may require a little less attention to formal equality, as it will require giving priority to the needs of marginalized people. In most countries, the question of whether such prioritization is permissible is based on a standard of proportionality, where government officials must ensure that the formal inequality created is proportionate to the need to address significant substantive inequality. The United States uses a different approach, with three specific levels of constitutional scrutiny depending on the type of inequality in question.

Among the most common examples of these approaches are affirmative action and indigenous rights. Affirmative action has been used at various times in a number of countries, such as the United States, France, and India, to increase substantive equality in access to higher education, employment, or political office for women, racial minorities, those from peripheral geographical areas, or those of marginalized caste backgrounds. Indigenous groups, as was discussed in chapter 3, may be granted special rights to autonomy and self-determination due to their unique status as colonized people.

Countries continue to vary greatly in the extent of inequality within their borders. Scholars have devised a method for calculating each country's degree of economic inequality called the **Gini coefficient**. This measure calculates the distribution of economic resources in a given society on a scale of zero to one. Zero would mean every single person in the society had exactly the same economic resources, while one would mean that one person had everything and everyone else had nothing (Barr 2017). As of the most recent data available, from the period 2013 to 2016, Ukraine, Slovenia, Iceland, and the Czech Republic have the lowest Gini coefficients, meaning they have the greatest degree of economic equality, while South Africa and Zambia have the highest. Obviously, most countries are somewhere in between, as shown in map 26, though no score is available for a number of countries. There are a variety of other similar calculations of economic inequality that result in somewhat different rankings of countries. It is important to note here that measures of economic freedom (as shown in map 25) and measures of economic

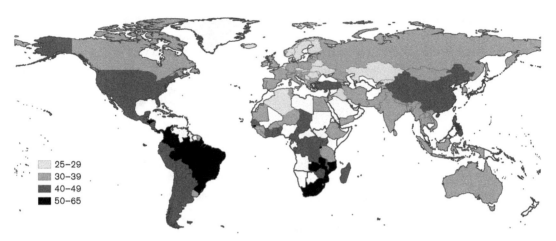

Map 26 Gini coefficient, most recent data available, 2013–2016 (World Bank n.d.). Darker colors illustrate a greater degree of economic inequality.

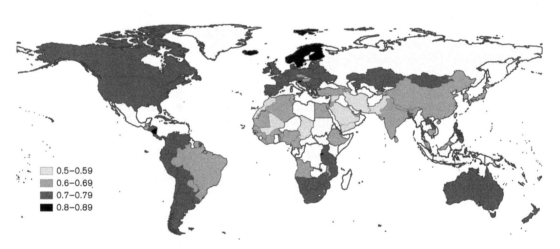

Map 27 Gender Inequality Index, 2017 (Leopold, Zahidi, and Ratcheva 2017). Darker colors illustrate a lesser degree of gender inequality.

equality do not necessarily coincide. The lack of regulation and taxes that the Heritage Foundation considers fundamental to economic freedom may reduce societies' ability to provide for the rights of substance and maintain economic equality.

The World Economic Forum has created a comparable measure, called the Global Gender Gap Score, which looks specifically at gender inequality, examining male-female ratios in labor force participation, political participation, education, and health (Leopold, Zahidi, and Ratcheva 2017). It is coded in the opposite direction from the Gini coefficient, with higher scores meaning a more gender-equal society. The 2017 Global Gender Gap Score, shown in map 27, ranks Iceland, Norway, Finland, and Rwanda as the most gender-equal countries. While data is not available for all countries, Yemen, Pakistan, and Syria are ranked as having the largest gender gap among those countries included in the rankings. This measure does not consider gender inequality beyond the male-female binary, as many countries do not even acknowledge the presence of a transgender or nonbinary population within their borders. It is also generally not possible to obtain useful cross-national data about racial and ethnic inequality given the vast differences between nations in terms of how—and even whether—data on population subgroups is collected.

CONCLUSION

As this chapter has shown, different countries have very different perspectives on fundamental rights. And even within countries, as in the case of the Bojayá massacre, different groups may have different perspectives on which rights are most fundamental or important. Examining these differences tells us a lot about how countries see the role of government, the balance between collective obligations and individual prerogatives, and the role of culture (as will be discussed further in chapter 11). It also helps us think more deeply about the extent to which it is possible to make universal claims about law, rights, and morality.

Scholars interested in this question focus on two main approaches: the doctrines of **natural law** and **positive law** (George 2001). The doctrine of natural law holds that law is not really created by people. Rather, it stems from an essential and universal human morality. In contrast, the doctrine of positive law holds that law is created by people without any inherent connection to morality (though of course humans can choose to create law that reflects moral precepts). So how do these ideas matter to considerations of legal rights?

Well, some scholars argue that the very idea of human rights requires a foundation in natural law. The notion here is that human rights stem from some "general moral standards" (Brown 1997:44) that apply to everyone, universally. Such scholars posit that rights created in positive law can of course exist but that they must by virtue of their creation within a particular legal system be limited to existing as civil rights. The difficulty for such scholars, though, is that a detailed examination of rights as they exist, both as spelled out in legal systems and as informally practiced and understood by people in society, shows little common agreement across the world. Some societies believe sex must occur only in marriage and anything else is immoral; others believe true freedom requires sexual autonomy. Some societies believe it is a moral imperative to provide the means of subsistence to all people, while others believe the height of moral behavior is creating a society where businesses have freedom of contract, regardless of the impact this has on ordinary folks. Advocates of natural law can attempt to resolve this dilemma by suggesting that there is an underlying morality that certain societies have chosen to reject or ignore or have been deprived of the opportunity to embrace (Brown 1997).

In contrast, since positive law is created by people, it has no essential claim to **universalism**. The doctrine of positive law, when applied to global human rights standards, would tend to suggest that these standards are simply a reflection of the views of the people who created them. Such a perspective leaves a lot of room for people who do not agree with human rights standards, such as those spelled out in the United Nations' Universal Declaration of Human Rights, to say that such standards are simply reflections of some cultural perspective that does not apply to everyone.

But perhaps there is more agreement than we might suspect. An analysis of constitutions in effect in 188 countries in 2006 (Law and Versteeg 2012) found freedom of religion, freedom of expression, the right to private property, and equality each mentioned in 97 percent of them, with privacy, prohibitions against arbitrary arrest and detention, rights to assembly and association, and women's rights each mentioned in over 90 percent. Sixteen more rights were found in at least 70 percent of the constitutions. Yet this body of similarities need not necessarily point to natural law as its explanation. Rather, it may be that, in making positive law, lawmakers look to common examples, and thus legal systems come to resemble one another through some process of imitation, competition, convergence, or allegiance that has led to the emergence of a set of generic rights and a growth in the overall number of rights included in constitutions (Law and Versteeg 2011). Of course, the real lived experience of people in these countries may suggest that the many rights their constitutions spell out are not actually protected.

One further complicating factor is that many of these human rights are today the subject of various international treaties. These treaties have been crafted in an attempt to further universalize human rights, to take them beyond the limitations of any one legal system and create a truly global regime of protection and enforcement. Chapter 10 will detail the system of global justice such as it exists. As will be clear, it does not live up to the dreams of those who wish to see truly global protection for all people's human rights. But it does do more than it once did, as we will see.

Global Justice 10

CHAPTER GOALS

1. Become familiar with institutions of global justice, especially the International Criminal Court, the United Nations, and the International Court of Justice.
2. Understand the sources of international law.
3. Be able to explain the impact and consequences of statelessness and the process of asylum-seeking.

Consider the legal context surrounding a cruise ship. Those sailing on the ship may hail from one country and work for or be customers of a company based in a second country that runs a ship that flies a flag from a third country, while sailing both in the waters of still other countries and in international waters. If a legal dispute arises, where does the case go? For a worker, this question may be resolved by the terms of her employment contract (W. Terry 2009). In the case of a passenger, complex terms and conditions she agreed to, most likely without reading them, govern the forum and law that will be applied (Wilson 2012). And beyond these provisions, there is the historical body of law that governs the high seas (Epps and Graham 2011), law with which neither worker nor passenger is likely to be familiar.

When we think about legal systems, we are generally focused on individual countries. After all, countries determine for themselves how to make laws, what counts as a crime, how particular crimes will be punished, and what civil rights to protect. But there is law that extends beyond the borders of individual countries. There are places such as the high seas, Antarctica, and outer space that belong to no country, and yet human activity goes on in these places. Countries squabble over borders, and they fight wars against one another and must grapple with the legal consequences of such armed conflict, including how to handle prisoners of war. Economic activity, crime, and disease cross borders, and countries sometimes disagree about how to handle these issues and who is to blame. As the cruise ship example above shows, these questions can be extremely complicated.

As discussed in chapter 1, globalization has increased the extent to which legal and other issues cross borders. Long ago, most trade occurred within individual countries, and wars tended to involve neighboring countries. But today, these types of issues are global in scope. As the reach and extent of globalization intensified, the need for global legal institutions grew. World War II, and the global devastation it was responsible for, made this need even more clear. Thus, while international law of a sort has existed for centuries, a new international legal order and new institutions of global justice developed in the postwar period. This chapter will explore what international law is, how it works, and what institutions of global justice—especially the International Criminal Court and the United Nations—our world has built.

WHAT IS INTERNATIONAL LAW?

International law is law that governs relations across borders. Public international law governs relations between nations; private international law governs relations between people or corporations that are implicated in more than one national context. The majority of international law is based either on tradition (customary international law) or on treaties (conventional international law), though there are other sources, such as judicial decisions in international courts, that are sometimes important.

Customary international law is a body of legal practices and understandings that has developed over time, otherwise known as tradition. There is a long history of international law around issues like piracy that is in some cases still treated as binding on nations. In particular, customary law is treated as binding when it is "adhered to in practice by most nations . . . because they feel compelled by legal duty" (Findlay, Kuo, and Wei 2013:53).

Conventional international law is law made through treaties. The use of the term "conventional" here does not mean ordinary but rather indicates that this body of law is based on conventions, another word for treaties. Treaties can also be called protocols, charters, or any number of other names and can be made between any two or more nations, though they must be in written form. In order for a country to be bound by a treaty, a domestic lawmaking process such as a legislative vote in favor of ratification may be required by that country's legal system (Epps and Graham 2011). For the most part, a nation must have signed on to a treaty in order to be governed by it, though losing parties in military conflicts may be subjected to treaty rules, and some treaties become part of customary international law and get applied to all nations in that way. In addition, state parties to a treaty sometimes incorporate elements of customary law into the treaty text (Epps and Graham 2011). It is important to note that not all countries sign all treaties, a fact that can limit their impact.

To take one example of a common type of treaty, consider **regional trade agreements** (RTAs). RTAs are treaties between two or more countries about trade-related issues (World Trade Organization 2018), including free trade agreements and customs unions, which eliminate taxes on imports from treaty partners (Hirsch 2015). When countries craft and then sign an RTA, they agree to a particular set of trade and economic practices, varying according to the treaty itself. As of 2019, there were 302 RTAs in effect around the world (World Trade Organization 2019).

How Is International Law Enforced?

The enforcement mechanisms of formal international law are themselves set out in treaties. Typically, parties that violate a treaty are subject to specific penalties, such as fines or increased monitoring. But there are no global police, and countries cannot be sentenced to prison. Despite the lack of strong enforcement mechanisms, most countries comply with international law most of the time (Koh 1997). Thus, scholars have long been interested in why countries comply and what increases the likelihood of compliance, and scholars continue to disagree about the answers to these questions.

There are several different lines of thought about why countries comply. Some scholars argue that countries may comply with international law because they make rational calculations about the potential consequences of noncompliance and decide that compliance is better for them (Koh 1997). This sort of rational decision-making perspective is consistent with the idea that treaties can provide for a deterrent effect by laying out potential unfavorable consequences of noncompliance. There can also be more coercive means of exacting compliance, such as the imposition of economic sanctions (Hirsch 2015), which similarly might have a deterrent effect. In this perspective, the power of international law is to create rules and lay out consequences for their violation so as to provide a shared conception of proper behavior by countries.

Other scholars point to the importance of global norms, arguing that countries comply for cultural, social, or other normative reasons (Hirsch 2015) or because international treaties are part of a process of discourse that encourages compliance through participation (Koh 1997). It is possible to use norm-based means to encourage compliance, such as statements of disapproval or decisions about whether or not to admit or expel countries from particular international organizations. In addition, global monitoring organizations, including nongovernmental organizations (NGOs), can use naming and shaming approaches to encourage countries to conform to global norms and global regulatory regimes (Hirsch 2015). In this perspective, the power of international law is to shape and reshape global norms to encourage compliance.

Finally, some scholars suggest that countries do not change their behavior due to international law; advocates for this perspective may even go so far as to argue that international law is not law at all (Koh 1997). This perspective suggests that countries make decisions about how to act in response to their own goals and intentions and their perceptions of the balance of power with other countries, which also have their own goals and intentions (Hirsch 2015). Much like the first perspective, this one assumes that countries will make rational decisions, but here the decisions are based on perceptions of the global power structure and the likely response of other individual countries, not based on international law per se.

International legal institutions—and individual countries—do have various tools available to them to encourage compliance. It is important to note that, unlike statutory sentencing regimes in place in some countries, the response to noncompliance in international law is not "rigid and formulaic" (Epps and Graham 2011:55) but includes a variety of flexible options depending on the circumstances. For example, a noncompliant country may be encouraged to apologize or to pay restitution for the harms it has caused. States can refer violations of international law by other states to the United Nations Security Council (to be discussed later in this chapter), which can impose penalties ranging from economic sanctions to authorizations for the use of force up to and including war (Epps and Graham 2011).

INSTITUTIONS OF GLOBAL JUSTICE

As law has globalized and international law has become more complex and incorporated more measures beyond what was customary, global legal institutions developed to help manage this complexity. Global legal institutions exercise their jurisdiction on a global scale (Findlay, Kuo, and Wei 2013). There are also regional legal institutions, with jurisdiction that goes beyond national boarders but that is more limited in scope than is the jurisdiction of global institutions, and global regulatory agencies with more limited foci (such as organizations that deal with transportation, postal mail, and weather monitoring). The first attempts at tribunals with jurisdiction extending beyond national

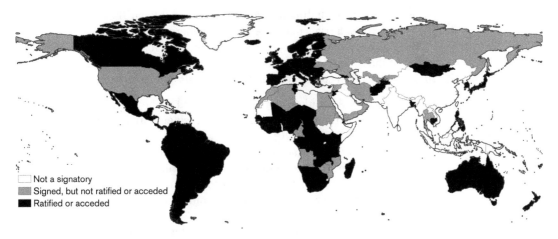

Map 28 Signatories to the Rome Treaty of the International Criminal Court (American Bar Association 2018).

borders were the international military tribunals in Nuremberg, Germany, and Tokyo, Japan, after World War II, though these were not global in nature (Schabas 2001). Subsequently, other areas where severe human rights abuses occurred also developed local or regional tribunals, such as Rwanda and the former Yugoslavia (Findlay, Kuo, and Wei 2013). Today, some disputes under international law are heard by specialized local or regional tribunals, some by international courts, and some by other bodies. For example, disputes related to RTAs, when they cannot be resolved by the parties themselves, go before arbitrators under the auspices of the Court of Arbitration in The Hague, Netherlands, which hears the disputes and issues binding decisions (Epps and Graham 2011).

The International Criminal Court

The **International Criminal Court** (ICC) is a tribunal for international crimes, specifically genocide, crimes against humanity, war crimes, and (since 2017) crimes of aggression. The Rome Statute, the treaty establishing the ICC, which was drafted beginning in the mid-1990s (Schabas 2001; Rome Statute of the International Criminal Court 1998), came into power in 2002, and the ICC can prosecute only crimes committed after that date. In order for the ICC to have jurisdiction over a particular crime, those accused of the crime must be nationals of a nation that participates in the ICC, the crime must have taken place in a nation that participates in the ICC, or the case must be brought by the UN Security Council (ICC n.d.-c). As of 2018, as shown in map 28, 123 states are parties to the Rome Statute, with additional states having signed but not ratified the treaty, including the United States and Russia. The ICC is housed in The Hague, though trials may take place anywhere.

The ICC has a detention center with twelve cells in which it holds those on trial and those convicted in the course of ICC proceedings. As of February 2019, the detention center held seven individuals (ICC n.d.-a):

- Al Hassan Ag Abdoul Aziz, the de facto head of the Islamic police in Timbuktu, Mali, who allegedly persecuted residents and destroyed historic monuments in 2012 and 2013;
- Ahmad Al Faqui Al Madhi, found guilty of war crimes in relation to the destruction of historic monuments in Timbuktu;
- Patrice-Edouard Ngaïssona, alleged to have committed war crimes and crimes against humanity in his role as commander of a coalition of militia groups in the Central African Republic;
- Bosco Ntaganda, who allegedly commanded operations of a military force in the Democratic Republic of Congo, resulting in thirteen counts of war crimes and five counts of crimes against humanity in 2002 and 2003;
- Dominic Ongwen, an alleged commander in the Lord's Resistance Army in Uganda, charged with seventy counts of crimes against humanity and war crimes in the post-2002 period; and
- Alfred Yekatom, former *caporal-chef* in the Forces Armées Centrafricaines and member of parliament in the Central African Republic, accused of crimes against humanity and war crimes.

The ICC has undertaken preliminary investigations in many parts of the world, but most official investigations have taken place in Africa. This focus on Africa has been one aspect of the ICC's existence that has been controversial, given that human rights abuses occur all around the globe. As the ICC is specifically focused on those crimes enumerated in international law, it does not have jurisdiction over the hundreds of other ways rights can be violated. Yet it is the only international legal institution that can act to protect or affirm rights beyond national borders.

The administrative structure of the ICC is complex (ICC n.d.-c). The Assembly of State Parties, which provides administrative oversight for the court, includes one representative from each state that is party to the ICC treaty. It is responsible for electing judges and prosecutors and determining budgets. There are then four bodies of ICC officials: the Presidency, the Judicial Divisions (three), the Office of the Prosecutor, and the Registry. The Presidency oversees the administration of the court, liaises with state parties, and assigns judges to cases. The Judicial Divisions are staffed by eighteen judges with nine-year terms assigned to three divisions: pretrial, trial, and appeals. The judges elect the president and two vice-presidents to three-year terms. The Office of the Prosecutor is responsible for investigating and prosecuting cases. Its primary officers are an elected prosecutor and deputy prosecutor, who are supported by professional staff. Finally, the Registry provides judicial support, such as maintaining court records, providing translation support, running the detention center, and supporting victims and witnesses; oversees external affairs; and manages court operations, including security, finances, and human resources.

The varied purposes and goals of the ICC do not always line up well— providing justice for victims, holding perpetrators accountable, deterring future international crimes, preserving a historical record of the violations and, to a more limited extent, restoring peace in conflict-ridden areas (Findlay, Kuo, and Wei 2013). Some of these functions are served well by trials that might be understood almost as show trials, providing a needed sense of closure and perhaps deterrence (Douglas 2005), though there is little evidence of deterrence for severe crimes generally (Findlay, Kuo, and Wei 2013). One of the central complications here is that the types of crimes the ICC has jurisdiction over involve a tangled web of individual and state responsibility. However, the ICC can only try and imprison individuals—states clearly cannot be held in the detention center. Another is that for people and communities who have suffered the unimaginable harm of being victims of international crimes, the ICC's justice does little. Imprisoning the warlord who slaughtered your family and destroyed your property does not bring your family back to life, nor does it restore your way of life or your ability to make a living.

The United States is not a party to the ICC's Rome Statute. While U.S. president Bill Clinton's administration was deeply involved with the negotiations that lead to the creation of the ICC and signed the treaty, it was never ratified, and President George W. Bush even attempted to retract Clinton's signature (Bava and Ireland 2016). The U.S. Congress prohibited the expenditure of any funds to support the ICC in 2000. And in 2002, it passed the American Servicemembers' Protection Act (the ASPA) due to fears that the ICC could prosecute U.S. officials, including the president, for international crimes—most notably the crime of aggression (Bava and Ireland 2016). The ASPA prevents U.S. courts, governments, and funds from assisting the ICC, including by providing information. However, it exempts certain actions taken by the president (Bava and Ireland 2016), as well as any initiatives related to bringing foreign nationals accused of war crimes, crimes against humanity, and genocide to justice (note that crimes of aggression are *not* included here).

The ASPA also includes a provision authorizing the use of military force to extract members of the U.S. armed forces and government and elected officials, as well as similar personnel of United States allies, who have been imprisoned by or on behalf of the ICC. In response, the ASPA has become known in some quarters as The Hague Abduction Act (Murphy 2002). In the 2000s, the United States also suspended funding to countries that did not sign agreements promising to grant immunity from prosecution to United States personnel, resulting in losses of millions of dollars in foreign aid that low-income countries relied on to fund security operations (*BBC News* 2003). But the ICC itself offers no mechanism for addressing disputes around issues such as these—they are the province of another set of international institutions.

THE UNITED NATIONS AND THE INTERNATIONAL COURT OF JUSTICE

The **United Nations** (UN) was founded in 1945 by a group of 51 countries. Today, it has 193 member states (United Nations n.d.). The most recent to join was South Sudan, on July 14, 2011, and nonmember countries tend to be those that are not fully recognized by the international community (such as Taiwan) or that have limited self-government (such as the Cook Islands and Western Sahara). The Vatican and the Palestinian Territories have nonmember permanent observer status. The UN was not the first attempt at a global organization of states. After World War I, a group of countries formed the League of Nations, which grew to fifty-eight members by the mid-1930s. But many countries, including the United States, never joined, and others withdrew, so it was not able to live up to its purpose. The organization of the UN was designed to address these limitations, creating an international organization with the mission to "maintain international peace and security," "develop friendly relations among nations based on respect for the principle of equal rights and self-determination," "achieve international co-operation," and "be a centre for harmonizing the actions of nations" (United Nations Charter 1945).

The UN is headquartered in New York City, but the land on which it stands is not considered part of the United States. It is **extraterritorial** land, exempt from local laws, as are the UN's subsidiary facilities. Map 29 shows the locations of United Nations agencies around the world, as well as the location of the ICC. The structure of the UN is complicated, as it is made up of a number of branches and agencies. The most well-known part of the UN is the Security Council, which is responsible for maintenance of international peace and security. It has five permanent member countries, the five Allied world powers at the end of World War II, when the UN was established: China, France, Russia, the United Kingdom, and the United States; as well as ten temporary members that are elected by the general assembly and serve two-year terms. For procedural matters, nine of the fifteen members must agree. For substantive matters, nine of fifteen members must agree, but this must include *all five* of the permanent members—meaning each permanent member has veto power. The UN Security Council can refer cases to the ICC and make other decisions related to world security, including authorizing the use of force (Epps and Graham 2011; United Nations n.d.-a).

The UN General Assembly is a legislative body with one vote per member state, regardless of population. Its powers include budgetary decision-making and elections to other UN bodies; it can also issue nonbinding advisory

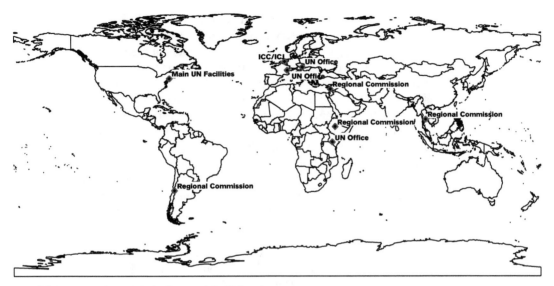

Map 29 Locations of Main UN facilities and the ICC.

opinions on other issues. The Economic and Social Council, with twenty-seven countries elected as members, studies and develops programs on economic and social issues, such as crime, the environment, indigenous issues, and women's rights. It has also established subsidiary bodies to carry out its mandate, such as the United Nations International Children's Emergency Fund (UNICEF) and the World Health Organization (WHO). A fourth body of the UN, formerly very important but with a reduced workload these days, is the Trusteeship Council. Its responsibility is to help colonized or otherwise dependent areas work toward autonomy (Epps and Graham 2011; United Nations n.d.-a).

Administrative functions of the UN are carried out by the Secretariat, the executive branch of the UN. It has just under forty thousand staff members around the world that carry out day-to-day business in jobs ranging from professional managers to data analysts, and from peacekeeping forces to language teachers (United Nations Secretary-General 2018). It is administered by the secretary-general, who is appointed to a five-year term by the General Assembly after a recommendation by the Security Council (Epps and Graham 2011; United Nations n.d.-a).

Finally, the judicial branch of the UN is the **International Court of Justice** (ICJ), which (unlike the rest of the UN's branches) is located in The Hague alongside other international courts. The ICJ settles legal disputes between nations and can also issue advisory opinions on matters referred by other branches of the UN (United Nations n.d.-a). It is staffed by fifteen judges elected to nine-year terms by the UN General Assembly and the UN Security Council, along with a registry of professional staff. The judges are required to represent all families of law and all of the permanent members of the Security Council. Judicial candidates are nominated by the Permanent Court of Arbitration, which serves as an arbitration body for international treaties, though ad hoc judges can also be nominated by parties in contentious cases (ICJ 2018).

While all UN member states are parties to the treaty that created the ICJ, the court only has jurisdiction over a case if member states choose to bring the case forward (Epps and Graham 2011). It hears cases about a wide variety of issues, ranging from border conflicts to water and fishing resources, from armed conflict to disputes over the imposition of economic sanctions, and from the rights of asylum and nationality to nuclear weapons tests (Epps and Graham 2011). In February 2019, there were seventeen pending cases (ICJ 2019). Among these cases were

- a dispute between Hungary and Slovakia over the Gabčíkovo-Nagymaros Project, a series of hydroelectric dams on the Danube River;
- a dispute between the Democratic Republic of Congo and Uganda about cross-border armed activities;
- disputes related to access to the ocean, the measurement of the continental shelf under the ocean, and other maritime rights, involving a variety of countries in South America, as well as a case dealing with similar issues between Somalia and Kenya;
- a dispute over the use of an underground aquifer between Chile and Bolivia;
- a challenge to the criminal investigation and seizure of diplomatic property in France by Equatorial Guinea;
- a dispute over economic sanctions imposed by the United States on Iran;
- a dispute over the relocation of the U.S. embassy in Israel to Jerusalem;
- a case in which India seeks to overturn a sentence of death imposed on an Indian national by a Pakistani military court; and
- two cases related to the International Convention on the Elimination of All Forms of Racial Discrimination, a treaty calling on signatories to work to prevent discrimination and criminalize hate speech, one of which involves allegations by Ukraine that Russia encourages and finances both hate and terrorism, while the other was filed by Qatar claiming that the United Arab Emirates discriminates against Qataris.

CITIZENSHIP AND STATELESSNESS

As discussed in chapter 3, citizenship is the legal term for belonging to a particular country and having access to the rights and protections of that country. People who are not citizens of the country in which they live may or may not have

Chevron in Ecuador

Chevron is one of the world's largest oil companies. Headquartered in California, in 2016 it had over US$100 billion in revenue and over 55,000 employees around the world, and it has been ranked as high as number five on the Fortune 500 list of top global companies (Fortune 2017). The company has a storied history. It was one of the earliest oil companies in the Western United States and traces its legacy to the behemoth monopoly Standard Oil (Chevron Corporation 2018). Besides the Chevron brand, it also owns the Gulf, Texaco, and Caltex brands and sells petrochemical products to a variety of industries.

Texaco, which merged with Chevron in 2001, operated in the Oriente region of Ecuador from 1967 to 2002. This northeastern region of the country used to be an impenetrable part of the Amazon rainforest populated by indigenous groups. But when Texaco left, according to the local people, it left behind widespread environmental destruction with significant health consequences, including an alleged eighteen billion gallons of toxic waste, some in open sludge pits. Texaco's activities are alleged to have caused the deaths of livestock and people, resulting in a significant reduction in the indigenous population (Keefe 2012).

During the period in which Texaco was active in Ecuador, the country had little in the way of environmental regulations. So Texaco's activities were not formally illegal. But it is clear that they had a major impact on local communities. Oil was everywhere—sprayed on dusty surfaces, used as a folk remedy for illnesses, and left in pools to sit. And indigenous people, from whose land the oil was extracted, earned none of the profits (Keefe 2012). In 1995, Texaco even agreed to remediate some of the harms it committed in the Ecuadorian Amazon, but since it had worked in coalition with other companies, it cleaned up only 37 percent of

the oil pits the coalition had left behind. This was enough to get it a release from future claims from the Ecuadorian government (Keefe 2012).

A coalition of American and Ecuadorian lawyers filed a class action lawsuit in federal court in the United States, *Maria Aguinda, et al. v. Texaco, Inc.,* in 1993, seeking US$1.5 billion in damages (Epstein 1995). The suit alleged that Texaco chose less-safe methods for disposing of toxic waste in Ecuador than it used in the United States, largely to save money; that doing so harmed the health of local people, who came to be known as *los afectados* (the affected ones); and that the actions were taken under the direction of the company's U.S. headquarters (Epstein 1995). This suit relied on a U.S. law called the Alien Tort Claims Act, which permits residents of other countries to sue in U.S. courts when they are harmed by actions in violation of international law. It alleged that environmental crimes constituted violations of international law under customary law. As part of a public relations strategy, the legal team brought indigenous people from Ecuador to New York, where they attended press conferences in traditional garb few wore anymore (Keefe 2012).

After fighting the case for eight years, Texaco was victorious—a federal judge dismissed the case, agreeing with Texaco's argument that it belonged in Ecuadorian rather than U.S. courts because the actions were not directed from the United States. But the legal team forged ahead, refiling the case in an Ecuadorian court with local lawyers representing the plaintiffs. Operating in the Ecuadorian courts was a struggle for the American lawyers, who were used to the United States' adversarial system rather than Ecuador's inquisitorial one (Keefe 2012). Ecuadorian courts, as is typical in inquisitorial systems, do not use juries, and the judges are civil servants. Contrary to U.S. practice, lawyers are permitted to meet with the judge *ex parte* (without the opposing side present), a practice common in inquisitorial systems. This, along with a general perception of local corruption and the government's reliance on oil revenues, led the lawyers to fear that bribery might undermine the case (Keefe 2012). And there was considerable turnover in judges, in part due to Chevron's similar worries.

But things changed in the mid-2000s. A new Ecuadorian president, Rafael Correa, called Chevron/Texaco's actions "crimes against humanity" in 2006, and in 2008 a geological engineer issued a report on Chevron's responsibility for the environmental degradation in the Oriente (Keefe 2012). In 2011, Judge Nicolás Zambrano decided *Maria Aguinda y otros v. Chevron Corporation* (Texaco was by then part of Chevron). He found for the plaintiffs, awarding them US$18 billion in damages (Keefe 2012), though the judgment was reduced to US$9.5 billion in 2013 by the Ecuadorian Supreme Court (Uram 2018).

Chevron has a long history of involvement in extensive litigation, including a practice of filing countersuits when people who believe they have been harmed by its actions file suit against it. For example, in a Nigerian case involving protestors who were shot to death, it tried to win attorney's fees from the widows and children of the dead men after their families sued for wrongful death; it lost (Keefe 2012). Continuing with this practice, it sued one of the lead lawyers in the *Maria Aguinda* litigation, Steven Donziger, in New York, charging that he engaged in extortion and fraud to win in Ecuador and alleging violation of the RICO statute used to prosecute organized crime.

The *Maria Aguinda* cases have been the center of Donziger's entire legal career. He graduated from Harvard Law School in 1991, and by 1993 he had been invited to join a group of lawyers and health experts looking into filing the lawsuit

(Keefe 2012). As Donziger had prior experience working in Latin America and a head for public relations, he eventually took on a leadership role as an architect of the case and of the publicity around it—including suggesting that a filmmaker make a documentary about the case (2009's *Crude*). He also raised money to support the litigation, including by creating litigation finance instruments (Keefe 2012). Litigation finance typically involves investors advancing money in exchange for a percentage of the proceeds from a lawsuit.

It was his involvement with *Crude* that may have ultimately been his undoing. A viewer on Chevron's legal team noticed a tiny difference between the DVD version of the film and the one shown at the Sundance Film Festival. Relying on this difference and a U.S. law permitting litigants in non-U.S. cases to use the U.S. courts to gain access to evidence through the discovery process, Chevron was able to obtain six hundred hours of film footage. In some of this footage, Donziger expresses disdain for the Ecuadorian legal system, disregards the scientific data presented in the case, and notes that the Ecuadorian judge may fear for his life.

This evidence provided the foundation for Chevron to gain access to Donziger's case files and to question him directly (Keefe 2012). Lawyers who are asked to turn over their work product are permitted to label certain documents confidential, but Donziger did not have the resources to go through two decades of documents—so he had to turn over the whole lot. Even his personal diary became part of the public court record (Keefe 2012). Many of the materials Chevron obtained through the discovery process would not have been discoverable in Ecuador. Issues like this one can lead to a phenomenon known as "venue shopping," where litigants look for the country or jurisdiction most hospitable to their case. For example, the United Kingdom has libel laws that are more generous to plaintiffs than those in many other countries, so plaintiffs sometimes bring their libel cases in the United Kingdom rather than in the country in which the libel initially occurred. This has come to be called libel tourism.

As the litigation against Donziger progressed, Chevron briefly won an injunction that would have forbidden the *Maria Aguinda* litigation team from seeking to collect on the court's judgment in any other country's courts. Chevron's lawyers argued that U.S. courts should not tolerate "judgements procured by fraud . . . anywhere in the world." But a panel of judges for the Second Circuit Court of Appeals quickly overturned the injunction (Keefe 2012), given the jurisdictional limits of U.S. courts.

In March 2014, the judge in *Chevron Corporation v. Stephen Donziger* issued a 485-page ruling finding that Donziger obtained the Ecuadorian judgment through "fraud, bribery, and other racketeering acts" by engaging in "extortion, wire fraud, obstruction of justice, witness tampering, money laundering, bribery, and Foreign Corrupt Practices Act violations in a pattern of conduct that also amounted to a violation of the Racketeer Influenced and Corrupt Organizations Act (RICO)." This decision barred Donziger and the plaintiffs from using the U.S. courts to try to enforce the Ecuadorian judgment and barred Donziger from "profiting" from the frauds (Parloff 2014). In 2016, the United States Court of Appeals for the Second Circuit held that the plaintiffs could not collect on the judgment in the U.S. courts. They upheld a lower court decision finding that the Ecuadorian court decision had been obtained through fraud and barred Donziger from further efforts to collect on the judgment (Diaz 2016). Other U.S. courts have come to similar conclusions.

In 2018, a Canadian court determined that Chevron Canada could not be liable in Canada in relation to this case, as it was not the Canadian

subsidiary that was responsible for the harm (Uram 2018). Argentine courts have also held for Chevron, and the plaintiffs have filed cases in Brazil and other countries but have not yet been successful in finding a way to collect on the judgment anywhere (Reuters 2017). They cannot rely on the Ecuadorian courts to collect because Chevron does not have existing operations or assets in the country (Keefe 2012).

Simultaneously with the Ecuadorian, U.S., and other domestic cases, the plaintiffs brought their case to relevant international legal institutions. Due to the existence of treaties between Ecuador and the United States concerning investment-related issues, Chevron was able to institute international arbitration proceedings. These proceedings generally found in Chevron's favor. Ecuador ultimately appealed to the District Court of The Hague, a court that hears appeals from international arbitration panels, which again found mostly in Chevron's favor (Mealy's 2016). Ecuador appealed that decision, but the court again ruled in Chevron's favor. The story continues, as Ecuador seeks additional avenues to hold Chevron accountable for the harms the country believes it caused, while Chevron seeks monetary damages to compensate it for what it sees as fraudulent and corrupt litigation (*BBC News* 2018).

The story of this case highlights what is so complicated about international law. Here is a case that, by its very nature, crosses borders—it involves a corporation incorporated in one country harming people in another in a way that at least some observers see as a violation of customary international law relating to environmental protection. And yet, after twenty-five years, the people harmed in this case have been unable to obtain compensation for their injuries. They have tried every avenue—courts in their own country, courts in other countries, international legal bodies. But because the harms occurred entirely in one country and the company responsible is no longer in that country, no country has the jurisdiction both to hold the company legally responsible for what it did and to facilitate collection of the money. Add in the fraud allegations and Chevron's deep pockets for legal defense, and things look even dimmer for the people of the Oriente.

Why is this so difficult? Well, international law was not developed for individual people, or even for class actions like the one the plaintiffs here filed. It was really developed for countries to take action against one another, with more recent pro-

cedures allowing countries to take action against individual perpetrators of individual crimes and for permitting certain kinds of legal actions for corporations (Hirsch 2015). If a state harms a citizen of another state, there is a procedure for the state in which the person holds citizenship to pursue a remedy on the international stage—but that does not work if the offending party is a corporation (Epps and Graham 2011). Thus, the people of the Oriente, and people like them all around the world, are left with little recourse for the harms they suffer.

citizenship in a different country. If they do, it is that other country that is supposed to protect their rights. For instance, as the International Court of Justice case involving an Indian national sentenced to death in Pakistan demonstrates, a country can file suit to protect their citizens from harm by other states. Of course, such processes are rare—and in many cases, people who leave their country of citizenship do so specifically because their country is not protecting their rights. In other cases, individuals may not hold citizenship in any state. People without citizenship are **stateless** people. In other words, statelessness is the condition of being without the right to protection by any sovereign state. Statelessness can be understood as the opposite of citizenship, defined as being entitled by right to such protection either by birth or naturalization (Achiron 2005).

For philosopher Hannah Arendt, statelessness is a type of "**state of exception**" (Agamben 2005; Arendt 1951), a circumstance where the ordinary rights of people are suspended. There are other kinds of states of exception, such as various types of internment camps and detention facilities as well as declared states of emergency, but statelessness creates a state of exception linked to a person rather than a place or moment. In French, the term *sans-papiers* (without papers) is often used to refer to both stateless people and migrants who may hold citizenship in some country but who do not have legal authorization to live in their country of residence. Both groups of *sans-papiers* may be understood as living in a state of exception. This French term points to the fundamental importance of being able to document one's legal status, because it is from this documentation that one demonstrates one's "right to have rights" (Krause 2008). Furthermore, the public discourse around stateless people leads not to their construction as individual human beings but rather to their Othering as strangers (Simmel 1950).

This same public discourse often blames individuals for their choice to cross borders, criminalizing their movement without regard for the circumstances driving their decision to migrate. In some cases, migration decisions are not decisions at all, as migrants see migration as the only way to stay alive. These individuals may be **refugees**, whose situation will be discussed later in this chapter; they may also be desperate economic migrants. But even where people are not driven to move across borders simply to survive, it may not be reasonable to understand the nature of their actions as a choice to commit a crime.

It is important to remember, as noted in chapter 4, that law creates illegality. In other words, crossing a border is not illegal by its very nature but rather *becomes* illegal because the lawmaking apparatus of a country chooses to declare the act of crossing borders a crime. And in many cases, the *sans-papiers* have legal status at the time at which they cross an international border but lose that status later on. National regimes for regulating migration and legal status can be specifically structured to ensure illegality in such cases (Calavita 1998). For example, a migrant worker may lose their legal status if their employer refuses to comply with certain government conditions, even if compliance was promised as part of the hiring contract and even if the worker remains employed. Even more difficult to navigate are permit-renewal requirements. In Spain in the 1990s, one particular type of work permit (Type A) lasted for nine months, but workers were not eligible to renew it until twelve months after issuance and then sometimes had to wait more than six months to receive the new document, so there was no way for Type A workers to maintain legal status without interruption (Calavita 1998). Ecuador offers another example. Its 2008 constitution provides for "universal citizenship," a situation in which everyone within the territory of Ecuador is entitled to the same rights and protections, regardless of formal citizenship status. Yet by 2011, Ecuador backed away from this legal principle and began detaining some migrants who had entered the country legally (Ortiz 2011).

The post–World War II global order—quite in opposition to the idea of universal citizenship—is predicated in part on the idea that everyone is supposed to live in a sovereign state and that state is supposed to guarantee civil rights to its own citizens. This conception of civil rights is therefore standing in for the concept of human rights. Citizenship, then, provides access to rights and benefits: "In liberal democracies, the national government acquires its authority from its role as representative government arising from the notion of the social contract, and consequently its dominion to control migration onto territory and to bestow (and deny) citizenship. With the decline of the welfare state, the values attached to citizenship have eroded, and arguable the value of citizenship is demonstrated by the risks associated with the absence of citizenship" (Findlay, Kuo, and Wei 2013:184).

The absence of citizenship means, in most cases, losing access to government protection and legal and political status. So long as they are not imprisoned and detained, the *sans-papiers* may be—formally—free, but they do not have many of the rights discussed in chapter 9 (Krause 2008). Not all states deprive *sans-papiers* of all rights, but the general lack of the right to have rights, which may go as far as rendering them legally not people, has wide-ranging consequences for people's lives.

Sans-papiers first of all lack legal rights. This often means they do not have standing to sue in court. If they are detected by law enforcement, they often face detention, deportation, or mistreatment, so they typically fear discovery when going to the police. This means they lack protection from crime and economic and sexual exploitation and are unable to seek a remedy when they are victimized. They also lack economic protections. The ability to work in the legal economy, purchase property, and even use financial institutions like banks is often dependent on the ability to demonstrate legal status. In addition, countries typically deny the *sans-papiers* (along with, in many cases, immigrants with legal status) access to government benefits like health care and social insurance.

Lacking legal and economic rights can have profound social and individual consequences. *Sans-papiers'* fear of discovery means they are unable to tell others, whether friends, employers, health care professions, or teachers, the truth about their lives. Their lack of access to decent and ongoing health care can exacerbate the medical problems the stress of their existence creates. One of the most stressful elements of living *sans-papiers* is the inability to ensure stable family arrangements. Parents, spouses, and other loved ones may go off to work in the morning and never come home, having been apprehended by law enforcement and placed into detention or deported.

Those *sans-papiers* who have citizenship somewhere retain legal rights in their country of nationality, but those who are stateless have no government to speak for them, and so they can become invisible to the world community (Arendt 1951). The body of international law concerned with rights is built upon the notion that people have the protection of a state (Hirsch 2015). So how, then, does the global community respond to statelessness?

The main tool of international law for responding to statelessness has been refugee status. Under international law, refugees are those who face a well-founded fear of persecution in their home country and thus appeal to another country to grant them **asylum**, or safety with temporary legal status. This idea developed as a global concept in the late 1940s in response to the vast numbers of displaced people after World War II—as many as two million in Europe alone—who did not have a country to return to (United States Holocaust Museum n.d.). The 1951 Refugee Convention grants refugee status to those who fear persecution on the basis of their political views, ethnicity or nationality, religious beliefs or affiliation, or membership in a particular social group (Convention Relating to the Status of Refugees 1954). Countries do have some leeway in assessing whether individuals qualify for asylum and setting out the categories of persecution and discrimination that may qualify individuals to seek asylum. For instance, different countries have different conceptions of what qualifies as a social group for the granting of refugee status. Some examples include those subjected to female genital mutilation, forced marriage, or other gender-based violence; those fearing persecution based on sexual orientation; children forced into military service or prostitution; and those fleeing slavery (Jans 2010). Protection may also be granted to those fleeing torture or other inhumane treatment, as well as those fleeing indiscriminate violence, as well as the close family of asylum-seekers, even if these relatives do not themselves have a well-founded fear of persecution.

Refugees can be citizens of some country, or they can be stateless (Achiron 2005). While statelessness on its own is not sufficient grounds for a person to qualify as a refugee, United Nations treaties signed by a minority of countries discourage countries from expelling stateless people (Achiron 2005). The expectation is that if and when their homeland becomes safe, refugees will return to it, an expectation that stateless people cannot fulfill. For example, at the conclusion of World War II, surviving Jewish people were liberated from concentration camps or came out of hiding. Most had lost their citizenship in their home countries as part of the persecution they faced during the Holocaust. By 1947, there were about 250,000 Jewish displaced persons in Europe (United States Holocaust Museum n.d.). There was nowhere for them to go. Very few ever returned to their prior homes, instead being resettled as refugees in the United States, Israel, and other countries after international pressure forced open doors that had previously been closed to refugees.

Today, there are multiple ways for an individual to claim asylum (Gammelt-oft-Hansen 2011). He or she may state the asylum claim to an official of the county by which he or she hopes to be granted refugee status at the embassy or airport, long before crossing any borders. The claim may be made upon reaching the border, whether the individual is crossing by land, air, or sea. Or an individual may cross the border without being detected and state his or her asylum claim later, once already inside the destination country. If an individual must enter the territory of a country in order to claim asylum there but border crossing is constructed as illegal, it is impossible to fully comply with the law—the asylum seeker will be "illegal" and *sans-papiers* until they are able to apply for asylum.

Once the claim of asylum is made, it is up to the destination country how to proceed. International law does not require countries to accept asylum seekers, but once an individual seeking asylum has reached the border or territory of a country, the legal norm is that they not be returned to any country where they may face persecution, a doctrine known as **non-refoulement** (Gammeltoft-Hansen 2011). Of course, if an asylum-seeker states his or her claim to an embassy official of the destination country while still in his or her country of origin, this issue does not apply. Where it does, countries develop internal legal processes for evaluating asylum claims; they may reject claims of asylum because they do not believe that individuals face persecution or because the

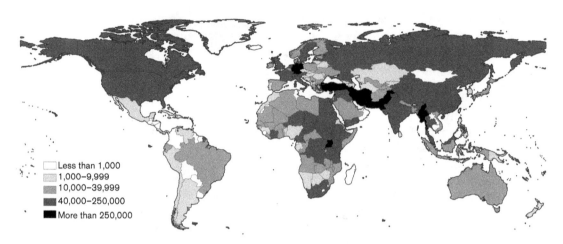

Map 30 Country of residence for refugees, asylum-seekers, and stateless people, 2016 (UNHCR 2017).

persecution they face is not based on membership in any of the particular categories the destination country believes qualify for protection.

The United Nations High Commissioner for Refugees (UNHCR), the United Nations agency tasked with providing shelter to refugees and facilitating the asylum-seeking process, estimates that in 2016, there were 25.4 million refugees worldwide, in addition to 3.1 million asylum seekers, 10 million stateless people, and 40 million people displaced within their countries of origin (UNHCR 2018b). Map 30 depicts the countries of origin of refugees and asylum seekers around the world as of 2016. The greatest numbers of refugees come from South Sudan, Afghanistan, Somalia, and Syria; over 1 million people from each of those countries—and over 5.5 million from Syria—have sought refuge elsewhere (UNHCR 2018b). Unsurprisingly, most of the countries hosting the largest numbers of refugees, asylum seekers, and stateless people are those neighboring countries of origin of large numbers of refugees, as shown in map 31: Turkey hosts more than 3 million; Pakistan, Lebanon, and Germany more than 1 million each; and Uganda, Myanmar/Burma, and Iran each host more than 800,000 (UNHCR 2018b).

As of February 2019, the UNCHR currently lists among the most profound crises the following, involving people who have fled

- Burundi in 2015 to Tanzania, Rwanda, and the Democratic Republic of Congo;
- the Central African Republic in 2013 and are now living in Cameroon, Chad, the Democratic Republic of Congo, Sudan, and South Sudan;
- the Democratic Republic of Congo in several waves, the most recently having begun in 2017, to Angola, Zambia, and other countries;

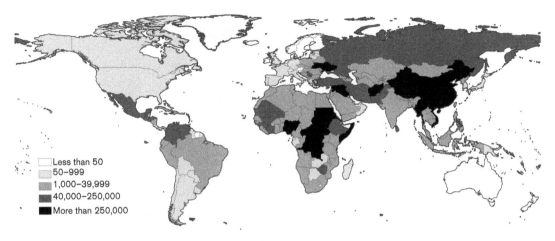

Map 31 World refugee population by country of origin, 2016 (UNHCR 2017).

- their homes in Iraq since 2014, many of whom remain internally displaced;
- Nigeria since 2014 to Cameroon, Chad, and Niger;
- Myanmar since 2017 to Bangladesh, especially members of the Rohingya ethnic and religious minority, considered to be a stateless group;
- South Sudan since 2013 to Ethiopia, Sudan, and Uganda;
- Syria to Lebanon, Turkey, Jordan, and other countries since 2011, a continuing refugee flow; and
- Venezuela to nearby countries in South America, Central America, and the southern Caribbean since 2014.

The UNHCR is also concerned with a complex situation in Yemen involving both those fleeing Africa to Yemen and those fleeing Yemen to other countries (UNHCR 2018a). There are also people from many different countries striving to reach European Union countries, the United States, Australia, Canada, and other perceived countries of safety, traveling across land and sea. The flow of migrants and refugees to Europe across the Mediterranean since 2016 has become a significant concern for the UNHCR. Large numbers of people seeking asylum are trapped in locations like the border between Mexico and the United States, various Australian and South Pacific islands, and the Greek island of Lesbos, hoping that some country will take them in. Instead, they face indefinite detention, often for years. In the United States in 2018 and 2019, some asylum-seekers have been prevented from stating their claim for asylum; many have been mistreated, including having their young children taken away. Many observers believe these actions to be a violation of international law, but U.S. officials pursue these policies in the hopes of reducing the number of refugees entering the country.

CONCLUSION

Global justice is a big topic—as big as the entire world—and this chapter has provided only a brief introduction to the workings of international law. It has explored some of the most important institutions of global justice, the International Criminal Court and the United Nations. And it has considered some examples of the thorny problems that international law must confront, especially the problem of statelessness and refugees. International legal institutions and treaties are the only tools our world has for the international assertion of human rights standards, such as those discussed in chapter 9. But they remain a weak tool, dependent on each individual country to determine for itself whether to sign on. For instance, forty-two countries have not signed the Rome Statute, the treaty establishing the International Criminal Court, including population powerhouses India and China; the United States and Russia signed but subsequently signaled that they did not wish to pursue formal ratification. The ICC is the only institution designed to enforce rights beyond national and regional borders, and yet its ability to do so is constrained by the lack of universal membership, as well as by the fact that it can exercise jurisdiction only over specific international crimes and not the hundreds of other ways rights can be violated.

As discussed above, the unwillingness of the United States to participate in the ICC has been based on fears that the court's legal tools would be turned against U.S. government and military officials who have engaged in actions that other countries see as violations of international law. For those who believe the United States should have the legal right to act with impunity—free from consequences—the decision not to participate makes sense. For those who believe robust institutions of global justice, made stronger by universal participation, are good for the entire world, the failure of the United States to ratify the Rome Statute is troubling.

And yet countries choose not to sign or ratify treaties for reasons far less profound than those motivating the decision of the United States to stay out of the ICC. For example, in 2006, the United Nations adopted the Convention on the Rights of Persons with Disabilities, a treaty designed to protect the human rights of people living with physical, mental, and other disabilities around the world (Convention on the Rights of Persons with Disabilities 2007). At least 175 countries have ratified this treaty, but the United States (along with Libya, Uzbekistan, Kyrgyzstan, Belarus, Ireland, Somalia, Botswana, and several other countries) has not. U.S. Senate Republicans opposed it, arguing that it would violate United States sovereignty. Mike Lee, a senator from Utah, argued that it would prevent Americans from homeschooling their children (Milbank 2012)—though the treaty did not impose any binding obligations on the United States.

Another real complexity of global legal institutions is that they must develop procedures that make sense to all their members, despite the important differences among domestic legal systems. Given the dominance of the global north in international affairs, institutions have often tried to resolve this issue by developing compromise systems incorporating elements of both common and civil law (Findlay, Kuo, and Wei 2013). However, this course of action leaves out the legal ideas and traditions of other parts of the world, such as traditional and theocratic systems. For instance, many indigenous and tribal societies conceive of rights in a collective fashion, while Western international law is focused on individual rights (Perrin 2017). In addition, people are no longer as connected to specific territories as they once were—global diasporas and borderlands complicate the notion that a people is tied to a particular state (Berman 2005). These kinds of disjunctures and omissions can leave many people feeling that international courts do not provide the kind of justice they seek.

In part due to these disjunctures, as well as to other factors such as the increasing complexity of the issues global justice must contend with, scholars of global justice argue that notions of international law must be expanded or transformed (Berman 2005; Hadfield 2017). For example, nongovernmental entities, ranging from groups like Al Qaeda to transnational corporations, exercise significant power and influence over global affairs, yet global justice systems are primarily structured around the conception of state power. And domestic legal systems may no longer be fully able to contend with the regulatory issues they are faced with in a globalized world in which certain legal issues, such as the diffusion of environmental pollutants or the nature of borderless electronic communication, cross borders. The existing nature of international law creates its own complexities, as the growing fragmentation and specialization of bodies of international law and specific international legal institutions increases the potential for conflicts of law to emerge (Koskenniemi 2006).

Conflicts of law are not just about legal rules, procedures, and institutions. Legal culture—as well as other aspects of culture—play an important role in shaping the way legal systems function and drive many international legal issues. For example, in the United States, scholars conducting research with human subjects are required to have this research vetted by an institutional review board (IRB) to verify that it will not inappropriately harm the participants. One of the most important requirements IRBs impose on research is the requirement that participants give their informed consent for research, generally by signing consent forms. A recent revision of the Common Rule (CITI Program n.d.), a U.S. government administrative regulation governing IRBs, has finally reckoned with the fact that informed-consent rules relied on a set of assumptions about the way people interact with documents that are not shared around the world. People do not routinely sign official documents in all parts of the world. They may not even have signatures, especially if they are illiterate. In some countries, thumbprints are used as an alternative to signatures, but keeping research participants' thumbprints on file raises its own ethical questions. Thus, the revised Common Rule creates procedures for using an alternative to "standard" informed consent for research in contexts where people do not ordinarily sign documents (CITI Program n.d.), in keeping with procedures in other countries for regulating research (which do not typically involve IRBs). This is just one small example of how cultural differences can affect legal provisions. Chapter 11 will discuss many more.

Law and Culture

CHAPTER

11

CHAPTER GOALS

1. Develop an understanding of how legal culture matters to legal systems.
2. Become familiar with the idea of the cultural defense to crime.
3. Be able to explain the difference between universalist and relativist ideas of legal culture.
4. Be able to articulate why understanding culture enhances understandings of law and legal systems.

As noted in chapter 1, legal culture is the set of perceptions, values, and opinions that people have about the law. Throughout this book, we have seen examples of instances where examining legal culture helps us understand more about what happens in a legal system than just looking at legal structures or laws themselves would. For example, chapter 3 discusses factors such as rates of voting and the representation of women among elected officials. Legal structures clearly influence these outcomes—where voting is easier, more people are likely to do it, and at some times and in some places women have been banned from voting and running for office. But structures are insufficient to explain the outcomes we observe. Chapter 6 explores litigiousness, or the likelihood that people will choose to settle their disputes by using the formal dispute resolution options provided by courts. While the accessibility of courts matters in these decisions, cultural factors matter too. Chapter 7 discusses different types of punishment that may be imposed on those convicted of crimes. Most societies provide for a variety of types of punishments, such as fines, control-in-freedom, incarceration, and in some cases corporal or capital punishment. Given this set of options, there is still substantial variation in the distribution of punishments imposed. Some of this variation can be explained by statutory sentencing guidelines and other structural concerns, but some of it is better explained by reference to cultural views on the purposes of punishment. The case study in chapter 8 discusses name changing after marriage. Certainly, legal systems set out rules that regulate this decision. In Japan, for instance, married couples must have the same surname. But the rule cannot explain why almost all married heterosexual couples end up with the husband's surname rather than the wife's. One final example comes from chapter 9, where the regulation of obscenity is discussed. Legal definitions of obscenity are rarely spelled out clearly. Rather, a vague sense of "community standards" is typically used to determine what counts as obscene, and this is clearly cultural in nature.

This chapter, then, will delve more deeply into the concept of legal culture. After reviewing the concept of legal culture, it will investigate notions of cultural universalism, cultural relativism, and cultural pluralism. Then it will discuss a variety of examples of conflicts in legal culture, including the cultural defense to crime and conceptions of childhood.

THE CONCEPT OF LEGAL CULTURE

As noted in chapter 1, the term legal culture refers to "the network of values and attitudes relating to law, which determines when and why and where [and how] people turn to law or government, or turn away" (Friedman 1969:34). Legal culture thus concerns the ideas, values, and perspectives a society has with respect to law and legal practices. When social scientists talk about culture, they typically include elements like traditions, values and beliefs, language, rituals, and symbols. All of these elements are part of legal culture as well. Thinking about legal culture reminds us that law is not just what it says it is or how it is structured but also how people live in and with the law. Indeed, some scholars argue that law is only created through "the life of a people" (Mautner 2011:845), a perspective that highlights the importance of culture for understanding law. A related concept, **legal consciousness**, refers to how ordinary people think about and understand law and legal practices (Berman 2005; Silbey 2005).

The legal *system* refers to the body of laws and supporting institutions in a given jurisdiction or entity (Friedman 1969). The laws themselves are, in Friedman's terms, substance, while the institutions and personnel are structure. Cultural elements are, then, values, attitudes, habits, and ways of relating to and using law. Legal cultures may not necessarily overlap with legal substance and structure. For example, as detailed in chapter 2, many countries adopted their legal systems nearly wholesale from France. Some of these countries even continue to speak French as their primary national language, and most were once colonized by France. But it is unlikely that any have quite the same legal culture as France does—or as each other. Legal systems and structures can, though, shape legal cultures. Researchers have found that where institutionalized opportunities for dispute resolution exist beyond the courts, these will be used. Where courts are available and accessible, they may seem more useful to people than they do in contexts where access to them is limited, even where courts are unlikely to result in true dispute resolution (Merry 1979).

Legal culture, legal substance, and legal structure all work together to shape the workings and outcomes of law in given contexts. Consider just a few potential research or policy questions (Friedman 1969): How much money will a new proposed income tax raise? In what circumstances do individuals turn to courts or other formal mechanisms to resolve their disputes rather than settling them informally or choosing to just live with the problem? How often do people have sexual relations with those to whom they are not married, and what are the consequences of such actions? What happens when an individual backs out of a commercial agreement he or she has made? Answering each of these questions requires an investigation into the actual laws and legal procedures of a jurisdiction, but just knowing the law is insufficient. We cannot understand from the law itself, or even from a study of legal institutions, how people perceive those institutions, when they choose to use them, how much compliance those institutions can extract, and what other social dynamics might occur alongside them.

It is important to remember that just because some phenomena are cultural does not mean they are unchanging. Culture can change just as structure and substance can—sometimes more easily and sometimes less easily, depending on the context and on how hard it is to revise laws in a given legal system (Nelken 2010b). And even within a given legal system, there are multiple legal cultures. Legal culture as a property of the legal profession (including judges, lawyers, other legal personnel, and maybe even police officers) is often called **internal legal culture**, whereas that of the broader population is often called **external legal culture** (Nelken 2010a). Internal legal culture can be distinct from external legal culture (Mautner 2011). For example, lawyers give certain professional courtesies to opposing counsel, such as extensions on deadlines, whereas nonlawyers would assume that treating the opposing side as an enemy or adversary would be more appropriate. And lawyers in the United States have an ethical obligation to zealously advocate for their clients, advocacy that might conflict with ethical norms in the broader society that place more value on broader social goods.

Beyond this, different ethnic groups, economic classes, religious traditions, or other categories of people may have somewhat different legal cultures from one another. Even individuals of the same class, ethnicity, and religion may have different legal cultures depending on where they live or whether they are recent immigrants (Nelken 2010b). This means that when we think about legal culture, we need to be clear about whether we are talking about the dominant culture of a nation or the culture of a specific community. And mixed systems may have mixed legal cultures. Some scholars refer to this as **bricolage**, a term that comes from artistic practices in which an artist creates art from an assemblage of found objects. In the cultural context, bricolage refers to practices that have been drawn from a diverse set of cultural backgrounds and assembled anew. International legal institutions have their own legal cultures, too, which can become intertwined with national legal cultures, and a nation's legal culture can be altered through contact with other legal cultures. One example of such dynamics might be European punishment policy, as described by David Nelken: "When comparative European prison rates first began to be published in the 1980s, Finland, which came high in the list, decided to cut back on prison building, whereas Holland felt entitled to build more. What mattered was to stay within the norm. Likewise, for many European countries the continued use of the death penalty in the USA serves as a significant marker of the superiority of their own legal culture" (2010a:285).

Consider another example—how long it takes for a court case to conclude. Writing about Italy in the late 1990s, Nelken (2010a) says the average civil case took five years from initiation through trial, and over nine years if you include the first appeal (which is somewhat standard in Italy). This trial duration led to a backlog of millions of cases awaiting trial. In one area of Sicily, the average case took 7.5 years just for the initial trial stage! Similar delays and backlogs are found in criminal cases. As might be expected, these delays have real consequences for the people seeking justice in the courts. So why do they occur? Well, there are a variety of factors. First of all, as discussed in chapter 6, Italian courts operate with a hybrid inquisitorial and adversarial procedure. In practice, this has largely meant that a series of adversarial processes were added on to the existing inquisitorial ones, thus producing delays. And when female judges go out on maternity leave—as shown in map 23, in chapter 8, Italy provides for a minimum of fourteen weeks of paid leave—their cases remain on their caseload, with no forward movement until they return. To some extent, these are both issues of legal structure. But there has also been a vast increase in litigiousness in Italy without a concomitant increase in judicial personnel. And unlike in other litigious countries, such as the United States, litigants are unlikely to pursue settlements or use alternative dispute resolution mechanisms (Nelken 2010a).

What is particularly interesting is how this culture and structure of delay interplays with Italy's political sphere. Italy has experienced a number of

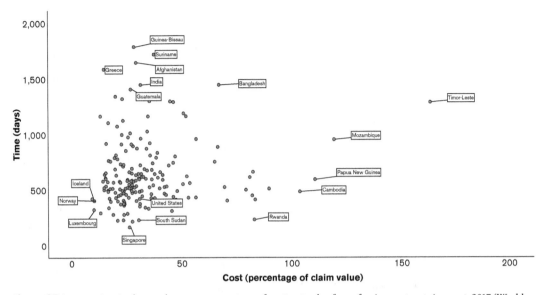

Figure 25 Average time in days and cost as a percentage of contract value for enforcing contracts in court, 2017 (World Bank 2018a).

political corruption scandals over the years. Because there is a strict separation of powers in the Italian government, the courts are able to investigate and try politicians for these crimes (Nelken 2010a). But the extensive trial delays, and the possibilities for exploiting procedural rules to delay cases even further, mean politicians have been able to stay in office for years while the wheels of justice grind very, very slowly (Nelken 2010a). For example, former Italian prime minister Silvio Berlusconi held office for three terms despite being under investigation for a variety of crimes, including tax evasion, bribery, corruption, embezzlement, money laundering, prostitution, sexual activity with underage women, and other crimes (McNally 2016). He continues to be active in politics as the leader of a far-right political party despite ongoing criminal trials and a six-year ban on serving in public office due to his 2013 conviction for tax fraud, for which he never had to serve prison time (Ognibene 2017). Some of the trials dragged on for so many years that the law did not allow punishment even after he was found guilty. In other cases, his administration implemented legal changes to throw a wrench into proceedings against him (McNally 2016). Similar delays have benefited members of organized crime, who can use the delays to try to intimidate witnesses (Perry 2018). As Nelken (2010a) argues, these kinds of delays benefit those who have engaged in wrongdoing the most, as they can draw out the process to avoid or delay unpleasant consequences.

Italy is far from the worst country in terms of court delays—the average contract case there takes a little more than three years, while cases in Greece, Afghanistan, Suriname, and Guinea-Bissau take on average just a month less than five years, as shown in figure 25. In contrast, in seventeen countries, such cases take less than a year to resolve, most notably in Singapore, with an average of 164 days. Countries vary considerably in terms of the cost of taking a dispute to court as well. Including attorney's fees, court costs, and costs for enforcing a judgment, the cost can be as little as 9–10 percent of the value of the contract claim in Iceland, Luxembourg, and Norway and as much as more than 100 percent of the value of the claim in Cambodia, Papua New Guinea, Mozambique, and Timor-Leste. In the United States, the average contract claim takes 420 days from filing until payment, and the costs are 30.5 percent of the value of the claim.

CULTURAL UNIVERSALISM, CULTURAL RELATIVISM, AND CULTURAL PLURALISM

As discussed in chapter 9, the universalist perspective suggests that there are universal basic rights across the entire world, with little or no room for exceptions or variations depending on cultural context. In keeping with the natural law perspective, universalism suggests these rights stem from some underlying moral truth and that this truth is universally applicable around the world. It is then possible for analysts to study cultures in comparative perspective through the lens of these rights or this truth.

Cultural relativism, in contrast, suggests that understandings of culture must remain sensitive to local variation. There are different schools of relativistic thought. First, relativism as theory, the strongest version of relativism, holds that it is generally impossible to compare cultures (White 1999), in large part due to their unique body of experiences. This body of thought indeed suggests that different cultures and legal traditions are incommensurable (Glenn 2001). Second, relativism as morals/politics permits comparison on a basic level but holds that rules and institutions stem inextricably from culture (White 1999). To such commentators, cultures and legal traditions may not necessarily be incommensurable, but they may be incompatible (Glenn 2001). Finally, relativity is a weaker version of relativism that provides space for deeper analytical investigation while still requiring that analysts keep their eyes open "to the variety of human ideology and practice" (White 1999:137). This perspective understands that there is often great diversity even within a given cultural context (Glenn 2001) and that we must begin our analysis by attending to that diversity. Note that cultural relativism does not necessarily imply that we must regard all cultural practices as valid or right—just because relativism requires taking a contextually informed perspective does not mean we must accept all practices (Renteln 2010).

Generally, cultural relativism is opposed to universalism, though some relativists do provide space for a strictly limited universalism in which a few extremely fundamental rights, such as freedom from torture and arbitrary state killings, are understood as universal (Tesón 1985). Given the linkages between universalism and natural law, it is clear that relativists are more likely to embrace positive law. But this need not necessarily be the case—it is also possible to argue that there are *multiple* bodies of natural law, with each culture having a body of natural law stemming from its own specific cultural codes.

Debates such as these are of recent origin. Historically, comparative scholarship was often overtly judgmental, and even if scholars sought to understand the different cultures they studied, this did not keep them from labeling others as "primitive," "savage," or otherwise inferior. The perspective of most governments was—and indeed often remains—that their own institutions and approaches are superior to all others. But contemporary comparative scholarship requires that we move beyond the limits of these historical approaches in order to fully develop our understanding of legal systems, legal cultures, and legal practices.

Conflicts between universalists and relativists take many forms and shapes. One example is that around the Islamic practice of veiling for women. There are a wide variety of styles of veiling, including the hijab, a scarf that typically covers the hair, ears, and neck; the chador, a shawl covering the head and upper body that is held closed at the neck; the niqab, which covers everything but the eyes; and the burqa, which has a mesh panel over the eyes. Different Islamic subcultures and Muslim-majority nations vary greatly in terms of their veiling practices. One study (Pipes 2014) looking at the most common response to a question about which style of veiling—or not veiling at all—is most appropriate for women in public in seven Muslim-majority countries found that respondents in Lebanon were most likely to prefer that women be unveiled; in Tunisia and Egypt, that she wear the hijab; and in Saudi Arabia, that she wear the niqab. Other countries were more divided: in Turkey, responses were split between remaining unveiled and the hijab; in Iraq, between the hijab and the chador; and in Pakistan, between the hijab, the chador, and the niqab.

Practices of veiling can be imposed by law, as in Saudi Arabia and Iran, but they may also occur in the absence of—or to extents that go well beyond—legal requirements (Lila 2002). When non-Muslims argue that women who choose to veil are oppressed, some Muslim women (and most cultural relativists) see these arguments as a form of cultural imperialism that ignores the choices, interests, and desires of women themselves. Some Muslim feminists, such as Katharine Bullock in her book *Rethinking Muslim Women and the Veil,* have argued in response to critiques of veiling that the sexualization of women in

Western cultural contexts is, in their eyes, a greater form of oppression, or that Western culture's emphasis on individualism and success is more harmful than living in a culture that values community and social support (Bullock 2002; Lila 2002). Such perspectives suggest that it is a form of oppression to forbid veiling, as some European countries now do, just as it is to require it.

The diversity of views about veiling, even within individual Muslim-majority countries, points to the importance of the concept of **cultural pluralism**. Cultural pluralism refers to the situation in which different cultural groups within a society are able to maintain their unique cultural identities and practices. It may be, but need not be, accompanied by real access to the political sphere and by systems of legal pluralism (as discussed in chapter 2). Considering the case of veiling, different subgroups or subcultures within a country may prefer different veiling practices, or some groups may prefer veiling while others do not. In a culturally pluralist country, each group is able to live according to its preferences, even if there is also a national culture (Mautner 2011); a nonpluralist country will instead impose some sort of majority practice on everyone. But this majoritarianism does not mean that nonpluralist countries are culturally uniform, as the example of language policy in Quebec and Latvia in chapter 9 shows. Consider Iran, for example (Beehner 2006; DaBell 2013). While the majority of Iranians are Shiite Muslims who are ethnically and linguistically Persian, there are a variety of minority groups living in the country. The largest of these is the Azeris, who make up nearly a quarter of the population and speak a Turkic language, though they are Shiite. Other large minority groups include Kurds, Baluchis, Arabs, and Lors, and there are smaller groups of Baha'i, Christian, Turkmen, and Jewish people. While the Iranian Constitution officially permits the teaching of minority languages and provides for equal rights to all ethnic and linguistic groups, official correspondence and textbooks must be in Persian, and freedom of religion is not protected. Thus, Kurdish, Baluchi, and Arab Sunni Muslims, who make up around 10 percent of the population, are prohibited from building mosques or publicly displaying their religious practices.

In pluralist countries, groups with different sets of cultural practices, norms, and values may come into conflict (Bracey 2006). These conflicts may find their way to the legal or justice system, which is then tasked with finding a way to resolve or ameliorate the disputes—often through procedures that are not equally culturally relevant to all of the groups involved. In nonpluralist countries, similar conflicts may emerge. The difference is that the legal and justice systems in these countries can respond by imposing adherence to officially sanctioned practices rather than by seeking some more accommodative response. Such conflicts may arise in relation to a vast array of cultural and religious practices and legal phenomena, such as norms in relation to education and childcare, the use of technology, beliefs about criminal responsibility and when violence is acceptable, and the way groups understand and respond to death, among many other issues. A number of these examples will be discussed below.

CONFLICTS IN LAW AND CULTURE

Consider sorcery, witchcraft, and black magic. In many Western countries, people no longer believe that such practices work and, other than perhaps regulating fraud and truth in advertising, would not imagine regulating a practice that has so little real impact on the world. But in many countries, such as the Central African Republic, Cameroon, Papua New Guinea, South Africa, Saudi Arabia, and Ghana, these beliefs remain alive and well, and individuals may be accused of engaging in sorcery or witchcraft when someone falls ill, dies in an accident, or experiences other bad fortune. Such accusations can result in the use of countermagic, forced exorcisms or torture, exile or incarceration, or the killing of the accused witch (Forsyth 2016).

Some countries have criminalized witchcraft, along with pretending to be a witch or possessing objects used in witchcraft (Forsyth 2016). Such laws may be passed because the society in general believes witchcraft is a real social harm or, in the absence of such a belief, where incorporation of witchcraft accusations into the formal justice system enables the state to combat vigilante violence by those who accuse their neighbors of being witches. Such laws also permit states and communities to target noncomformists and social outsiders. Other countries have increased sentence lengths for those convicted of killing accused witches. There have been some attempts to criminalize witchcraft accusations, but the evidence suggests that these practices have little deterrent effect and may increase vigilante actions (Forsyth 2016).

The example of sorcery and witchcraft highlights how culture and formal law may conflict. A legal system that operates based on rules of evidence and is confronted with a witchcraft accusation may be unable to contend with that accusation. Some countries, such as Zimbabwe, have addressed the issue by criminalizing practices *associated with* witchcraft, rather than witchcraft itself (Forsyth 2016). Others, however, have found it difficult to proceed with trials in the absence of the kinds of evidence normally acceptable in courts. Yet where trials cannot proceed despite the presence of antiwitchcraft laws, and community members believe they have been victimized by witches, individuals may lose trust in the formal judicial system and take matters into their own hands. And efforts to change community beliefs about witchcraft may be understood as the imposition of external Western values that ignore real traditions and concerns in the community. Scholars thus have asked whether it is possible to construct practices that both respect community beliefs around witchcraft and provide for due process for those accused as witches. Good answers to this question may not yet exist, though efforts to focus legal responses on conduct rather than belief and to engage in restorative practices may yield results (Forsyth 2016).

Where people believe in witchcraft, they may assume that injuries occur because they have been the victims of sorcery. Where people believe in individual responsibility, they may believe injuries are accidents—or that they were caused by individual criminals acting out of malice. Another perspective comes from the Thai Buddhist ideas of karma and fate. Karma is a spiritual principle of cause and effect that suggests that actions individuals take will have future consequences, sometimes even in another lifetime after reincarnation. Fate is sometimes used interchangeably with karma, but it may also refer to outcomes that do not occur as a result of individuals' actions (Engel 2005). If an accident occurs and the victim attributes the accident to karma or fate, she is likely to respond by doing good deeds, engaging in acts of religious observance, and forgiving the party outside observers might see as responsible for the accident so as to avoid repeating a karmic cycle in her next life.

In the past, local villages in Thailand had mechanisms for traditional justice relying on mediation infused with an understanding of Buddhist beliefs, but today's increasingly mobile and urban Thai society no longer has access to these local mechanisms (Engel 2009). Thus, victims are unlikely to seek formal legal remedies and may even turn down offers of compensation when they believe injuries are due to their own karma (Engel 2005). Scholars of dispute resolution would perceive the victims as choosing inaction—or what chapter 6 calls "lumping it." But the victims would not think of their own choices in this way. They believe they are actively pursuing a strategy that will benefit themselves and their families in the future, a strategy based in religion and more appropriate than would be seeking relief in the formal legal system (Engel 2009). As of 2015, over 94 percent of Thai residents were Buddhist—more than 96 percent in the urban areas where access to traditional justice has most broken down (National Statistical Office of Thailand n.d.)—and thus cultural conflicts over understandings of injury and approaches to dispute resolution are perhaps less likely to occur. But it is easy to imagine how complex dispute resolution would be if a person who did not share these beliefs sought to hold someone responsible for her injury and the accused perpetrator and the surrounding community believed it was her karma and/or fate that explained the injury.

So what happens when cultural or religious minorities have practices and beliefs that are at odds with those of the surrounding population? An examination of Amish groups in the United States sheds some light on that question. There are extensive variations between different Amish subgroups; here we will consider the Old Order Amish, the most traditionalist of all of these groups, but even among them there are differences in practices across congregations and communities. What Old Order Amish groups have in common is a commitment to maintaining their traditional way of life and limiting outside influence, along with their language, a Germanic dialect. Common practices include refusing to use electricity, telephones, central heat, and modern machinery in their homes; wearing traditional, unornamented attire and beards (but no moustaches) for men; stopping formal education before high

Figure 26 A traffic sign in Illinois Amish country (Daniel Schwen, CC BY-SA 4.0).

school; and enforcing rules against mixing with or creating business partnerships with those outside the community (Hostetler 1984).

One of the greatest commonalities between Amish groups is that they do not use modern vehicles, instead getting around by horse and buggy. Obviously, a horse and buggy move much more slowly than a car—while speeds vary with terrain and cargo, the horse is generally going to travel at less than eight miles per hour, often much less. Thus, even on slow neighborhood roads, Amish vehicles can present a traffic hazard, as the road sign in figure 26 suggests. Many states require vehicles traveling under twenty miles per hour, including buggies, to be marked with symbols indicating that they are slow-moving, most commonly a triangle in red and florescent orange (Zook 2003). Some Amish groups have willingly adopted these symbols, but others—especially the Swartzentruber group of Old Order Amish living in Ohio—object to them on the basis of their bright color and their implication that human rather than divine action is needed for protection and see their imposition as a violation of their religious freedom (Zook 2003). Some Amish individuals have been fined or even jailed for their refusal to use the symbol. In response, some states have negotiated a compromise, permitting Amish buggy owners to use large amounts of reflective tape along with hanging lanterns to make their vehicles visible at night, while others continue to require the standard emblem (Zook 2003).

Amish groups generally take a very strict view of nonresistance and pacifism, including refusing to participate in military service when conscripted (Keim 2003). This extends as far as discouraging the use of lawsuits to settle disputes or collect on debts (Hostetler 1984) and, unless court ordered to comply, the hiring of lawyers. When arrested for a criminal offense, Amish people may waive their Miranda right to silence and answer questions they are asked, and they are unlikely to report being criminally victimized to the police (Cates 2014). In addition, they do not take oaths, run for office, or serve on juries, though they do vote, especially in local elections (Hostetler 1984).

They also do not use insurance, as they see doing so—like in the case of the orange triangles—as suggesting a lack of faith that the divine will provide. Thus, while they pay ordinary payroll taxes, they object to social security and have won an exemption that permits individuals who are members of religious communities that provide for their congregants and who are self-employed to forgo the tax (Hostetler 1984). Those who are employed by others still must pay, even though they will never draw on the social security program in old age. They also do not use private or public health insurance, though they do use much of modern medicine, including blood transfusions and organ transplants, and they are willing to donate blood and to share samples with medical researchers (Cates 2014; Huntington 2003).

While the Amish live in closed communities, these communities exist in close proximity to non-Amish people (who are called the English by Amish groups) and Amish people are subject to the same legal system as the English. Thus, it is clear that a variety of conflicts in law and culture are likely to arise, ranging from the disputes over warning symbols on buggies, as discussed above, to arguments over appropriate schooling for Amish children and efforts to avoid otherwise mandatory insurance programs. Law enforcement officers may be baffled when they encounter Amish people who will willingly answer the questions posed during an investigation yet will not press charges against a criminal suspect.

Thus, the Amish provide a useful example for thinking about cultural pluralism. There are some cultural practices that Amish people engage in that, while they may be considered unusual by the surrounding community, do not become a source of conflict, such as the refusal to carry cell phones or wear blue jeans. There are some practices that may give rise to conflict or confusion but that, given our pluralist system, are permitted, such as the refusal to pay social security tax when self-employed. And there are others that have led to extensive legal conflict, such as the buggy warning symbols and the refusal to permit high school education (Hostetler 1984). These conflicts sometimes result in compromises, such as the use of reflective tape and lanterns, and sometimes they do not, with Amish individuals facing jail time and other criminal sanctions. Does this mean that there are limits to cultural pluralism?

One area in which people often struggle over the limits of cultural pluralism is around definitions of life, such as in debates over whether it is acceptable to terminate a pregnancy, to use physician-assisted suicide or euthanasia to end the life of someone suffering from a terminal or incurable illness, or to withdraw life support and permit someone to die (Bracey 2006). Depending on one's moral, religious, cultural, and/or ethical perspective, these three actions may be entirely acceptable and indeed even laudable actions taken out of the deepest care for one's family, or they may be considered the most heinous kind of murder. Of course, many people have positions in between these extremes, and people may think differently about some of these actions than they do about others. Where people believe these actions are acceptable, they may not see them as involving the taking of a life—they believe the terminally ill are already dying and that fetuses are not yet alive and thus cannot be killed. Yet even in cases where people agree that a life is being taken, they may not agree about whether it is acceptable to take that life—even though most societies and cultures criminalize murder. For example, is the death penalty the imposition on Earth of the divine will that criminals must be struck down, or is it a sinful taking of a life? Are war and the killing of armed combatants that it entails immoral, or is engaging in military actions a fully justified act of national self-preservation?

The Cultural Defense to Crime

The examples above highlight the fact that an action that is criminalized in a particular country may not be considered wrong by people with other cultural or religious backgrounds. This inevitably leads to conflicts of law and culture, when the person who believes their actions to be acceptable or even necessary finds themselves arrested and charged with a crime. Some courts permit such individuals to use what has come to be called the **cultural defense** when they are put on trial by explaining that in their culture, such actions are acceptable, encouraged, or even mandatory and that they could not have been expected to assimilate to the dominant standard or even to be familiar with it (Bracey 2006). The cultural defense can be used in both criminal and noncriminal contexts and may be used either as part of claiming an affirmative defense (one in which the defendant asserts that even if she did what she is accused of doing, she should not be held liable for it) or as mitigation evidence to reduce sentences or damages imposed (Renteln 2004).

There are wide variations across legal systems in the degree to which the cultural defense is permitted. Even within a given legal system, the cultural defense may be admitted to court in some cases and not others, whether due to the type of charges, the whims of the judge, or other factors. Some legal systems entirely prohibit considerations of culture, seeing cultural considerations as merely a way to treat people differently from one another. Yet there are many circumstances in which human behavior cannot be explained without reference to cultural beliefs, attitudes, and values (Renteln 2004). The cultural defense and related claims for exemptions from legal provisions may thus arise in the context of a vast array of issues, including homicide, child abuse and neglect, the use or abuse of animals, and in many other circumstances. When permitting the cultural defense to be raised in the context of a case, courts have several options about how to proceed. They may permit cultural practices to be used as an affirmative defense, with the defendant arguing that culture made her actions necessary, foreclosed other paths, or otherwise explained what occurred. They may use cultural practices as part of sentencing guidelines or in determining the extent to which an action was premeditated. Or they may use culture to modify the "reasonable person" standard, suggesting that reasonableness be interpreted in light of the specific cultural background of the defendant (Dearth 2011).

In cases in which the cultural defense arises, legal anthropologists may be called to testify as to the cultural practices and beliefs of the group to which the defendant belongs (Good 2008; Renteln 2004). Their role is to draw on their expertise and knowledge about a group to contextualize the events and explain why people may have acted as they did so that the judge or jury can come to their own conclusions as to whether such actions may be understandable given the defendant's cultural background. Without such testimony, the judge and jury would have nothing to rely on but the defendant's own explanations for their behavior, which are obviously less persuasive than the perspective of a disinterested expert.

Homicide

Courts typically permit factors like self-defense or mental incapacity (such as insanity) to be used as affirmative defenses to charges of murder. In other words, an individual accused of murder can admit that she killed someone but defend herself from the murder charge in court by arguing that she did not have the required mental intention to kill and/or that she should not be held responsible for the killing due to such factors. But there are considerable cultural differences in our understandings of such circumstances. For example, if someone kills a person that she believes had been engaging in witchcraft for the purpose of harming her (Forsyth 2016), do we understand this killing as self-defense in the face of a sincere fear, as the act of an insane person who is out of touch with reality, or as a premeditated cold-blooded crime? What if someone believes that twins or albino people are bad omens who will bring destruction to the community if they are allowed to live and thus kills her neighbor's albino child or newborn twins?

On a related note, adherents of many religious faiths beleive that individuals can become possessed by demons or evil spirits and that these demons can injure the person they possess as well as use them to inflict great harm upon those around him and the broader world. In response, clergy or lay people may carry out exorcisms in hope of chasing the demons from the person's body. Depending on the particular faith tradition, the exorcism ritual can be quite dangerous, and it is not unheard of for the person being exorcized to die. While the individuals carrying out the exorcism are not seeking death, they may prefer that their loved one die free of demons than that he live possessed and ultimately end up in hell. So are the exorcists guilty of murder—an intentional killing? Or are they guilty of some lesser degree of homicide, a criminal act but one they did not intend? Or is the death an unfortunate outcome of their best efforts to save their loved one, something to regret but not to prosecute?

In common law jurisdictions, a reasonable provocation defense can, if successful, result in a lessening of charges from murder to manslaughter. Such a defense might be used if a defendant kills someone who has killed their pet or harmed their child. In earlier times in some Western societies, a wide variety of affronts and insults might have resulted in one man challenging another to a duel, resulting in the death of one of them, and until antidueling statutes were enacted, such deaths would not in most cases have been considered criminal (Cohan 2010). A similar cultural defense is used in the case of honor killings. Honor killings typically involve the killing of young women by their male relatives after the women have become suspected of acting in ways that "stain the honor" of the family (Renteln 2004), most commonly by engaging in sexual or romantic relationships contrary to their family's wishes or norms, but also for transgressions as minor as talking to a male stranger or wearing clothes considered immodest by their families (Cohan 2010). For example, in 2012, a man who had emigrated from Jordan to Houston, Texas, killed his daughter's husband and his daughter's friend after they allegedly helped her leave home and convert to Christianity (Rogers 2018b). He intended to kill his daughter and two others as well in order to "wash his honor in blood." Other family members may have helped carry out the plan. This man was convicted of his crime in 2018 and sentenced to death (Rogers 2018a). Men are rarely the victims of honor killings, but some cases are recorded, especially among gay men (Cohan 2010). While honor killings are typically planned in advance, some countries, such as Jordan and Pakistan, treat them as if they were crimes of passion carried out under extreme emotional distress in the moment of discovering the transgression (Cohan 2010), which generally results in a much less severe punishment.

Child Abuse and Neglect

Child abuse occurs when someone actively does something that is understood to harm a child, while **child neglect** occurs when someone does not do the things seen as necessary for the child. So, for example, forcibly breaking a child's arm would be understood as abuse; not seeking medical attention for an injury that occurred accidentally would be understood as neglect. There are a wide variety of traditional practices that are seen as appropriate and even necessary in some cultural contexts but have become understood as abuse in other cultural contexts. For example, many cultures have traditional practices involving various kinds of body modifications, such as male circumcision, ritual scarification, and female genital mutilation (FGM), that occur early in children's lives (Kalev 2004; Renteln 2004). When courts consider the cultural defense in such contexts, they are asked to balance the cultural (and sometimes religious) significance of the practices with judgments about the degree of harm the child has experienced or will experience in the future.

Parents who use corporal punishment may also be charged with child abuse. While most countries do allow parents to engage in some degree of corporal punishment (see chapter 7), rules about how far parents are permitted to go in physically disciplining their children vary. Sociologist Mary Waters (2001) documents in her research on West Indian immigrants in New York that children rapidly become aware of the differences in standards between their immigrant parents and the state child welfare system and threaten to report their parents when they are physically disciplined. One common governmental standard permits physical discipline so long as it does not leave visible marks or injuries (Renteln 2004; 2010), a standard that also comes into play in cases where parents use traditional medicinal practices, like cupping. The practice of cupping involves the placement of cups on the skin and the use of suction to draw skin, and sometimes blood, into the cups. While Western medicine dismisses cupping as a medical technique, it has long been practiced as part of traditional medicine in some Asian countries, and there is even scholarly research on its efficacy (Kim et al. 2011). However, since it leaves visible marks on the skin, parents who seek cupping as a treatment for their children may be charged with child abuse.

Parents may also face child abuse charges for touching their children in ways that the state believes are inappropriate. For example, in 1993, Mohammad Kargar, an Afghan refugee living in Maine, was found guilty of sexual assault and required to register as a sex offender after a young neighbor saw him kissing his eighteen-month-old son's penis. Kargar and his witnesses argued that this is a typical cultural practice in Afghanistan. Parents kiss the penis, a body part viewed as unclean, to show their love for their child, though they do so only when the child is quite young. On appeal to the Supreme Judicial Court of Maine, the case was dismissed as having been an unjust conviction (*State of Maine v. Mohammad Kargar* 1996). It is important to note here that, when Kargar arrived in the United States, no one informed him that this cultural practice would be considered criminal in his new country, though of course after the court case concluded he could be expected to know of these standards.

And consider the practice of child marriage. In many countries today, individuals must be eighteen years old in order to marry, or sometimes slightly younger if they have parental consent, and they must themselves consent to the marriage. In other countries, it remains common for parents to arrange marriages for young people and move forward with limited consultation. This presents a clear opportunity for conflicts when people move from one context to another. In Nebraska in 1996, a father arranged the marriages of his two daughters, aged thirteen and fourteen, to considerably older men (aged thirty-four and twenty-eight). All the individuals involved were at the time recent immigrants from Iraq (D. Terry 1996). Though the father claimed he had his daughters' consent to go forward with the weddings, one ran away with a boyfriend shortly after the marriage. And the marriages were illegal, as the minimum age for marriage in the state was seventeen. The girls' parents and both grooms were charged with crimes (as was the twenty-year-old boyfriend), given the girls' young ages. But the Iraqis involved had never been told how marriage laws work in the United States. They simply knew that the United States protects the free exercise of religion and went forward with the marriages assuming they would be protected as religious practices (D. Terry 1996).

The cultural defense is used commonly in child neglect cases involving the denial of education, such as in the Amish case, where children are withdrawn from formal education before high school, as well as in cases involving the refusal to provide medical care. While courts often give parents wide latitude to make medical decisions for their children, the state may step in when medical conditions become life-threatening. But religious and cultural traditions may conflict with Western medical practices in some circumstances. For example, Hmong people, an ethnic group with roots in China who today live primarily in Southern China, Vietnam, and Laos, tend to be very reluctant to permit surgical interventions due to religious beliefs about surgery's effects on the spirit and the afterlife. This has caused intractable conflict between Hmong families and the child welfare authorities in cases where parents refuse surgeries to remove cancerous tumors (Renteln 2004). They also have different, spiritually informed interpretations of diseases like epilepsy that may result in noncompliance with Western treatment regimens (Fadiman 1997). Thus, children may be removed from their parents' care so that the state can ensure they receive prescribed Western treatment.

Similar conflicts have emerged in relation to Christian Scientists and Jehovah's Witnesses. Jehovah's Witnesses believe the Bible prohibits blood transfusions, so accepting a transfusion may lead to eternal damnation (they use all other forms of medical care), and courts routinely order the children of Jehovah's Witnesses to have transfusions over the strenuous objections of their parents (Hickey and Lyckholm 2004). Christian Scientists use prayer as a source of healing and avoid medical care other than dentistry, basic orthopedic care, glasses, hearing aids, and the dressing of wounds (Merrick 1994). They do also permit obstetric care (Merrick 1994). While many U.S. states have passed laws specifically exempting parents who choose faith healing from child neglect charges, these laws may draw the line when the child's life is at stake (Merrick 1994), and Canada and Great Britain have no such exemptions (Asser and Swan 1998; Hickey and Lyckholm 2004).

The Use and Abuse of Animals

The status of nonhuman animals varies widely across human societies. To some societies, all animals exist for human benefit, and there are few regulations on which species can be consumed or how animals must be treated. To others, some animals are fair game while others must be spared misuse or abuse. For still others, some animals are sacred, such as the cow in Hinduism, or all use of animals is to be avoided, as is the case in the Jain religion. These differences are frequently a source of conflict.

One circumstance in which such conflict arises is where animals are used in religious ceremonies or as part of cultural traditions. For example, some Orthodox Jews engage in a ritual prior to the holiday of Yom Kippur, the Day of Atonement, in which a chicken or rooster is swung over the head and then slaughtered, a practice called *kapparot*. Others, including some other Jewish people, object to this practice on the grounds that it can be cruel to animals, is wasteful, and can lead to litter or public health violations, and some of these opponents have worked to enact laws and policies limiting or prohibiting *kapparot*. But to the people who practice the ritual, it is an essential part of their observances.

Groups may kill endangered animals or hunt out of season in order to obtain carcasses or body parts for rituals, or they may engage in animal sacrifice in public parks or inside buildings not zoned for slaughter. For example, a number of cultural groups, including Inuit peoples and the Japanese, claim that whale hunting and the consumption of whale meat are important traditional cultural practices and continue to kill whales, despite global norms against such activities. There are also cultural differences around the use of animals in sporting events, such as cockfights and rodeos, and in views about the keeping of so-called "exotic" animals as pets or beasts of burden.

Conflicts may also arise over the use of animals for food. Both Jews and Muslims have religious requirements about the slaughter of animals to be consumed as meat, involving a specific method of cutting the animals' throats. If animals have not been slaughtered in this fashion, their meat is not considered suitable for consumption. While historically this method of slaughter was more humane than other alternatives, some people today believe that it induces more suffering than certain more modern techniques. Thus, a number of European countries have banned or severely restricted the practice of Jewish and Muslim ritual slaughter (Global Legal Research Center 2018). Of course, taken from the perspective of some practitioners of Hinduism, Buddhism, and Jainism, *any* slaughter of animals induces torment, and those individuals who ban Jewish and Muslim ritual slaughter but continue to fill their dinner plates with meat are thus continuing to perpetuate suffering. Cultures further differ in their perspectives on which animals are suitable for consumption and which are not. Commentators who discuss this issue tend to focus on the consumption of dogs, as people in Western countries tend to think of dogs as beloved household pets and thus view their consumption as particularly outrageous. But the issue arises in other contexts as well—such as in the consumption of endangered species or primates.

Other Examples

Of course, there are many other circumstances in which the cultural defense may arise. For example, as discussed in chapter 4, countries and cultures vary considerably in which drugs or other intoxicating substances they criminalize. Substances that are used as part of cultural traditions or religious rituals in one country may thus be entirely prohibited in another. This difference affects users of khat, a chewable stimulant commonly used by people from Yemen and East Africa; ayahuasca, a psychedelic tincture from South America used in shamanistic rituals; marijuana, which has medicinal uses as well as, for Rastafarians, religious uses; and even alcohol, which is prohibited in some Muslim countries. If courts are willing to consider the cultural defense, they may reduce the penalties imposed or, as in the case of the use of peyote (a cactus with psychoactive properties) by the Native American Church in the United States, create specific exemptions to drug laws to permit the use of substances for religious or cultural purposes. If courts are not so willing, individuals may face lengthy prison sentences for engaging in traditional cultural or religious practices.

Another circumstance in which the cultural defense may arise is when countries adopt legal restrictions on certain types of attire or types of personal grooming, whether more generally or in certain circumstances, such as in the course of police employment, while at school, or while incarcerated. These may include restrictions on hairstyles, such as prohibiting dreadlocks, cornrows, or uncut hair; prohibitions on facial hair; and bans on the wearing of head coverings such as hats, turbans, or the Muslim veil (as discussed earlier in this chapter) as well as on the wearing or display of religious or cultural symbols, such as kente cloth or necklaces bearing a crucifix or a Jewish star. One of the most interesting examples of this type of issue, which has resulted in criminal justice system involvement, is the Sikh kirpan. The kirpan is a ceremonial dagger, and Sikhs are required to wear it at all times, usually under their clothing, as a symbol of their commitment to justice on behalf of the defenseless (Lal 1996). Indeed, the kirpan is never to be used as an offensive weapon. As might be expected, authorities often prohibit the kirpan in courtrooms, public busses, schools, airplanes, and other places where weapons are not permitted, though in some cases they are allowed if they are as small as eating utensils or Swiss army knives (Renteln 2004). Different jurisdictions have come to different conclusions about the extent to which Sikhs' wearing of kirpans must be accommodated (Juss 2012). One compromise that has been used in some places is to blunt the edges of the kirpans or encase them in a sheath such that they could not be used; some more secular Sikhs wear symbolic kirpans, such as necklace charms. For some believers, though, these compromises are unacceptable, as they consider carrying a genuine kirpan to be a religious necessity (Juss 2012).

The cultural defense may also arise in relation to the treatment of the dead. For example, Jews, Muslims, Hmong, Navajo (Dine), and other groups are generally opposed to autopsies, believing that the autopsy may result in the desecration of the body and thus harm the spirit or inhibit the afterlife; some of these groups also have religious beliefs requiring a speedy burial with which an autopsy may interfere. Yet the authorities may require an autopsy in cases where crimes are suspected or for public health reasons (Renteln 2004). For some religious groups, cremation is a necessity; for others, the cremation of a loved one may mean that any hope of seeing her in the afterlife has been lost. The funerary practices of the Zoroastrians (sometimes referred to as Parsis), a faith with historical roots in Iran whose believers are concentrated in India today, are of particular interest here. The Zoroastrian faith requires that the dead be left in a high place for their flesh to be consumed by vultures or other scavengers (Solanki 2017). Due to the sacred nature of earth, water, and fire, bodies cannot be buried in the ground or at sea or cremated. Thus, Zoroastrians build stone structures atop mountains, called Towers of Silence, and secure their dead to them (Solanki 2017). When local vulture populations are healthy, it takes only a few hours for the flesh to be removed. Outside of India, it has been difficult for Zoroastrians to practice these traditions. Laws against mutilation of a corpse as well as those designed to protect public health have prevented the establishment of Towers of Silence in countries such as the United States, though there is no evidence that these practices present health risks (Solanki 2017). Even in India, however, the Zoroastrians' traditional practices are at risk. This is because the Asian vulture has become critically endangered, largely due to deaths caused by their ingestion of a common livestock antibiotic, diclofenac (Swan et al. 2006).

One of the claims made by those asserting the cultural defense is that their status as cultural outsiders or newcomers—especially in societies without provisions for robust adult cultural and legal education programs—means they could not have been expected to know or understand the legal provisions they are now accused of having violated. It is important to note that even those born and raised among the mainstream of a given society may not be very familiar with the legal provisions of that society. About three fifths of U.S. states do not even require a full civics curriculum (Shapiro and Brown 2018), and such a curriculum would provide students only with a framework for knowing how to find out what the laws are—not a detailed understanding of the criminal laws themselves.

Another claim those asserting the cultural defense make is that, in pluralist societies, people should be able to preserve their own distinct cultural practices rather than being expected to conform to dominant standards. This argument further suggests that even when people are expected to conform—and even when they face harsh punishment for their nonconformity—they will not necessarily discard or even be able to change their deeply held beliefs and practices (Renteln 2004). Data suggests, for example, that in the years after migration, parents continue to engage in childrearing practices much as they would have had they stayed in their native countries (Strasburger 2013).

Yet there are many opponents of the cultural defense (Renteln 2004). Opponents argue that a central purpose of the law is deterrence and that allowing people to use their cultural practices and backgrounds as an excuse for noncompliance with law will reduce the deterrent effect of laws. They also worry that the cultural defense is too often used to enable the oppression of women and other socially disadvantaged groups (Dearth 2011). Other opponents argue that implementing the cultural defense is simply too complicated, because it is hard to tell when it is legitimate, in which circumstances it should be permitted, and where to draw the line (Renteln 2004).

LEGAL CULTURES OF CHILDHOOD

As the examples of the cultural defense above in relation to child abuse and neglect and honor killings highlight, cultural conceptions of what childhood is, what it means, and the extent to which it is deserving of special status or protection are very different across social contexts. Today, many legal systems incorporate the principle that legal decisions involving children (leaving aside criminal prosecutions of children) should take into account the best interests of the child (Sutherland 2012). Such a standard is, of course, rather vague. Is it in the best interests of the child to be brought up by unmarried, or same-sex, or atheistic parents? Or is it in the best interests of the child to be removed from those parents and placed in what the courts consider an appropriately moral institution? Is it in the best interests of the child to participate in the complete school curriculum? Or is it in the best interests of the child to be shielded from learning about evolution, sexual health, or theology? Is it in the best interests of the child to take up arms to defend her community from military invasion? Or does the use of child soldiers violate international human rights standards?

The best guesses of Child Soldiers International (n.d.), a nongovernmental organization, as to areas of the world in which child soldiers are being used in the current time period by state *or* nonstate actors are shown in CS 11.1 Map a, in the case study. This data is the best currently available, but it is important to note that it is limited in reliability and validity as states and organizations that make use of child soldiers are unlikely to honestly report this. Furthermore, as noted above, countries have different perceptions of what constitutes a child soldier. In the United States, for instance, those who are seventeen can join the armed forces (though they are not supposed to see combat), a clear violation of the Straight 18 position. Yet the United States is not shown in the map as a

Child Soldiers

BY CARSE RAMOS

> Childhood is not from birth to a certain age and at
>   a certain age
> The child is grown, and puts away childish things.
> Childhood is the kingdom where nobody dies.
> Nobody that matters, that is.

—Edna St. Vincent Millay ([1934] 1956)

At the time of this writing, the International Criminal Court is attempting to try its first case involving a former child soldier. Dominic Ongwen was a high-ranking officer in the Lord's Resistance Army (LRA), a notoriously brutal rebel group led by Joseph Kony, which was fighting against the Ugandan government forces in the 1990s and 2000s. Ongwen is being charged with seventy counts of crimes against humanity and war crimes, including, amongst others, murder, torture, sexual slavery, forced marriage, and the conscription of children under the age of fifteen. This case is made all the more complicated by the fact that Ongwen himself was conscripted into the LRA as a young boy; it is said that he was kidnapped at around age nine while walking to his primary school. He then grew up within the LRA, rising through the ranks and ultimately becoming a commander (see, e.g., Chothia 2015; ICC n.d.-b; Wrong 2016).

Brought squarely into international discourse through cases in Liberia and Sierra Leone, the issue of child soldiers has, to date, been addressed through other mechanisms, such as Sierra Leone's short-lived Truth and Reconciliation Commission. Ongwen's case has both the court and the wider society asking how to make sense of a situation like this. Is Ongwen a victim? A perpetrator? What should he be held accountable for? Do we differentiate between what he did as a child and as an adult, and if so, how? What do we mean by these

categories? Child soldiers present a complex case, because they are at once situated between and occupying all of these spaces. Their very existence also forces questions about what childhood is, what it is supposed to be, when someone stops being a child and starts being an adult, and who has the power to decide.

To many of us, the figure of the child soldier is inherently shocking. Indeed, the term itself seems paradoxical. Fighting in a war seems directly opposite to the idyllic portrayal of childhood innocence that many of us were brought up with, whether or not the latter mirrors our own individual reality. Photographs of child soldiers are often designed to play on these contrasts: they frequently picture a young boy, usually African, wearing a torn T-shirt or fatigues and wielding a Kalashnikov or another automatic weapon that is as big as he is. Such images are designed to shock the conscience, raise awareness, and frequently, inspire action.

While perhaps effective as an advocacy tool, this image is problematic for any number of reasons. First, it is misleading. While data on child soldiers is lacking and ambiguous, reports in the past five years suggest that roughly 40 percent of child soldiers are girls (Office of the Secretary-General's Envoy on Youth 2015). Second, sometimes younger children conscripted into a military or rebel group do not primarily participate in combat, leaving this to their older peers. Instead, such young recruits are often in support roles, acting as porters, cooks, and in a variety of other capacities. To be sure, the portrait painted above does exist and is common, but it does not represent all child soldiers; it may not even represent what is "typical." Third, as has been pointed out by a number of scholars, historically and around much of the world, youth and war have not been at odds but rather have gone hand in hand (see, e.g., Drumbl

2012; Honwana 2007; Rosen 2005). Even in the United States during the Revolutionary War and Civil War, young boys commonly joined in the efforts, signing up as drummers and musicians and, at times, as "boy soldiers" who engaged directly in combat.

The idea, then, that the figure of the child soldier is paradoxical and tragic is rooted in both temporal and cultural assumptions and norms—about childhood, adulthood, war, and age more broadly—which are largely reflective of those held by modern "Western" cultures. These assumptions and norms have been codified into statutes and conventions, both at the domestic and international levels.

Most current international law—and bodies like the International Criminal Court, which flow from it—takes a position referred to as Straight 18 (Rome Statute of the International Criminal Court 1998, art. 26). Under this conceptualization, adulthood universally begins at age eighteen. The protections afforded to children extend until this cutoff, and accountability for one's actions largely attaches at and after. Following this definition, then, a child soldier is any combatant—either recruited or active—who has not yet reached his or her eighteenth birthday. Further, individuals cannot be held accountable for acts committed prior to reaching this age.

Other legal sources frequently cited in terms of child protection in the context of armed conflict, such as the Optional Protocol to the Convention on the Rights of the Child (CRC), largely follow this design. The convention goes on to acknowledge the right to special protection for individuals under age eighteen and then specifies the conditions under which such individuals can be voluntarily recruited by government forces. Article 4 is the sole provision dealing with nonstate actors and explicitly prohibits all recruitment before age eighteen.

There is, however, a separate delimiter of age fifteen given in a number of legal conventions, which has been the basis for both confusion and controversy. The Rome Statute, for example, has elevated the use of child conscripts under age fifteen to a war crime, creating a three-year bracket whereby conscription is not a war crime but the conscripted individual is not held accountable (Rome Statute of the International Criminal Court art. 8(2)(b)(xvii)). Some argue that this second age cutoff reinforces the gravity of using young

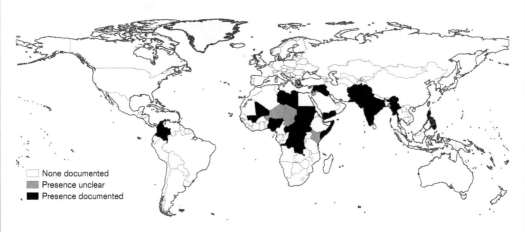

CS 11.1 Map a Reports of child soldiers by state or nonstate actors, 2016 (Child Soldiers International n.d.).

children and that assigning this the status of a war crime acts as an effective deterrent; others disagree, observing that this discrepancy creates a three-year window of effective impunity, something that governments and nonstate actors alike may be eager to exploit. Whether the cutoff is placed at eighteen or fifteen, however, law still operates according to bright-line rules and the assumption that there is a specific age of majority.

There are a number of critiques of this idea, relating to differing ideas of childhood and shifting societal norms. Even practically, however, the use of a strict cutoff proves problematic. Firstly, in many places where the use of child soldiers is prevalent, age is not so easy to ascertain. Records are frequently lacking, especially in rural areas, and age might not be counted in the same way across cultures and societies. This is more prevalent among older generations but not their exclusive province. Dominic Ongwen provides a good example of just how messy this can be. Many sources state that he was conscripted at age nine; others have given this age as ten. He himself has stated that this happened when he was fourteen (see, e.g., *BBC News* 2016b; Drumbl 2015). A related but different issue is that not all societies use the Gregorian calendar for counting time, meaning years could be counted differently. Issues like these make documenting the presence of child soldiers in any given context challenging, though the data from one attempt to do so can be seen in CS 11.1 map a.

Secondly, wars are frequently long endeavors. Even a given conflict or event within a larger war can last for a number of days. How, then, does it make sense to differentiate what one does today as a seventeen-year-old versus tomorrow as an eighteen-year-old? Did the members of the Rwandan *Interahamwe,* the name used for groups of civilians responsible for killing Tutsis during the genocide which were notoriously comprised of youth gangs, the members of which were on the cusp of the internationally recognized legal marker for establishing adulthood, become more responsible for their actions at the stroke of midnight? Were they somehow less culpable the day before?

David Rosen has observed that "age and childhood are contested domains. Chronological age has no absolutely fixed meaning in either nature or culture. Like ethnicity, age categories such as 'child,' youth,' and 'adult' are situationally defined within a larger system and cannot be understood without consideration of conditions and circumstances" (Rosen 2005:132). Societies that organize themselves around age categories, he suggests, do so through continual tension about the social and political implications of these categories. Many other societies instead organize their understandings of childhood, adolescence, and adulthood around particular events, rituals, or achievements. To this end, ideas of childhood are better understood as pluralistic and dynamic, varying in relation to sociocultural norms and practices.

Even if we take a pluralistic and constructivist perspective on age categories, child soldiers add yet another layer of complexity as their experiences disrupt the very processes that establish categorical parameters. Lieutenant-General Roméo Dallaire asks, "Is a child still a child when pressing the barrel of a gun to your chest?" (Dallaire 2011:9). This question, while intended to be evocative, makes a crucial point, namely that childhood and adulthood mean very different things when you grow up in conflict, and different things still when you are brought up among rebels or military forces.

country that uses child soldiers. It is even less possible to obtain figures about the numbers of child soldiers worldwide.

While the use of child soldiers may be limited to certain armed conflicts, child labor is much more common, though its prevalence has decreased markedly over the past several decades (Ortiz-Ospina and Roser 2018). The United Nations Children's Fund (UNICEF), the source of the data in map 32, recognizes that a small amount of paid work or a moderate amount of household labor may be appropriate for older children, and so it defines child labor as one or more hours of paid work or twenty-eight or more hours of household work per week for children aged five to eleven, fourteen or more hours of paid work or twenty-eight or more hours of household work per week for children aged twelve to fourteen, and forty-three or more hours of paid or household work per week for children aged fifteen to seventeen (United Nations Children's Fund 2017).

In some countries, such as Somalia, Guinea-Bissau, Chad, and Benin (as can be seen in map 32), half or more than half of children are working—but child labor is not just an African issue! More than a quarter of children work in Nepal, Afghanistan, Kyrgyzstan, and a number of Latin American countries. In addition, data is not available for many countries, including both countries where child labor is likely to be common and those in which it is generally illegal. Most commonly, children are employed as domestic workers or farm laborers, but they can also be found working in fishing, forestry, hospitality, manufacturing, construction, and other fields (Ortiz-Ospina and Roser 2018). Children who are working may or may not also be able to attend school, and working hours vary considerably. Among children aged seven to fourteen who were working, the average child in 2013 in Bangladesh worked thirty-two hours a week; in 2013 in Jordan, twenty hours per week; and in 2014 in Nepal, under nine hours per week (Ortiz-Ospina and Roser 2018).

International child labor standards suggest that young children should not be employed at all and that older children under age eighteen be protected from work that involves abuse, physical hazards or danger, health hazards, long hours, and overnight shifts (White 1999). It seems this body of suggestions would preclude some work that is common for teenagers in some cultures, such as work as an overnight camp counselor.

One interesting question that arises in the context of the regulation of child labor is whether children themselves have had a say in these regulations (Sutherland 2012). Modern rulemaking, especially in democratic or representative contexts, tends to assume the importance of consultation with or at least input from the communities and populations to be impacted by a body of regulations. But children—even older teens—may be left out of such discussions, and as detailed in chapter 3, they rarely have the ability to vote. Children may have a different perspective on these regulations than do adults. For example, adults may assume that it would be in children's best interest if they were entirely

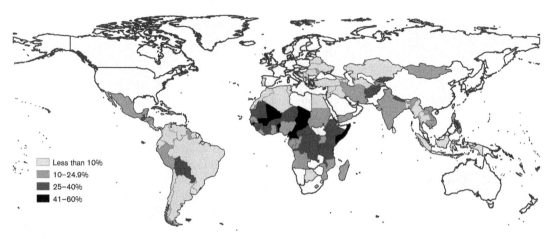

Map 32 Percent of children aged five to seventeen years engaged in child labor (United Nations Children's Fund 2017).

prohibited from working until they reached the age of majority so as to protect their opportunities for education and personal development. But in international discussions around child labor regulations, young people have said they valued the opportunity to work within reasonable limits and did not approve of or appreciate attempts to prevent child labor entirely (White 1999). Notably, child soldiers are not part of such discussions, though international treaties discourage the participation of those under eighteen in armed conflict, especially where that participation is not voluntary and occurs without parental consent, and prohibit participation by those under fifteen, as discussed in this chapter's case study. During the negotiations for these treaties, a number of countries pushed for an absolute minimum age of eighteen, but the United States was among the countries that opposed such a standard given its practice of recruiting those aged seventeen (*New York Times* 1988).

Anti-child-labor advocates continue to seek to develop global standards against child labor, but the discussion of child labor is an interesting case for questions of universalism. Children in different countries, and sometimes even within the same country, live in very different contexts and under very different conditions, and what may imperil a child's future in one country may help that child to survive in a different context. Understanding the context and consequences of child labor requires answering a number of questions. For example, to what extent are educational opportunities available to that child? If he or she is not working, would he or she be able to go to school, or is that simply not an option? Does the child's work provide funds necessary to the child's survival or to their family's survival, or could the family do without or access government benefits to make up the difference? Will entering the workforce negatively impact the child's future life options? Does paid labor provide an opportunity for children to escape abusive home situations, forced domestic labor, early marriage, or other problematic circumstances? Considering such questions highlights the fact that while child labor may be extremely problematic for a young person in a postindustrial economy who needs to complete school in order to ensure a beneficial future, the consequences may be entirely different for a young person in a subsistence agricultural economy who has few other options in any case.

CONCLUSION

Imagine that it is winter in a part of the world in which snowfall is common and you are driving through a major city in the aftermath of a series of heavy snows. The snowplows have made large, densely packed snowbanks where there would normally be spaces for parking cars—in some places, the snow is so high that it covers parking meters and trash cans. As you drive down the street, you come upon a parking space that has been neatly shoveled out, the snow placed in adjacent areas. The empty space is not occupied by a car or other vehicle, though. Instead, a folding chair, the kind more at home on a sunny beach, has been placed in the center of the space, as shown in figure 27.

If you are from Boston, Chicago, Pittsburgh, or certain other snowy cities in the United States, this practice might be familiar to you. But in other cities that routinely get heavy snowfall, such as Buffalo, Minneapolis, Montreal, and pretty much anywhere else outside the United States, it is unheard of. In places where people claim parking spots, it is routine for people to do the hard physical labor of shoveling out spaces and then place objects on the now-clear asphalt to reserve their spot for when they return so that they can continue to benefit from their labor when they next need a spot. They believe their labor entitles them to a property interest in the spot, at least until the surrounding snow melts, and the object they place in the spot—be it a chair, an ironing board, a picnic cooler, or whatever—serves as public notice that the spot has been claimed (Silbey 2012). When others violate the unwritten rules by parking in the cleared spaces, they risk receiving nasty notes from the spot's "rightful owner," having their car buried in snow, or worse, having their car keyed or their tires slashed (Silbey 2012).

The fact that this practice is common does not mean it is legally sanctioned. In Philadelphia, despite widespread community support for space saving, the police launched a #NoSavsies campaign to discourage the (already illegal) practice, tweeting to one resident "@maddieles your lawn chair will be thrown in jail with its accomplices, Orange Cone and Trash Can. #NoSavsies" (Philadelphia Police 2014). Yet in the communities where it takes place, the legal culture clearly shapes people's behavior and understandings such that pretty much anyone familiar with the practice will respect the claims represented by the

Figure 27 A parking space claimed by beach chairs (Meryddian Photography 2009, CC BY-ND 2.0).

chair in the parking space. And sometimes, this legal culture is so powerful that it overpowers regular law. For example, in January 2018, after a snowfall of over a foot, Boston mayor Marty Walsh explained to a local television program that the streets are not private property. The outcry was immediate, and Walsh soon clarified that the city would stick with the policy that has been in place since 2005, permitting space saving for forty-eight hours after a snowfall (Glatter 2018). Disputes over space saving have even ended up in federal court, as in a Chicago case in which a man was awarded $20,500 plus attorney's fees after the police entered his house without a warrant (D. Weiss 2014). The man, Oscar Flores, had saved a parking space; when someone else moved his objects and tried to take his spot, Flores threatened the man's car and police were called. The police told Flores he was not permitted to save the space, and Flores cursed at them, and they then entered his house.

The example of saving parking spaces highlights the importance of understanding legal culture in addition to legal systems. Law is not only what it says and does but also how people interact with it, think about it, and create informal structures and procedures that work alongside or against it. While the rules of legal culture may be unwritten, they are rules nonetheless—rules that can have real consequences for people's lives. And while provisions like the cultural defense can, in jurisdictions that permit it, help individuals who have unwittingly become tangled in the web of justice, they are not always available and do not help those who have violated unwritten rules. A driver from Toronto who gets her tires slashed after moving a lawn chair aside to park on a snowy Boston street has no recourse for her cultural ignorance.

Thus, it is clear that we cannot fully understand law and legal systems without looking to culture, including both its broader elements (such as when homicide is acceptable or what sorts of medical procedures people are willing to undergo) and specifically legal culture. In pluralist countries especially, the different cultural backgrounds and practices of diverse peoples will shape legal interactions and conflicts. What we do in response to the understandings we develop through the study of law and culture depends considerably on our perspective in terms of universalism and relativism. A universalist is likely to argue that such cultural differences must be overcome through a move into a "culturally neutral" space (Choudhury 2015) and that cultural concerns should not be elevated above other kinds of concerns in legal decision-making (Phillips 2009). For example, a universalist would argue that if a judge permits the cultural defense when a family chooses to pursue potentially harmful medical treatments due to their value in the family's culture of origin, that judge should also find in favor of a family choosing those treatments because of philosophical beliefs in opposition to Western medicine that they developed from reading articles on the Internet.

In contrast, a relativist is likely to believe that we must at least attempt to understand the diversity of beliefs and practices that exists—and that it is impossible to be culturally neutral. While the strongest type of relativism would suggest that criticism and comparison of such beliefs and practices is largely impossible and generally inadvisable, many relativists would instead suggest that criticism is indeed possible, but only under certain circumstances. For example, Alison Renteln (2010:257), an expert on the cultural defense, argues that relativists can mount a critique when "the society violates its own internal standards; . . . the custom violates the relativist's external standard, which renders the criticism ethnocentric but nevertheless possible; [or] . . . the custom violates a cross-cultural universal, an international standard supported by global consensus," such as customary international law as discussed in chapter 10.

It has long been the case that some legal systems have had to struggle with these questions. For example, the Roman Empire of antiquity ruled as much as a quarter of the world's population, including peoples as diverse as those living in what is now England, North Africa, Syria, and Spain. But our globalized world has expanded the magnitude of this struggle. Flows of people across borders have expanded, increasing the diversity of cultures found in localities around the world. And people are more likely than they have been in the past to find that they need to interact across borders and cultural boundaries, whether to transact business or to solve global social problems. Thus, the future of law will require that both universalists and relativists understand cultural differences, even if they come to varied conclusions about how to respond to these differences.

Considering Comparative Law and Justice

CHAPTER GOALS

1. Reinforce an understanding of why the study of comparative law and justice is important and what the benefits of such study are.
2. Become familiar with future challenges legal systems face, including technological and climate change.

The highest court in Egypt upheld death sentences for twenty people who had been convicted of attacking a police station, with fatal results, in the context of a political demonstration. In the United States, a lawsuit sought more information on remarks the U.S. National Security Advisor made about the International Criminal Court. A nongovernmental organization filed a lawsuit in the European Court of Human Rights against Hungary, which had enacted laws providing for a 25 percent tax on activities and organizations that promote international migration. The European Union planned litigation against Poland in relation to Polish legislation that would lower the retirement age of judges and thus require twenty-seven out of the then-current seventy-two Supreme Court judges to retire. Italy passed a law making it easier to deport migrants who have been convicted of crimes. Scotland sought a judgment from the high court of the European

Union about what happens if the EU and Britain could not agree on a plan for terminating Britain's membership in the EU. The international nongovernmental organization Amnesty International published a study on the Venezuelan human rights crisis and launched a campaign about suppression of public dissent in Egypt. A Danish court upheld a request by Rwanda to send a man who was originally from Rwanda but who had gained Danish citizenship back to Rwanda to stand trial for crimes against humanity. The Malaysian Anti-Corruption Commission filed charges against a former prime minister for corruption. A human rights group in Mexico claimed that Mexican police and military personnel were responsible for the extrajudicial killing of two people suspected of stealing fuel. A United Nations official encouraged Guatemala to enact measures to ensure judicial independence. A European Union court held that Britain's process of leaving the EU did not prevent a man from standing trial for crimes committed in other EU countries. A court in Pakistan suspended the sentence of a former prime minister in a corruption case. Hong Kong announced that it would henceforth grant immigration visas to dependent same-sex partners who seek to immigrate. The Supreme Court of Honduras temporarily suspended the trial of a suspect accused of murdering an environmental activist, which may have involved state security officials and a hydroelectric company. United Nations officials accused Kyrgyzstan of continuing to permit bride kidnapping, a practice discussed in chapter 8, and encouraged South Sudan to develop a new type of court for hearing war crimes cases. Ireland repealed a constitutional ban on abortion following a national vote. The International Criminal Court announced an investigation into the deportation of Rohingya people, a Muslim ethnic group, from Myanmar, while United Nations officials argued that Myanmar military personnel should face genocide charges. A Romanian court approved a ballot measure that would redefine family in the Romanian constitution and make it more difficult to pursue legalization of same-sex marriage.

This is a list of events that all occurred in one week in September 2018 and were detailed by the Jurist (2018) world legal news site. The array of issues and challenges the list includes demonstrates the complex diversity of global law and justice questions our world faces as it looks to the future. Understanding and responding to these questions requires the study of comparative law and justice.

What are we comparing when we study comparative law and justice? As this book has shown, we can compare many elements of law and legal systems. We can compare the historical development of legal systems. We can compare the structural and procedural elements of legal systems themselves, such as the frameworks of governments, the organization of courts, and the practices of law enforcement. We can compare cultural factors related to law, seeking an understanding of legal cultures as well as of those elements of nonlegal culture that happen to impact law and legal systems, such as religion. And we can compare the ways that different societies and nations have dealt with the challenges they face, such as seeking to reduce crime or increase social equality.

Thus, this concluding chapter takes up two final questions. First, it examines the reasons and motivations for engaging in the study of comparative law and justice. And second, it considers the future of law, exploring some of the issues and problems that legal scholars, policymakers, and practitioners will be faced with in years to come, issues like megacorporations, computer algorithms and machine learning, drones, the law of space, and environmental degradation and climate change. Such a review cannot possibly be exhaustive, and there are undoubtedly many more cutting-edge issues just around the corner with which both domestic and global legal systems will have to grapple. But before thinking about the future, let us think more about comparison itself.

WHY COMPARE?

So why do we study comparative law and justice? There are a variety of motivations driving such study. Academic and intellectual motivations drive us to study law and justice in different countries as well as global law and justice simply so that we can know more about the world. To scholars, increasing knowledge is a goal in itself, and such research designed to increase knowledge for its own sake is called **basic research**. Thus, the study of comparative law and justice lets us learn more about how, and maybe why, things are done in different countries and contexts.

The study of comparative law and justice can also involve **applied research** when it focuses on the practical, professional, and/or policy lessons that can be learned from comparative analysis. Comparative study helps make it possible to understand, for example, the roots and dynamics of international crime, terrorism, and other cross-border criminal offenses, an understanding without which it might be difficult, if not impossible, to detect, combat, and prosecute such offenses. And it enables us to learn about the approaches other societies or nations have tried, permitting us to examine them and consider whether they might be a good fit for our own contexts. There are many types of policies in place in some parts of the world that might—or might not—turn out to be worth adopting elsewhere. To take just a few examples: restorative justice, day fines, compulsory elections, the right to be forgotten, and community policing are all policies discussed earlier in this book that have been used in some places but that are not common across the entire world. Through comparative study, analysts and policymakers could determine if these policies have the desired effects and whether they might be able to be adapted for other national contexts.

But comparison is not always this simple. As David Nelken (2009) points out, when we compare, we run the risk of ethnocentrism, or of applying our own understandings of law, crime, and culture to the other legal systems and societies we study. And we run the risk of overly ascribing to what Ben White (1999) calls relativism as theory (discussed in chapter 11), the strict version of cultural relativism that tells us comparative understanding is impossible (Nelken 2009). Instead, Nelken argues, we must attend to what actors in other places, other countries, and other legal systems are working toward—what their policies and laws are really seeking to accomplish. For example, if we compare per capita rates of imprisonment across countries and stop with just this one piece of data, we may come to remarkably incorrect views about the workings of criminal justice. Imprisonment rates may reflect views about punishment. But they may also reflect demographic trends, crime rates, and periodic fluctuations due to amnesties and pardons. Furthermore, examining imprisonment rates without understanding prisons on a more qualitative level may give us the wrong idea. Do prisons provide rehabilitative and mental health services, or are those in need of such services placed elsewhere? Does the society have the capacity to sentence offenders to control-in-freedom, or are prisons the only way to restrict an offender's movements? Are individuals subject to incarceration when they cannot come up with the money to pay a fine, or are fines assessed in a way that is sensitive to economic resources? The list of questions could go on.

Nelken further points out that even linguistic differences can muddy our comparative understanding, an issue referred to in chapter 2 as the translation problem. He provides the example of the Dutch word *gedogen,* which he argues cannot accurately be translated into English. Sometimes rendered as "tolerance," *gedogen* really refers to a complex philosophical attitude toward criminality, an understanding that some illegal behavior is inevitable, accompanied by a belief that law enforcement is only one tool among many that may be used to achieve desired social ends (Uitermark 2004). Thus, the Dutch state uses what may be perceived as selective enforcement or inconsistent application of the rules in order to achieve the priorities it has set for itself. So how do we understand what it is that the Dutch state is trying to accomplish—is it tolerance of illegality, or is it a pragmatic perspective on criminal justice efficacy (Nelken 2009)?

These questions highlight another reason why people engage in the study of comparative law and justice, and that is to develop international understanding in our increasingly globalized world (Breyer 2018). Such understanding is particularly important to those who will work in the arena of international law, of course. They must be able to work across world legal systems, languages, and cultural contexts, whether they are crafting bilateral or multilateral treaties, negotiating agreements within the structure of the United Nations or the European Union, litigating in the International Criminal Court or the International Court of Justice, or drafting contracts between companies coming from different places.

But understanding can be important in so many other ways. Consider the cultural defense, as discussed in chapter 11. People from different cultures and legal systems may have differing understandings of what is criminal and how to respond to legal investigations. Thus, those who work as police officers, lawyers, and court officials in contexts of cultural diversity will be better able to carry out their duties if they have an understanding of comparative law and justice. This extends to other areas of life as well. Teachers, social workers, therapists, and so many other professionals are increasingly faced with clientele from diverse cultural backgrounds whose interactions with legal systems may have had important impacts on their lives. And if one wants to make money in the global economy, understanding the different mechanisms of dispute resolution and corporate regulation across borders may be essential to success.

Frank Zimring, an eminent criminologist, spent much of his career (by his own admission) not very concerned with international comparison. But his mind was changed after he embarked on a study of comparative crime rates. His study was designed to test several assumptions that pundits, policy makers, and researchers had long made about the United States, assumptions based on a sense that the United States is in some ways unique. These assumptions were (Zimring 2006:616):

1. crime is a bigger problem in the United States than it is elsewhere in the developed world;
2. most kinds of crime rates are higher in United States than in other developed countries; and
3. the reason why there is more crime in the United States is because there are more criminals in United States.

But Zimring and his coauthor, Gordon Hawkins, found that this set of assumptions did not hold up to scrutiny. They found that the United States was similar to other countries when rates of theft, burglary, and nonlethal assault were compared (Zimring 2006). However, *homicide* rates were much higher—at the time the study was conducted, they were four to seven times that of the rates in countries like Australia and Canada (Zimring 2006). In another study, Zimring found that the United States and Canada both experienced greater declines in the crime rate in the 1990s than did other comparable countries—but that Canada did not do any of the things people in the United States assume lead to crime declines, like increasing imprisonment or hiring more police officers. Zimring concludes from his analysis that ramping up the war on crime probably is not the most effective method for reducing crime rates. He points out that without studies like his, policymakers looking to fight crime would turn to the wrong kinds of solutions. Instead, if we want to reduce deaths due to homicide and suicide, we must focus on the factors that lead assaults in the United States to be more deadly. Public health research suggests that the unusual access to lethal weapons—guns—found in the United States, as discussed in chapter 5, is a key factor, though research on the relationship between guns and deaths suffers from a lack of funding and support for collecting relevant data in the United States (Hemenway 2017). If we want to understand the crime decline in the United States and Canada, we may need to turn to an analysis of demographic factors—Zimring found that the proportion of the population consisting of young people declined markedly in both countries during the time period he considered.

Zimring's and Nelken's research points out the importance of remembering that analyses of comparative law and justice must extend beyond the legal system if they are to fully account for the policies, practices, and impacts we can observe. Without understanding such factors as demographic change, economic contexts, and cultural beliefs, it may be difficult to understand just what is occurring in a legal system, why it is occurring, and what may result. Additionally, Zimring points out the importance of attending to societal change. While from the perspective of a person living in a country with a stable government it may seem that legal systems are enduring and slow to change, a study of legal history shows that things are not so stable as they may seem. This book has shown that legal systems themselves have changed over time, as have more specific practices like approaches to punishment and social control. The apparatus of international law itself is continually evolving, and today there is a considerably body of settled international law that barely existed a few centuries ago, when almost all international law was customary. Thus, as we consider the future of law, we must remember that it may look very different from the past or the present.

THE FUTURE OF LAW

As discussed elsewhere in this book, our increasingly globalized world will continue to lead to changes in law and legal systems. The increased magnitude of global military conflicts and immigrant and refugee flows, the expansion of global business and personal relationships, the continuing threat of cross-border crime (including cybercrime and trafficking in goods and people), and the internationalization or regionalization of some forms of governance and regulation all have important consequences for law and legal systems at the domestic and global levels. As legal scholar Gillian Hadfield (2017) argues, today's complex global economy crosses state boundaries and involves flows of goods, services, digital content, and information that cannot easily be contained by the regulatory systems of the past.

The law of the past was charged with regulating human conduct, along with in some cases the conduct of nonhuman animals, such as pigs and goats, who may have been accused of crimes (as discussed in chapter 6). It also was charged with regulating the conduct of corporate entities, which were once relatively small or at least primarily located under the control of a single jurisdiction. Today, corporations are increasingly global, and they may venue-shop for the most attractive countries in which to register their corporate existence or hold their profits. Thus, the corporations—and in some cases even the corporate executives—of today may have nomadic existences, being everywhere at once while living nowhere in particular. Furthermore, many corporations today are even larger than states, whether we reckon by economic or demographic scales. Indeed, sixty-nine of the hundred largest global economic entities as of 2016 were corporations rather than countries, with Walmart ranked the tenth largest and a number of oil companies ranking in the top twenty-five (Myers 2016). And many legal systems, including the United States, today recognize corporations as a kind of legal person (Brölmann and Nijman 2017). Global and domestic legal systems will thus be forced to reckon with how to regulate corporate behavior and protect human rights in a context (Bilchitz 2016) in which corporations may be responsible for crimes as varied as human trafficking and slavery, corporate bribery, tax noncompliance (Lord and Broad 2017), money laundering (Bromwich 2018), and global economic degradation (Spapens, White, and Kluin 2016).

While global regulation schemes have been developed with the goal of keeping the global financial system stable (Sciurba 2018), these schemes cannot always keep up with the ongoing development of criminal enterprises, as they were not developed or designed for that purpose (Søreide 2019). In 2016, a criminal enterprise attempted to steal $951 million from the Bangladeshi central bank by exploiting software weaknesses (Hammer 2018). While alert bank officers around the world stopped some of the transactions and others got flagged by the coincidental similarity of a bank's name to that of a sanctioned shipping company in Greece, the criminals made off with $81 million. But it was not only software weaknesses that made this heist possible. It was also the fact that weekends begin and end at different times in different countries: in Bangladesh, banks are closed on Fridays, while in the United States, where the New York Federal Reserve plays a central role in managing the global banking system, they are closed on Saturdays and Sundays. This meant that a fraudulent transaction executed on Thursday night in Bangladesh might not be able to be addressed until Monday morning in New York. By the time that New York could respond, the money transfers these criminals had set into motion had already been completed, with the money being transferred to a Filipino bank. Investigators recovered some of the stolen money, but they believe the rest has made its way to North Korea. And while the Filipino banker responsible for transforming Bangladeshi funds into ready cash has been imprisoned, what law could possibly reach the North Koreans who absconded with the funds?

This story highlights some of the many possibilities our globalized and technologized world offers for financial crimes, but there are others. E-payments and cryptocurrencies like Bitcoin (Burge 2016) open up new possibilities for financial crimes such as tax evasion (Künnapas 2016) and money laundering. On the other hand, some scholars argue that new technologies might reduce the potential for financial crimes. For example, a mandatory electronic tax invoicing system implemented in South Korea seems to have increased tax compliance while reducing compliance costs for both taxpayers and tax authorities (Lee 2016).

The law of the future will have to reckon with not only the behavior of living beings and corporate entities but also the behavior of computer algorithms. Today's computer algorithms often incorporate a technology called "machine learning," which enables a computer to come to conclusions by examining a large amount of already-existing data with little or no human input. Machine learning algorithms are already used in a wide variety of areas of human life, from medical decision-making to dropping bombs, from evaluating prison inmates' parole applications to assessing credit risk. But when the machine makes a decision based on these algorithms, it may not be able to provide an explanation as to why it made that particular decision (Kuang 2017). In some cases, the algorithm itself is considered protected intellectual property, thus preventing courts from fully examining the decision-making process (Pasquale 2017). And indeed, the decisions the algorithms make may re-encode existing systems of inequality or discrimination that are baked into the data the machine has examined (see, for instance, Eubanks 2017; O'Neil 2016).

The European Union has already begun to craft a legal regulatory regime to address algorithmic decision-making, a step most other jurisdictions have not yet taken. The European Union's new General Data Protection Regulation (GDPR), discussed in chapter 9 in the context of information privacy, contains a provision prohibiting decisions based on any kind of automated processing without consent and the ability to provide for human intervention, and further prohibits the use of such algorithms in circumstances that may result in discriminatory outcomes (Goodman and Flaxman 2016). Where algorithmic decision-making is used, the GDPR provides for the right to an explanation (Goodman and Flaxman 2016). Other jurisdictions will face the need to grapple with these questions as algorithmic decision-making becomes more widespread.

Technological change may impact the future of law in many other ways that extend across borders. For example, as more and more of life is lived online, the law must contend with such new dilemmas as international property rights disputes about virtual property (Lastowka 2010) and intellectual property (Cheslow 2013). And, as recent events around the world have demonstrated, the risk of cross-border election interference and hacking of election infrastructure and other government apparatus has become a new global threat, as have other forms of cybercrime such as large-scale identity theft, ransomware, the hacking of banking or utility companies, and distributed denial-of-service attacks that disrupt websites and Internet infrastructure (Fidler 2017; Hamilton 2017; Shackelford, Russell, and Kuehn 2016). Securing physical borders, the

Figure 28 A U.S. soldier prepares to launch a Black
Hornet 3 surveillance drone (Olson n.d.).

historical response countries have had toward cross-border threats, is of little
use against these sorts of attacks.

Another area of technological change with significant legal implications is
the development of robotics. While domestic legal systems are already beginning to contend with the legal issues raised by driverless cars (Cheslow 2013),
what happens when such cars cross borders? Or when they become airborne?
What about robots performing other functions—can a robot board an airplane
without a human minder and fly itself to another country? What if the robot *is*
the airplane, as in the case of drones? Indeed, drones raise many questions
(Saura 2016), including those about the legality of automated, targeted assassi-
nations and cross-border surveillance. For example, military forces are now
using stealth drones so small they may not be detected by opposing forces
(Vergun 2018), as shown in figure 28, a technology that could easily be adapted
to other purposes with which international law has not yet contended. And
this is just a small sampling of the cross-border legal issues raised by new technology. There are so many more—like DNA privacy, control over the apparatus
of the Internet (Ruotolo 2017), cloning and genetic engineering, and even the
legal personhood of animals as our biological science discovers more about
their intelligence, emotions, and selves.

Changes in technology have also increased the legal issues represented by
space exploration. A series of international treaties has sought to develop an
international regulatory regime governing space. These treaties have positioned space as a common territory not subject to occupation or domination by
any one country, an area to be used for peaceful purposes and for the better-
ment of all humanity (Epps and Graham 2011). There are also a variety of
regional and global agencies that focus on space law, including the United
Nations Office for Outer Space Affairs, the Committee on the Peaceful Uses of
Outer Space, and the European Space Agency (Lyall and Larson 2018). Space
law continues to present new frontiers as space technology advances. For
example, there is a variety of space junk, including defunct satellites, currently
in orbit around the Earth (Listner 2011). If a spacecraft or newly launched

CASE STUDY 12.1

Regulating the Environment

When people discuss global climate change, they tend to focus on warming air and ocean temperatures. As important as those factors are to the future of humanity, they are not the only consequences of climate change. An increase in the frequency of severe weather, including tornadoes, hurricanes, floods, blizzards, and droughts, is expected, and in some parts of the world is already being observed. Climate change increases the geographical range of such tropical and subtropical diseases as malaria, yellow fever, and Zika and increases the prevalence of other diseases, like Lyme disease, West Nile virus, and many parasites. Such incidents will also have legal implications, including the obvious ones, like battles involving international insurance companies or the question of how to address natural disasters that occur along international borders. Others are less obvious. For example, current migration laws can make it difficult for large numbers of people to move across the globe quickly in response to disasters and epidemics (Cheslow 2013).

Scientists believe that much of the global climate change they predict, though not all, is due to human activity, in particular the release of greenhouse gasses like methane and carbon dioxide that warm the globe, melt the polar ice caps, change oceanic and air currents, and lead to sea level rise. Humans have also been responsible for a variety of other forms of environmental degradation. These include plant and animal extinction due to habitat loss and overconsumption; deforestation; and a vast array of different kinds of pollution, such as the release of toxic, nuclear, agricultural, and human waste.

Pollution does not respect national borders (Epps and Graham 2011), and neither do the impacts of global climate change and other environmental problems. Thus, the global environment is a key example of a phenomenon that is known as the "**tragedy of the commons.**" This phrase has its roots in the old arrangement of towns in England and New England (Lloyd 1833). Such towns typically would have involved a cluster of houses, along with a church, arranged around a common green space, as shown in figure CS 12.1 figure a. This green space was used for communal activities, markets, and sometimes the grazing of livestock. Given that no one

CS 12.1 Figure a A town common in England (Forbes 1921).

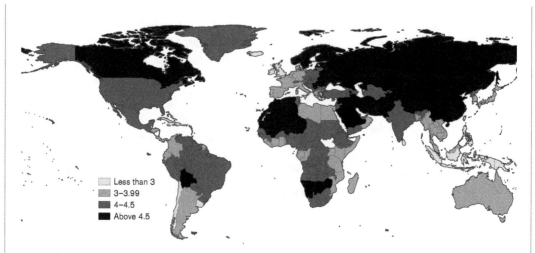

CS 12.1 Map a Average predicted warming by 2045–2065 in degrees Fahrenheit (World Bank 2011).

individual was responsible for the maintenance of the commons but that its grass supplied feed for everyone's livestock, it was in each individual's self-interest to graze as many animals as possible on the commons. However, if too many animals grazed, the grass would be destroyed, and none of the animals would have enough to eat. While it is unclear if the tragedy of the commons actually affected such old towns, the metaphor of the commons' destruction became a powerful one, motivating movements for enclosure of the commons into individual plots of grazing land (Fairlie 2009).

However weak the tragedy of the commons may be as a historical truth, it is a powerful way to understand global environmental problems. If individuals, companies, and countries around the world each act according to their own rational self-interest—releasing greenhouse gasses to power air conditioners, cutting down trees in the rainforest to make room for palm oil plantations, overfishing to feed a ravenous appetite for sushi, and tossing trash without concern for the space needed in landfills—the limited resources we

share on our planet Earth will face destruction. And this can occur even when everyone knows the likely outcome, since each individual cannot themselves do much to forestall a bad long-term result for everyone.

This means that, as hard as individual countries may try to adopt environmental policies, practices, and regulations designed to forestall or reverse environmental damage, they will not be able to succeed on their own. Without universal standards and collaborative efforts, the Earth will suffer a vast array of consequences. The global average temperature is projected to rise by 3.6 degrees Fahrenheit or more by the year 2100, leading to longer and more frequent heat waves, changes in precipitation, severe weather patterns, and other negative impacts (IPCC 2014), and these impacts will be distributed differentially across countries (see CS 12.1 map a). Sea levels are likely to rise as a consequence, perhaps by more than two meters by 2100 (see CS 12.1 map b), and this will flood island nations that are predominantly low-lying, like Kiribati and the Maldives (Keating 2018), as well as the islands and coastlines of other

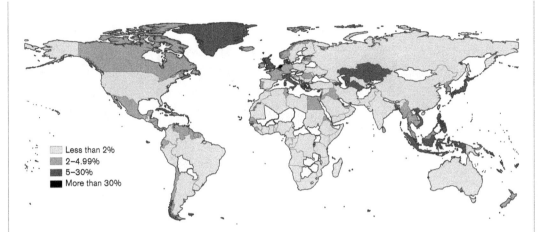

CS 12.1 Map b Percent of land below 5 meters (16.4 feet) in elevation as of 2000 (World Bank 2011).

Legend:
- Less than 2%
- 2–4.99%
- 5–30%
- More than 30%

countries, such as Virginia's Tangier Island (Plott 2018). Overuse of water, along with climatic factors related to global climate change, is leading to the spread of deserts like the Sahara and the Gobi (Huang et al. 2016) and a lack of drinking water in major urban centers like Cape Town, South Africa (Fallon 2018). Trash is collecting in outer space, as discussed elsewhere in this chapter, as well as in the Great Pacific Garbage Patch, where it can harm ocean life, and in landfills and informal dumps all around the globe, where chemicals in the trash can leach out and pollute waterways. Overfishing, habitat destruction, and other human activities are leading to the mass extinction of species (Kolbert 2014). And these are only a few examples of the impact human activity is having on the global environment.

There are a wide variety of international treaties governing behavior and activities that can have environmental impacts, including fishing and other resource extraction on the high seas (waters beyond oceanic territorial boundaries); pollution and other emissions; endangered plant and animal species and other natural resources; and the use of radioactive materials; as well as instituting the requirement to conduct environmental impact assessments before embarking on projects (Epps and Graham 2011). Many such international legal documents have articulated standards based on concern about future generations.

It is important to note that the environmental damage intensifying these problems is not equally caused by all countries, as can be seen in CS 12.1 map c. Developed countries have had decades, and in some cases centuries, to emit greenhouse gasses, pollute the waterways, and extract natural resources with little limit. They continue to be disproportionately responsible for greenhouse gas emissions, though some less-developed countries are catching up. Thus, one interesting element of current international environmental regulation regimes is that they tend to provide different standards for developed and less-developed countries (Epps and Graham 2011). These differences are based on the fact that through years of engaging freely in pollution and environmental destruction, developed countries had opportunities to grow their national economies, while less developed countries may not yet have had such opportunities. In addition, many environmentally

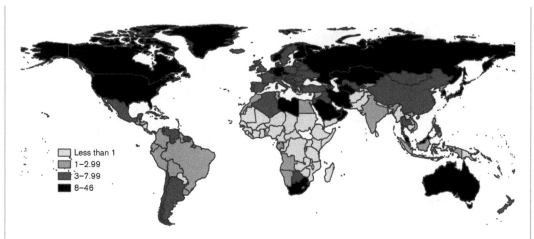

CS 12.1 Map c Metric tons of CO_2 emitted per capita, 2014 (Carbon Dioxide Information Analysis Center 2018).

friendly technologies, such as electric cars, solar power, and single-stream recycling, are considerably more expensive than their high-pollution alternatives, like high-emission gasoline-powered vehicles, coal power, and open pit landfills.

In response to the urgent pressures presented by climate change, world nations gathered in Paris in December 2015 to negotiate an agreement about global climate change policy and regulation, an event that is referred to as COP21 (COP stands for Conference of Parties and refers to the parties, or state signatories, to the United Nations Framework Convention on Climate Change, which includes nearly all countries in the world). Countries agreed to plans designed to mitigate, though not forestall, global climate change, including a standard protocol for measuring greenhouse gas emissions; a series of future meetings, including those scheduled for 2018 and 2023; and a process for developed countries to provide both financial and technical assistance to less-developed countries (Robbins 2016); along with a system through which countries articulate their own individual pledges for reducing their national contributions to global climate change (Bach 2016). The agree-

ment was ratified in 2016 (UNFCCC 2018) and has been signed by nearly all countries in the world (Paris Agreement 2015), though the United States has indicated its intention to withdraw from the treaty in 2019, effective in 2020, in accordance with the withdrawal procedure specified in the COP21 agreement (Shear 2017).

The COP21 agreement's goal is to reduce greenhouse gas emissions to net zero levels, meaning that any greenhouse gas emitted is offset by carbon capture or other technologies to remove such gasses from the atmosphere, in order to keep the global average temperature increase to somewhere between 2.7 and 3.6 degrees Fahrenheit above that of preindustrial times (Rhodes 2016). However, the likelihood that such goals will be achieved may be limited given the reality of nations' individual articulated commitments, which do not add up to the sum necessary to avoid warming beyond 3.6 degrees Fahrenheit (Bach 2016; Rhodes 2016).

It is clear that in the context of global environmental regulation, some of the divides and debates around universalism and relativism break down. When global environmental regulations are created and imposed on others, these regulations are not only a form of cultural imperialism imposed on others whose cultural practices may not conform to the regulatory intent. They are also a tool designed to protect all of us, including those opposed to them, from an environmentally uncertain future, one that may not be as hospitable to human life as the past has been. The tragedy of the commons highlights the fact that when we all act in our own self-interest in the short term, the long-term impacts may harm us all. Global environmental regulations seek to avoid this fate.

But though agreements like COP21 lay out innovative pathways that may provide the promise of some forward movement on environmental protection, they remain a tool of international law, with all the same limitations and caveats that are part of all treaties. As chapter 10 has shown, the international community faces serious constraints in its ability to ensure compliance among those who are signatories to a treaty. And that is without considering the case of countries that choose not to sign in the first place or that later withdraw. The promised withdrawal of the United States, for instance, would revoke compliance by the world's second-largest emitter of greenhouse gasses, responsible, according to 2017 data, for over 14 percent of global emissions (Friedrich, Ge, and Pickens 2017). While COP21 may facilitate novel uses of international justice institutions to regulate emissions and pollution (Bach 2016), it cannot fully escape the limitations of all international agreements. So what does this mean for the future of our global commons? That depends on whether we as a planetary community can get beyond a limited-term perspective on national self-interest and instead concern ourselves with our planet's future.

satellite collides with some of this debris and is damaged, or if the collision results in debris landing on someone's house and destroying it, who is responsible? Many such items were launched by governmental entities, but today all manner of private companies have gotten into the space business. Imagine a case where a corporation based in England launches a satellite from Mongolia that collides with space debris originally traceable to Russia and subsequently lands in Argentina. In which courts will such a dispute be heard? And by what means might the international community move forward on developing mechanisms for dealing with the backlog of space junk (Imburgia 2011)?

Many other legal issues are raised by space exploration. For example, how do property claims work in space? Can people, corporations, or governments claim ownership or exclusive dominion over bits of moon, an asteroid, or territory on another planet? Are outer space lands meant to be free of ownership claims, as Antarctica is today? Or should some other system of property interests, such as leases or licenses, be developed (Widgerow 2011)? And what about when such systems break down and, say, a series of lunar-mining companies get into a dispute about who has the right to extract helium (Gilson 2011)? Private businesses are also seeking to get into the commercial spaceflight business (Laisné 2013). Such commercial endeavors present a variety of problems of personal injury, investment, contract, and administrative law. Some of these have easy historical precedents, such as in the invention of airplane flight, which presented similar types of personal risk and similarly transcended national boundaries, but space—of course—is a new frontier.

CONCLUSION

The pages of this book have provided a journey through law, legal systems, and justice systems around the globe. This tour has considered categories of legal systems, the structure of state governments and the process of lawmaking and elections, domestic variations in crime as well as international and transnational crime, law enforcement, courts and dispute resolution processes, punishment and social control, family law and the regulation of intimate relationships, human and civil rights and legal inequality, institutions of global justice, legal culture, and the future of law. Such a tour cannot be complete, as the legal and justice systems even within a given country are vast, complex, and ever changing, and the labyrinth of global justice even more complex. This tour did not devote many words to the nature of domestic administrative law, to legal battles about intellectual property or contract disputes, to social security and pension law, or to the many other issues that matter for the daily lives of people living under the law's authority. Yet here at least there has been a beginning, a first few steps in the direction of comprehending the diversity of approaches to law and justice our world holds and has held over time.

There is a long tradition of comparative legal scholarship, but there is much work left to be done as scholars and policymakers continue seeking to enhance their and our understanding of law and justice around the world. The many questions this chapter raises about the future challenges our global and domestic legal systems may face are just a few of the avenues scholars and policymakers may travel as they continue such investigations. For those who are interested in pursuing scholarly research in comparative law and justice, there are a wide variety of avenues for such scholarship. Any chapter in this book presents dozens, if not hundreds, of topics about which additional scholarly research could be conducted. And this research can be done in many disciplines: comparative law and justice is studied in the field of law and legal studies, of course, but it is also studied in sociology, anthropology, political science, international relations, public administration, philosophy, geography, and many other fields.

But the work of comparative law and justice is not limited to scholars. Policymakers benefit greatly from this work, as it provides them with a greater array of potential ideas as they seek to refine and innovate in policy domains, and it allows them to see the potential impacts and outcomes of policies they might be considering. And practitioners can learn from comparative analysis, too. Law enforcement officers might learn new ways to detect, investigate, and prevent crime by looking at how police in other countries operate. Those who supervise correctional institutions may gain insight into the kinds of programs they can implement in their facilities to reduce recidivism or increase opportunities for rehabilitation by looking at the practices in place at facilities in other parts of the world. Lawyers who are involved in litigation that crosses borders, or who are tasked with negotiating deals among parties located in different countries, benefit from an understanding of the distinct legal structures and cultures in which their clients and those other parties operate. And the staff of international nongovernmental organizations dealing with human rights, international migration, or other cross-border issues will better be able to pursue their mission when they are familiar with the workings of both international and domestic legal institutions.

And what of those of us who do not foresee a future as scholars, policymakers, or practitioners in any area of work directly relevant to comparative law and justice? Our lives in the increasingly globalized context in which we live will still be touched by these important issues. We will travel across borders. We will engage in commercial transactions across legal systems. We will struggle to understand complex geopolitical realities that affect our governments and our economies. We will fall in love with those who grew up in a different legal culture. We will collectively face global problems like environmental change. Law permeates our lives, and as our lives continue to globalize, that means global, international, and comparative legal realities touch us all.

Glossary

absolute monarchy: A government system characterized by a hereditary ruler with absolute power.

accountability: A characteristic of electoral systems measuring whether elected officials are responsible to a specific body of constituents.

adjudication: Formal dispute resolution in a court.

administrative law: Law relating to the work of government administrative agencies.

adoption: The creation of a parent-child relationship by law rather than biology.

adversarial trial: The trial form associated with common law, involving two competing sides that present evidence to a judge and jury.

alimony: Payments made after a divorce to support a former spouse.

alternative dispute resolution (ADR): A term encompassing a variety of forms of formal dispute resolution other than the court process.

alternative voting: A method of voting in which voters rank candidates in order of preference. Candidates with the fewest number of first-choice votes are eliminated, and those votes are transferred to the voters' next-place choice. This process is repeated until a candidate receives 50 percent of the votes. See also **instant-runoff voting** and **ranked-choice voting**.

annulment: Declaring a marriage void as if it had never occurred.

applied research: Research carried out to answer specific practical questions.

arbitration: A system of third-party, binding dispute resolution occurring outside the courts.

aristocracy: A hereditary ruling class, as well as government by this class.

asylum: A legal status granted to individuals who cannot return to their country of origin due to persecution based on their membership in particular social groups.

authoritarian government: A government featuring strong central control with little individual freedom.

authoritarian law: A system of law in which law issues from the control of a leader rather than from texts, traditions, or other sources.

barrister: A type of lawyer in common law systems specializing in trial work.

basic research: Research designed to increase knowledge about the world.

bicameral: Having two houses, as in a legislature.

bricolage: Creation of something out of the materials at hand.

bride price: Money paid by a groom or his family to the bride's family at the time of marriage.

capital punishment: Punishing a person by death. Also called the death penalty.

centralized police structure: When control over a country's police is consolidated in a national command.

checks and balances: The process whereby each part of government can exercise powers to limit the actions of other parts.

child abuse: Actions that harm children and are not considered acceptable by the broader society.

child neglect: Failing to meet a child's basic needs.

citizen: A person who has the legal right to protection from a state and owes allegiance to it.

citizenship: The status of being a citizen.

city-state: A sovereign state consisting entirely of a city and its surrounding lands.

civil disobedience: The refusal to obey certain laws, typically those considered unjust, and typically as an act of protest against the government.

civil law (legal system): A legal system characterized by reliance on legal codes (written law), especially those derived from continental Europe.

civil law (type of law): Noncriminal law, especially that related to settling private disputes.

civil policing: A model of policing in which law enforcement and military functions are fully separated.

civil rights: Individual legal rights to equal treatment, often including the right to political participation.

common law: A legal system characterized by reliance on precedent derived from the English legal tradition.

common law marriage: A legal framework in which people can be considered married without having formally undertaken to become married, usually requiring cohabiting for a certain number of years.

communism: A political system characterized by common ownership of the means of production, the elimination of private property, and collective or state control over the economy and consumption.

community policing: An approach to policing in which police work with and build ties to people in the communities they police.

compensatory damages: Money awarded in a court case to compensate a person for the injuries or losses they have experienced.

compurgation: A trial process used in early common law based on oath-taking by a number of witnesses.

Condorcet winner: The candidate in a given election who, compared to all other candidates, is most preferred by the greatest number of voters.

consanguinity: Kinship or blood relation through a common ancestor.

constitution: A set of principles establishing the legal groundwork for a political entity, along with how it is to be governed.

control-in-freedom: A form of punishment in which the individual is not imprisoned but is monitored or supervised.

conventional international law: International law established through treaties.

corporal punishment: Punishment inflicted upon the body to cause pain.

corporatism: A political system in which large organizations like businesses and trade unions exercise control.

covenant marriage: An alternative system of marriage with more limited grounds for divorce; used in certain U.S. states.

coverture: A legal doctrine under which women lost their separate legal rights upon marriage and their legal personhood merged into that of their husbands.

crimes against humanity: International crimes involving attacks on civilian populations committed in accordance with policy or in a systematic fashion.

crimes of aggression: International crimes of mounting military action for reasons other than self-defense.

criminal law: The body of law related to crime.

criminalization: The process of making an action punishable as a crime in law.

cross-border crime: Criminal acts that involve activity in more than one country. See also **transnational crime**.

cultural defense: A defense to crime relying on cultural differences as justification or explanation for actions.

cultural pluralism: When social groups are able to maintain their cultural values and identities within a larger society.

cultural relativism: The idea that values and practices can be understood only within the context of a specific culture.

culture: The way of life of a group of people, including values, norms, expression, tradition, and behavior.

custody: Legal responsibility for control and care of an individual.

customary international law: International law based on custom or tradition.

day fine: A fine calculated based on an offender's personal income.

decentralized police structure: When control over a country's police is not consolidated in a national command.

decriminalization: The removal of criminal penalties for specific acts.

defamation: False statements that are harmful to the reputation of another individual.

defense attorney: A lawyer charged with representing a criminal defendant.

democracy: Government by the people.

democratic republic: A form of government in which people elect representatives to govern on their behalf. See also **representative democracy**.

depenalization: A reduction in penalties for a specific criminal act.

deterrence: A theory of punishment focusing on the use of punishments to discourage potential offenders from committing crimes.

dictatorship: An authoritarian government with a single leader.

direct democracy: A form of government in which people directly make policy decisions.

direct social control: Social control that is exercised deliberately and overtly.

dispute: A disagreement that has become public.

domestic crime: Crime occurring within a given country.

dowry: Money or goods given by a bride's family to the couple or the groom's family at the time of marriage.

dual citizenship: Holding citizenship in more than one country at the same time.

durable government: A government able to maintain its power until the next scheduled election.

electoral college: An electoral process in which specific electors, rather than regular voters, choose the winner of the election.

electronic monitoring (EM): The use of electronic surveillance devices to track individuals.

empire: A group of nations ruled over by a single government.

exclusionary rule: A legal rule preventing the use of illegally gathered evidence in court.

executive branch: The branch of government charged with administering and enforcing the law.

external legal culture: The legal culture of those outside the legal system.

extraterritorial: Can mean both the ability of a government to exercise power outside its boundaries and being exempt from the authority of local law.

fascism: A system of authoritarian government typically characterized by economic control, a lack of personal freedom, and ethnic nationalism.

families of law: Groups of legal systems that have central features in common.

federation: A political entity in which a common government is shared by political subunits that also maintain their own governments.

feudalism: A political and economic system in which lords provide land to vassals in return for service.

fine: A monetary penalty.

first-past-the-post voting: An electoral system in which the candidate receiving the plurality of votes wins.

formal equality: A condition in which all people receive equal treatment.

formal social control: Social control stemming from prescribed rules.

gender: An individual's social role and personal identification. Gender categories include maleness and femaleness as well as other identities that vary by society.

genocide: Action taken against an ethnic or religious group with the intention of destroying it completely.

gerontocracy: A system of government in which elders rule.

Gini coefficient: A statistical measure of inequality in economic distribution within a society.

globalization: The increasing interconnectedness of people and practices on a worldwide scale.

grievance: Something that someone is upset about.

gross domestic product (GDP): A measure of the value of all goods produced and services provided in a specific area in a given year.

human rights: Rights that all humans are considered to have.

human trafficking: The moving of people into conditions of exploitation through use of threat, force, or deception, typically for labor or sexual exploitation.

ideal types: An abstract representation of social reality taking together the essential characteristics of a phenomenon.

illegitimate (child): A child born outside of marriage.

incapacitation: A type of punishment designed to make it impossible for an individual to commit future crimes.

incarceration: Imprisonment.

incommensurable: A circumstance in which direct comparison is not possible.

indirect social control: Social control that occurs due to an internalized sense of obligation.

informal social control: Social control that is maintained through norms, stigma, or other social practices that have not been written down or formalized.

informational privacy: The ability to have control over one's own personal data.

inquisitorial trial: The trial form associated with civil law systems, in which the court actively participates in investigation.

instant-runoff voting: A voting method in which voters rank candidates in order of preference and low-ranked candidates are eliminated until a winner is determined. See also **alternative voting** and **ranked-choice voting**.

intelligence-led policing: A system of policing based on analyzing crime data to determine law enforcement priorities.

internal legal culture: The legal culture of those inside the legal system, like lawyers and judges.

International Court of Justice (ICJ): The court of the United Nations, which hears disputes between countries.

international crime: Crimes defined as such under international law, specifically genocide, war crimes, crimes against humanity, and the crime of aggression.

International Criminal Court (ICC): The international tribunal responsible for prosecuting alleged international crimes.

international law: Law governing relations between states.

Interpol: An international organization tasked with facilitating cooperation between police departments around the world.

judge: An official who presides over court hearings and makes legal decisions.

judicial branch: The branch of government responsible for interpreting laws and managing disputes.

jury: A body of people selected to determine questions of fact in trials, especially in common law systems.

jury equity: The British term for **jury nullification**.

jury nullification: A situation in which a jury finds a criminal defendant not guilty because the members of the jury do not believe it is appropriate to apply the law as it stands, even though they believe the defendant committed the act he or she is accused of. See also **jury equity**.

legal code: A systematic, written set of laws.

legal consciousness: How people think about and understand law and legal practices.

legal culture: The values, attitudes, and ideas people have in relation to law and legal practices.

legal custody: The right to make decisions about a dependent's care and upbringing.

legal pluralism: When multiple legal systems coexist in a specific area.

legal structure: The institutions, processes, and personnel that make up the legal system.

legal system: The body of laws and supporting institutions in a given jurisdiction or entity.

legalization: The process of making it legal to do something that was previously illegal.

legislative branch: The branch of government responsible for making laws.

legitimacy: The general acceptance that a government or other authority is valid. Also refers to children born within marital unions. See also **illegitimate**.

lèse-majesté: A criminal offense involving insults or defamation of a ruler or state.

macro: Large-scale.

majority: An amount over 50 percent.

martial law: Military control over a civilian population, especially during temporary emergencies.

mediation: A process of dispute resolution in which a neutral third party facilitates the resolution of conflict between disputants.

mercenaries: Hired military personnel who are not part of any state's military forces.

meso: Medium-scale.

micro: Small-scale.

mixed legal system: A legal system incorporating elements of multiple families of law.

monarchy: A government ruled by a (usually hereditary) ruler who rules until he or she dies or chooses to step down.

multiple coordinated police structure: A system of policing in which multiple law enforcement agencies exist and they have a formal process for working together to coordinate their activities.

multiple uncoordinated police structure: A system of policing in which multiple law enforcement agencies exist without any formal process for coordination.

nation-state: A country featuring a population that is largely homogenous in ethnic and cultural terms, where political and cultural boundaries match up.

natural law: The philosophy that certain rights and legal principles are endowed by nature or the divine.

negative rights: Rights requiring the government to avoid doing something in order to protect them.

non-governmental organization (NGO): A group operating independently of government to provide services or engage in advocacy; typically but not always nonprofit.

non-refoulement: A legal principle forbidding states from returning asylum seekers to countries where they would face persecution.

oligarchy: A form of government in which power is held by a small group.

panopticon: A prison design in which prison cells are arranged around a central guard tower so that prisoners are always visible to guards. Also used to describe similar systems of surveillance outside of prisons.

parliamentary system: A system of government in which the executive comes from within the legislative body and there is less separation of powers between these branches.

parole: The release of a prisoner under certain conditions, usually involving continued supervision, before his or her term is completed.

peremptory challenge: The rejection of a potential juror without the need to provide a reason.

physical custody: The legal right to have a dependent live with you.

physical privacy: The ability to protect one's body, belonging, and personal spaces from search or access.

piracy: Refers to both acts of violence and theft on the high seas and acts of theft of intellectual property, especially via electronic means.

plural marriage: A marriage involving more than two partners. See also **polygamy**.

plurality: When counting votes, members in a group, etc., the amount that is higher than any other amount but does not reach above 50 percent.

political rights: Rights related to voting, holding office, and engaging in other elements of participation in government.

polygamy: Being married to more than one spouse at the same time. See also **plural marriage**.

positive law: The philosophy that rights and legal principles are actively created by people.

positive rights: Rights requiring the government to act in order to provide them.

precedent: A rule established in a prior legal case that becomes a standard for subsequent decisions.

prenuptial agreement: A contract entered into prior to marriage, especially one governing the distribution of property and other issues upon divorce.

presidential system: A system of government in which the executive branch is fully separate from the legislative branch.

private law: Law governing relationships between individuals.

pro se: When an individual argues on their own behalf in court without being represented by a lawyer.

proactive policing: A system of policing in which police actively seek to prevent crime before it occurs.

probation: A punishment involving supervision as an alternative to incarceration.

problem-oriented policing: A policing strategy focused on tackling public concerns to address the root causes of crime and disorder.

procedural law: Law laying out the rules for the functioning of legal systems, especially the processes of courts.

progressive tax: A system of taxation in which the tax rate increases for those who have a greater ability to pay.

proportional representation voting: An electoral system in which electoral results reflect the proportion of support each group or party has among voters.

proportionality: The degree to which a party's number of seats in the legislature reflects the share of votes it received in an election.

prosecutor: A lawyer responsible for bringing criminal actions to court and litigating them.

public law: Law dealing with relationships between people and the state as well as between parts of the state.

punishment: Penalties assessed in response to a determination of guilt or responsibility.

punitive damages: Money awarded to an injured party in a court case for the purpose of punishing the responsible party.

quasi-military policing: A model of policing in which police are organized in close relation to military command and use military structures and tactics.

racial profiling: When an individual is suspected of illegal behavior on the basis of race, ethnicity, religion, or national origin rather than due to their individual actions or evidence linking them to the crime.

ranked-choice voting: A voting method in which voters rank candidates in order of preference and low-ranked candidates are eliminated until a winner is determined. See also **alternative voting** and **instant runoff voting**.

reactive policing: A policing practice in which police wait for calls for service or reports of crime before acting.

reconciliation: Seeking to settle or resolve problems between people. In the justice context, this refers to practices designed to restore relationships and community trust in the wake of a crime rather than simply mete out punishment.

refugee: A person who has fled their home, usually traveling across national borders, due to threats to their safety.

regional trade agreement (RTA): A treaty between two or more countries defining rules regarding international commerce.

regressive tax: A system of taxation in which those with a lower ability to pay end up paying a larger share of their income in taxes

rehabilitation: Practices designed to restore a person to healthy or properly functioning. In the justice context, this refers to helping resolve whatever issues might have led an individual to commit crimes, such as by providing education or mental health treatment, so that they will not commit crimes in the future.

relative deprivation: A person's feeling that he or she has less resources or status than others do and less than she or he deserves.

representative democracy: A form of government in which people elect representatives to govern on their behalf. See also **democratic republic**.

republic: A form of government in which power is vested in a legal system rather than a single individual, such as a monarch.

restorative justice: An approach in which victims, offenders, and often community members work together to repair harm.

retention election: An election held after an official, usually a judge, has been appointed to office, in which voters determine whether the official will keep their position or be removed.

retribution: A punishment determined to be proportionate to the offense and administered via appropriate systems as a societal response to wrongdoing.

revenge: Actions taken to harm others in response to a grievance, usually outside of the justice system.

rule of law: A characteristic of legal systems in which law is written down, publicly available, and fairly applied.

sanctions: Penalties applied to instances of wrongdoing. Can also be used in a positive sense to refer to permission to engage in a course of action.

sans-papiers: Literally "without papers." Refers to migrants who do not have legal documentation permitting them to dwell or work where they live.

semi-presidential system: A system of government with two heads of state, one an elected president and the other a prime minister responsible to the legislature.

separation of powers: The division of government into branches, each with its own areas of responsibility.

sex: Biological characteristics determining whether an individual is male, female, or intersex, such as chromosomes, hormones, and physical features.

Shari'a: Islamic religious law.

show trial: A trial in which the outcome is predetermined. Used as a public warning to others.

single police structure: When a state has only one police force covering all aspects and areas of policing.

social control: Mechanisms for increasing conformity within society in terms of norms, rules, attitudes, and behavioral expectations.

social disorganization theory: The idea that crime occurs due to neighborhood characteristics, especially the inability to exercise social control over community members.

social structure: The arrangement of institutions that make up society

socialism: An economic system characterized by public or cooperative ownership of the means of production. Designed to ensure a more equal distribution of resources across society.

solicitor: A type of lawyer in common law systems specializing in advising clients.

sovereignty: The condition of having authority over one's own government and not being subject to any other foreign state.

stare decisis: Literally "let the decision stand." Refers to the practice of abiding by precedent in common law courts.

state: A set of institutions and personnel with centrally located control over a specific territory, including control over rule making and the legitimate use of violence.

state of exception: A situation in which normal rights and the rule of law are suspended and the state's power is extended.

state policing: A model of policing in which there is some, but limited, separation between military and law enforcement functions. May also refer to law enforcement agencies established by U.S. states.

stateless: Used to describe a person who is without the protection of any sovereign state, especially one who does not have citizenship anywhere.

statute: A written law.

substantive equality: Going beyond equal treatment to ensure equality of opportunity and to correct for past disadvantage.

substantive law: Law governing rights, responsibilities, crimes, punishments, and relationships but not procedures.

superstate: A large state formed by combining other states.

surveillance: Observation or monitoring.

taking: When the government seizes someone's private property for public use or the use of others, not as punishment for a crime or as a tax levied on people in general.

terrorism: The calculated use or threat of violence against civilians to further policy or ideological goals.

theocracy: A form of government in line with religious precepts in which the divine is considered the source of state power.

theocratic law: A system of law based on religious teachings and texts.

traditional law: A system of law based on custom and tradition.

traditional policing: A system of policing developed early in the history of policing in which reactive policing is primary.

tragedy of the commons: A situation in which individual exploitation of shared resources exceeds sustainable levels.

transitional justice: Mechanisms and processes used in the aftermath of war and/or significant human rights violations to help a society come to terms with its past.

transnational crime: Criminal acts that involve activity in or that impact more than one country. See also **cross-border crime**.

transnational policing: Police work that occurs across national borders.

trial by ordeal: A practice of determining guilt or innocence by subjecting the accused to a difficult or dangerous experience.

tribalism: When a society is organized in terms of tribes (groups of extended kin).

unitary state: A state in which the central government has control and subdivisions do not have separate power, in contrast to a **federation**.

United Nations: An international organization of countries tasked with encouraging international cooperation and maintaining international order.

universalism: The idea that there are principles, especially morals, that extend to the entire world.

vigilante: Someone who takes law into their own hands without any legal authority to do so.

war crimes: Acts that violate international laws concerning the fighting of wars.

warehousing: Long-term incarceration without rehabilitative services.

writ: A formal, written order issued by a court directing someone to do or stop doing something.

Works Cited

LEGAL AUTHORITIES

Airey v Ireland. 2 E.H.R.R. 305. (European Court of Human Rights, 1979).

Ashford v. Thornton. 1 Barnewell and Alderson's Reports 405. (Court of King's Bench, 1818).

Brown v. Plata. 563 U.S. 493. (2010).

Constitucion Politica de los Estados Unidos Mexicanos, art. 37.

Constitution of the Republic of Singapore, art. 120–141.

Convention on the Civil Aspects of International Child Abduction, Oct. 25, 1980, T.I.A.S. No. 11,670 (entered into force Dec. 1, 1983).

Convention on the Rights of the Child, Optional Protocol 1. May 25, 2000, A/RES/54/263.

Convention on the Rights of Persons with Disabilities, G.A. Res. 61/106, U.N. Doc. A/RES/611106 (Jan. 24, 2007).

Convention Relating to the Status of Refugees, opened for signature 28 July 1951, 189 UNTS 150 (entered into force 22 April 1954).

D.G.G. v. B.B.G., v. R.R.F. and S.B.R. 2012 No. A-5783–10T3 WL 2813824. (N.J. App., 2012).

Health (Regulation of Termination of Pregnancy) Act 2018 (Act No. 31/2018) (Ir.) https://data.oireachtas.ie/ie/oireachtas/act /2018/31/eng/enacted/a3118.pdf (last visited June 6, 2018).

International Criminal Court, Assembly of States Parties, Review Conference, The Crime of Aggression, ICC Doc. RC/Res.6 (June 11, 2010).

Judgment Concerning Article 750 of the Civil Code and Article 13 of the Constitution, 69 Minshu 2586 (Japan Sup. Ct., Dec. 16, 2015).

"Loi fédérale sur les armes, les accessoires d'armes et les munitions." L'Assemblée fédérale de la Confédération suisse.

Moore v. City of East Cleveland. 431 US 494. (1977).

Nardone v. United States. 308 U.S. 338. (1939).

Paris Agreement (adopted 12 December 2015, entered into force November 2016), UNTS Registration No. 54113.

Rhode Island General Laws § 11–6-2 (2012) (Adultery).

Rome Statute of the International Criminal Court. July 17, 1998, 2187 U.N.T.S. 90.RS 514.51. 1997.

Sean and David Goldman International Child Abduction Prevention and Return Act of 2014, 22 U.S.C. § 9101–9141.

State of Maine v. Mohammad Kargar. 679 A.2d 81. (Supreme Judicial Court of Maine, 1996).

UN Charter (1945).

UN Code of Conduct for Law Enforcement Officials, G.A. Res. 169, U.N. GAOR, 34th Sess., U.N.Doc. A/34/169 (Dec. 17, 1979) (available at https://www.ohchr.org/Documents /ProfessionalInterest/codeofconduct.pdf).

Universal Declaration of Human Rights, G.A. Res. 217A (III), U.N. Doc. A/810 (1948).

OTHER WORKS CITED

Achiron, Marilyn. 2005. *Nationality and Statelessness: A Handbook for Parliamentarians.* Lausanne, Switzerland: United Nations High Commissioner for Refugees.

Addati, Laura, Naomi Cassirer, and Katherine Glichrist. 2014. "Maternity and Paternity at Work: Law and Practice across the World." *International Labor Organization.* Report accessed 07/20/2018, (http://www.ilo.org/global /publications/ilo-bookstore/order-online/books/WCMS_ 242615/lang--en/index.htm).

Administrative Office of the U.S. Courts. 2017. "Judicial Facts and Figures 2017." *United States Courts.* Website accessed 02/10/2019, (https://www.uscourts.gov/statistics-reports /judicial-facts-and-figures-2017).

Aebi, Marcelo F., Mélanie M. Tiago, and Christine Burkhardt. 2017. "Annual Penal Statistics: SPACE I—Prison Populations." *Council of Europe.* Website accessed 07/05/2017, (http:// wp.unil.ch/space/files/2017/04/SPACE_I_2015_ FinalReport_161215_REV170425.pdf).

AFP-JIJI. 2017. "Philippines to Implement Family Planning Law in a Blow to the Church." *Japan Times.* Website accessed 07/18/2018, (https://web.archive.org/web/20171118040315 /https://www.japantimes.co.jp/news/2017/11/17/asia- pacific/social-issues-asia-pacific/philippines-implement- family-planning-law-blow-church/).

Agamben, Giorgio. 2005. *State of Exception.* Chicago: University of Chicago Press.

Agence France-Presse. 2013. "Pink Panther Thief among Escapees in Dramatic Prison Break." *Telegraph.* Website accessed 03/12/2018, (https://www.telegraph.co.uk/news/worldnews /europe/switzerland/10057627/Pink-Panther-thief-among- escapees-in-dramatic-prison-break.html).

———. 2016. "French Workers Win Legal Right to Avoid Checking Work Email Out-of-Hours." *Guardian.* Website accessed 08/06/2018, (https://www.theguardian.com/money/2016 /dec/31/french-workers-win-legal-right-to-avoid-checking- work-email-out-of-hours).

Aiken, Nevin T. 2010. "Learning to Live Together: Transitional Justice and Intergroup Reconciliation in Northern Ireland." *International Journal of Transitional Justice* 4(2): 166–88.

Allen, Peter, Darren Boyle, and Gareth Davies. 2018. "All £3.5million of Jewels Stolen in Armed Heist at the Paris Ritz Hotel Are Recovered after Bungling Thieves Dropped the Lot as They Fled." *Daily Mail.* Website accessed 03/13/2018, (http:// www.dailymail.co.uk/news/article-5260737/All-3– 5million-jewels-stolen-Paris-Ritz-raid-recovered.html).

Almazán, Marco A. 1999. "The Aztec States-Society: Roots of Civil Society and Social Capital." *Annals of the American Academy of Political and Social Science* 565:162–75.

Alper, Mariel, Alessandro Corda, and Kevin R. Reitz. 2016. "American Exceptionalism in Probation Supervision." *Robina Institute of Criminal Law and Criminal Justice*. Data brief accessed 02/04/2019, (https://robinainstitute.umn .edu/publications/data-brief-american-exceptionalism-probation-supervision).

Altheimer, Irshad. 2008. "Do Guns Matter? A Multi-Level Cross-National Examination of Gun Availability on Assault and Robbery Victimization." *Western Criminology Review* 9(2):9–32.

Altindag, Duha T. 2012. "Crime and Unemployment: Evidence from Europe." *International Review of Law and Economics* 32(1):145–57.

American Bar Association. 2018. "State Parties to the ICC." *ABA-ICC Project*. Website accessed 06/28/2018, (https://www .aba-icc.org/about-the-icc/states-parties-to-the-icc/).

Amnesty International. 2014. "Torture in 2014: 30 Years of Broken Promises." Report accessed 02/12/2018, (https://www .amnestyusa.org/files/act400042014en.pdf).

———. 2015. "'I'm Nothing But a Prisoner'—Qatar: Release the Poet, Mohammed al-Ajami." Website accessed 08/20/2018, (https://www.amnesty.org/download /Documents/MDE2227602015ENGLISH.PDF).

———. 2017. "Death Sentences and Executions, 2016." *Amnesty International*. Website accessed 01/21/2019, (https://www .amnestyusa.org/wp-content/uploads/2017/05/death_ penalty_2016_report_embargoed.pdf).

———. 2018a. "Amnesty International Report 2017/18: The State of the World's Human Rights." Report accessed 07/25/2018, (https://www.amnesty.org/download/Documents /POL1067002018ENGLISH.PDF).

———. 2018b. "Death Sentences and Executions, 2017." *Amnesty International*. Website accessed 01/21/2019, (https://www .amnesty.org/download/Documents/ACT5079552018 ENGLISH.PDF).

Anderson, Gerard F., and Peter Sotir Hussey. 2000. "Population Aging: A Comparison among Industrialized Countries." *Health Affairs* 2000(May/June):191–203.

Anderson, Michelle J. 2016. "Marital Rape Laws Globally: Rationales and Snapshots around the World." Pp. 177–88 in *Marital Rape: Consent, Marriage, and Social Change in Global Context*, edited by Kersti Yllö and M. Gabriela Torres. New York: Oxford University Press.

Anderson, Nick. 2016. "Texas University Gets $76 Million Each Year to Operate in Qatar, Contract Says." *Washington Post*. Website accessed 08/17/2018, (https://www .washingtonpost.com/news/grade-point/wp/2016/03/08 /texas-university-gets-76-million-each-year-to-operate-in-qatar-contract-says).

Anderson, Siwan. 2007. "The Economics of Dowry and Brideprice." *Journal of Economic Perspectives* 21(4):151–74.

Andreas, Peter, and Ethan Nadelmann. 2006. *Policing the Globe: Criminalization and Crime Control in International Relations*. Oxford, UK: Oxford University Press.

Arendt, Hannah. 1951. *The Origins of Totalitarianism*. New York: Harcourt Brace Jovanovich.

———. 1963. *Eichmann in Jerusalem: A Report on the Banality of Evil*. New York: Penguin Books.

Arthur, Paige. 2009. "How 'Transitions' Reshaped Human Rights: A Conceptual History of Transitional Justice." *Human Rights Quarterly* 31(2):321–67.

Ashwood, Daniel, Karen B. Farris, Shelly Campo, Mary L. Aquilino, and Mary Losch. 2011. "Unlocking the Condoms: The Effect on Sales and Theft." *Pharmacy Practice* (Granada) 9(1):44–47.

Asser, Seth M., and Rita Swan. 1998. "Child Fatalities from Religion-Motivated Medical Neglect." *Pediatrics* 101(4):625–29.

Austrian Embassy in Washington. n.d. "Austrian Citizenship." *Consular Services for Austrians in the U.S.* Website accessed 06/06/2018, (http://www.austria.org/citizenship/).

Avalos, Francisco. 1994. "An Overview of the Legal System of the Aztec Empire." *Law Library Journal* 86(2):259–76.

Awal, Noor Aziah Mohd. 2012. "Malaysia: What Lies Ahead?" Pp. 205–34 in *The Future of Child and Family Law: International Predictions*, edited by Elaine E. Sutherland. Cambridge, UK: Cambridge University Press.

Bach, Tracy. 2016. "Human Rights in a Climate Changed World: The Impact of Cop21, Nationally Determined Contributions, and National Courts." *Vermont Law Review* 40(3):561–95.

Baderin, Mashood. [2006] 2017. "Effective Legal Representation in 'Shari'ah' Courts as a Means of Addressing Human Rights Concerns in the Islamic Criminal Justice System of Muslim States." Pp. 135–67 in *Issues in Islamic Law*, vol. 2, edited by Mashood Baderin. London, UK: Routledge.

Bain News Service. 1908. "New York City Police Dept. Activities: Information Bureau at HQ—4 Men at Work." Bain Collection, Library of Congress, Washington, DC. LOT 10920.

Baker, Al. 2015. "U.S. Police Leaders, Visiting Scotland, Get Lessons on Avoiding Deadly Force." *New York Times*. Website accessed 03/14/2018, (https://www.nytimes.com/2015 /12/12/nyregion/us-police-leaders-visiting-scotland-get-lessons-on-avoiding-deadly-force.html).

Barbagli, Marzio, and Laura Sartori. 2004. "Law Enforcement Activities in Italy." *Journal of Modern Italian Studies* 9(2):161–85.

Barnett, Corey. 2018. "Jainist Monk Gives Support for India's Landmark Euthanasia Legalization." *World Religion News*. Website accessed 08/03/2018, (https://www.worldreligion news.com/religion-news/jainist-monk-gives-support-indias-landmark-euthanasia-legalization).

Barr, Caelainn. 2017. "Inequality Index: Where Are the World's Most Unequal Countries?" *Guardian*. Website accessed 08/06/2018, (https://www.theguardian.com/inequality /datablog/2017/apr/26/inequality-index-where-are-the-worlds-most-unequal-countries).

Bar Standards Board. n.d. "When Might I Need a Barrister?" Website accessed 01/28/2019, (https://www.barstandards board.org.uk/using-a-barrister/when-might-i-need-a-barrister/).

Bartlett, Jamie. 2017. "Return of the City-State." *Aeon*. Website accessed 06/06/2018, (https://aeon.co/essays/the-end-of-a-world-of-nation-states-may-be-upon-us).

Bartlett, Katharine T. 1995. "Tradition, Change, and the Idea of Progress in Feminist Legal Thought." *Wisconsin Law Review* 1995(2):303–43.

Barton, Roy Franklin. 1919. "Ifugao Law." *University of California Publications in American Archeology and Ethnology* 15(1):1–186.

Bassiouni, Cherif. 2014. "Is Amanda Knox Extraditable from the United States to Italy?" *Oxford University Press Blog*. Website accessed 02/27/2015, (https://blog.oup.com/2014 /04/is-amanda-knox-extraditable-from-the-united-states-to-italy/).

Bauböck, Rainer, Iseult Honohan, and Maarten Vink. 2018. "How Citizenship Laws Differ: A Global Comparison." *GLOBALCIT, Florence, Italy*. Delmi Policy Brief no. 2018:9. Brief accessed 02/26/2019, (http://globalcit.eu

/wp-content/uploads/2018/11/Policy_Brief_Delmi_
GLOBALCIT.pdf).

Bava, Julian, and Kiel Ireland. 2016. "The American
Servicemembers' Protection Act: Pathways to and
Constraints on U.S. Cooperation with the International
Criminal Court." *Eyes on the ICC* 12(1):1–29.

Bayley, David H. 1975. "The Police and Political Development in
Europe." Pp. 328–79 in *The Formation of the National States
of Europe*, edited by Charles Tilly. Princeton, NJ: Princeton
University Press.

———. 1990. *Patterns of Policing: A Comparative International
Analysis*. New Brunswick, NJ: Rutgers University Press.

BBC Monitoring. 2016. "Who Are Islamic 'Morality Police'?" *BBC
News*. Website accessed 02/04/2019, (https://www.bbc.com
/news/world-middle-east-36101150).

BBC News. 2003. "US Blocks Aid over ICC Row." Website accessed
06/20/2018, (http://news.bbc.co.uk/2/hi/americas/3035296
.stm).

———. 2009. "Nigeria Police Hold 'Robber' Goat." Website accessed
01/08/2017, (http://news.bbc.co.uk/2/hi/africa/7846822.stm).

———. 2013. "Defamation Act 2013 Aims to Improve Libel Laws."
Website accessed 07/27/2018, (https://www.bbc.com/news
/uk-25551640).

———. 2016a. "Anders Breivik: Just How Cushy Are Norwegian
Prisons?" *BBC News Magazine*. Website accessed
06/29/2017, (http://www.bbc.com/news/magazine-
35813470).

———. 2016b. "Former LRA Child Soldier Dominic Ongwen and
the Quest for Justice." Website accessed 09/04/2018,
(https://www.bbc.com/news/world-africa-38207086).

———. 2016c. "Qatar Poet Mohammed al-Ajami Released after
Pardon." Website accessed 08/20/2018, (https://www.bbc
.com/news/world-middle-east-35830372).

———. 2017. "Lese-Majeste Explained: How Thailand Forbids Insult
of Its Royalty." Website accessed 07/04/2018, (https://www
.bbc.com/news/world-asia-29628191).

———. 2018. "Chevron Wins Ecuador Rainforest 'Oil Dumping'
Case." Website accessed 01/28/2019, (https://www.bbc.com
/news/world-latin-america-45455984).

Beehner, Lionel. 2006. "Iran's Ethnic Groups." *Council on Foreign
Relations*. Website accessed 08/23/2018, (https://www.cfr
.org/backgrounder/irans-ethnic-groups).

Belur, Jyoti. 2010. *Permission to Shoot? Police Use of Deadly Force in
Democracies*. London, UK: Springer.

Benko, Jessica. 2015a. "Prison Planet." *New York Times Magazine*.
Website accessed 04/01/2015, (http://www.nytimes.com
/2015/03/29/magazine/prison-planet.html).

———. 2015b. "The Radical Humanness of Norway's Halden Prison."
New York Times Magazine. Website accessed 05/04/2015,
(https://www.nytimes.com/2015/03/29/magazine/the-
radical-humaneness-of-norways-halden-prison.html).

Bentham, Jeremy. 1843. *The Works of Jeremy Bentham*, vol. 4.
Edinburgh, UK: William Tait.

Berman, Eric G., Keith Krause, Emile LeBrun, and Glenn McDonald.
2007. *Small Arms Survey 2007: Guns and the City*.
Cambridge, UK: Cambridge University Press.

Berman, Paul Schiff. 2005. "From International Law to Law and
Globalization." *Columbia Journal of Transnational Law*
43(2):485–556.

Beydoun, Nasser M., and Jennifer Baum. 2012. *The Glass Palace:
Illusions of Freedom and Democracy in Qatar*. New York:
Algora Publishing.

Bilchitz, David. 2016. "Corporations and the Limits of State-
Based Models for Protecting Fundamental Rights in
International Law." *Indiana Journal of Global Legal Studies*
23(1):143–70.

Bingham, Lord. 2007. "The Rule of Law." *Cambridge Law Journal*
66(1):67–85.

Blackburn, Carole. 2009. "Differentiating Indigenous Citizenship:
Seeking Multiplicity in Rights, Identity, and Sovereignty in
Canada." *American Ethnologist* 36(1):66–78.

Blackwell, Christopher W. 2003. "Athenian Democracy: A Brief
Overview." *Stoa Consortium for Electronic Publication in
the Humanities*. Website accessed 06/05/2018, (http://www
.stoa.org/projects/demos/article_democracy_overview?
page=all).

Blair, Marianne, and Merle H. Weiner. 2005. "Resolving Parental
Custody Disputes—A Comparative Exploration." *Family
Law Quarterly* 39(2):247–66.

Blevins, Ethan. 2016. "A Fixed Meaning of 'Religion' in the First
Amendment." *Willamette Law Review* 53(1):1–32.

Bogos, Kristina. 2016. "American Universities in a Gulf of
Hypocrisy." *New York Times*. Website accessed 08/16/2018,
(https://www.nytimes.com/2016/12/15/opinion/american-
univisities-nyu-georgetown-in-a-gulf-of-hypocrisy.html).

Bowler, Natasha. 2015. "When Bahrain Says You're Not Bahraini
Anymore." *Foreign Policy*. Website accessed 06/06/2018,
(http://foreignpolicy.com/2015/08/18/when-bahrain-says-
youre-not-bahraini-anymore/).

Boyce, Bret. 2018. "Obscenity and Nationalism: Constitutional
Freedom of Sexual Expression in Comparative
Perspective." *Columbia Journal of Transnational Law*
56(3):681–749.

Bracey, Dorothy. 2006. *Exploring Law and Culture*. Long Grove, IL:
Waveland Press.

Bracha, Mor, and Yehonatan Kamil. 2016. "Hamdinah shma sof
lehitdechat nash llo rashon" [The state puts an end to the use
of weapons without a license]. *Calcalist*. Website accessed
03/15/2018, (https://www.calcalist.co.il/articles/0,7340,L-
3704739,00.html).

Brennan Center for Justice. 2015. "Judicial Selection: Significant
Figures." *New York University School of Law*. Website
accessed 01/29/2018, (https://www.brennancenter.org
/rethinking-judicial-selection/significant-figures).

Breyer, Stephen. 2018. "America's Courts Can't Ignore the World."
Atlantic. Website accessed 01/28/2019, (https://www
.theatlantic.com/magazine/archive/2018/10/stephen-
breyer-supreme-court-world/568360/).

Bring Sean Home Foundation. 2012. "Nine Days in December: 'The
Christmas Miracle'" *Bring Sean Home Foundation*. Website
accessed 07/24/2017, (http://bringseanhome.org/goldman-
case/nine-days-in-december/).

Broadhurst, Roderic G. 2017. "Cybercrime: Thieves, Swindlers,
Bandits and Privateers in Cyberspace." *SSRN*. Paper
accessed 05/25/2018, (https://papers.ssrn.com/sol3/papers
.cfm?abstract_id=3009574).

Brogden, Mike, and Preeti Nijhar. 2005. *Community Policing:
National and International Models and Approaches*. Devon,
UK: Willan Publishing.

Brölmann, Catherine, and Janne Nijman. 2017. "Legal Personality as
a Fundamental Concept of International Law." In *Concepts
for International Law: Contributions to Disciplinary
Thought*, edited by Jean d'Aspremont and Sahib Singh.
London, UK: Edward Elgar.

Bromwich, Rebecca. 2018. "(Where Is) the Tipping Point for
Governmental Regulation of Canadian Lawyers? Perhaps It
Is in Paradise: Critically Assessing Regulation of Lawyer
Involvement with Money Laundering after *Canada*

(Attorney General) v Federation of Law Societies of Canada." *Manitoba Law Journal* 41(4):1–26.

Brown, Chris. 1997. "Universal Human Rights: A Critique." *International Journal of Human Rights* 1(2):41–65.

Buckley, Chris. 2016. "Chinese Jews of Ancient Lineage Huddle under Pressure." *New York Times.* Website accessed 08/03/2018, (https://www.nytimes.com/2016/09/25/world/asia/china-kaifeng-jews.html).

Budiani-Saberi, Deborah A., and Francis L. Delmonico. 2008. "Organ Trafficking and Transplant Tourism: A Commentary on the Global Realities." *American Journal of Transplantation* 8(5):925–29.

Bullock, Karen, and Nick Tilley. 2003. *Crime Reduction and Problem-Oriented Policing.* Abingdon, UK: Routledge.

Bullock, Katherine. 2002. *Rethinking Muslim Women and the Veil: Challenging Historical and Modern Stereotypes.* Herndon, VA: International Institute of Islamic Thought.

Bullough, Vern L. 2004. "Age of Consent: A Historical Overview." *Journal of Psychology & Human Sexuality* 16(2/3): 25–42.

Burge, Mark Edwin. 2016. "Apple Pay, Bitcoin, and Consumers: The ABCs of Future Public Payments Law." *Hastings Law Journal* 67(6):1493–549.

Burke, Jason. 2019a. "African Nations Call for Recount in DRC Election." *Guardian.* Website accessed 01/28/2918, (https://www.theguardian.com/world/2019/jan/13/african-nations-call-for-recount-in-drc-election).

———. 2019b. "DRC Electoral Fraud Fears Rise as Internet Shutdown Continues." *Guardian.* Website accessed 01/28/2019, (https://www.theguardian.com/world/2019/jan/01/drc-electoral-fears-rise-as-internet-shutdown-continues).

Burnet, Jennie. 2011. "(In)Justice: Truth, Reconciliation, and Revenge in Rwanda's *Gacaca.*" Pp. 95–118 in *Transitional Justice: Global Mechanisms and Local Realities after Genocide and Mass Violence,* edited by Alexander Laban Hinton. New Brunswick, NJ: Rutgers University Press.

Buti, Antonio. 2004. "The Removal Of Indigenous Children from Their Families." *University of Western Sydney Law Review* 8(1):126–53.

Calavita, Kitty. 1998. "Immigration, Law, and Marginalization in a Global Economy: Notes from Spain." *Law & Society Review* 32(3):529–66.

California Department of Corrections and Rehabilitation. 2006. "Prison Overcrowding Photos." *California Department of Corrections and Rehabilitation: News.* Website accessed August 27, 2010, (https://web.archive.org/web/20100731061702/http://www.cdcr.ca.gov/News/prisonovercrowding.html).

Cambell, Colm, and Fionnuala Ní Aoláin. 2002. "Local Meets Global: Transitional Justice in Northern Ireland." *Fordham Internationa Law Journal* 26(4):871–92.

Capell, Heather Lynn. 1998. "After the Glass Has Shattered: A Comparative Analysis of Orthodox Jewish Divorce in the United States and Israel." *Texas International Law Journal* 33(2):331–47.

Carbon Dioxide Information Analysis Center. 2018. "CO2 Emissions (Metric Tons per Capita)." World Bank. Website accessed 09/26/2018, (https://data.worldbank.org/indicator/EN.ATM.CO2E.PC?view=chart).

Carey, Christopher. 2012. *Trials from Classical Athens.* 2nd ed. London, UK: Routledge.

Carey, Corinne, Sarah Tofte, and Jamie Fellner. 2007. "No Easy Answers: Sex Offender Laws in the US." *Human Rights Watch.* Website accessed 05/10/2018, (https://www.hrw.org/report/2007/09/11/no-easy-answers/sex-offender-laws-us).

Carlsen, Audrey, and Sahil Chinoy. 2018. "How to Buy a Gun in 15 Countries." *New York Times.* Website accessed 03/15/2018, (https://www.nytimes.com/interactive/2018/03/02/world/international-gun-laws.html).

Carlsson, Ulla. 2016. "Freedom of Expression and the Media in a Time of Uncertainty: A Brief Introduction." Pp. 9–18 in *Freedom of Expression and Media in Transition: Studies and Reflections in the Digital Age,* edited by Ulla Carlsson. Göteborg, Sweden: Nordicom and UNESCO.

Carroll, Aengus, and Lucas Ramón Mendos. 2017. "State-Sponsored Homophobia 2017: A World Survey of Sexual Orientation Laws: Criminalisation, Protection and Recognition." International Lesbian, Gay, Bisexual, Trans and Intersex Association. Website accessed 07/20/2018, (https://ilga.org/maps-sexual-orientation-laws).

Carter, Robert F. 1964. "The Amazing Aztec Jurisprudence." *American Bar Association Journal* 50(7):667–69.

Cates, James A. 2014. *Serving the Amish: A Cultural Guide for Professionals.* Baltimore, MD: Johns Hopkins University Press.

Center for Reproductive Rights. 2010. "The Right to Contraceptive Information and Services for Women and Adolescents." *United Nations Population Fund.* Briefing paper accessed 07/18/2018, (https://www.unfpa.org/sites/default/files/resource-pdf/Contraception.pdf).

Central Intelligence Agency. n.d.-a. "Field Listing: Government Type." *CIA World Factbook.* Website accessed 06/11/2018, (https://www.cia.gov/LIBRARY/publications/the-world-factbook/fields/299.html).

———. n.d.-b. "Field Listing: Legal System." *CIA World Factbook.* Website accessed 07/03/2018, (https://www.cia.gov/LIBRARY/publications/the-world-factbook/fields/308.html).

———. n.d.-c. "Field Listing: Military Service Age and Obligation." *CIA World Factbook.* Website accessed 03/12/2018, (https://www.cia.gov/LIBRARY/publications/the-world-factbook/fields/333.html).

Centre for Human Rights. 1997. "International Human Rights Standards for Law Enforcement: A Pocket Book on Human Rights for the Police." *United Nations Office of the High Commissioner for Human Rights.* Document accessed 03/07/2018, (https://www.un.org/ruleoflaw/blog/document/international-human-rights-standards-for-law-enforcement-a-pocket-book-on-human-rights-for-the-police/).

Chambers, Robert. 1869. *The Book of Days: A Miscellany of Popular Antiquities in Connection with the Calendar.* London, UK: W. and R. Chambers.

Chambers and Partners. 2019. "What Kind of Lawyer Do You Want to Be?" *Chambers Student.* Website accessed 01/28/2019, (https://www.chambersstudent.co.uk/where-to-start/what-kind-of-lawyer-do-you-want-to-be).

Chambliss, William J., and Elizabeth Williams. 2012. "Transnational Organized Crime and Social Sciences Myths." Pp. 52–64 in *Routledge Handbook of Transnational Organized Crime,* edited by Felia Allum and Stan Gilmour. Abingdon, UK: Routledge.

Chan, Nicholas. 2019. "Europe Rights Court Orders Italy to Compensate Amanda Knox for Human Rights Violations." *Jurist.* Website accessed 01/28/2019, (https://www.jurist.org/news/2019/01/europe-rights-court-orders-italy-to-compensate-amanda-knox-for-human-rights-violations/).

Chan, Sewell. 2017. "Sex for Women after 50 Is Important after All, European Court Rules." *New York Times*. Website accessed 03/06/2018, (https://www.nytimes.com/2017/07/25/world /europe/sex-after-50-portugal-european-court.html).

Chawla, Sandeep, Angela Me, and Thibault le Pichon. 2009. "Global Report on Trafficking in Persons." *United Nations Office on Drugs and Crime*. Report accessed 05/23/2018, (http://www .unodc.org/documents/Global_Report_on_TIP.pdf).

Chen, Alice, Emily Oster, and Heidi Williams. 2016. "Why Is Infant Mortality Higher in the United States Than in Europe?" *American Economic Journal: Economic Policy* 8(2):89–124.

Chen, Elsa Y. 2008. "Impacts of 'Three Strikes and You're Out' on Crime Trends in California and Throughout the United States." *Journal of Contemporary Criminal Justice* 24(4):345–70.

Cheslow, Joshua F. 2013. "The Future of Law: Four Practice Areas on the Horizon." *New Jersey Lawyer* 283(August): 60–65.

Chevron Corporation. 2018. "History." Website accessed 06/19/2018, (https://www.chevron.com/about/history).

Child Rights International Network. 2017. "The Minimum Age of Criminal Responsibility." Website accessed 01/21/2019, (https://home.crin.org/issues/deprivation-of-liberty /minimum-age-of-criminal-responsibility).

Child Soldiers International. n.d. "Child Soldiers World Index." Website accessed 08/28/2018, (https:// childsoldiersworldindex.org/).

Chothia, Farouk. 2015. "Profile: Dominic Ongwen of Uganda's LRA." *BBC News*. Website accessed 09/04/2018, (https://www.bbc .com/news/world-africa-30709581).

Choudhury, Cyra Akila. 2015. "Beyond Culture: Human Rights Universalisms versus Religious and Cultural Relativism in the Activism for Gender Justice." *Berkeley Journal of Gender, Law & Justice* 30(2):226–67.

Chuang, Janie A. 2017. "Using Global Migration Law to Prevent Human Trafficking." *American Journal of International Law Unbound* 111:147–52.

Chung, Jean. 2018. "Felony Disenfranchisement: A Primer." *Sentencing Project*. Website accessed 02/04/2019, (https:// www.sentencingproject.org/publications/felony- disenfranchisement-a-primer/).

Cismas, Ioana. 2014. *Religious Actors and International Law*. Oxford, UK: Oxford University Press.

CITI Program. n.d. "Final Rule Resources." *Collaborative Institutional Training Initiative*. Website accessed 06/28/2018, (https://about.citiprogram.org/en/final-rule- resources/).

City of London. 2018. "About the City." Website accessed 06/11 /2018, (https://www.cityoflondon.gov.uk/about-the-city /Pages/default.aspx).

Clark, Phil. 2007. "Hybridity, Holism and Traditional Justice: The Case of the Gacaca Courts in Post-Genocide Rwanda." *George Washington International Law Review* 39(4): 765–837.

———. 2008. "Establishing a Conceptual Framework: Six Key Transitional Justice Themes." Pp. 191–205 in *After Genocide: Transitional Justice, Post-Conflict Reconstruction and Reconciliation in Rwanda and Beyond*, edited by Phil Clark and Zachary Kaufman. London, UK: Hurst and Company.

Clarke, Ronald V., and Patricia M. Harris. 1992. "Auto Theft and Its Prevention." *Crime and Justice* 16:1–54.

Clark-Flory, Tracy. 2018. "It's 2018 and Sweden Finally Recognizes Sex without Consent as Rape." *Jezebel*. Website accessed 08/06/2018, (https://jezebel.com/its-2018-and-sweden- finally-recognizes-sex-without-cons-1826258513).

Cmiel, Kenneth. 2004. "The Recent History of Human Rights." *American Historical Review* 109(1):117–35.

Cohan, John Allan. 2010. "Honor Killings and the Cultural Defense." *California Western International Law Journal* 40(2):177– 252.

Coker, Margaret. 2018. "How Guardianship Laws Still Control Saudi Women." *New York Times*. Website accessed 07/13/2018, (https://www.nytimes.com/2018/06/22/world/middleeast /saudi-women-guardianship.html).

Colbran, Nicola. 2010. "Realities and Challenges in Realising Freedom of Religion or Belief in Indonesia." *International Journal of Human Rights* 14(5):678–704.

Committee on Obstetric Practice. 2017. "Methods for Estimating the Due Date: Committee Opinion no. 700." *American College of Obstetricians and Gynecologists*. Report accessed 07/17/2018, (https://www.acog.org/Clinical-Guidance-and-Publications /Committee-Opinions/Committee-on-Obstetric-Practice /Methods-for-Estimating-the-Due-Date).

Consulado General de México en El Paso. 2018. "Requistos para Obtener la Declaratoria de Nacionalidad Mexicana por Nacimiento." *Secretaría de Relaciones Exteriores*. Website accessed 06/06/2018, (https://consulmex.sre.gob.mx /elpaso/index.php/2016–03–16–20–44–26/2016–03– 16–21–00–22).

Corda, Alessandro, and Michelle S. Phelps. 2017. "American Exceptionalism in Community Supervision." *APPA- Perspectives* 41(2):20–27.

Cordner, Gary W. 2014. "Community Policing." Pp. 432–49 in *The Oxford Handbook of Police and Policing*, edited by Michael D. Reisig and Robert J. Kane. Oxford, UK: Oxford University Press.

Corey, Allison, and Sandra F. Joireman. 2004. "Retributive Justice: The *Gacaca* Courts in Rwanda." *African Affairs* 103(410):73–89.

Cornell, Stephen. 2015. "Processes of Native Nationhood: The Indigenous Politics of Self-Government." *International Indigenous Policy Journal* 6(4):1–27.

Cornell Law School. n.d. "8 U.S. Code § 1409—Children Born out of Wedlock." *Legal Information Institute*. Website accessed 07/13/2018, (https://www.law.cornell.edu/uscode/text/8 /1409).

Crane, Megan, Laura Nirider, and Steven A. Drizin. 2016. "The Truth about Juvenile False Confessions." *Insights on Law & Society* 2(Winter):10–15.

Crilly, Rob. 2012. "Pakistan Children 'Grow Up Faster Than Others Because of Spicy Food.'" *Telegraph*. Website accessed 07/05/2017, (http://www.telegraph.co.uk/news/newstopics /howaboutthat/9128476/Pakistan-children-grow-up-faster- than-others-because-of-spicy-food.html).

Criminal Justice Policy Group. 2000. "Review of Monetary Penalties in New Zealand." *Ministry of Justice, New Zealand*. Report accessed 07/12/2011, (https://web.archive.org /web/20130207123549/http://justice.govt.nz/publications /global-publications/r/review-of-monetary-penalties-in- new-zealand).

Cumming-Bruce, Nick. 2018. "Taking Migrant Children from Parents Is Illegal, U.N. Tells U.S." *New York Times*. Website accessed 07/25/2018, (https://www.nytimes.com/2018/06/05/world /americas/us-un-migrant-children-families.html).

Currie, Elliott. 1968. "Crimes without Criminals: Witchcraft and Its Control in Renaissance Europe." *Law & Society Review* 3(1):7–32.

DaBell, Bijan. 2013. "Iran Minorities 2: Ethnic Diversity." *Iran Primer: United States Institute of Peace*. Website accessed 08/23/2018, (https://iranprimer.usip.org/blog/2013/sep/03/iran-minorities-2-ethnic-diversity).

Dallaire, Roméo. 2011. *They Fight Like Soldiers, They Die Like Children*. London, UK: Walker Books.

Daly, Erin. 2002. "Between Punitive and Reconstructive Justice: The Gacaca Courts in Rwanda." *New York University Journal of International Law and Politics* 34(2):355–96.

Damme, Catherine. 1978. "Infanticide: The World of an Infant under Law." *Medical History* 22(1):1–24.

Davies, Aled. 2017. *The City of London and Social Democracy: The Political Economy of Finance in Britain, 1959–1979*. Oxford, UK: Oxford University Press.

Davies, Sara E. 2010. "Reproductive Health as a Human Right: A Matter of Access or Provision?" *Journal of Human Rights* 9(4):387–408.

Davis, Lois M., Robert Bozick, Jennifer L. Steele, Jessica Saunders, and Jeremy N. V. Miles. 2013. *Evaluating the Effectiveness of Correctional Education: A Meta-Analysis of Programs That Provide Education to Incarcerated Adults*. Santa Monica, CA: RAND Corporation.

Dearth, Megan H. 2011. "Defending the 'Indefensible': Replacing Ethnocentrism with a Native American Cultural Defense." *American Indian Law Review* 35(2):621–60.

Deflem, Mathieu. 2005. "History of International Police Cooperation." Pp. 795–98 in *Encyclopedia of Criminology*, edited by Richard A. Wright and J. Mitchell Miller. New York: Routledge.

Delmonico, Francis L. 2008. "The Development of the Declaration of Istanbul on Organ Trafficking and Transplant Tourism." *Nephrology Dialysis Transplantation* 23(11):3381–2.

DePalma, Donald. 2016. "A Slippery Slope: Measuring the Quality of Extra Virgin Olive Oil and Translation." *Common Sense Advisory*. Website accessed 03/19/2018, (https://web.archive.org/web/20170202050832/http://www.commonsenseadvisory.com/Default.aspx?Contenttype=ArticleDetAD&tabID=63&Aid=36459&moduleId=390).

Department of Justice and Constitutional Development. n.d. "African Charter on Human and Peoples' Rights." *Department of Justice and Constitutional Development, South Africa*. Website accessed 05/10/2018, (http://www.justice.gov.za/policy/african%20charter/africancharter.htm).

Department of Official Language. 2015. "Languages Included in the Eighth Schedule of the Indian Constitution." *Government of India*. Website accessed 03/27/2018, (http://rajbhasha.gov.in/en/languages-included-eighth-schedule-indian-constitution).

De Schutter, Olivier, and Julie Ringelheim. 2008. "Ethnic Profiling: A Rising Challenge for European Human Rights Law." *Modern Law Review* 71(3):358–84.

Determann, Lothar, and Robert Sprague. 2011. "Intrusive Monitoring: Employee Privacy Expectations Are Reasonable in Europe, Destroyed in the United States." *Berkeley Technology Law Journal* 26(2):979–1036.

Deutsche Welle. 2017. "Spaghetti Monster Goes to Germany's Constitutional Court." Website accessed 08/03/2018, (https://www.dw.com/en/spaghetti-monster-goes-to-germanys-constitutional-court/a-40359916).

DeVore, Veronica. 2017. "Regulating Firearms in Gun-Loving Switzerland." *Swiss Broadcasting Corporation*. Website accessed 03/14/2018, (https://www.swissinfo.ch/eng/society/bearing-arms_how-gun-loving-switzerland-regulates-its-firearms/43573832).

Diaz, Alonso. 2016. "Federal Appeals Court Rules for Chevron in Ecuador Pollution Case." *Jurist*. Website accessed 01/04/2018, (http://www.jurist.org/paperchase/2016/08/federal-appeals-court-rules-for-chevron-in-ecuador-pollution-case.php).

Dienst, Jonathan, Rich McHugh, Nancy Ing, and Michelle Neubert. 2016. "NYPD Embeds Intelligence Officers in 13 Cities Overseas Since 9/11." *NBC4 New York*. Website accessed 03/12/2018, (https://www.nbcnewyork.com/news/local/NYPD-Stationed-Overseas-Increasing-Global-Terror-Threat-401186455.html).

DiFonzo, J. Herbie, and Ruth C. Stern. 2007. "Addicted to Fault: Why Divorce Reform Has Lagged in New York." *Pace Law Review* 27(4):559–603.

Dinan, Desmond. 2014. *Europe Recast: A History of the European Union*. Boulder, CO: Lynne Rienner Publishers.

Dixon, Jo, and Alan J. Lizotte. 1987. "Gun Ownership and the 'Southern Subculture of Violence.'" *American Journal of Sociology* 93(2):383–405.

Dodd, Vikram. 2017. "Majority of Police Officers Are Prepared to Carry Guns, Survey Finds." *Guardian*. Website accessed 03/14/2018, (https://www.theguardian.com/uk-news/2017/sep/22/one-in-three-uk-officers-want-all-police-to-carry-guns-survey-finds).

Donnelly, Jack. 2013. *Universal Human Rights in Theory and Practice*. 3rd ed. Ithaca, NY: Cornell University Press.

Douglas, Lawrence. 2005. *The Memory of Judgment: Making Law and History in the Trials of the Holocaust*. New Haven, CT: Yale University Press.

Drumbl, Mark. 2012. *Reimagining Child Soldiers*. Oxford, UK: Oxford University Press.

———. 2015. "The Ongwen Trial at the ICC: Tough Questions on Child Soldiers." *OpenDemocracy*. Website accessed 09/04/2018, (https://www.opendemocracy.net/openglobalrights/mark-drumbl/ongwen-trial-at-icc-tough-questions-on-child-soldiers).

Du Mont, Janice, and Deborah White. 2007. "The Uses and Impacts of Medico-Legal Evidence in Sexual Assault Cases: A Global Review." *World Health Organization*. Report accessed 02/04/2019, (http://apps.who.int/iris/bitstream/10665/43795/1/9789241596046_eng.pdf).

Duncan, Martha Grace. 2017. "What Not to Do When Your Roommate Is Murdered In Italy: Amanda Knox, Her 'Strange' Behavior, and the Italian Legal System." *Harvard Journal of Law & Gender* 41:1–78.

Ebrahimi, Seyed Nasrollah. 2005. "Child Custody (Hizanat) under Iranian Law: An Analytical Discussion." *Family Law Quarterly* 39(2):459–76.

Eco, Umberto. 1995. "Ur-Fascism." *New York Review of Books*. Website accessed 06/01/2018, (http://pegc.us/archive/Articles/eco_ur-fascism.pdf).

Electoral Knowledge Network. 2018a. "Comparative Data." *Administration and Cost of Election Project*. Website accessed 06/05/2018, (http://aceproject.org/epic-en).

———. 2018b. "Voting from Abroad: Cape Verde." *Administration and Cost of Elections Project*. Website accessed 05/31/2018, (http://aceproject.org/ace-en/topics/va/annex/country-case-studies/cape-verde-a-large-diaspora-and-low-turnout-by).

Ellison, Christopher G. 1991. "An Eye for an Eye? A Note on the Southern Subculture of Violence Thesis." *Social Forces* 69(4):1223–39.

EMCDDA (European Monitoring Centre for Drugs and Drug Addiction). n.d.-a. "The EU Drugs Strategy (2013–20) and

Its Action Plan (2013–16)." *European Monitoring Centre for Drugs and Drug Addiction.* Website accessed 05/10/2018, (http://www.emcdda.europa.eu/topics/pods/eu-drugs-strategy-2013–20_en).

———. n.d.-b. "Penalties for Drug Offences in Europe at a Glance." *European Monitoring Centre for Drugs and Drug Addiction.* Website accessed 05/10/2018, (http://www.emcdda.europa.eu/topics/law/penalties-at-a-glance).

Emens, Elizabeth F. 2007. "Changing Name Changing: Framing Rules and the Future of Marital Names." *University of Chicago Law Review* 74(3):761–863.

Emsley, Clive. 2014. *The English Police: A Political and Social History.* 2nd ed. London; UK: Routledge.

Engel, David M. 2005. "Globalization and the Decline of Legal Consciousness: Torts, Ghosts, and Karma in Thailand." *Law & Social Inquiry* 30(3):469–514.

———. 2009. "Landscapes of the Law: Injury, Remedy, and Social Change in Thailand." *Law & Society Review* 43(1):61–94.

Epps, Valerie, and Lorie Graham. 2011. *International Law: Examples and Explanations.* New York: Wolters Kluwer.

Epstein, Jack. 1995. "Ecuadorans Wage Legal Battle against US Oil Company." *Christian Science Monitor.* Website accessed 06/19/2018, (https://www.csmonitor.com/1995/0912/12101.html).

Estin, Ann Laquer. 2009. "Unofficial Family Law." *Iowa Law Review* 94(2):449–80.

Estival, Dominique, and Alastair Pennycook. 2011. "L'Académie Française and Anglophone Language Ideologies." *Language Policy* 10(4):325–41.

Eubanks, Virginia. 2017. *Automating Inequality: How High-Tech Tools Profile, Police, and Punish the Poor.* New York: St. Martin's Press.

European Citizens' Initiative. 2018. "FAQ on the EU Competences and the European Commission Powers." *European Commission.* Website accessed 06/06/2018, (http://ec.europa.eu/citizens-initiative/public/competences/faq).

European Union. 2018. "About the EU." Website accessed 06/06/2018, (https://europa.eu/european-union/about-eu_en).

European University Institute. 2018. "Bahrain: Bahraini Citizenship Act—1963." *Gulf Labour Markets and Migration.* Website accessed 06/06/2018, (http://gulfmigration.eu/bahrain-bahraini-citizenship-act-1963–2/).

Evans, Sandra S., and Joseph E. Scott. 1984. "The Seriousness of Crime Cross-Culturally: The Impact of Religiosity." *Criminology* 22(1):39–59.

Ewald, Alec C., and Brandon Rottinghaus. 2009. *Criminal Disenfranchisement in an International Perspective.* Cambridge, UK: Cambridge University Press.

Ewulum, Boniface, and Ikenga K. E. Oraegbunam. 2014. "Ethnic Profiling in Terrorist Investigation in Nigeria: A Violation of the Fundamental Right of Freedom from Discrimination." *Academia.* Paper accessed 02/04/2019, (https://www.academia.edu/26126352/ETHNIC_PROFILING_IN_TERRORIST_INVESTIGATION_IN_NIGERIA_A_VIOLATION_OF_THE_FUNDAMENTAL_RIGHT_OF_FREEDOM_FROM_DISCRIMINATION).

Fadiman, Anne. 1997. *The Spirit Catches You and You Fall Down: A Hmong Child, Her American Doctors, and the Collision of Two Cultures.* New York: Farrar, Straus and Giroux.

Fairlie, Simon. 2009. "A Short History of Enclosure in Britain." *The Land.* Website accessed 09/24/2018, (http://www.thelandmagazine.org.uk/articles/short-history-enclosure-britain).

Fallon, Amy. 2018. "A Perfect Storm: The Hydropolitics of Cape Town's Water Crisis." *Global Water Forum.* Website accessed 09/24/2018, (http://www.globalwaterforum.org/2018/04/17/the-hydropolitics-of-cape-towns-water-crisis-a-perfect-storm/).

Fan, Jiayang. 2014. "Can China Stop Organ Trafficking?" *New Yorker.* Website accessed 05/25/2018, (https://www.newyorker.com/news/news-desk/can-china-stop-organ-trafficking).

Farrell, Graham, and Ken Clark. 2004. "What Does the World Spend on Criminal Justice?" *European Institute for Crime Prevention and Control, Helsinki, Finland.* HEUNI Paper no. 20. Paper accessed 03/06/2018, (https://www.heuni.fi/material/attachments/heuni/papers/6KtlkZMtL/HEUNI_papers_20.pdf).

Faruqi, Anwar. 2000. "Saudis Defend Beheadings as Mandated by Religion." *Associated Press.* Article accessed via Lexis-Nexis 06/29/2017.

Fazel, Seena, and Achim Wolf. 2015. "A Systematic Review of Criminal Recidivism Rates Worldwide: Current Difficulties and Recommendations for Best Practice." *PLOS One* 10(6):e0130390. Paper accessed 07/06/2017, (https://www.ncbi.nlm.nih.gov/pmc/articles/PMC4472929/).

Federal Bureau of Investigation. n.d. "Overseas Offices." Website accessed 03/12/2018, (https://www.fbi.gov/contact-us/legal-attache-offices).

Felder, Brittany. 2015. "India Top Court Stays Order Banning Extreme Religious Fasting." *Jurist.* Website accessed 08/03/2018, (https://www.jurist.org/news/2015/08/india-top-court-stays-order-banning-extreme-religious-fasting/).

Félix, Sónia, Pedro Portugal, and Ana Tavares. 2017. "Going after the Addiction, Not the Addicted: The Impact of Drug Decriminalization in Portugal." *IZA Institute of Labor Economics, Bonn, Germany.* Discussion Paper Series no. 10895. Paper accessed 2/11/2019, (https://www.iza.org/publications/dp/10895).

Felter, Claire, and Danielle Renwick. 2017. "Colombia's Civil Conflict." *Council on Foreign Relations.* Website accessed 08/06/2018, (https://www.cfr.org/backgrounder/colombias-civil-conflict).

Ferreira, Susana. 2017. "Portugal's Radical Drugs Policy Is Working. Why Hasn't the World Copied It?" *Guardian.* Website accessed 05/10/2018, (https://www.theguardian.com/news/2017/dec/05/portugals-radical-drugs-policy-is-working-why-hasnt-the-world-copied-it).

Ferrell, Jeff. 1996. *Crimes of Style: Urban Graffiti and the Politics of Criminality.* Boston, MA: Northeastern University Press.

Fick, Nicolé. 2006. "Enforcing Fear: Police Abuse of Sex Workers When Making Arrests." *South African Crime Quarterly* 16:27–33.

Fidler, David P. 2017. "The U.S. Election Hacks, Cybersecurity, and International Law." *AJIL Unbound* 110:337–342.

Findlay, Mark, Lousie Boon Kuo, and Lim Si Wei. 2013. *International and Comparative Criminal Justice: A Critical Introduction.* London, UK: Routledge.

Fisher, Max, and Josh Keller. 2017. "What Explains U.S. Mass Shootings? International Comparisons Suggest an Answer." *New York Times.* Website accessed 05/23/2018, (https://www.nytimes.com/2017/11/07/world/americas/mass-shootings-us-international.html).

Flam, Lisa. 2014. "5 Years after Their Reunion, a 'Happy' David and Sean Goldman Talk Family and Future." *Today.* Website accessed 07/24/2017, (http://www.today.com/news/david-sean-goldman-talk-family-future-5-years-after-their-1D80385661).

Flores, Sam Morales. 2014. "International Perspectives on Indigent Defense and Legal Aid: Shared Challenges and the Road Forward." *American University.* Report accessed 02/12/2018, (https://jpo.wrlc.org/bitstream/handle /11204/3584/April%2024%20International%20 Perspectives%20on%20Indigent%20Defense%20and%20 Legal%20Aid.FINAL.pdf?sequence=1).

Florida Legislature. 2018. "Justifiable Use of Force 776.013." Website accessed 02/12/2019, (http://www.leg.state.fl.us/statutes /index.cfm?App_mode=Display_Statute&URL=0700–0799 /0776/Sections/0776.013.html).

Florquin, Nicolas. 2011. "A Booming Business: Private Security and Small Arms." Pp. 100–33 in *Small Arms Survey 2011*, edited by Keither Krause and Eric G. Berman. Geneva, Switzerland: Graduate Institute of International and Development Studies.

Forbes, Allen, ed. 1921. "Market Place, Yarmouth, England." P. 222 in *Towns of New England and Old England, Ireland, and Scotland*, pt. 1. New York: G. P. Putnam's Sons.

Forsyth, Miranda. 2016. "The Regulation of Witchcraft and Sorcery Practices and Beliefs." *Annual Review of Law and Social Science* 12:331–51.

Fortune. 2017. "Chevron." *Fortune Global 500*. Website accessed 06/19/2018, (http://fortune.com/global500/chevron/).

Foucault, Michel. 1977. *Discipline and Punish: The Birth of the Prison.* Translated by Alan Sheridan. New York: Vintage Books.

Frank, David John, Bayless J. Camp, and Steven A. Boutcher. 2010. "Worldwide Trends in the Criminal Regulation of Sex, 1945 to 2005." *American Sociological Review* 75(6):867–93.

Fredericks, John, III. 1999. "America's First Nations: The Origins, History and Future of American Indian Sovereignty." *Journal of Law and Policy* 7(2):347–410.

Freedom House. 2017. "Freedom on the Net 2017." Report accessed 07/25/2018, (https://freedomhouse.org/report/freedom-net/freedom-net-2017).

Freshfields Bruckhaus Deringer LLP. 2017. "The Disappearing Trial: Towards a Rights-Based Approach to Trial Waver Systems." *Fair Trials, London, UK.* Report accessed 01/29/2018, (https://www.fairtrials.org/campaigns/the-disappearing-trial/).

Friedkin, William. 2016. "The Devil and Father Amorth: Witnessing 'the Vatican Exorcist' at Work." *Vanity Fair.* Website accessed 06/30/2017, (http://www.vanityfair.com /hollywood/2016/10/father-amorth-the-vatican-exorcist).

Friedman, Lawrence M. 1969. "Legal Culture and Social Development." *Law & Society Review* 4(1):29–44.

Friedrich, Johannes, Mengpin Ge, and Andrew Pickens. 2017. "This Interactive Chart Explains World's Top 10 Emitters, and How They've Changed." *World Resources Institute.* Website accessed 09/25/2018, (https://www.wri.org/blog/2017/04 /interactive-chart-explains-worlds-top-10-emitters-and-how-theyve-changed).

Fronius, Trevor, Hannah Persson, Sarah Guckenberg, Nancy Hurley, and Anthony Petrosino. 2016. "Restorative Justice in U.S. Schools: A Research Review." *WestEd Justice and Prevention Research Center.* Report accessed 02/04/2019, (http://www .antoniocasella.eu/restorative/Fronius_feb16.pdf).

Fung, Katherine. 2018. "A Bill to Allow Divorce in the Philippines Could Mean Freedom for Some Women in New York." *Public Radio International.* Website accessed 07/24/2018, (https://www.pri.org/stories/2018-06-05/bill-allow-divorce-philippines-could-mean-freedom-some-women-new-york).

Galanter, Marc. 1983. "Reading the Landscape of Disputes: What We Know and Don't Know (And Think We Know) about our Allegedly Contentious and Litigious Society." *UCLA Law Review* 31(1):4–71.

Gammeltoft-Hansen, Thomas. 2011. *Access to Asylum: International Refugee Law and the Globalisation of Migration Control.* Cambridge, UK: Cambridge University Press.

Garrison, Marsha. 2011. "What's Fair in Divorce Property Distribution? Cross-National Perspectives from Survey Evidence." *Louisiana Law Review* 72(1):57–88.

Gau, Jacinta M., and Travis C. Pratt. 2010. "Revisiting Broken Windows Theory: Examining the Sources of the Discriminant Validity of Perceived Disorder and Crime." *Journal of Criminal Justice* 38(4):758–66.

George, Robert P. 2001. "Natural Law, the Constitution, and the Theory and Practice of Judicial Review." *Fordham Law Review* 69(6):2269–83.

Gettleman, Jeffrey. 2011. "Taken by Pirates." *New York Times Magazine.* Website accessed 05/10/2018, (https://www .nytimes.com/2011/10/09/magazine/taken-by-pirates .html).

Ghana Consulate General. 2018. "Dual Nationality." *Ghana Consulate New York.* Website accessed 06/06/2018, (https:// ghanaconsulatenewyork.org/dual_nationality.php).

Giddens, Anthony. 1990. *The Consequences of Modernity.* Stanford, CA: Stanford University Press.

Gilliani, Syed Yasir Mahmood, Hafeez Ur Rehman, and Abid Rasheed Gill. 2009. "Unemployment, Poverty, Inflation, and Crime Nexus: Cointegration and Causality Analysis of Pakistan." *Pakistan Economic and Social Review* 47(1):79–98.

Gilson, Blake. 2011. "Defending Your Client's Property Rights in Space: A Practical Guide for the Lunar Litigator." *Fordham Law Review* 80(3):1367–405.

Glatter, Hayley. 2018. "Marty Walsh Threatened to End the Space Saver Rule in Boston." *Boston Magazine.* Website accessed 08/21/2018, (https://www.bostonmagazine.com/news/2018 /01/11/walsh-space-saver-change/).

Glendon, Mary Ann, Paolo G. Carozza, and Colin B. Picker. 2008. *Comparative Legal Traditions in a Nutshell.* St. Paul, MN: Thomson West.

Glenn, H. Patrick. 2001. "Are Legal Traditions Incommensurable?" *American Journal of Comparative Law* 49(1):133–45.

———. 2007. *Legal Traditions of the World.* 3rd ed. Oxford, UK: Oxford University Press.

———. 2008. "A Concept of Legal Tradition." *Queen's Law Journal* 34(1):427–45.

Global Initiative to End All Corporal Punishment of Children. 2017. "Global Progress towards Prohibiting all Corporal Punishment." Website accessed 07/10/2017, (https:// web.archive.org/web/20171118042626/http://www .endcorporalpunishment.org/assets/pdfs/legality-tables /Global-progress-table-commitment.pdf).

Global Legal Research Center. 2018. "Legal Restrictions on Religious Slaughter in Europe." *Law Library of Congress.* Report accessed 09/03/2018, (https://www.loc.gov/law/help /religious-slaughter/europe.php).

Goldin, Claudia, and Maria Shim. 2004. "Making a Name: Women's Surnames at Marriage and Beyond." *Journal of Economic Perspectives* 18(2):143–60.

Goldman, David. 2012. "David's Story." *Bring Sean Home Foundation.* Website accessed 07/24/2017, (http:// bringseanhome.org/goldman-case/davids-story).

Good, Anthony. 2008. "Cultural Evidence in Courts of Law." *Journal of the Royal Anthropological Institute* 14(S1):S47-S60.

Gooding, Gretchen E., and Rose M. Kreider. 2010. "Women's Marital Naming Choices in a Nationally Representative Sample." *Journal of Family Issues* 31(5):681–701.

Goodman, Bryce, and Seth Flaxman. 2016. "EU Regulations on Algorithmic Decision-Making and a 'Right to Explanation.'" *2016 ICML Workshop on Human Interpretability in Machine Learning*. Conference paper accessed 09/17/2018, (https://arxiv.org/abs/1606.08813).

Goodwin, Jeff. 2006. "A Theory of Categorical Terrorism." *Social Forces* 84(4):2027–46.

Goris, Indira, Fabien Jobard, René Lévy, James A. Goldston, William Kramer, and Rachel Neild. 2009. "Profiling Minorities: A Study of Stop-and-Search Practices in Paris." *Open Society Institute*. Report accessed 02/04/2019, (https://www.opensocietyfoundations.org/sites/default/files/search_20090630.Web.pdf).

Goss, Ernest, Scott Strain, and Jackson Blalock. 2016. "The Economic Impact of the Death Penalty on the State of Nebraska: A Taxpayer Burden?" *Goss and Associates Economic Solutions, Denver, CO*. Report accessed 07/06/2017, (https://www.omaha.com/the-economic-impact-of-the-death-penalty-on-the-state/pdf_a6de772c-7515–11e6–8138–1f408072cffb.html).

Government of Ghana. 2018. "Citizenship." *Government of Ghana Official Portal*. Website accessed 06/06/2018, (http://www.ghana.gov.gh/index.php/component/content/category/92-citizenship).

Government of Iceland. n.d. "Equal Pay Certification." Website accessed 08/06/2018, (https://www.government.is/topics/human-rights-and-equality/equal-pay-certification/).

Government of the Netherlands. n.d. "Toleration Policy Regarding Soft Drugs and Coffee Shops." Website accessed 05/10/2018, (https://www.government.nl/topics/drugs/toleration-policy-regarding-soft-drugs-and-coffee-shops).

Greenberg, David F., and Valerie West. 2008. "Siting the Death Penalty Internationally." *Law & Social Inquiry* 33(2):295–343.

Greenwald, Glenn. 2009. *Drug Decriminalization in Portugal: Lessons for Creating Fair and Successful Drug Policies*. Washington, DC: Cato Institute.

Griffin, Richard. 2017. "The Traditional Courts Bill: Are They Getting It Right?" *Helen Suzman Foundation*. Website accessed 02/19/2018, (http://hsf.org.za/resource-centre/hsf-briefs/the-traditional-courts-bill-are-they-getting-it-right).

Grimm, Beca. n.d. "What Are the Penalties for Public Urination in Cities around the World?" *H&F Weekly*. Website accessed 05/10/2018, (http://www.hopesandfears.com/hopes/city/city_index/215327-public-urination).

Grinberg, Emanuella. 2018. "Spain Might Be Next to Criminalize Sex without Consent." *CNN*. Website accessed 08/06/2018, (https://www.msn.com/en-us/news/world/spain-might-be-next-to-criminalize-sex-without-consent/ar-AAAhm8B).

Grinshteyn, Erin, and David Hemenway. 2016. "Violent Death Rates: The US Compared with Other High-Income OECD Countries, 2010." *American Journal of Medicine* 129(3):266–73.

Gross, Samuel R., and Katherine Y. Barnes. 2002. "Road Work: Racial Profiling and Drug Interdiction on the Highway." *Michigan Law Review* 101(3):651–754.

Haberfeld, M. R., and Ibrahim Cerrah. 2008. *Comparative Policing: The Struggle for Democratization*. Thousand Oaks, CA: Sage.

Hadfield, Gillian K. 2017. *Rules for a Flat World: Why Humans Invented Law and How to Reinvent It for a Global Economy*. New York: Oxford University Press.

Hagan, John, Kim Lane Sheppele, and Tom R. Tyler. 2013. "Sex Laws and Sexuality Rights in Comparative and Global Perspective." *Annual Review of Law and Social Science* 9:149–67.

Hague Conference on Private International Law. 2019. "Status Table: 28; Convention of 25 October 1980 on the Civil Aspects of International Child Abduction." Website accessed 01/21/2019, (https://www.hcch.net/en/instruments/conventions/status-table/?cid=24).

Hall, Philippa. 2018. "The Global Education Market, Criticality, and the University Curriculum in the Overseas Campuses of Qatar and the United Arab Emirates." *International Journal of Critical Pedagogy* 9(1):73–94.

Hamilton, Logan. 2017. "Beyond Ballot-Stuffing: Current Gaps in International Law Regarding Foreign State Hacking to Influence a Foreign Election." *Wisconsin International Law Journal* 35(1):179–204.

Hammer, Joshua. 2018. "The Billion-Dollar Bank Job." *New York Times*. Website accessed 01/28/2019, (https://www.nytimes.com/interactive/2018/05/03/magazine/money-issue-bangladesh-billion-dollar-bank-heist.html).

Hans, Valarie P. 2008. "Jury Systems around the World." *Annual Review of Law and Social Science* 4:275–297.

Hanson, Hillary. 2016. "Behold, the World's First Official Pastafarian Wedding." *Huffington Post*. Website accessed 08/03/2018, (https://www.huffingtonpost.com/entry/pastafarian-wedding-flying-spaghetti-monster_us_5712b212e4b0060ccda37a86).

Harkness, Geoff, and Peggy Levitt. 2017. "Professional Dissonance: Reconciling Occupational Culture and Authoritarianism in Qatar's Universities and Museums." *Sociology of Development* 3(3):232–51.

Harris, David A. 1999. "The Stories, the Statistics, and the Law: Why 'Driving While Black' Matters." *Minnesota Law Review* 84:265–326.

———. 2002. "Flying While Arab: Lessons from the Racial Profiling Controversy." *Civil Rights Journal* 6(1):8–13.

Hasday, Jill Elaine. 2000. "Contest and Consent: A Legal History of Marital Rape." *California Law Review* 88(5):1373–505.

Hayner, Priscilla. 2001. *Unspeakable Truths: Confronting State Terror and Atrocity*. London, UK: Routledge.

Head, John W. 2014. "Criminal Procedure in Transition: Observations on Legal Transplantation and Italy's Handling of the Amanda Knox Trial." In *Festschrift in Honor of Feridun Yenisey*, edited by Ayse Nohuoglu. Istanbul: Beta Publishers.

Hemenway, David. 2017. *Private Guns, Public Health*. Ann Arbor, MI: University of Michigan Press.

Heritage Foundation. 2018. "2018 Index of Economic Freedom." Website accessed 08/17/2018, (https://www.heritage.org/international-economies/commentary/2018-index-economic-freedom).

Herz, John H. 1957. "Rise and Demise of the Territorial State." *World Politics* 9(4):473–93.

Herzog, Ben. 2010. "The Revocation of Citizenship in Israel." *Israel Studies Forum* 25(1):57–72.

Hickey, Kenneth S., and Laurie Lyckholm. 2004. "Child Welfare versus Parental Autonomy: Medical Ethics, the Law, and Faith-Based Healing." *Theoretical Medicine* 25(4):265–76.

HiiL (Hague Institute for Innovation of Law). 2017. "The Hague Institute for Innovation of Law." Website accessed 07/25/2017, (http://www.hiil.org).

Hinton, Alexander Laban. 2010. "Introduction: Toward an Anthropology of Transitional Justice." Pp. 1–24 in

Transitional Justice: Global Mechanisms and Local Realities after Genocide and Mass Violence, edited by Alexander Laban Hinton. New Brunswick, NJ: Rutgers University Press.

Hirsch, Moshe. 2015. *Invitation to the Sociology of International Law.* Oxford, UK: Oxford University Press.

Hobbes, Thomas. 1909–14. *Leviathan.* New York: P. F. Collier and Son.

Hobgood, Hamilton H. 1981. "When Should a Trial Judge Intervene to Question a Witness?" *Campbell Law Review* 3(1):69–76.

Hobsbawm, Eric, and Terence Ranger. 1983. *The Invention of Tradition.* Cambridge, UK: Cambridge University Press.

Hoffman, Elizabeth A. 2003. "Legal Consciousness and Dispute Resolution: Different Disputing Behavior at Two Similar Taxicab Companies." *Law & Social Inquiry* 28(3):691–716.

Hoffman, Stephanie B. 2009. "Behind Closed Doors: Impotence Trials and the Trans-Historical Right to Marital Privacy." *Boston University Law Review* 89(5):1725–52.

Hojecká, Pavlína. 2003. "Regina v Dudley and Stephens." *Common Law Review* 4(1):31–36.

Holmes, Oliver Wendell, Jr. 1897. "The Path of the Law." *Harvard Law Review* 10:457–78.

Holmquist, Kate. 2015. "Divorce, Irish Style." *Irish Times.* Website accessed 07/17/2018, (https://www.irishtimes.com/life-and-style/divorce-irish-style-1.2068656).

Honwana, Alcinda. 2007. *Child Soldiers in Africa.* Philadelphia: University of Pennsylvania Press.

Horowitz, Donald L. 2003. "Electoral Systems: A Primer for Decision-Makers." *Journal of Democracy* 14(4):115–27.

Hostetler, John A. 1984. "The Amish and the Law: A Religious Minority and Its Legal Encounters." *Washington and Lee Law Review* 41(1):33–47.

Houseman, Lilith. 2010. "Reducing Reliance on Incarceration in Texas: Does Finland Hold Answers?" *Texas International Law Journal* 46:209.

Howard, Gregory J., Graeme Newman, and William Alex Pridemore. 2000. "Theory, Method, and Data in Comparative Criminology." Pp. 139–211 in *Measurement and Analysis of Crime and Justice,* Criminal Justice 2000, edited by David Duffee. Washington DC: National Institute of Justice.

Htun, Mala, and S. Laurel Weldon. 2011. "State Power, Religion, and Women's Rights: A Comparative Analysis of Family Law." *Indiana Journal of Global Legal Studies* 18(1):145–65.

Huang, Jianping, Haipeng Yu, Xiaodan Guan, Guoyin Wang, and Ruixia Guo. 2016. "Accelerated Dryland Expansion under Climate Change." *Nature Climate Change* 6:166–71.

Human Rights Watch. 2011. "World Report 2011: Events of 2010." Website accessed 03/14/2018, (https://www.hrw.org/sites/default/files/world_report_download/wr2011_book_complete.pdf).

———. 2017. "World Report 2018: Events of 2017." Report accessed 07/25/2018, (https://www.hrw.org/world-report/2018).

Hunt, Alex, and Brian Wheeler. 2019. "Brexit: All You Need to Know about the UK Leaving the EU." *BBC News.* Website accessed 01/28/2019, (https://www.bbc.com/news/uk-politics-32810887).

Hunt, Stephen. 2011. "Social Structure." Pp. 578–79 in *The Concise Encyclopedia of Sociology,* edited by George Ritzer and Michael Ryan. Malden, MA: Wiley-Blackwell.

Huntington, Gertrude Enders. 2003. "Health Care." Pp. 163–90 in *The Amish and the State,* edited by Donald B. Kraybill. Baltimore, MD: Johns Hopkins University Press.

ICC (International Criminal Court). n.d.-a. "Defendants." Website accessed 02/18/2019, (https://www.icc-cpi.int/Pages/defendants-wip.aspx).

———. n.d.-b. "Ongwen Case." Website accessed 09/04/2018, (https://www.icc-cpi.int/uganda/ongwen).

———. n.d.-c. "International Criminal Court." Website accessed 06/20/2018, (https://www.icc-cpi.int).

ICJ (International Court of Justice). 2018. "The Court." Website accessed 06/26/2018, (http://www.icj-cij.org/en/court).

———. 2019. "Pending Cases." Website accessed 02/18/2019, (http://www.icj-cij.org/en/pending-cases).

ICVS (International Crime Victims Survey). 2018. "About the ICVS." *Institut de Criminologie et de Droit Pénal, University of Lausanne.* Website accessed 05/23/2018, (http://wp.unil.ch/icvs/).

Imburgia, Joseph S. 2011. "Space Debris and Its Threat to National Security: A Proposal for a Binding International Agreement to Clean Up the Junk." *Vanderbilt Journal of Transnational Law* 44(3):589–640.

Independent Diplomat. n.d. "Independent Diplomat: The Diplomatic Advisory Group." Website accessed 07/25/2017, (https://independentdiplomat.org/).

Information Resource of Maine. 2015. "2010 Governor General Election Tabulations." *State of Maine, Department of the Secretary of State.* Website accessed 05/30/2018, (http://www.maine.gov/sos/cec/elec/results/2010–11/gen2010gov.html).

Ingelaere, Bert. 2009. "Does the Truth Pass across the Fire without Burning? Locating the Short Circuits in Rwanda's *Gacaca* Courts." *Journal of Modern African Studies* 47(4):507–28.

———. 2016. *Inside Rwanda's Gacaca Courts: Seeking Justice after Genocide.* Madison, WI: University of Wisconsin Press.

INSEE (Institut national de la statistique et des études économiques). 2018. "Mariages—Pacs—Divorces." *Tableaux de L'Économie Française, Édition 2018.* Website accessed 07/13/2018, (https://www.insee.fr/fr/statistiques/3303338?sommaire=3353488&q=mariages#tableau-T18F033G2).

Institute for Criminal Policy Research. n.d. "World Prison Brief: Highest to Lowest—Prison Population Total." *Birckbeck, University of London.* Website accessed 06/30/2017, (http://www.prisonstudies.org/highest-to-lowest/).

Institute for Economics and Peace. 2017. "Global Terrorism Index 2017." Report accessed 05/23/2018, (http://visionofhumanity.org/app/uploads/2017/11/Global-Terrorism-Index-2017.pdf).

Instituto Português da Droga e da Toxicodependência. 2000. "Annual Report on the Drug Phenomena, 2000." *European Monitoring Centre on Drugs and Drug Addiction.* Website accessed 05/10/2018, (http://www.emcdda.europa.eu/attachements.cfm/att_34676_EN_NR2000Portugal.PDF).

Inter-Parliamentary Union. 2018. "Women in National Parliaments." Website accessed 06/05/2018, (http://archive.ipu.org/wmn-e/world.htm).

International Center for Transitional Justice. 2018. "What Is Transitional Justice?" Website accessed 01/14/2019, (https://www.ictj.org/about/transitional-justice).

———. 2019. "Colombia." Website accessed 01/18/2019, (https://www.ictj.org/our-work/regions-and-countries/colombia).

International Chamber of Commerce. n.d. "IMB Piracy Reporting Centre." *Commercial Crime Services.* Website accessed 05/25/2018, (https://www.icc-ccs.org/piracy-reporting-centre).

International IDEA (Institute for Democracy and Electoral Assistance). 2018a. "Compulsory Voting." Website accessed 06/05/2018, (https://www.idea.int/data-tools/data/voter-turnout/compulsory-voting).

———. 2018b. "Voter Turnout Database." Website accessed 06/05/2018, (https://www.idea.int/data-tools/data/voter-turnout).

International Institute for Strategic Studies. 2018. "The Military Balance 2018." Website accessed 03/12/2018, (www.iiss.org /publications/the-military-balance/the-military-balance-2018).

Interpol. 2018a. "About Interpol." Website accessed 03/12/2018, (https://web.archive.org/web/20180308194712/https:// www.interpol.int/About-INTERPOL/Overview).

———. 2018b. "Interpol Expertise." Website accessed 03/12/2018, (https://web.archive.org/web/20180218154722/https:// www.interpol.int/INTERPOL-expertise/Overview

———. 2018c. "Project Pink Panthers." Website accessed 03/13/2018, (http://web.archive.org/web/20180127100254 /https://www.interpol.int/Crime-areas/Organized-crime /Project-Pink-Panthers).

IPCC (Intergovernmental Panel on Climate Change). 2014. "Climate Change 2014: Synthesis Report; Contribution of Working Groups I, II and III to the Fifth Assessment Report of the Intergovernmental Panel on Climate Change." Website accessed 09/24/2018, (http://ipcc.ch/report/ar5/syr/).

Israel, David K. 2010. "Oh No, You Can't Name Your Baby THAT!" Mental Floss, CNN. Website accessed 07/17/2018, (http:// www.cnn.com/2010/LIVING/07/03/mf.baby.naming.laws /index.html).

Israel Government Print Office. 1961. "Defendant Adolf Eichmann Stands as He Is Sentenced to Death by the Court." United States Holocaust Memorial Museum. Photograph accessed 02/05/2018. (https://www.ushmm.org/wlc/en/media_ph .php?ModuleId=0&MediaId=5635).

Ivkovic, Sanja Kutnjak. 2005. Fallen Blue Knights: Controlling Police Corruption. Oxford, UK: Oxford University Press.

Iyi, John-Mark. 2016. "Fair Hearing without Lawyers? The Traditional Courts Bill and the Reform of Traditional Justice System in South Africa." Journal of Legal Pluralism and Unofficial Law 48(1):127–52.

Jafar, Tazeen H. 2009. "Organ Trafficking: Global Solutions for a Global Problem." American Journal of Kidney Disease 54(6):1145–57.

Jaffe, Justin, and Laura Hautala. 2018. "What the GDPR Means for Facebook, the EU and You." CNET. Website accessed 07/25/2018, (https://www.cnet.com/how-to/what-gdpr-means-for-facebook-google-the-eu-us-and-you/).

James, Erwin. 2013. "The Norwegian Prison Where Inmates Are Treated Like People." Guardian. Website accessed 07/05/2017, (https://www.theguardian.com/society/2013 /feb/25/norwegian-prison-inmates-treated-like-people).

Jans, Jeroen. 2010. "Profiling of Asylum Seekers." Federale Overheidsdienst Binnenlandse Zaken. Website accessed 06/26/2018, (http://www.unhcr.org/50aa05599.pdf).

Jenks, Chris. 2011. "Culture: Conceptual Clarifications." Pp. 114–15 in The Concise Encyclopedia of Sociology, edited by George Ritzer and Michael Ryan. Malden, MA: Wiley-Blackwell.

Johnson, Vincent R. 2017. "Comparative Defamation Law: England and the United States." University of Miami International and Comparative Law Review 24(1):2–97.

Jones, Rhett. n.d. "What Are the Penalties for Possession of a Gram of Weed around the World?" H&F Weekly. Website accessed 05/10/2018, (http://www.hopesandfears.com/hopes/city /city_index/168691-city-index-gram-of-weed).

Jones, Tobias. 2011. "Amanda Knox Case Is Typical of Italy's Inconclusive Justice." Guardian. Website accessed 02/19/2018, (https://www.theguardian.com/commentisfree /2011/oct/04/amanda-knox-case-italy-justice).

Judicial Appointments Commission. n.d. "Judicial Appointments Commission." Website accessed 01/29/2018, (https://jac .judiciary.gov.uk/).

Judkins, Benjamin N. 2015. "Through a Lens Darkly (32): The Chinese Police and the Romance of the Sword." Kung Fu Tea: Martial Arts History, Wing Chun, and Chinese Martial Studies. Website accessed 03/06/2018, (https:// chinesemartialstudies.com/2015/09/07/through-a-lens-darkly-32-the-chinese-police-and-the-romance-of-the-sword/comment-page-1/).

Jurist. 2018. "World Legal News." Website accessed 09/26/2018, (https://www.jurist.org/news/tag/international/).

Juss, Satvinder Singh. 2012. "Kirpans, Law, and Religious Symbols in Schools." Journal of Church and State 55(4):758–95.

Kadri, Sadakat. 2005. The Trial: A History, from Socrates to O. J. Simpson. New York: Random House.

Kaempf, Joseph W., Mark Tomlinson, Cindy Arduza, Shelly Anderson, Betty Campbell, Linda A. Ferguson, Mara Zabari, and Valerie T. Stewart. 2006. "Medical Staff Guidelines for Periviability Pregnancy Counseling and Medical Treatment of Extremely Premature Infants." Pediatrics 117(1):22–29.

Kalev, Henriette Dahan. 2004. "Cultural Rights or Human Rights: The Case of Female Genital Mutilation." Sex Roles 51(5/6):339–48.

Katzman, Kenneth. 2017. "Qatar: Governance, Security, and U.S. Policy." Congressional Research Service. Report accessed 08/17/2018, (https://digital.library.unt.edu/ark:/67531 /metadc980503/m2/1/high_res_d/R44533_2017Mar15.pdf).

Kawachi, Ichiro, Bruce P. Kennedy, and Richard G. Wilkinson. 1999. "Crime: Social Disorganization and Relative Deprivation." Social Science & Medicine 48(6):719–31.

Keating, Joshua. 2018. "The Sinking State." Washington Post. Website accessed 09/24/2018, (https://www.washingtonpost.com /news/posteverything/wp/2018/07/26/feature/this-is-what-happens-when-climate-change-forces-an-entire-country-to-seek-higher-ground/).

Keefe, Patrick Radden. 2012. "Reversal of Fortune." New Yorker. Website accessed 06/15/2018, (https://www.newyorker.com /magazine/2012/01/09/reversal-of-fortune-patrick-radden-keefe).

Keim, Albert N. 2003. "Military Service and Conscription." Pp. 43–66 in The Amish and the State, edited by Donald B. Kraybill. Baltimore, MD: Johns Hopkins University Press.

Kelly, Emily. 2013. "International Organ Trafficking Crisis: Solutions Addressing the Heart of the Matter." Boston College Law Review 54(3):1317–49.

Kennedy, David M. 2009. Deterrence and Crime Prevention: Reconsidering the Prospect of Sanction. Routledge: New York.

Kennedy, Randall. 1997. Race, Crime, and the Law. New York: Vintage Books.

Khedr, Ahmed Aly. 2016. "Update: Qatar's Legal System Governance and Business." Hauser Global Law School Program, New York University School of Law. Website accessed 08/20/2018, (http://www.nyulawglobal.org/globalex/Qatar1.html).

Khory, Kavita R. 2005. "The Shah Bano Case: Some Political Implications." Pp. 213–26 in Sociology of Law, Oxford in India Readings in Sociology and Anthropology, edited by Indra Deva. New Delhi, India: Oxford University Press.

Kilmurray, Avila. 2017. Community Action in a Contested Society: The Story of Northern Ireland. Oxford, UK: Peter Lang.

Kim, Jong-In, Myeong Soo Lee, Dong-Hyo Lee, Kate Boddy, and Edzard Ernst. 2011. "Cupping for Treating Pain:

A Systematic Review." *Evidence-Based Complementary and Alternative Medicine* 2011:1–7.

Kim, Ryang Hui, and David Clark. 2013. "The Effect of Prison-Based College Education Programs on Recidivism: Propensity Score Matching Approach." *Journal of Criminal Justice* 41(3):196–204.

Kingdom of Saudi Arabia. n.d. "Elections in the Kingdom of Saudi Arabia." *Saudi National Portal.* Website accessed 05/30/2018, (https://www.saudi.gov.sa/wps/portal/snp /pages/electionsInTheKingdomOfSaudiArabia/).

Kishi, Katayoun. 2018. "Global Uptick in Government Restrictions on Religion in 2016." *Pew Research Center.* Report accessed 08/03/2018, (http://assets.pewresearch.org/wp-content /uploads/sites/11/2018/06/19155938/Restrictions-IX-FULL-REPORT-WITH-APPENDIXES.pdf).

Kleibach, Russ, and Lilly Salimjanova. 2007. "*Kyz Ala Kachuu* and *Adat:* Non-Consensual Bride Kidnapping and Tradition in Kyrgyzstan." *Central Asian Survey* 26(2):217–33.

Kleiman, Mark A. R. 2009. *When Brute Force Fails: How to Have Less Crime and Less Punishment.* Princeton, NJ: Princeton University Press.

Koh, Harold Jongiu. 1997. "Why Do Nations Obey International Law?" *Yale Law Journal* 106(8):2599–2659.

Kolbert, Elizabeth. 2014. *The Sixth Extinction: An Unnatural History.* New York: Henry Holt.

Komiya, Nobuo. 1999. "A Cultural Study of the Low Crime Rate in Japan." *British Journal of Criminology* 39(3):369–90.

Koskenniemi, Martti. 2006. "Fragmentation of International Law: Difficulties Arising from the Diversification and Expansion of International Law." *United Nations General Assembly, International Law Commission.* Report accessed 06/19/2018, (http://legal.un.org/ilc/documentation/english/a_cn4_l682 .pdf).

Koss, Mary P., Karen J. Bachar, and C. Quince Hopkins. 2003. "Restorative Justice for Sexual Violence: Repairing Victims, Building Community, and Holding Offenders Accountable." *Annals of the New York Academic of Sciences* 989:384–96.

Kovandzic, Tomislav V., John J. Sloan, III, and Lynne M. Vieraitis. 2004. "'Striking Out' as Crime Reduction Policy: The Impact of 'Three Strikes' Laws on Crime Rates in U.S. Cities." *Justice Quarterly* 21(2):207–39.

Koyana, Digby Sqhelo. 2011. "Traditional Courts in South Africa in the Twenty-First Century." Pp. 227–46 in *The Future of African Customary Law,* edited by Jeanmarie Fenrich and Paolo Galizzi. Cambridge, UK: Cambridge University Press.

Krause, Monika. 2008. "Undocumented Migrants: An Arendtian Perspective." *European Journal of Political Theory* 7(3): 331–48.

Kuang, Cliff. 2017. "Can A.I. Be Taught to Explain Itself?" *New York Times Magazine.* Website accessed 12/29/2017, (https:// www.nytimes.com/2017/11/21/magazine/can-ai-be-taught-to-explain-itself.html).

Kulish, Nicholas. 2011. "Germany's Anti-Chaos Crusaders." *New York Times Magazine.* Website accessed 07/26/2013, (http:// www.nytimes.com/2011/05/22/magazine/you-are-here-germanys-anti-chaos-crusaders.html).

Künnapas, Kaido. 2016. "From Bitcoin to Smart Contracts: Legal Revolution or Evolution from the Perspective of *De Lege Ferenda?*" Pp. 111–32 in *The Future of Law and eTechnologies,* edited by Tanel Kerikmäe and Addi Rull. Basel, Switzerland: Springer.

Kuo, Lily. 2018. "Chinese Province Introduces 'Divorce Test' for Couples Planning to Split." *Guardian.* Website accessed 07/24/2018, (https://www.theguardian.com/world/2018 /may/23/chinese-province-introduces-divorce-test-for-couples-planning-to-split).

Kurtzleben, Danielle. 2015. "Canada Reminds Us That American Elections Are Much Longer." *National Public Radio.* Website accessed 06/05/2018, (https://www.npr.org/sections /itsallpolitics/2015/10/21/450238156/canadas-11-week-campaign-reminds-us-that-american-elections-are-much-longer).

Laisné, Michael. 2013. "Space Entrepreneurs: Business Strategy, Risk, Law, and Policy in the Final Frontier." *John Marshall Law Review* 46(4):1039–54.

Lal, Vinay. 1996. "Sikh Kirpans in California Schools: The Social Construction of Symbols, Legal Pluralism, and the Politics of Diversity." *Amerasia Journal* 22(1):57–89.

Landes, William M., and Richard A. Posner. 1976. "Legal Precedent: A Theoretical and Empirical Analysis." *Journal of Law & Economics* 19(2):249–307.

Lanni, Adriaan. 2006. *Law and Justice in the Courts of Classical Athens.* Cambridge, UK: Cambridge University Press.

Laplante, Lisa J., and Kimberly Susan Theidon. 2007. "Truth with Consequences: Justice and Reparations in Post-Truth Commission Peru." *Human Rights Quarterly* 29(1): 228–50.

Lartey, James. 2015. "By the Numbers: US Police Kill More in Days than Other Countries Do in Years." *Guardian.* Website accessed 03/14/2018, (https://www.theguardian.com/us-news/2015/jun/09/the-counted-police-killings-us-vs-other-countries).

Lastowka, Greg. 2010. *Virtual Justice: The New Laws of Online Worlds.* New Haven, CT: Yale University Press.

Law, David S., and Mila Versteeg. 2011. "The Evolution and Ideology of Global Constitutionalism." *California Law Review* 99(5):1163–258.

———. 2012. "The Declining Influence of the United States Constitution." *New York University Law Review* 87(3):762–858.

Lee, Hyung Chul. 2016. "Can Electronic Tax Invoicing Improve Tax Compliance? A Case Study of the Republic of Korea's Electronic Tax Invoicing for Value-Added Tax." *World Bank Group.* Policy Research Working Paper no. 7592. Working paper accessed 01/28/2019, (http://documents.worldbank .org/curated/en/712881467994710005/pdf/WPS7592.pdf).

Lemahieu, Jean-Luc, and Angela Me. 2014. "Global Study on Homicide, 2013." *United Nations Office on Drugs and Crime.* Report accessed 05/22/2018, (https://www.unodc.org /documents/gsh/pdfs/2014_GLOBAL_HOMICIDE_BOOK_ web.pdf).

Leopold, Till Alexander, Saadia Zahidi, and Vesselina Ratcheva. 2017. "The Global Gender Gap Report 2017." *World Economic Forum.* Report accessed 08/06/2018, (https:// www.weforum.org/reports/the-global-gender-gap-report-2017).

Letsch, Constanze. 2015. "Istanbul Hospitals Refuse Abortions as Government's Attitude Hardens." *Guardian.* Website accessed 07/17/2018, (https://www.theguardian.com /world/2015/feb/04/istanbul-hospitals-refuse-abortions-government-attitude).

Levine, Samuel J. 2006. "An Introduction to Self-Incrimination in Jewish Law, with Application to the American Legal System: A Psychological and Philosophical Analysis." *Loyola of Los Angeles International and Comparative Law Review* 28:257–77.

Lewis, James. 2018. "Economic Impact of Cybercrime—No Slowing Down." *McAfee.* Report accessed 05/25/2018, (https://www .mcafee.com/us/resources/reports/restricted/economic-impact-cybercrime.pdf).

Lewis, Mark, and Alan Cowell. 2012. "On Witness Stand, Norwegian Says He Would Kill Again." *New York Times*, 04/18/2012, section A, p. 9.

Lewy, Guenter. 2014. *Outlawing Genocide Denial: The Dilemmas of Official Historical Truth.* Salt Lake City, UT: University of Utah Press.

Leydet, Dominique. 2017. "Citizenship." *Stanford Encyclopedia of Philosophy.* Website accessed 06/06/2018, (https://plato.stanford.edu/entries/citizenship/).

Libell, Henrik Pryser. 2016. "Norway Violated Rights of Anders Behring Breivik, Mass Killer, Judge Rules." *New York Times*, 04/21/2016, section A, p. 6.

Licht, Amir N., Chanan Goldschmidt, and Shalom H. Schwartz. 2007. "Culture Rules: The Foundations of the Rule of Law and Other Norms of Governance." *Journal of Comparative Economics* 35(4):659–88.

Lila, Abu-Lughod. 2002. "Do Muslim Women Really Need Saving? Anthropological Reflections on Cultural Relativism and Its Others." *American Anthropologist* 104(3):783–90.

Liptak, Adam. 2008. "U.S. Voting for Judges Perplexes Other Nations." *New York Times.* Website accessed 01/29/2018, (http://www.nytimes.com/2008/05/25/world/americas/25iht-judge.4.13194819.html).

Listner, Michael J. 2011. "International Space Law: An Overview of Law and Issues." *New Hampshire Bar Journal* 2011 (Spring):62–71.

Liu, Can, and Chiung-Fang Chang. 2006. "Patterns of Sterilization." Pp. 35–47 in *Fertility, Family Planning, and Population Policy in China*, edited by Dudley L. Poston, Che-Fu Lee, Chiung-Fang Chang, Sherry L. McKibben, and Carol S. Walther. Abingdon, UK: Routledge.

Liu, Hung-En. 2001. "Mother or Father: Who Received Custody? The Best Interests of the Child Standard and Judges' Custody Decisions in Taiwan." *International Journal of Law, Policy, and the Family* 15(2):185–225.

Liu, Sida, and Terence C. Halliday. 2016. *Criminal Defense in China: The Politics of Lawyers at Work.* Cambridge, UK: Cambridge University Press.

Lloyd, William Forster. 1833. *Two Lectures on the Checks to Population.* Oxford, UK: S. Collingwood.

Locke, John. [1690] 2008. "Second Treatise of Government." *Early Modern Texts.* Website accessed 07/25/2017, (http://www.earlymoderntexts.com/assets/pdfs/locke1689a.pdf).

Lord, Nicholas, and Rose Broad. 2017. "Corporate Failures to Prevent Serious and Organised Crimes: Foregrounding the 'Organisational' Component." *European Review of Organised Crime* 4(2):27–52.

Low, Harry. 2017. "How Japan Has Almost Eradicated Gun Crime." *BBC News.* Website accessed 03/15/2018, (http://www.bbc.com/news/magazine-38365729).

Lubell, Maayan. 2013. "Israeli Couples Say 'I Don't' to Orthodox Jewish Weddings." *Reuters.* Website accessed 07/17/2018, (https://www.reuters.com/article/us-israel-marriage/israeli-couples-say-i-dont-to-orthodox-jewish-weddings-idUSBRE9AJ0Q120131120).

Luna, Eri. 2004. "A Place for Comparative Criminal Procedure." *University of Louisville Brandeis Law Journal* 42:277–327.

Lundin, Susanne Maria. 2010. "Organ Economy: Organ Trafficking in Moldova and Israel." *Public Understanding of Science* 1:1–16.

Lutze, Faith E., Jeffrey W. Rosky, and Zachary K. Hamilton. 2013. "Homelessness and Reentry: A Multisite Outcome Evaluation of Washington State's Reentry Housing Program

for High Risk Offenders." *Criminal Justice and Behavior* 41(4):471–91.

Lyall, Francis, and Paul B. Larson. 2018. *Space Law: A Treatise.* Oxon, UK: Routledge.

Lynch, James P., and William Alex Pridemore. 2010. "Crime in International Perspective." Pp. 5–52 in *Crime and Public Policy*, edited by James Q. Wilson and Joan Petersilia. New York: Oxford University Press.

Lynch, James P., and William J. Sabol. 1997. "Did Getting Tough on Crime Pay?" *Urban Institute.* Crime Policy Report no. 1. Report accessed 05/22/2018, (http://webarchive.urban.org/publications/307337.html).

MacClintock, Heather. 2010. "Sexism, Surnames, and Social Progress: The Conflict of Individual Autonomy and Government Preferences in Laws Regarding Name Changes at Marriage." *Temple International & Comparative Law Journal* 24:277–312.

Mail Foreign Service. 2010. "Inside Tokyo's Death House." *Daily Mail.* Website accessed 06/29/2017, (http://www.dailymail.co.uk/news/article-1306683/Pictured-time-Japan-opens-doors-death-chambers.html).

Malhotra, Anil, and Ranjit Malhotra. 2012. "India: A Perspective." Pp. 144–74 in *The Future of Child and Family Law: International Predictions*, edited by Elaine E. Sutherland. Cambridge, UK: Cambridge University Press.

Mandal, Saptarshi, and Sachin Dhawan. 2016. "Religious Family Law and Legal Change in Comparative Perspective." *Jindal Global Review* 7(1):1–8.

Mann, Michael. 1986. "The Autonomous Power of the State: Its Origins, Mechanisms, and Results." Pp. 109–36 in *States in History*, edited by John A. Hall. New York: Basil Blackwell.

Marke, Julius J. 1979. "The Last Trial by Battle." *Litigation* 5(2):39–40, 81.

Marotta, Manny. 2018. "South Korea Court: Citizens Can Legally Reject Mandatory Military Service on Conscientious or Religious Grounds." *Jurist.* Website accessed 01/29/2019, (https://www.jurist.org/news/2018/11/south-korea-court-citizens-can-legally-reject-mandatory-military-service-on-conscientious-or-religious-grounds/).

Martin, Justin D., Ralph J. Martins, and Robb Wood. 2016. "Desire for Cultural Preservation as a Predictor of Support for Entertainment Media Censorship in Saudi Arabia, Qatar, and the United Arab Emirates." *International Journal of Communication* 10:3400–422.

Martin, Susan Taylor. 2013. "Florida 'Stand Your Ground' Law Yields Some Shocking Outcomes Depending on How Law Is Applied." *Tampa Bay Times.* Website accessed 03/06/2018, (http://www.tampabay.com/news/publicsafety/crime/florida-stand-your-ground-law-yields-some-shocking-outcomes-depending-on/1233133).

Marx, Karl, and Frederick Engels. [1848] 1906. *Manifesto of the Communist Party.* Chicago: Charles H. Kerr and Company.

Maskin, Eric, and Amartya Sen. 2017. "The Rules of the Game: A New Electoral System." *New York Review of Books.* Website accessed 05/30/2018, (http://www.nybooks.com/articles/2017/01/19/rules-of-the-game-new-electoral-system/).

Matas, Caroline. 2016. "Federal Court Rules Church of Flying Spaghetti Monster Not a Religion." *Harvard Divinity School Religious Literacy Project.* Website accessed 08/03/3018, (https://rlp.hds.harvard.edu/news/federal-court-rules-church-flying-spaghetti-monster-not-religion).

Mautner, Menachem. 2011. "Three Approaches to Law and Culture." *Cornell Law Review* 96(4):839–67.

McDonald, Henry, Emma Graham-Harrison, and Sinead Baker. 2018. "Ireland Votes by Landslide to Legalise Abortion." *Guardian.* Website accessed 02/18/2019, (https://www .theguardian.com/world/2018/may/26/ireland-votes-by-landslide-to-legalise-abortion).

McEvoy, Kieran. 2012. "Commentary on Locality and Legitimacy." Pp. 311–18 in *Critical Perspectives in Transitional Justice, Series on Transitional Justice,* edited by Nicola Palmer, Phil Clark, and Danielle Granville. Cambridge, UK: Intersentia.

McMillian, Lance. 2012. "Adultery as Tort." *North Carolina Law Review* 90(6):1987–2031.

McNally, Darragh. 2016. "Norms, Corruption, and Voting for Berlusconi." *Politics & Policy* 44(5):976–1008.

Mealy's. 2016. "Court at The Hague Rules Ecuador's Lago Agrio Claims Fail to 'Hit Their Mark.'" *Mealey's International Arbitration Report.* Website accessed 06/19/2018, (https:// www.lexislegalnews.com/articles/5648).

Mears, John A. 1969. "The Emergence of the Standing Professional Army in Seventeenth-Century Europe." *Social Science Quarterly* 50(1):106–15.

Meierhenrich, Jens. 2010. "Through a Glass Darkly." *Harvard University.* Website accessed 01/18/2019, (http://maps.cga .harvard.edu/rwanda/home.html).

Merrick, Janna C. 1994. "Christian Science Healing of Minor Children: Spiritual Exemption Statutes, First Amendment Rights, and Fair Notice." *Issues in Law and Medicine* 10(3):321–42.

Merry, Sally Engle. 1979. "Going to Court: Strategies of Dispute Management in an American Urban Neighborhood." *Law & Society Review* 13(4):891–925.

———. 1988. "Legal Pluralism." *Law & Society Review* 22(5):869–96.

Merton, Robert. 1968. *Social Theory and Social Structure.* New York: Free Press.

Michaels, Ralph. 2018. "Banning Burqas: The Perspective of Postsecular Comparative Law." *Duke Journal of Comparative and International Law* 28(2):214–45.

Michelson, Ethan. 2018. "Lawyers Every Country." Unpublished data provided 1/20/2018 (on file with author).

Milbank, Dana. 2012. "Mike Lee vs. the Disabled." *Salt Lake Tribune.* Website accessed 06/26/2018, (http://archive.sltrib.com /article.php?id=55357260&itype=CMSID).

Miles, Hugh. 2012. "Qatari Poet Appeals over Life Prison Sentence." *BBC News.* Website accessed 08/20/2018, (https://www.bbc .com/news/world-middle-east-20550160).

Millay, Edna St. Vincent. [1934] 1956. "Childhood Is the Kingdom Where Nobody Dies." Pp. 286–88 in *Collected Poems,* edited by Edna St. Vincent Millay. New York: Harper and Row.

Miller, Richard E., and Austin Sarat. 1980–81. "Grievances, Claims, and Disputes: Assessing the Adversary Culture." *Law & Society Review* 15(3/4):525–66.

Ministry of Justice. 2014. "Court Statistics Quarterly: January to March 2014." *National Statistics UK.* Report accessed 01/22/2018, (https://www.gov.uk/government/uploads /system/uploads/attachment_data/file/321352/court-statistics-jan-mar-2014.pdf).

Ministry of Social Affairs. 2018. "New Icelandic Law on Equal Pay Certification Entered into Force on January 1, 2018." *Government of Iceland.* Website accessed 08/06/2018, (https://www.government.is/news/article/2018/01/04 /New-Icelandic-law-on-Equal-Pay-Certification-entered-into-force-on-January-1–2018/).

Minow, Martha. 1998. *Between Justice and Forgiveness: Facing History after Genocide and Mass Violence.* Boston, MA: Beacon Press.

Mirabella, Julia Grace. 2012. "Scales of Justice: Assessing Italian Criminal Procedure through the Amanda Knox Trial." *Boston University International Law Journal* 30(1):229–60.

Mokgoro, Yvonne. 2002. "Report on Traditional Courts and the Judicial Function of Traditional Leaders." *South African Law Commission, Pretoria, South Africa.* Traditional Law no. 90. Report accessed 02/25/2018, (http://www.justice.gov.za /salrc/reports/r_prj90_tradlead_2003jan.pdf).

Monnet, Charles. 1794. "The Execution of Queen Marie Antoinette of France." Copper engraving, Bibliothèque nationale de France, département Estampes et photographie, RESERVE QB-370 (33)-FT 4. Image accessed 06/30/2017, (http:// chnm.gmu.edu/revolution/d/183).

Montagne, Renee, and Nina Martin. 2017. "U.S. Has the Worst Rate of Maternal Deaths in the Developed World." *National Public Radio.* Website accessed 08/03/2018, (https://www .npr.org/2017/05/12/528098789/u-s-has-the-worst-rate-of-maternal-deaths-in-the-developed-world).

Moody, Barry, and Roberto Landucci. 2012. "Insight: Overloaded Justice System Ties Italy in Knots." *Reuters.* Website accessed 02/19/2018, (https://www.reuters.com/article /us-italy-justice/insight-overloaded-justice-system-ties-italy-in-knots-idUSBRE83409E20120405).

Mosbergen, Dominique. 2015. "Pastafarian Allowed to Wear Colander in Driver's License Photo." *Huffington Post.* Website accessed 08/03/2018, (https://www.huffingtonpost .com/entry/pastafarian-colander-license-photo_us_ 56498e42e4b08cda34897b27).

Mosher, Clayton J., Terance D. Miethe, and Timothy C. Hart. 2011. "Introduction: The Pervasiveness (and Limitations) of Measurement." Pp. 1–29 in *The Mismeasure of Crime.* Thousand Oaks, CA: Sage.

Moyn, Samuel. 2010. *The Last Utopia: Human Rights in History.* Cambridge, MA: Belknap Press of Harvard University Press.

Murphy, Sean D. 2002. "American Servicemembers' Protection Act." *American Journal of International Law* 96(4):975–7.

Myers, Joe. 2016. "How Do the World's Biggest Companies Compare to the Biggest Economies?" *World Economic Forum.* Website accessed 09/18/2018, (https://www.weforum.org /agenda/2016/10/corporations-not-countries-dominate-the-list-of-the-world-s-biggest-economic-entities).

National Center for State Courts. 2015. "The Landscape of Civil Litigation in State Courts." *Civil Justice Initiative.* Report accessed 01/22/2018, (https://www.ncsc.org/~/media/Files /PDF/Research/CivilJusticeReport-2015.ashx).

National Conference of State Legislators. 2018. "Felon Voting Rights." Website accessed 06/05/2013, (http://www.ncsl .org/research/elections-and-campaigns/felon-voting-rights.aspx).

National Police Agency. 2011. "Rainichi Gaikokujin Hanzai no Kenkyo Jōkyō" [Report on criminal arrests of foreigners visiting Japan]. Tokyo: National Police Agency.

National Policing Improvement Agency. 2011. "Manual of Guidance on the Management, Command and Deployment of Armed Officers, 3rd Edition." *Specialist Operations Centre.* Report accessed 03/14/2018, (http://www.npcc.police.uk /documents/FoI%20publication/Disclosure%20Logs /Uniformed%20Operations%20FOI/2012/093%2012%20 %20Att%2001%20of%201%20Management%20 Command%20and%20delpyment%20of%20Firearms%20 Officers.pdf).

National Statistical Office of Thailand. n.d. "Population by Religion, Sex and Area, 2015." Website accessed 08/23/2018, (http://

web.nso.go.th/en/survey/popchan/data/2015–2016-Statistical%20tables%20PDF.pdf).

Ndulo, Muna. 2011. "African Customary Law, Customs, and Women's Rights." *Indiana Journal of Global Legal Studies* 18(1):87–120.

Neily, Clark. 2017. "If the Law Is This Complicated, Why Shouldn't Ignorance Be an Excuse?" *CATO Institute.* Website accessed 05/22/2018, (https://www.cato.org/publications /commentary/law-complicated-why-shouldnt-ignorance-be-excuse).

Nelken, David. 2009. "Comparative Criminal Justice: Beyond Ethnocentricism and Relativism." *European Journal of Criminology* 6(4):291–311.

———. 2010a. *Comparative Criminal Justice.* London, UK: Sage.

———. 2010b. "Using the Concept of Legal Culture." Pp. 279–304 in *Legal Theory and the Social Sciences*, vol. 2 of *The Library of Essays in Contemporary Legal Theory*, edited by Maksymilian Del Mar and Michael Giudice. Surrey, UK: Ashgate.

Nellis, Mike, Kristel Beyens, and Dan Kamnski. 2013. "Introduction: Making Sense of Electronic Monitoring." Pp. 1–18 in *Electronically Monitored Punishment: International and Critical Perspectives*, edited by Mike Nellis, Kristel Beyens, and Dan Kamnski. London, UK: Routledge.

New York Times. 1988. "U.S. Opposes Raising Minimum Combat Age to 18." Website accessed 08/23/2018, (https://www .nytimes.com/1988/12/01/world/us-opposes-raising-minimum-combat-age-to-18.html).

Nickel, James. 2014. "Human Rights." *Stanford Encyclopedia of Philosophy.* Website accessed 07/25/2018, (https://plato .stanford.edu/entries/rights-human/).

Nicola, Fernanda G. 2010. "Family Law Exceptionalism in Comparative Law." *American Journal of Comparative Law* 58(4):777–810.

Noack, Rick. 2015. "When Peeing in Public in This German City, Beware Walls That Pee Back." *Washington Post.* Website accessed 05/10/2018, (https://www.washingtonpost.com /news/worldviews/wp/2015/03/12/when-peeing-in-public-in-this-german-city-beware-walls-that-pee-back/).

Noor, Farish. 2010. "From Empire to War on Terror: The 1915 Indian Sepoy Mutiny in Singapore as a Case Study of the Impact of Profiling of Religious and Ethnic Minorities." *S. Rajaratnam School of International Studies, Singapore.* RSIS Working Paper no. 206. Working paper accessed 02/04/2019, (https://www.rsis.edu.sg/rsis-publication /idss/206-wp206-from-empire-to-the-war/).

Nordmeyer, Kristijane, Nicole Bedera, and Trisha Teig. 2016. "Ending White Saviorism in Study Abroad." *Contexts* 15(4):78–79.

Northern Ireland Human Rights Commission. 2013. "Dealing with Northern Ireland's Past: Towards a Transitional Justice Approach." Report accessed 01/18/2019, (http://www.nihrc .org/uploads/publications/NIHRC_Transitional_Justice_ Report.pdf).

Nutt, David J., Leslie A. King, and Lawrence D. Phillips. 2010. "Drug Harms in the UK: A Multicriteria Decision Analysis." *Lancet* 376(10):1558–65.

Odinokova, Veronika, Maia Rusakova, Lianne A. Urada, Jay G. Silverman, and Anita Raj. 2014. "Police Sexual Coercion and Its Association with Risky Sex Work and Substance Use Behaviors among Female Sex Workers in St. Petersburg and Orenburg, Russia." *International Journal of Drug Policy* 25(1):96–104.

O'Donnell, Guillermo A. 2004. "Why the Rule of Law Matters." *Journal of Democracy* 15(4):32–46.

OECD (Organisation for Economic Co-operation and Development). 2016. "OECD Data." Website accessed 05/24/2016, (https://data.oecd.org/).

———. n.d.-a. "Family Database: By Country—The Structure of Families." *OECD.Stat.* Website accessed 07/13/2018, (https://stats.oecd.org/index.aspx?queryid=68249#).

———. n.d.-b. "Real Minimum Wages." *OECD.Stat.* Website accessed 08/06/2018, (https://stats.oecd.org/Index .aspx?DataSetCode=RMW).

Office of the Secretary-General's Envoy on Youth. 2015. "4 Out of 10 Child Soldiers Are Girls." *United Nations.* Website accessed 09/04/2018, (http://www.un.org/youthenvoy/2015/02 /4–10-child-soldiers-girls/).

Offner, Jerome A. 2017. "The Future of Aztec Law." Pp. 1–32 in *Legal Encounters on the Medieval Globe*, edited by Elizabeth Lambourn. Kalamazoo, MI: Arc Humanities Press.

Ognibene, Silvia. 2017. "Italy's Berlusconi Sent to Trial Accused of Bribing Witness." *Reuters.* Website accessed 08/08/2018, (https://www.reuters.com/article/us-italy-berlusconi-trial /italys-berlusconi-sent-to-trial-accused-of-bribing-witness-source-idUSKBN1DU2NE).

Ohnesorge, John K. M. 2007. "The Rule of Law." *Annual Review of Law and Social Science* 3:99–114.

Oldenquist, Andrew. 1988. "An Explanation of Retribution." *Journal of Philosophy* 85(9):464–78.

Olson, Kyle J. O. n.d. "Sgt. Justin L. Bertoniere, 3rd Brigade Combat Team, 10th Mountain Division, Looks at His Display as He Prepares to Launch the Black Hornet III during Field Testing at Fort A.P. Hill, Va." U.S. Army. Image accessed 09/18/2018, (https://www.army.mil/article/205997/small_ birdlike_uas_to_provide_eyes_in_the_sky_for_soldiers).

O'Neil, Cathy. 2016. *Weapons of Math Destruction: How Big Data Increases Inequality and Threatens Democracy.* New York: Broadway Books.

Oomen, Barbara. 2005. *Chiefs in South Africa: Law, Power, and Culture in the Post-Apartheid Era.* New York: Palgrave.

O'Rourke, Clara. 2019. "The Desperado." *Atavist.* Website accessed 02/12/2019, (https://magazine.atavist.com/the-desperado-ed-averill-bank-robbery-austin-texas).

Ortiz, Gonzalo. 2011. "Ecuador: 'Universal Citizenship' Clashes with Reality." *Inter Press Service News Agency.* Website accessed 06/26/2018, (http://www.ipsnews.net/2011/02/ecuador-universal-citizenship-clashes-with-reality/).

Ortiz-Ospina, Esteban, and Max Roser. 2018. "Child Labor." *Our World in Data.* Website accessed 08/23/2018, (https:// ourworldindata.org/child-labor).

Ovuga, Emilio, and Charles Madrama. 2006. "Burden of Alcohol Use in the Uganda Police Department." *African Health Sciences* 6(1):14–20.

Pacuit, Eric. 2011. "Voting Methods." *Stanford Encyclopedia of Philosophy.* Website accessed 05/30/2018, (https://plato .stanford.edu/entries/voting-methods/).

Pap, András. 2009. "Police Ethnic Profiling in Hungary—Lessons from an International Research." *Acta Juridica Hungarica* 50(3):253–67.

Pardo, Osvaldo F. 2006. "How to Punish Indians: Law and Cultural Change in Early Colonial Mexico." *Comparative Studies in Society and History* 48(1):79–109.

Parker, Kim, Juliana Menasce Horowitz, Ruth Igielnik, Baxter Oliphant, and Anna Brown. 2017. "America's Complex Relationship with Guns." *Pew Research Center.* Website accessed 03/14/2018, (http://www.pewsocialtrends .org/2017/06/22/the-demographics-of-gun-ownership/).

Parker, L. Craig, Jr. 2001. *The Japanese Police System Today: A Comparative Study.* Armonk, NY: M. E. Sharpe.

Parker, Sarah. 2011. "Balancing Act: Regulation of Civilian Firearm Possession." Pp. 261–351 in *Small Arms Survey 2011*, edited by Keither Krause and Eric G. Berman. Geneva, Switzerland: Graduate Institute of International and Development Studies.

Parloff, Roger. 2014. "Judge: $9.5 Billion Ecuadorian Verdict against Chevron Was Product of Bribery." *Fortune.* Website accessed 06/19/2018, (http://fortune.com/2014/03/05/judge-9-5-billion-ecuadorian-verdict-against-chevron-was-product-of-bribery/).

Pasquale, Frank. 2017. "Secret Algorithms Threaten the Rule of Law." *MIT Technology Review.* Website accessed 09/17/2018, (https://www.technologyreview.com/s/608011/secret-algorithms-threaten-the-rule-of-law/).

Paterson, Craig. 2013. "Commercial Crime Control and the Development of Electronically Monitored Punishment: A Global Perspective." Pp. 211–27 in *Electronically Monitored Punishment: International and Critical Perspectives*, edited by Mike Nellis, Kristel Beyens, and Dan Kamnski. London, UK: Routledge.

Pattinson, Shaun D. 2008. "'Organ Trading, Tourism, and Trafficking within Europe." *Medicine and Law* 27(1):191–201.

Paxton, Pamela, and Melanie M. Hughes. 2017. *Women, Politics, and Power: A Global Perspective.* Thousand Oaks, CA: CQ Press.

Perelli-Harris, Brienna, and Nora Sánchez Gassen. 2012. "How Similar Are Cohabitation and Marriage? Legal Approaches to Cohabitation across Western Europe." *Population and Development Review* 38(3):435–67.

Perrin, Jonas. 2017. "Legal Pluralism as a Method of Interpretation: A Methodological Approach to Decolonising Indigenous Peoples' Land Rights under International Law." *Universitas, Revista de Ciencias Sociales y Humanas* 15(26):25–62.

Perry, Alex. 2018. "The Women Who Took On the Mafia." *New Yorker.* Website accessed 08/08/2018, (https://www.newyorker.com/magazine/2018/01/22/the-women-who-took-on-the-mafia).

Peters, Edward. 2013. "A Catechist's Introduction to Canon Law." *CanonLaw.Info.* Website accessed 07/05/2018, (http://www.canonlaw.info/a_catechistintro.htm).

Philadelphia Police (@PhillyPolice). 2014. "@maddieles your lawn chair will be thrown in jail with its accomplices, Orange Cone and Trash Can. #NoSavsies." Twitter, 1/2/2014, 4:34 P.M. Post accessed 08/21/2018, (https://twitter.com/PhillyPolice/status/418903081179709440).

Phillips, Anne. 2009. *Multicultualism without Culture.* Princeton, NJ: Princeton University Press.

Pierotti, Rachael S. 2013. "Increasing Rejection of Intimate Partner Violence: Evidence of Global Cultural Diffusion." *American Sociological Review* 78(2):240–65.

Pinto-Duschinsky, Michael. 2002. "Financing Politics: A Global View." *Journal of Democracy* 13(4):69–86.

Pipes, Daniel. 2014. "Here's How the Muslim World Believes Women Should Dress." *National Review.* Website accessed 08/21/2018, (https://www.nationalreview.com/corner/heres-how-muslim-world-believes-women-should-dress-daniel-pipes/).

Plott, Elaina. 2018. "The Country's First Climate Change Casualties?" *Pacific Standard.* Website accessed 09/24/2018, (https://psmag.com/magazine/the-countrys-first-climate-change-casualties).

Pollack, Danielle, Moshe Bleich, Charles J. Reid, Jr., and Mohammed H. Fadel. 2004. "Classical Religious Perspectives of Adoption Law." *Notre Dame Law Review* 79(2):693–52.

Pont, Vivian Newman, Maria Paula Ángel, and María Ximena Dávila. 2018. "Victims and Press After the War: Tensions Between Privacy, Historical Truth, and Freedom of Expression." *Dejusticia.* Report accessed 08/07/2018, (https://www.dejusticia.org/en/column/victims-press-war-said-unsaid-lessons/).

Public's Radio. 2019. "Saudi Arabia Allows Women to Travel without Male Consent." Website accessed 08/02/2019, (https://thepublicsradio.org/article/saudi-arabia-allows-women-to-travel-without-male-consent).

Punch, Maurice. 2009. *Police Corruption: Deviance, Reform, and Accountability in Policing.* Devon, UK: Willan Publishing.

Quigley, John. 1989. "Socialist Law and the Civil Law Tradition." *American Journal of Comparative Law* 37(4):781–808.

Quinn, Job. 2004. "Constraints: The Un-Doing of the Ugandan Truth Commission." *Human Rights Quarterly* 26(2):401–27.

Raffaele, Paul. 2007. "The Pirate Hunters." *Smithsonian Magazine.* Website accessed 08/03/2009, (https://www.smithsonianmag.com/innovation/the-pirate-hunters-159331252/).

Ramsay, George Daniel. 1975. *The City of London in International Politics at the Accession of Elizabeth Tudor.* Manchester, UK: Manchester University Press.

Ramseyer, J. Mark, and Eric B. Rasmusen. 2010. "Comparative Litigation Rates." *Harvard University, Cambridge, MA.* John M. Olin Discussion Paper no. 681. Working paper accessed 02/19/2018, (http://www.law.harvard.edu/programs/olin_center/papers/pdf/Ramseyer_681.pdf).

Rashad, Hoda, Magued Osman, and Farzaneh Roudi-Fahimi. 2005. "Marriage in the Arab World." *Population Reference Bureau.* Website accessed 1/13/2012, (https://www.prb.org/marriageinthearabworld/).

Ratcliffe, Jerry H. 2008. "Intelligence-Led Policing." Pp. 263–82 in *Environmental Criminology and Crime Analysis*, edited by Richard Wortley and Lorraine Mazerolle. Cullompton, UK: Willan Publishing.

Ray, Rebecca, Milla Sanes, and John Schmitt. 2013. "No-Vacation Nation Revisited." *Center for Economic and Policy Research.* Report accessed 08/06/2018, (http://cepr.net/publications/reports/no-vacation-nation-2013).

Raymond, Elizabeth G., and David A. Grimes. 2012. "The Comparative Safety of Legal Induced Abortion and Childbirth in the United States." *Obstetrics & Gynecology* 119(2):215–19.

Reichel, Philip L. 2007. *Comparative Criminal Justice Systems.* 5th ed. New York: Pearson.

Renteln, Alison Dundes. 2004. *The Cultural Defense.* Cary, NC: Oxford University Press.

———. 2010. "Corporal Punishment and the Cultural Defense." *Law and Contemporary Problems* 73(2):253–79.

República Portuguesa. 2000. "Lei n.º 30/2000" *Diário da República.* Website accessed 05/10/2018, (https://dre.pt/pesquisa/-/search/599720/details/).

Reputation VIP. 2018. "Discover What Is the Right to Be Forgotten." *Forget.me.* Website accessed 07/25/2018, (https://www.forget.me/).

Research Institute for Higher Education. 2018. "Table 33: Number of Graduates, Universities (Undergraduates), Males and Females." *Hiroshima University.* Dataset accessed 01/20/2018, (rihe.hiroshima-u.ac.jp/wp/wp-content/uploads/date_en/pdf/EG33.pdf).

Reuters. 2009. "Indonesian District Launches Unique Reforestation Plan." Website accessed 07/13/2018, (https://www.reuters .com/article/us-indonesia-marriage-trees/indonesian-district-launches-unique-reforestation-plan-idUSTRE52320G20090304).

———. 2017. "Justicia Argentina Rechaza Apelación Contra Chevron en Caso de Contaminación en Ecuador" [Argentine justice denies appeal against Chevron in case of pollution in Ecuador]. *El Universo.* Website accessed 06/19/2018, (https://www.eluniverso.com/noticias/ 2017/11/02/nota/6462619/justicia-argentina-rechaza-apelacion-contra-chevron-caso).

Reynolds, Andrew, Ben Reilly, and Andrew Ellis. 2008. "Electoral System Design: The New International IDEA Handbook." *International Institute for Democracy and Electoral Assistance.* Report accessed 05/30/2018, (https://www.idea .int/sites/default/files/publications/electoral-system-design-the-new-international-idea-handbook.pdf).

Reyntjens, Filip. 1990. "Le Gacaca ou la Justice du Gazon au Rwanda." *Politique Africaine* 40:31–41.

Rhodes, Christopher J. 2016. "The 2015 Paris Climate Change Conference: COP21." *Science Progress* 99(1):97–104.

Rhodes, Tim, Milena Simić, Sladjana Baroš, Lucy Platt, and Bojan Žikić. 2008. "Police Violence and Sexual Risk among Female and Transvestite Sex Workers in Serbia: A Qualitative Study." *BMJ* 337(a118):1–6.

Richburg, Keith B. 2009. "Rabbis, New Jersey Politicians among 44 Arrested in Corruption Probe." *Washington Post.* Website accessed 05/25/2018, (http://www.washingtonpost.com /wp-dyn/content/article/2009/07/23/AR2009072301449 .html).

Riddell, William Renwick. 1926. "Appeal of Death and Its Abolition." *Michigan Law Review* 24(8):786–808.

Riddle, John M. 1991. "Oral Contraceptives and Early-Term Abortifacients during Classical Antiquity and the Middle Ages." *Past & Present* 132(1):3–32.

Ritzer, George. 2011. *The McDonaldization of Society.* Thousand Oaks, CA: Pine Forge Press.

Robbins, Anthony. 2016. "How to Understand the Results of the Climate Change Summit: Conference of Parties21 (COP21) Paris 2015." *Journal of Public Health Policy* 37(2):129–32.

Rogers, Brian. 2018a. "Houston Death Penalty Trial Brings Focus to Scourge of 'Honor Killings.'" *Houston Chronicle.* Website accessed 08/30/2018, (https://www.houstonchronicle.com /news/houston-texas/houston/article/Houston-death-penalty-trial-brings-focus-to-13153602.php).

———. 2018b. "Jury Delivers Death Sentence for Jordanian Immigrant Convicted of Two Houston-Area 'Honor Killings.'" *Houston Chronicle.* Website accessed 08/30/2018, (https://www.chron.com/news/houston-texas/houston /article/Jury-gives-decides-on-death-sentence-for-Jordian-13155493.php).

Roht-Arriaza, Naomi, and Javier Mariecurrena. 2006. *Transitional Justice in the Twenty-First Century: Beyond Truth versus Justice.* Cambridge, UK: Cambridge University Press.

Rohter, Larry. 2005. "Divorce Ties Chile in Knots." *New York Times.* Website accessed 07/10/2018, (https://www.nytimes .com/2005/01/30/weekinreview/divorce-ties-chile-in-knots.html).

Romanowski, Michael H., and Ramzi Nasser. 2010. "Faculty Perceptions of Academic Freedom at a GCC University." *Prospects* 40(4):481–97.

Rønning, Helge. 2016. "On Press Freedom and Other Media Freedoms." Pp. 43–51 in *Freedom of Expression and Media in Transition: Studies and Reflections in the Digital Age,* edited by Ulla Carlsson. Göteborg, Sweden: Nordicom and UNESCO.

Rosen, David. 2005. *Armies of the Young: Child Soldiers in War and Terrorism.* New Brunswick, NJ: Rutgers University Press.

Ross, Jacqueline E. 2008. "Undercover Policing and the Shifting Terms of Scholarly Debate: The United States and Europe in Counterpoint." *Annual Review of Law and Social Science* 4:239–73.

Rotman, Edgardo. 1995. "The Inherent Problems of Legal Translation: Theoretical Aspects." *Indiana International & Comparative Law Review* 6(1):187–96.

Rounds, Jay. 1977. "The Role of the Tecuhtli in Ancient Aztec Society." *Ethnohistory* 24(4):343–61.

Royal Commission. 1893. *Statement as to the Origin, Position, Powers, Duties, and Finance of the Corporation of London.* London, UK: City of London.

Rueschemeyer, Dietrich. 1987. "Comparing Legal Professions Cross-Nationally: From a Professions-Centered to a State-Centered Approach." *American Bar Foundation Research Journal* 11(3):415–46.

Ruotolo, Gianpaolo Maria. 2017. "Fragments of Fragments. The Domain Name System Regulation: Global Law or Informalization of the International Legal Order?" *Computer Law & Security Review* 33(2):159–70.

Sabuj, Kudrate Khoda. 2018. "16-Year-Old Boy From Kushtia Has Been Married Four Times." *Dhaka Tribune.* Website accessed 07/24/2018, (https://www.dhakatribune.com /feature/2018/07/24/16-year-old-boy-from-kushtia-has-been-married-four-times).

Saiko saibansho [Supreme Court of Japan]. n.d. "Shiho tokei nempo" [Judicial statistics annual report]. Report accessed 01/08/2018, (http://www.courts.go.jp/app/sihotokei_jp/search).

Sampson, Robert J., and Stephen W. Raudenbush. 1999. "Systematic Social Observation of Public Spaces: A New Look at Disorder in Urban Neighborhoods." *American Journal of Sociology* 105(3):603–51.

Sampson, Robert J., and W. Byron Groves. 1989. "Community Structure and Crime: Testing Social-Disorganization Theory." *American Journal of Sociology* 94(4):774–802.

Samuels, David. 2010. "The Pink Panthers: A Tale of Diamonds, Thieves, and the Balkans." *New Yorker.* Website accessed 04/13/2010, (https://www.newyorker.com/magazine/2010 /04/12/the-pink-panthers).

Sang-Hun, Chloe. 2018. "South Korea Must Offer Alternatives to Military Draft, Court Rules." *New York Times.* Website accessed 07/27/2018, (https://www.nytimes.com/2018 /06/28/world/asia/south-korea-military-service-conscientious-objectors.html).

Santos-Ong, Milagros. 2015. "Philippine Legal Research." *Hauser Global Law School Program, New York University School of Law.* Website accessed 07/11/2018, (http://www .nyulawglobal.org/globalex/Philippines1.html).

Saudi Gazette. 2018. "A Rundown on Reasons for Rising Divorce Rate in Saudi Arabia." *Al Arabiya.* Website accessed 07/19/2018, (http://english.alarabiya.net/en/life-style/art-and-culture/2018/02/10/A-rundown-on-reasons-for-rising-divorce-rate-in-Saudi-Arabia-.html).

Saura, Jaume. 2016. "On the Implications of the Use of Drones in International Law." *Journal of International Law and International Relations* 12(1):120–50.

Sawyer, Bradley. 2017. "How Does the Quality of the U.S. Healthcare System Compare to Other Countries?" *Kaiser Family Foundation.* Website accessed 08/03/2018, (https://www

.healthsystemtracker.org/chart-collection/quality-u-s-healthcare-system-compare-countries/).

Sawyer, Bradley, and Cynthia Cox. 2018. "How Does Health Spending in the U.S. Compare to Other Countries?" Kaiser Family Foundation. Website accessed 08/03/2018, (https://www.healthsystemtracker.org/chart-collection/health-spending-u-s-compare-countries/).

Scarry, Elaine. 1985. *The Body in Pain: The Making and Unmaking of the World.* Oxford, UK: Oxford University Press.

Schabas, William A. 2001. *An Introduction to the International Criminal Court.* Cambridge, UK: Cambridge University Press.

Schanz, Deborah. n.d. "Tax Attractiveness Index." *Institute for Taxation and Accounting, Ludwig Maximilian University of Munich.* Website accessed 08/03/2018, (https://www.tax-index.org).

Schiavenza, Matt. 2013. "China's Big (and Growing) Problem with Its Elderly Population." *Atlantic.* Website accessed 07/20/2018, (https://www.theatlantic.com/china/archive/2013/07/chinas-big-and-growing-problem-with-its-elderly-population/277656/).

Schmid, Carol, Brigita Zepa, and Arta Snipe. 2004. "Language Policy and Ethnic Tensions in Quebec and Latvia." *International Journal of Comparative Sociology* 45(3/4):231–52.

Schneider, Friedrich. 2017. "The Dark Side: Crime Has Gone Global." Pp. 72–101 in *A Closer Look at Globalization: The Positive Facets and the Dark Faces of a Complex Notion,* edited by Jörg Habich. Gütersloh, Germany: Bertelsmann Stiftung.

Sciurba, Michele. 2018. *Anti-Money Laundering State Mechanisms: International Experiences, Current Issues and Future Challenges.* Frankfurt am Main, Germany: Edition Faust.

Secretaría de Servicios Parlamentarios. 2012. "Ley de Nacionalidad: Nueva Ley Publicada en el Diario Oficial de la Federación el 23 de Enero de 1998." *Cámara de Diputados del H. Congreso de la Unión.* Website accessed 06/06/2018, (http://www.diputados.gob.mx/LeyesBiblio/pdf/53.pdf).

Sedgh, Gilda, Lori S. Ashford, and Rubina Hussain. 2016. "Unmet Need for Contraception in Developing Countries: Examining Women's Reasons for Not Using a Method." *Guttmacher Institute.* Website accessed 07/18/2018, (https://www.guttmacher.org/report/unmet-need-for-contraception-in-developing-countries).

Semple, Kirk. 2009. "Court Battle over a Child Strains Ties in Two Nations." *New York Times,* 02/25/2009, section A, p. A21.

Setor de Administração Federal Sul. 2014. "An Increased Number of Brazilian Voters Are Eligible to Vote Abroad." *Superior Electoral Court.* Website accessed 05/31/2018, (http://english.tse.jus.br/noticias-tse-en/2014/Julho/an-increased-number-of-brazilian-voters-are-eligible-to-vote-abroad).

Seus, John M. 1969. "Aztec Law." *American Bar Association Journal* 55(7):736–39.

Shackelford, Scott J., Scott Russell, and Andreas Kuehn. 2016. "Unpacking the International Law on Cybersecurity Due Diligence: Lessons from the Public and Private Sectors." *Chicago Journal of International Law* 17(1):1–50.

Shadian, Jessica. 2010. "From States to Polities: Reconceptualizing Sovereignty through Inuit Governance." *European Journal of International Relations* 16(3):485–510.

Shafer, Emily Fitzgibbons. 2017. "Hillary Rodham versus Hillary Clinton: Consequences of Surname Choice in Marriage." *Gender Issues* 34(4):316–32.

Shahidulah, Shahid M. 2014. *Comparative Criminal Justice Systems: Global and Local Perspectives.* Burlington, MA: Jones and Bartlett Learning.

Shapiro, Martin. 1980. "Appeal." *Law & Society Review* 14(3):629–61.

Shapiro, Sarah, and Catherine Brown. 2018. "The State of Civics Education." *Center for American Progress.* Website accessed 08/23/2018, (https://www.americanprogress.org/issues/education-k-12/reports/2018/02/21/446857/state-civics-education/).

Shear, Michael D. 2017. "Trump Will Withdraw U.S. from Paris Climate Agreement." *New York Times.* Website accessed 09/24/2018, (https://www.nytimes.com/2017/06/01/climate/trump-paris-climate-agreement.html).

Shimazono, Yosuke. 2007. "The State of the International Organ Trade: A Provisional Picture Based on Integration of Available Information." *Bulletin of the World Health Organization* 85(12):901–80.

Shultz, Cynthia B. 1989. "Economic Crimes in the People's Republic of China: A Swinging Door Policy." *American University International Law Review* 5(1):161–206.

Siaroff, Alan. 2003. "Comparative Presidencies: The Inadequacy of the Presidential, Semi-Presidential and Parliamentary Distinction." *European Journal of Political Research* 42(3):287–312.

Sierra, Isabel Cristina Jaramillo, and Helena Alviar. 2015. "'Family' as a Legal Concept." *CS* (15):91–109.

Silbey, Susan S. 2005. "After Legal Consciousness." *Annual Review of Law and Social Science* 2005(1):323–68.

———. 2012. "J. Locke, Op. Cit.: Invocations of Law on Snowy Streets." *Journal of Comparative Law* 5(2):66–91.

Simmel, Georg. 1950. "The Stranger." Pp. 403–408 in *The Sociology of Georg Simmel,* edited by Kurt H. Wolff. New York: Free Press.

Simon, Matt. 2014. "Fantastically Wrong: Europe's Insane History of Putting Animals on Trial and Executing Them." *Wired.* Website accessed 01/22/2018, (https://www.wired.com/2014/09/fantastically-wrong-europes-insane-history-putting-animals-trial-executing/).

Simpson, Alfred William Brian. 1981. "Cannibals at Common Law." *Law School Record* 27(2):2–10.

Singh, Susheela, Lisa Remez, Gilda Sedgh, Lorraine Kwok, and Tsuyoshi Onda. 2018. "Abortion Worldwide 2017: Uneven Progress and Unequal Access." *Guttmacher Institute.* Website accessed 07/17/2018, (https://www.guttmacher.org/report/abortion-worldwide-2017).

Skakavac, Zdravko, Tatjana Skakavac, and Sanja Skakavac. 2016. "'Pink Panther'—Activities and Characteristics of the Criminal Activity." *Sovremennye Problemy Prava, Economiki i Upravleniya* [Modern problems of law, economics and management] 1(2):91–97.

Slater, Dashka. 2017. "Prison Break." *Mother Jones,* July/August, pp. 42–49.

Smith, Clive Stafford. 2013. *Injustice: Life and Death in the Courtrooms of America.* London, UK: Vintage.

Smith, Donald Eugene. 2005. "Religion, Law, and Secularism." Pp. 158–73 in *Sociology of Law, Oxford in India Readings in Sociology and Anthropology,* edited by Indra Deva. New Delhi, India: Oxford University Press.

Solanki, Khushbu. 2017. "Buried, Cremated, Defleshed by Buzzards? Religiously Motivated Excarnatory Funeral Practices are Not Abuse of Corpse." *Rutgers Journal of Law and Religion* 18(3):351–86.

Søreide, Tina. Forthcoming. "Regulating Corruption in International Markets: Why Governments Introduce Laws They Fail to Enforce." In *The Oxford Handbook of International Economic Governance and Market Regulation,* edited by Eric Brousseau, Jean Michel Glachant, and Jérôme Sgard. Oxford: Oxford University Press.

Sozialministerium and BM.I. n.d. "Citizenship." Living and Working in Austria. Website accessed 06/06/2018, (https://www.migration.gv.at/en/living-and-working-in-austria/integration-and-citizenship/citizenship/).

Spaht, Katherine Shaw. 2005. "Covenant Marriage Seven Years Later: Its as Yet Unfulfilled Promise." *Louisiana Law Review* 65(2):605–34.

Spapens, Toine, Rob White, and Marieke Kluin. 2016. *Environmental Crime and Its Victims: Perspectives within Green Criminology.* Oxon, UK: Routledge.

Spillman, Lyn. 2011. "Culture." Pp. 112–14 in *The Concise Encyclopedia of Sociology,* edited by George Ritzer and Michael Ryan. Malden, MA: Wiley-Blackwell.

Stark, Barbara. [2005] 2016. *International Family Law: An Introduction.* Abingdon, UK: Routledge.

Starr, Douglas. 2013. "The Interview: Do Police Interrogation Techniques Produce False Confessions?" *New Yorker,* 12/9/2013, pp. 42–49.

State of Israel. 2013. "Acquisition of Israeli Nationality." *Israel Ministry of Foreign Affairs.* Website accessed 06/06/2018, (http://www.mfa.gov.il/mfa/aboutisrael/state/pages/acquisition%20of%20israeli%20nationality.aspx).

State of Jersey. 2018. "Islanders Asked for their Views on Divorce." *Information and Public Services for the Island of Jersey.* Website accessed 07/24/2018, (https://www.gov.je/News/2018/Pages/DivorceReform.aspx).

Statistics Canada. 2016. "Table 6: Operating Expenditures of the Adult Correctional System, by Jurisdiction, 2014/2015." *Juristat.* Website accessed 07/06/2017, (http://www.statcan.gc.ca/pub/85–002-x/2016001/article/14318/tbl/tbl06-eng.htm).

Storti, Cláudia Costa, and Paul De Grauwe. 2012. *Illicit Trade and the Global Economy.* Cambridge, MA: MIT Press.

Strasburger, R. Lee, Jr. 2013. "The Best Interests of the Child? The Cultural Defense as Justification for Child Abuse." *Pace International Law Review* 25(1):161–208.

Subramanian, Ram, and Alison Shames. 2013. "Sentencing and Prison Practices in Germany and the Netherlands: Implications for the United States." *Vera Institute of Justice, New York.* Report accessed 01/12/2015, (https://www.vera.org/publications/sentencing-and-prison-practices-in-germany-and-the-netherlands-implications-for-the-united-states).

Supreme Court of Japan. 2006. "The Legal Training and Research Institute of Japan." Website accessed 01/30/2018, (http://www.courts.go.jp/english/institute_01/institute/index.html).

Sutherland, Elaine E. 2012. "Imperatives and Challenges in Child and Family Law: Commonalities and Disparities." Pp. 1–46 in *The Future of Child and Family Law: International Predictions,* edited by Elaine E. Sutherland. Cambridge, UK: Cambridge University Press.

Swan, Gerry, Vinasan Naidoo, Richard Cuthbert, Rhys E Green, Deborah J Pain, Devendra Swarup, Vibhu Prakash, Mark Taggart, Lizette Bekker, Devojit Das, Jörg Diekmann, Maria Diekmann, Elmarié Killian, Andy Meharg, Ramesh Chandra Patra, Mohini Saini, and Kerri Wolter. 2006. "Removing the Threat of Diclofenac to Critically Endangered Asian Vultures." *PLoS Biology* 4(3):395–402.

Swissinfo. 2007. "Soldiers Can Keep Guns at Home but Not Ammo." *Swiss Broadcasting Corporation.* Website accessed 03/14/2018, (http://www.swissinfo.ch/eng/soldiers-can-keep-guns-at-home-but-not-ammo/970614).

Syed, Sofie G. 2017. "Liberté, Égalité, Vie Privée: The Implications of France's Anti-Veil Laws for Privacy and Autonomy." *Harvard Journal of Law & Gender* 40(2):302–32.

Tanikawa, Miki. 2011. "A Japanese Legal Exam That Sets the Bar High." *New York Times.* Website accessed 01/30/2018, (http://www.nytimes.com/2011/07/11/world/asia/11iht-educLede11.html).

Teitel, Ruti G. 2000. *Transitional Justice.* New York: Oxford University Press.

———. 2003. "Transitional Justice Genealogy." *Harvard Human Rights Journal* 16(1):69–94.

———. 2010. "Global Transitional Justice." *George Mason University Project on Human Rights, Global Justice, and Democracy.* Working paper accessed 01/15/2019, (https://www.gmu.edu/centers/globalstudies/publications/hjd/hjd_wp_8.pdf).

Telegraph Reporters. 2012. "Would Be Juror Who Claimed 'Extremely Homophobic and Racist Views' Faces Prosecution." *Telegraph.* Website accessed 01/29/2018, (http://www.telegraph.co.uk/news/uknews/law-and-order/9532947/Would-be-juror-who-claimed-extremely-homophobic-and-racist-views-faces-prosecution.html).

Terry, Don. 1996. "Cultural Tradition and Law Collide in Middle America." *New York Times.* Website accessed 08/08/2018, (https://www.nytimes.com/1996/12/02/us/cultural-tradition-and-law-collide-in-middle-america.html).

Terry, William C. 2009. "Working on the Water: On Legal Space and Seafarer Protection in the Cruise Industry." *Economic Geography* 85(4):463–82.

Tesón, Fernando R. 1985. "International Human Rights and Cultural Relativism." *Virginia Journal of International Law* 25(4):869–98.

TheLocal. 2017. "Italian Man Granted Divorce after Claiming Wife 'Possessed by Devil.'" Website accessed 07/24/2018, (https://www.thelocal.it/20170410/italian-man-granted-divorce-after-claiming-wife-possessed-by-devil).

Theodorou, Angelina E. 2016. "Which Countries Still Outlaw Apostasy and Blasphemy?" *Pew Research Center.* Website accessed 08/03/2018, (http://www.pewresearch.org/fact-tank/2016/07/29/which-countries-still-outlaw-apostasy-and-blasphemy/).

Thompson, Anthony K. 2016. "The Liberties of the Church and the City of London in Magna Carta." *Ecclesiastical Law Journal* 18(3):271–90.

Thomson, Susan. 2011. "The Darker Side of Transitional Justice: The Power Dynamics behind Rwanda's Gacaca Courts." *Africa* 81(3):373–90.

Thuan, Willy. 2017. "Bangkok Correction Museum." *Bangkok.com.* Website accessed 07/05/2017, (http://www.bangkok.com/magazine/correction-museum.htm).

Tonry, Michael. 2011. "Reducing the Prison Population." Pp. 211–23 in *Confronting Crime: Crime Control Policy under New Labour,* edited by Michael Tonry. Abington, UK: Routledge.

Tonry, Michael, and Richard S. Frase. 2001. *Sentencing and Sanctions in Western Countries.* New York: Oxford University Press.

Torrum, Japheth Terande, and Cyprian Clement Abur. 2014. "The Relationship between Unemployment, Inflation and Crime: An Application of Cointegration and Causality Analysis in Nigeria." *Journal of Economics and Sustainable Development* 5(4):131–37.

Translation Bureau. 2015. "Twitter Terminology (Linguistic Recommendation from the Translation Bureau)." *Public Works and Government Services Canada.* Website accessed 07/27/2018, (https://www.btb.termiumplus.gc.ca

/tpv2guides/guides/wrtps/index-eng.html?lang=
eng&lettr=indx_catlog_t&page=9naZKRv2b_o0.html).

Transparency International. 2017. "Corruption Perceptions Index
2017." Website accessed 03/07/2018, (https://www
.transparency.org/news/feature/corruption_perceptions_
index_2017).

Truth and Reconciliation Commission. 2018. "The Official Truth
and Reconciliation Commission Website." Website accessed
01/18/2019, (http://www.justice.gov.za/trc/).

Turk, Austin T. 2004. "Sociology of Terrorism." *Annual Review of
Sociology* 30:271–86.

Tuttle, Gray. 2015. "China's Race Problem." *Foreign Affairs* 94(3):
39–46.

Uggen, Christopher, and Jeremy Staff. 2001. "Work as a Turning
Point for Criminal Offenders." *Corrections Management
Quarterly* 5(4):1–16.

Uitermark, Justus. 2004. "The Origins and Future of the Dutch
Approach towards Drugs." *Journal of Drug Issues* 34(3):511–32.

U.K. Parliament. n.d. "Chiltern Hundreds and the Manor of
Northstead." *Parliament.uk.* Website accessed 07/11/2017,
(https://www.parliament.uk/site-information/glossary
/chiltern-hundreds/).

UNDOC (United Nations Office on Drugs and Crime). 2010.
"Compiling and Comparing International Crime Statistics."
Website accessed 02/08/2010, (http://www.unodc.org/unodc
/en/data-and-analysis/Compiling-and-comparing-
International-Crime-Statistics.html).

———. 2018. "United Nations Surveys on Crime Trends and the
Operations of Criminal Justice Systems (UN-CTS)." Website
accessed 05/23/2018, (https://www.unodc.org/unodc/en
/data-and-analysis/United-Nations-Surveys-on-Crime-
Trends-and-the-Operations-of-Criminal-Justice-Systems
.html).

———. n.d. "Statistics and Data." *Research and Analysis Branch,
United Nations Office on Drugs and Crime.* Dataset
accessed 01/29/2018, (https://data.unodc.org/).

UNFCCC (United Nations Framework Convention on Climate
Change). 2018. "Paris Agreement—Status of Ratification."
Website accessed 09/24/2018, (https://unfccc.int/process
/the-paris-agreement/status-of-ratification).

UNHCR (United Nations High Commissioner for Refugees). 2017.
"Global Trends-Annex Tables." *Global Trends: Forced
Displacement in 2016.* Dataset accessed 06/28/2018, (http://
www.unhcr.org/globaltrends/2016-GlobalTrends-annex-
tables.zip).

———. 2018a. "Emergencies." *UNHCR USA.* Website accessed
06/27/2018, (http://www.unhcr.org/en-us/emergencies.html).

———. 2018b. "Figures at a Glance." *UNHCR Statistical Yearbooks.*
Website accessed 06/28/2018, (http://www.unhcr.org/en-us
/figures-at-a-glance.html).

United Kingdom General Secretariat. 2006. "A Guide to Names and
Naming Practices." *Interpol.* Website accessed 07/17/2018,
(https://www.fbiic.gov/public/2008/nov/Naming_practice_
guide_UK_2006.pdf).

United Nations. 2018. "World Contraceptive Usage 2018." *United
Nations Department of Economic and Social Affairs.*
Website accessed 07/24/2018, (http://www.un.org/en
/development/desa/population/publications/dataset
/contraception/wcu2018.shtml).

———. n.d. "About the UN." Website accessed 06/26/2018, (http://
www.un.org/en/about-un/index.html).

United Nations Children's Fund. 2017. "Child Labour." *UNICEF
Data.* Website accessed 08/23/2018, (https://data.unicef.org
/topic/child-protection/child-labour/).

United Nations Development Programme. 2016. "Global Study on
Legal Aid." *United Nations Office on Drugs and Crime.*
Report accessed 02/12/2018, (https://www.unodc.org
/documents/justice-and-prison-reform/LegalAid/Global-
Study-on-Legal-Aid_Report01.pdf).

———. n.d. "Governing Systems and Executive-Legislative
Relations." Website accessed 09/15/2008, (https://web
.archive.org/web/20080530212246/http://www.undp.org
/governance/docs/Parl-Pub-govern.htm).

United Nations Office of the High Commissioner for Human Rights.
2014. "Status of Ratification Interactive Dashboard."
Website accessed 07/25/2018, (http://indicators.ohchr
.org/).

United Nations Secretary-General. 2018. "Composition of the
Secretariat: Staff Demographics." *United Nations General
Assembly.* Website accessed 06/26/2018, (http://undocs.org
/A/73/79).

United States Citizenship and Immigration Services. 2018. "Volume
12—Citizenship and Naturalization." *USCIS Policy Manual.*
Website accessed 06/06/2018, (https://www.uscis.gov
/policymanual/HTML/PolicyManual-Volume12.html).

United States Holocaust Museum. n.d. "Postwar Refugee Crisis and
the Establishment of the State of Israel." *Holocaust
Encyclopedia.* Website accessed 06/26/2018, (https://www
.ushmm.org/wlc/en/article.php?ModuleId=10005459).

United States Office of Personnel Management Investigations
Service. 2001. "Citizenship Laws of the World." Report
accessed 06/09/2011, (https://web.archive.org/web
/20110610221202/http://www.opm.gov/EXTRA
/INVESTIGATE/is-01.PDF).

Uram, Zachary. 2018. "Ontario Court of Appeal Denies Liability for
Chevron Subsidiary." *Jurist.* Website accessed 06/19/2018,
(https://web.archive.org/web/20180605114428/http://www
.jurist.org/paperchase/2018/05/the-canadian-subsidiary-
of-us-based-oil-giant-chevron-corp-cannot-be-held-liable-
for-a-us95-billion.php).

van Dijk, Jan. 2007. "Mafia Markers: Assessing Organized Crime
and Its Impact upon Societies." *Trends in Organized Crime*
10(4):39–56.

———. 2009. "Approximating the Truth about Crime: Comparing
Crime Data Based on General Population Surveys with
Police Figures of Recorded Crimes." *Groupe Européen de
Recherche sur les Normativités.* Report accessed 05/23/2018,
(http://lodel.irevues.inist.fr/crimprev/index.php?id=67).

Varghese, John. 2010. "Police Structure: A Comparative Study of
Policing Models." *SSRN.* Website accessed 03/06/2018,
(https://papers.ssrn.com/sol3/papers.cfm?abstract_
id=1605290).

Vergun, David. 2018. "Small, Birdlike UAS to Provide Eyes in the Sky
for Soldiers." *Army News Service.* Website accessed
09/18/2018, (https://www.army.mil/article/205997/small_
birdlike_uas_to_provide_eyes_in_the_sky_for_soldiers).

Verini, James. 2015. "Escape or Die." *New Yorker,* 4/20/2015, pp.
66–75.

Vidmar, Neil, and Valarie P. Hans. 2007. *American Juries: The
Verdict.* Amherst, NY: Prometheus Books.

Villamor, Felipe. 2018. "'Your Concern Is Human Rights, Mine Is
Human Lives,' Duterte Says in Fiery Speech." *New York
Times.* Website accessed 07/25/2018, (https://www.nytimes
.com/2018/07/23/world/asia/philippines-duterte-speech-
muslims.html).

Villé, Renaud, Ugljesa Zvekic, and Jon F. Klaus. 1997. "Promoting
Probation Internationally." *United Nations Interregional
Crime and Justice Research Institute*, Valletta, Malta.

International Training Workshop on Probation, publication No. 58. Publication accessed 07/25/2017, (http://www .unicri.it/services/library_documentation/publications /unicri_series/Probation_international.pdf).

Waites, Matthew. 2005. *The Age of Consent: Young People, Sexuality, and Citizenship.* London, UK: Palgrave MacMillan.

Waldorf, Lars. 2008. "Rwanda's Failing Experiment in Restorative Justice." Pp. 422–35 in *Handbook of Restorative Justice,* edited by Dennis Sullivan and Larry Tifft. Abingdon, UK: Routledge.

Waldron, Jeremy. 2016. "The Rule of Law." *Stanford Encyclopedia of Philosophy.* Website accessed 07/05/2018, (https://plato .stanford.edu/entries/rule-of-law/).

Walmsley, Roy. 2014. "World Pre-Trial/Remand Imprisonment List. 2nd Edition." *International Centre for Prison Studies.* Report accessed 02/12/2018, (http://www.prisonstudies.org/sites /default/files/resources/downloads/world_pre-trial_ imprisonment_list_2nd_edition_1.pdf).

Wang, Shucheng. 2017. "Tripartite Freedom of Religion in China: An Illiberal Perspective." *Human Rights Quarterly* 39(4):783–810.

Ward, Alex. 2012. "Won't Sell Up? Enjoy Living in the Middle of a Motorway! Road Is Built around a House after Elderly Chinese Couple Refuse to Move." *Daily Mail.* Website accessed 08/03/2018, (http://www.dailymail.co.uk/news /article-2236746/Road-built-building-couple-refuse-China .html).

Washburn, Kevin K. 2006. "American Indians, Crime, and the Law." *Michigan Law Review* 104(4):709–77.

Waters, Mary. 2001. *Black Identities: West Indian Dreams and American Realities.* Cambridge, MA: Harvard University Press.

Watters, Ethan. 2014. "The Organ Detective." *PSMag.* Website accessed 05/25/2018, (https://psmag.com/economics /nancy-scheper-hughes-black-market-trade-organ- detective-84351).

Weale, Albert. 2008. "Between the Highest and the Attainable? Reflections on the Right to Health." *Essex Human Rights Review* 5(1):1–4.

Weaver, R. Kent. 2002. "A New Look at Federalism: Electoral Rules and Governability." *Journal of Democracy* 13(2):111–25.

Weber, Max. 1946. "Politics as a Vocation." Pp. 77–128 in *From Max Weber: Essays in Sociology,* edited by H. H. Gerth and C. Wright Mills. New York: Oxford University Press.

———. 1949. "'Objectivity' in Social Science and Social Policy." Pp. 49–112 in *The Methodology of the Social Sciences,* edited by Edward A. Shils and Henry A. Finch. New York: Free Press.

Weinstein, Jeremy D. 1986. "Adultery, Law, and the State: A History." *Hastings Law Journal* 38(1):195–238.

Weisbrod, Carol. 1999. "Universals and Particulars: A Comment on Women's Human Rights and Religious Marriage Contracts." *Southern California Review of Law and Women's Studies* 9(1):77–97.

Weiss, Debra Cassens. 2014. "Parking-Dibs Tradition Becomes a Federal Case in Chicago." *ABA Journal.* Website accessed 08/21/2018, (http://www.abajournal.com/news/article /parking-dibs_tradition_becomes_a_federal_case_in_ chicago/).

Weiss, Susan. 2009. "Divorce: The Halakhic Perspective." *Jewish Women: A Comprehensive Historical Encyclopedia.* Website accessed 07/20/2018, (https://jwa.org/encyclopedia/article /divorce-halakhic-perspective).

Weitzer, Ronald. 2014. "New Directions in Research on Human Trafficking." *Annals of the American Academy of Political and Social Science* 653(1):6–24.

Welchman, Lynn. 2012. "Gulf Women and the Codification of Muslim Family Law." Pp. 367–406 in *Gulf Women,* edited by Amira El-Azhary Sonbol. Syracuse, NY: Syracuse University Press.

White, Ben. 1999. "Defining the Intolerable: Child Work, Global Standards and Cultural Relativism." *Childhood* 6(1):133–44.

Widgerow, Davin. 2011. "Boldly Going Where No Realtor Has Gone Before: The Law of Outer Space and a Proposal for a New Interplanetary Property Law System." *Wisconsin International Law Journal* 28(3):490–520.

Wight, Ed. 2015. "Is This the End for the Pink Panthers?" *Daily Mail.* Website accessed 03/13/2018, (http://www.dailymail.co.uk /news/article-3340712/Is-end-Pink-Panther-jewel-thieves- Gang-world-s-elaborate-gem-heists-brink-founder-caught- flat-Croatian-ambassador-s-jewellery.html).

Williams, Jennifer, and Judith Klusener. 2013. "The Traditional Courts Bill: A Woman's Perspective." *South African Journal on Human Rights* 29(2):276–93.

Wilson, James Q., and George L. Kelling. 1982. "Broken Windows." *Atlantic Monthly,* March 1982, pp. 29–38.

Wilson, Richard. 2001. *The Politics of Truth and Reconciliation in South Africa: Legitimizing the Post-Apartheid State.* Cambridge, UK: Cambridge University Press.

Wilson, Robert H. 2012. "The Legal Strategy of the Cruise Line Industry: An Effective Use of Terms and Conditions to Manage Disputes." *Cornell Hospitality Quarterly* 53(4):347–56.

Witte, John, Jr. 2003. "Ishmael's Bane: The Sin and Crime of Illegitimacy Reconsidered." *Punishment & Society* 5(3):327–45.

Wolfe, Jonathan. 2018. "New York Today: The Right to Disconnect." *New York Times.* Website accessed 08/06/2018, (https:// www.nytimes.com/2018/03/23/nyregion/new-york-today- the-right-to-disconnect.html).

Woods, Amanda. 2017. "Pastafarian in Hot Water for Wearing Colander in Driver's License Photo." *New York Post.* Website accessed 08/03/2018, (https://nypost.com/2017/06/02 /pastafarian-in-hot-water-for-wearing-colander-in-drivers- license-photo/).

World Bank. 2011. "WB: Climate Change Data, World Bank Group." *World Bank Open Data.* Database accessed 09/25/2018, (http://databank.worldbank.org/data/download/catalog /climate_change_download_0.xls).

———. 2018a. "Enforcing Contracts." Doing Business: Measuring Business Regulations. Website accessed 08/21/2018, (http:// www.doingbusiness.org/data/exploretopics/enforcing- contracts).

———. 2018b. "Labor Market Regulation Data." *Doing Business: Measuring Business Regulations.* Report accessed 08/06/2018, (https://web.archive.org/web/20180928212057 /http://www.doingbusiness.org/en/data/exploretopics /labor-market-regulation).

———. n.d. "DataBank: World Development Indicators." Website accessed 08/06/2018, (http://databank.worldbank.org/data /reports.aspx?source=2&series=SI.POV.GINI&country=#).

World Health Organization. 2014. "Management of Substance Abuse: Country Profiles 2014." Website accessed 05/22/2018, (https://web.archive.org/web/20180516022237 /https://www.who.int/substance_abuse/publications /global_alcohol_report/profiles/en/).

World Justice Project. 2017. "Rule of Law Index, 2017–2018." Website accessed 07/05/2018, (http://data.worldjusticeproject.org/).

———. n.d. "What Is the Rule of Law?" Website accessed 07/05/2018, (https://worldjusticeproject.org/about-us /overview/what-rule-law).

World Trade Organization. 2018. "Regional Trade Agreements and the WTO." Website accessed 06/20/2018, (https://www.wto.org/english/tratop_e/region_e/scope_rta_e.htm).

———. 2019. "Regional Trade Agreements Database." Website accessed 09/07/2019, (http://rtais.wto.org/UI/PublicMaintainRTAHome.aspx).

Wright, Alan. 2013. *Policing: An Introduction to Concepts and Practice.* Abingdon, UK: Routledge.

Wrong, Michela. 2016. "Making a Murderer in Uganda." *Foreign Policy.* Website accessed 09/04/2018, (https://foreignpolicy.com/2016/01/20/making-a-murderer-dominic-ongwen-uganda-icc/).

Xueguan, Mu. 2017. "African Officials Hail Community Courts for Easing Access to Justice." *Xinhua News.* Website accessed 02/19/2018, (http://www.xinhuanet.com/english/2017–08/23/c_136547057.htm).

Yanick, Joe. n.d. "What Are the Penalties for Assaulting a Cop in Cities around the World?" *H&F Weekly.* Website accessed 10/05/2018, (http://www.hopesandfears.com/hopes/city/city_index/215849-city-index-the-penalties-for-assaulting-a-cop).

Yardley, Jim. 2016. "For Chinese Police Officers, Light Duty on Tourist Patrol in Italy." *New York Times.* Website accessed 03/12/2018, (https://www.nytimes.com/2016/05/13/world/europe/chinese-police-rome-italy.html).

Yarwood, Richard. 2007. "The Geographies of Policing." *Progress in Human Geography* 31(4):447–65.

Yi, Beh Lih. 2017. "From an Oscar to Church Weddings, Five Big Wins for LGBT Rights in 2017." *Reuters.* Website accessed 01/21/2019, (https://www.reuters.com/article/us-global-lgbt-2017-idUSKBN1EN04O).

Youth Restoration Project. 2016. "What Are Restorative Practices?" *Youth Restoration Project of RI.* Website accessed 06/30/2017, (http://yrpofri.org/what-are-restorative-practices/).

Zakariyah, Luqman. 2010. "Confession and Retraction: The Application of Islamic Legal Maxims in Safiyyatu and Amina's Cases in Northern Nigeria." *Journal of Muslim Minority Affairs* 30(2):251–63.

Zimring, Franklin E. 2006. "The Necessity and Value of Transnational Comparative Study: Some Preaching from a Recent Convert." *Criminology & Public Policy* 5(4):615–22.

Zion, James W., and Robert Yazzie. 1997. "Indigenous Law in North America in the Wake of Conquest." *Boston College International and Comparative Law Review* 20(1):55–84.

Zook, Lee. 2003. "Slow-Moving Vehicles." Pp. 145–62 in *The Amish and the State*, edited by Donald B. Kraybill. Baltimore, MD: Johns Hopkins University Press.

Zweigert, Konrad, and Hein Kötz. 1988. *Introduction to Comparative Law.* 3rd ed. Translated by Tony Weir. Oxford, UK: Oxford University Press.

Index